Secret Craft
The Journalism of Edward Farrer

Edward Farrer

CARMAN CUMMING

Secret Craft
The Journalism of Edward Farrer

UNIVERSITY OF TORONTO PRESS
Toronto Buffalo London

© University of Toronto Press Incorporated 1992
Toronto Buffalo London
Printed in Canada

ISBN 0-8020-2846-2

Printed on acid-free paper

Canadian Cataloguing in Publication Data

Cumming, Carman
  Secret craft : the journalism of Edward Farrer

  Includes index.
  ISBN 0-8020-2846-2

  1. Farrer, Edward. 2. Journalism — Canada —
  History. 3. Journalists — Canada — Biography.
  I. Title.

  PN4913.F37C86 1992   071'.1'092   C92-094451-5

All of the cartoons are from *Grip*, except as noted. The sources are listed below.

Collection of the Library of Congress: frontispiece (reference number 13770, from *New England Magazine*, December 1891)
Metropolitan Toronto Reference Library: pages 15, 70, 82, 89, 92, 99, 112, 121, 137 (from the Toronto *Globe*, 13 September 1890), 151, 165, 214
National Library of Canada: 75 (15740), 78 (15739), 114 (15732), 115 (15734), 125 (15735), 126 (15736), 136 (18071), 157 (15737), 194 (*Evening News*, 25 February 1891), 200 (15741), 210 (15738), 220 (15743)
National Archives of Canada: 184 (C6539)

This book has been published with the help of a grant from the Canadian Federation for the Humanities, using funds provided by the Social Sciences and Humanities Research Council of Canada.

Farrer was the most extraordinary figure in Canadian journalism ... He was a man of real convictions ...
> – O.D. Skelton, *Life and Letters of Sir Wilfrid Laurier*, 1:372

Edward Farrer was one of the most remarkable men I have known. Of wide range of intellect, of high culture, with virile gift of expression, a master of English prose, of impressive personality, his powerful mind was seemingly quite without moral convictions so far as he allowed himself to be known ... In turn he was editor of leading Conservative, Independent and Liberal newspapers in the Dominion, and he made mischief on them all.
> – P.D. Ross, *Retrospects of a Newspaper Person*, 269

In whatever he said or wrote, the impression created was of a tremendous, almost infinite, reserve of power.
> – Toronto *Star*, 28 April 1916

Whimsical, happy, alert, companionable, unpretentious, scholarly, simple, profound, mysterious and elusive, I have known no more remarkable man than Edward Farrer nor any of greater gifts or greater knowledge ... The story of his life would reveal remarkable connections and far-reaching influences. But no one can tell the story from the fragmentary material that remains.
> – Sir John Willison, *Reminiscences Political and Personal*, 214–15

- the intellectual — the master of words & ideas — the joy of dispute.
- games of truth: what convictions? Playing partisan. Changing sides. The mischief-maker. What is integrity?
- Causing sensations. The raising of a popular furore. Race & Religion. Commercial Union. The Jesuit Estates crisis. Binaries: us + them, The sense of panic. The enemy.
- The assumed power of the press.
- The impact of liberal ideology
- The bedeviling question: the annexation issue. Denied but not forgotten. The always possible solution. The gospel of despair. The issue of treason.
- The impossibility of Canada — race, religion, & the USA.
- Who speaks truth? And how is truth determined? So the press, the editorial, the conviction. Why Farrer tests the foundation of this game of truth.

- The newspaper & governmentality

Contents

ACKNOWLEDGMENTS ix

PREFACE xi

1 The Traitor 3

2 The Partisans 12

3 'Scalps Must Be Taken' 34

4 Making Mischief 44

5 Splendid Isolation 63

6 The Hidden Message 96

7 Master Craftsman 129

8 The *Globe*, the *Mail*, and the *Empire* 145

9 The Mercenary 163

10 The Plot 177

11 A Wicked and Ungovernable Force 204

viii Contents

12 The Forlorn Hope 225

13 Remarkable Connections 238

14 Backstairs Agent 247

15 A More Natural Passion 270

NOTE ON ATTRIBUTION 289

NOTES 293

SOURCES 321

INDEX 327

Acknowledgments

I am grateful to Professor Wilfred Kesterton, who first stimulated my interest in journalism history, for reading and commenting on an early draft of the manuscript, and for providing continued interest and support.

I also wish to thank Dr Paola Ludovici MacQuarrie, for research in Rome; Ms Mary Purcell, for her help in searching out materials at Clonliffe College, Dublin; Ms Mary Pat O'Malley, for research on Irish parish and tax records; Ms Mabel Charlesworth, for her aid in translating the unusual shorthand in Farrer's personal files; Professor J.R. Miller, for guiding me to important Justice Department files on the annexation movement of the 1890s; my son Chris, who helped with early stages of research; and the many staff people at the National Archives of Canada, the Carleton University library, and the Dalhousie University library who have been unfailingly helpful. I am grateful for the thoughtful work of editors Gerald Hallowell and Kenneth Lewis at University of Toronto Press. The book was researched with the assistance of Carleton University and published with help from the Canadian Federation for the Humanities. I acknowledge, too, the permission of the *Journal of Canadian Studies* to use material that originally appeared in that journal.

In particular I want to thank my wife, Betty, who has helped at every stage of the project and has been always a patient, generous, encouraging, and meticulous collaborator.

I dedicate the book to her.

Preface

My interest in Edward Farrer arose in this way: I had been looking at patterns of change in political journalism in Canada and had developed a special interest in that period of the late nineteenth century when the party press began to give way to the corporate press. In reading memoirs and other documents from that time, I was surprised that Farrer, an itinerant Irish journalist of mysterious habits and background, should have gained so much attention. There seemed no doubt that he was seen not just as an exceptionally prolific and humorous and entertaining writer, but also as the outstanding journalistic craftsman of the day, especially as guiding genius of the Toronto *Daily Mail* in the 1880s when it broke with Sir John A. Macdonald. I wondered – at first in only a casual way – why so little attention had been given to him later.

Over time I became convinced that he had indeed been neglected, for reasons that said much about Canadian journalism and about Canadian society. He was, it seemed (in the view of those who came just after him), something of an embarrassment. As P.D. Ross put it, he was a mischief-maker. He was regarded as a mercenary, ready to write any policy line for pay – and, paradoxically, as a rebel who could not be relied on to follow the party line. He was condemned by some (and quietly admired by others) for his attacks on Roman Catholic clericalism or on bilingualism. He was known to be dangerously anti-British. Above all he was condemned as a traitor, who had sold out his adopted country to American annexationists. In short, he was a troublemaker, thoroughly out of step with his time. The things others cared about – such things as party politics or family lineage or the glory of Empire – he cared about very little. The things that mattered to him, especially his hostility to imperialism and militarism and clericalism, were more likely to be seen by others as evidence of moral turpitude than as signs of moral consistency.

On a more subtle level Farrer was seen as not quite a gentleman. While he was known as the most delightful of companions, the most entertaining of storytellers, the most incisive of political analysts, he was still, after all, an Irishman of unknown antecedents, who drank. It could never be forgotten that he had (so the story went) trained at Rome for the priesthood, only to break with the church and become its devastating critic. It could never be forgiven that he rejected with amiable contempt the holy doctrines of Gritism or Toryism, the glories of United Empire Loyalism, or the sanctity of nationalism. Although he served as the brains of a number of newspapers, Farrer worked consistently for managers or publishers whose talent was much less than his own. His mischief-making, and perhaps his Irish background and his drinking, meant that he was distrusted by those in power, even when they admired his talent and picked up his ideas. No one ever left him entirely in charge of the shop.

Because he was seen as an uncaring mercenary on the things that *mattered*, most of his contemporaries failed to note the long-term consistency he displayed in other areas. The huge body of his work, stretching over more than four decades, shows that his most notable journalistic attribute was patience – a formidable restraint combined with care in writing so as to influence, not just to preach to the converted. The full flavour of this quality could hardly have been seen by contemporaries, unless they studied his work over a period of years. It also seems doubtful that people of the day, or of the immediately following years, could have realized how patiently and deviously and effectively Farrer worked, first, to separate the *Mail* from the Tory party, and second, to exploit the 'race and creed' turmoil of the 1880s, with the goal of breaking up Confederation and bringing on annexation. His later role as an agent for Sir Wilfrid Laurier – an agent who constantly edged the Liberal party towards continentalism – has also not been fully exposed, because of Farrer's intense, almost obsessive, habits of secrecy.

Aside from these political implications Farrer's career is also significant in the narrower history of Canadian journalism. He was indeed a fine craftsman, writing in a style that was clear and understated, in welcome contrast to the florid language of the time, and as well exceptionally imaginative, exceptionally subtle – full of surprises. His interests ranged far beyond imperialism and continentalism, through the difficult social and economic and cultural problems of a young and far from stable country. His arguments (and he was above all a journalist of ideas) were impressively backed by statistics and by historical or literary knowledge. He was clearly a man of extraordinary breadth in his reading and his memory, and his sense of irony was, in a somewhat stolid age, magnificent. All of these qualities were marked in the newspapers where he worked, and may have helped to lead others away from a style of journalism more notable for its righteous fury than for humour or insight. It is one of the many paradoxes of his career that while the *Mail* would be remembered as a fanatic champion of Protestantism, all those who praised Farrer's writing style were taken by his moderate and reasoned and ironic tone – a tone that undoubtedly gave all the more impact to his often destructive writing.

More important in the journalistic perspective, perhaps, and much more elusive, is the impact Farrer had on the partisan newspaper *system*. While the final verdict is not yet in, enough evidence exists to say that Farrer and the *Mail*, for all their manifold sins, opened new possibilities for independent newspapers. The journalist Walter Blackburn Harte was at least partly right when he wrote in 1891 that independence was then a new thing for Canadian journalism, and added: 'The Toronto *Mail*'s evolution as an independent paper has therefore been intensely interesting, and it is one of the most encouraging things in Canada today that it has had a successful issue.'[1] It could be argued, of course, that Farrer was not a typical journalist, and that one should not generalize from his experience to define patterns. Yet his actions do in a curious way highlight some features of the craft precisely when they diverge from usual standards: through his experience one can see not only the rules of the game, but also where the limits were drawn – where and how political masters reached out to curb him, as they did on successive newspapers.

In sum, Farrer was an original and unconventional journalist at a time when newspapers were more than ordinarily cheapened by outside influence, and some of his better qualities rubbed off on those around him. 'Those who know him familiarly,' wrote E.E. Sheppard, 'are aware that there are few men who have more thoroughly followed Carlyle's injunction – "clear your mind of cant." '[2] One item of 'cant' that Farrer rejected was the pretence, adopted by most journalists to protect their pride, that they shared the views of their political masters. Farrer worked under no such illusion. While he spent much of his career cheerfully writing the party line, whatever that line might be, he also worked, in his tightly restrained and measured way, against party control. His motivation on this may have been more political than journalistic, since he used the parties' papers to carry his own (or his clients') ideas, but the effect was to change newspapering. His editorship of the *Mail* during its period of 'splendid isolation' earned admiration from his fellow journalists and encouraged a different understanding of the power and function of journalism. Even when he worked inside the system, he showed that party journalists were by no means solely party instruments – that they were instead often active members of the party team, or of party factions, influencing as well as being influenced. His career thus serves as a caution against seeing the press in this era simply as a creature of the political party or as a creation of inexorable social forces. Farrer was both influential and highly idiosyncratic, and he was not alone in that.

More broadly, Farrer's story may say something about trends in historical writing. It may be fair to say that Canadian historians in the early twentieth century looked above all for icons of respectability, for mythic stature, in their subject matter. They tended to focus on Queenston Heights or Confederation or the building of the railway, or on heroic aspects of the Boer War or the First World War, or on those politicians or tycoons who achieved wealth or knighthoods. They neglected 'lower-class' social history. They were hopefully elitist in cultural matters, exalting minor poets or essayists while looking down on mere journalists. They accentuated nation-building while turning their eyes away from embarrassing episodes like the annexation movement of the 1890s. On all these counts Edward Farrer's career now deserves reassessment.

These thoughts on the impact of Farrer's work are necessarily tentative, however. Sir John Willison was undoubtedly right in thinking that Farrer's story could never be fully told from the fragmentary material that remains. In time, of course, more pieces of the story will be added, and perceptions will be revised. But even with additions and corrections to come, Farrer will remain something of an enigma.

I should confess, though, what may already be obvious to the reader: I have developed, together with the conviction that his work was significant, a certain *liking* for Farrer. He was in some ways a reprobate. In some ways he did great damage to his adopted country. To critics who say he inflamed 'race and religion' hatreds so as to break his country, I can only say that the evidence does indeed point to that conclusion. Yet he must also be one of the most mysterious, charming, and secretly influential minor characters of his era. One cannot help but admire his grace, his wit, his unconventionality, and his sardonic intelligence. He, too, has earned 'a place i' the story.'

SECRET CRAFT

1 The Traitor

The election rally in Toronto's Academy of Music on the night of 17 February 1891 was a remarkable affair. The Toronto *Empire*, Sir John A. Macdonald's slavish hand-organ, said it was not only the greatest rally in Canada's history but the greatest there ever would be – a meeting that would 'exist without a peer in the history of the Dominion.'[1] Even the *Mail*, once Sir John's paper but now a renegade, was awed by the spectacle. 'Such a crowd as surged outside the main entrance has seldom if ever been seen at a political meeting in this city,' it said, 'and those who were unfortunate enough to get caught in it will never forget the experience.'[2] In front of the ornate Academy, King Street, between York and Simcoe, was blocked for fully a hundred yards, said the *News*, and the unspeakable mud of it was sopped up in trouser legs and dainty skirts. Some women in the crowd tried to retreat but found themselves trapped. A *News* reporter heard one of them tell a companion that it was a good thing bustles had gone out of style. 'Yes,' said the other, 'but oh, my dear, ribs have not gone out of fashion yet.'[3]

In retrospect, the cause of the excitement is not hard to explain: Sir John A. Macdonald had become something of a living legend, and his presence alone was enough to create a stir, even without the talk in the newspapers of treason and of great revelations. It was an age when politics and journalism were taken with zest, passion, and sometimes a drop of whisky. Toronto had six daily newspapers, each a political entity and each with its team of 'young men' deployed inside the Academy and in the slush and clamour outside. They missed no detail that would help to build the political tension: even the *Globe* reporters, always conscious of the special status of their great Liberal organ, were well aware of the drama, though they did their best to suppress it. The others gave minute-by-minute detail.

Just after six o'clock, they noted, those Tories with tickets to the rally were allowed in by the stage door, while others left outside in the winter dusk surged against the main doors. Shortly after seven those doors were opened, and the crowd entered 'with a rush and a shout,' filling the hall within seconds. By 7:20, the *Empire* estimated, four thousand people filled the hall while another fifteen to twenty thousand milled outside. In the crush, a large gas lamp was carried away, rupturing the gas main to the theatre and 'rendering necessary the use of electricity.'

Within the hall 'ladies and their escorts' crowded the boxes and every corner of the gallery, while men covered every inch of the remaining space. 'They sat in the windows, perched on the gallery stairways and sat on the edges of the platform,' the Montreal *Star* correspondent noted. 'Looking up from the reporters' table the vast audience seemed, in the glittering light, a very mountain of humanity.' Very soon it was clear the damage would be formidable. Chairs were wrenched from moorings, the carpet was stained with mud and tobacco juice, and the 'fine blue plush' on railings at the back was soiled by dirty feet. In the orchestra pit a number of young rowdies were out of control, and the police finally organized a flying wedge to clear them into the street – 'whence from time to time came little yelps and cheers to show that the police and the people were in mild conflict.'[4]

At 7:30, said the *Mail*, the prime minister arrived at the stage door, but the crush was so great he had to remain in his carriage for ten minutes. At last his supporters managed to make way through the cheering crowd, but Macdonald was 'subjected to more pressure than was at all agreeable.' After this excitement people left in the frustrated crowd outside tried every ruse to get in. Some young men broke a window to crawl through the coal cellar, while at the back of the building an enterprising youngster put a ladder against the twelve-foot fence of the stage yard and charged his own admission: first a nickel, then a dime, and finally a quarter. Even the burly Sir Charles Tupper, lead-off speaker of the night, had trouble getting in. Tupper had come all the way from England to take part in the campaign, but the crowd would not make way for him and he had to resort to the ladder. Swathed in his greatcoat, the future prime minister balanced atop the fence while the ladder was transferred to the inside, and 'nearly came a cropper.'[5]

Sir Charles, somewhat out of breath, got a mixed reception in the hall, but there was no lack of warmth in the cheers for Sir John. Among those applauding was the *Empire's* 'Faith Fenton' (Alice Freeman), who a few months later, as Sir John lay paralysed and dying, wrote movingly of the mood of the rally. It had seemed, she said, as though a premonition of Macdonald's fate touched the audience, for never had there been a welcome so thrilling. 'It broke in great waves over the house, falling and rising again and again, spontaneous, irrepressible, magnetic ...'[6] When Macdonald actually rose to speak, much later in the evening, Fenton noted the scene in close detail: the prime minister's fur overcoat thrown across the back of an easy chair, the cluster of roses drooping nearby, the light flashing through a glass water ewer that sent scintillating sparkles across his face, a little pale with fatigue. A *News* reporter also tried to fix the scene in mind: the hats and handkerchiefs waving over the crowd, the prime minister's 'silvered hair and strong, lined face,' his immaculate morning coat and famous red tie.

For the audience there was a moment of suspense as Sir John stepped forward. For some it was also a moment of apprehension, for at least a sprinkling of those in the hall knew what was coming. Throughout this last of Macdonald's many campaigns there had been rumours of imminent revelations. Today the stories had become much more specific, and closer to home. John Willison, the young, idealistic editor-in-chief of the *Globe*, had heard earlier in the day the story that Sir John, in the keynote speech of the campaign, would be able to link the leading Liberal organ with a conspiracy to annex Canada to the United States. For Willison it was devastating news, coming at a time when he, as a good party editor, had been working to keep his own leaders from tearing at each other in public. Willison had heard the rumour from a friendly Conservative journalist and had been prevailed on to post guards at the *Globe*, in case a hostile Tory mob got out of hand.[7] While the rally warmed up, fifty police marched to the new *Globe* building at Yonge and Melinda, while another fifty were kept on reserve.[8] As Willison recalled it, he really did not consider the guard necessary, but thought it might make villains of the Tory mob and thus blunt the impact of Sir John's revelations. He must have been stung, though, when the *Empire* next day observed gleefully that the wicked ran where no man pursued.

Ned Farrer had also heard the story, which was not surprising since there were few things about Canadian politics he did not know, and this one concerned him personally. He had been dining at Webb's restaurant across from the *Globe* with a young protégé, Walter Dymond Gregory (later a figure in the annexation movement) when a newspaperman came to the table to pass on the bad news. Farrer's reaction must have been casual, because Gregory did not record it.[9] And Farrer may already have heard the story from John Willison. Willison was his nominal superior, even though everyone recognized Farrer as the brains of the *Globe*. In any event, Willison and Farrer certainly talked before the rally, for a *News* reporter saw them coming to the hall together, sauntering arm-in-arm through the crowd. The reporter even considered it worth noting that Farrer was disposed to linger outside and that Willison urged him on, Farrer turning with a deep sigh, as though he were 'thinking of other days.'

Edward (Ned) Farrer, the stout, bearded, amiable (and brilliant) chief editorial writer of the *Globe*, had already built much of the legend that would make him one of the most enigmatic figures in Canadian journalistic history. An Irishman, apparently of good family and classical education (his background was mysterious, but the story was that he had trained as a priest under the Jesuits in Rome), Farrer was known above all as a craftsman, who commanded extraordinary respect and affection from colleagues, even though some called him erratic or irresponsible. Some also called him the ultimate mercenary, because he had broken the code of the times and switched sides, writing for both the Tories and Grits. Part of his personal legend, in fact, was that he had written the campaign literature for both parties in the 1882 election, and that he would, using his Jesuit training, write anonymously for one publication and then attack his argument in another. A cartoon in *Grip* a year earlier had shown him with a quill pen in each hand, one labelled Grit and the other Tory.[10] A favourite press club story was that someone had met him once on an early morning stroll and found he was mentally drafting a reply to a piece he had written the night before. It was all more or less exaggerated, of course, but even his enemies respected his talent. In the late 1880s, as editor of the *Mail*, he had helped make that paper arguably the best in the country after it had broken from Sir John's control. His move to the *Globe* the previous summer had caused a small sensation. Yet now his career was in jeopardy, because he had 'made mischief' once too often.

This time he had laid a trail of gunpowder between the annexation movement and the Liberal party. The rumour was that the Tories had somehow laid hands on a secret pamphlet, written by Farrer, that told the Americans how to dragoon Canada into annexation. To the Tories it added up to a clear pattern: Farrer was already known to have made several trips to Washington to meet officials favouring commercial or political union, including James G. Blaine, the powerful, annexation-minded secretary of state. As a result, it seemed, Blaine had casually thrown sand into Macdonald's efforts for a better trade deal with the Americans and was leaning towards the Liberals' vague policy of 'unrestricted reciprocity.' Farrer, too, was clearly the tool of Sir Richard ('Blue Ruin') Cartwright, a morose veteran whose stature in the Liberal party, at least in Ontario, matched or surpassed that of his young leader, Wilfrid Laurier. As the Tories saw it, the potential for damaging the Grits by painting them as closet annexationists was considerable. In some cases it might even be true. Macdonald, in fact, was gambling that it would be enough to tip the election scales, and the result showed him to be right. It is probably fair to say that Farrer's indiscretion allowed Macdonald to die in office. More profoundly, it may have tipped a great national debate, one that could have gone the other way, towards a continental trade deal that would have set Canada on a path to total absorption.

So in the Academy of Music, on the night of 17 February 1891, both a personal drama and a national one were on the program. For anyone who knew the circumstances there was poignancy in the fact that Farrer had once been Macdonald's man, had felt admiration and affection for him. And Farrer certainly would have appreciated the Old Chieftain's skill as he began to play the rowdy Toronto audience. Like Farrer, Macdonald was a master of the soft opening, the modest, low-key approach that would enlist audience support. He could scarcely hope, Macdonald said (according to the *Empire*'s long verbatim report), to match the power of Sir Charles Tupper, whose warm-up speech had just ended. But it was always a pleasure to come to Toronto, where he had once worked, while he was in opposition in the 1870s, and had seen the need for a protective tariff, a protective National Policy, in a city laden with the sweepings of American warehouses.

This was the cue for his theme: the conflict of protection versus reciprocity that symbolized the real fight of the election, on whether Canada would stay in Britain's orbit or swing towards the mass of the United States. His critics, Sir John said smoothly, had accused him of inconsistency because he sought a better trade deal with the United States while maintaining the National Policy, but it was not so. Protection was consistent with a desire to extend trade to all countries, including the United States. The problem was that the government, in trying to promote freer trade, had encountered great obstruction in the United States. That, he said, warming to the thesis, was because Grit traitors had gone to Washington, had told the Americans not to concede anything to Canada, and thus to force her into annexation.

And now he must have felt that he had the audience in his hands, as he drew the incriminating document from his pocket, waited for silence, and spoke the portentous words: 'I now take the opportunity of making the charge.' The effect was all he could have wished for, at least in the view of the *News* reporter. The audience, he wrote, was struck with 'that chill feeling of dread which the unmasking of treachery must bring even when men are crowded together.'

There was, Macdonald said, a deliberate conspiracy, in which some of the leaders of the Grit opposition were more or less compromised:

I say that there is a deliberate conspiracy, by force, by fraud, or by both, to force Canada into the American union. In the first place, did you ever hear before of a statesman of one country going clandestinely to those of another and giving advice to them against the constituted authority of their own? (Cries of 'Never' and 'Name him.')

What is that I hear? You ask me to name him? Yes, I will name him. In the first place, you know Mr Farrer? (Hear, hear.) People know who Mr Farrer is. He was once the editor of the *Mail*, when it was a Tory paper. He is now the editor, philosopher and friend of Sir Richard Cartwright, and the controlling influence over that great, that glorious and consistent newspaper – the *Globe*. Mr Farrer has been down to Washington several times. Perhaps he is there yet.

A voice – 'He is here tonight.'

I am very glad that he is, because he will hear what I have to say ...

Cartwright, the prime minister went on, was the real villain of the piece, along with Erastus Wiman, known to everyone in the audience as the beefy, flamboyant Toronto journalist who had gone on to become a New York tycoon, and also a leader in the commercial union movement. Cartwright had sneaked down to Washington, coaxed there by Wiman. Like all conspirators, 'with their cloaks around them' they had sat at night with sundry U.S. statesmen and tried to sell Canada. It was a deliberate attempt by the Grits to get the United States to favour them, by holding out hope of annexation. And how was he to prove that? Well, he would tell them, he said, launching into the revelation of the secret pamphlet:

Mr Farrer, a man of great ability, as I happen to know, and a man of utter want of principle, as I happen to know, was the Tory editor of the Tory newspaper, the *Mail*. (Laughter) That newspaper has also fallen from grace, but Sir Richard Cartwright wanted to have a man of ability, and he brought him – no, leave out the letter 'r' in the word brought – (Laughter) – I say he bought him from the *Mail* and planted him in the *Globe*. Since then Mr Farrer has been the ambassador between the *Globe* or Sir Richard Cartwright and Washington.

Now a loyal man brought it to the notice of a member of the Government that this Mr Farrer, the conscience keeper of Sir Richard Cartwright – an easy task, by the way – with his own hand had prepared a document for the purpose to be used in the United States, and I have no doubt on his last visit there has used it.

He (Mr Farrer) prepared that manuscript with his own hand. He was afraid to publish it even with his own types in the *Globe* office. He took it to Hunter, Rose & Co. He got back the manuscript, and a loyal man bought [*sic*] some of the original galley proofs of that document, and it is now being collected, or is nearly all collected, by the officers of the police. (Hear, hear and cheers.)

The document, Sir John went on, told the Americans how to force Canada into the union. They were to grant Canada nothing; they were to stop the bonding privilege, under which Canadian goods went by rail through sections of the United States; they were to put a tax on everything Canada produced. In fact, they were being shown every way in which Canada could be injured and its people impoverished, with the view of eventually bringing about annexation.

Sir John then proceeded to read the conclusions of Farrer's document, slipping in occasional sarcastic comments. Farrer had paid him a great compliment, he said, in predicting that annexation could not make progress while he was at the head of affairs (cheers), but he had also noted that he was seventy-five years old (laughter). Then Macdonald brought the crowd back to serious attention and wound up with another plea for loyalty. He did not, later reports to the contrary, use the famous line that had already struck the campaign theme: 'A British subject I was born, a British subject I will die.' But he echoed it: if American millionaires were allowed to come into the country to buy up its people, he said, it would mark the end of Canada. And he himself would rather see grass growing over his grave than to see the degradation of the country he had loved so much and served so long.[11]

In a later perspective it might seem to be rather thin stuff in which to dress the major issue of the campaign, considering there was no proof that Farrer actually spoke for Cartwright or Laurier. But for the moment the audience was suitably stirred – to feelings of loyalty for the Old Flag and the Old Leader, and to feelings of revulsion for the traitor. Just before the national anthem and the 'three cheers,' the four thousand or so committed Tories bellowed a chorus of 'We'll hang Ned Farrer on the Sour Apple Tree.'

As the theatre emptied, an *Empire* reporter decided to follow Farrer, to see how he was reacting to the 'terrible indictment presented against himself.' Farrer was still with Willison, he noted, the two chatting casually about plans to go over to the Rossin House for a word with Samuel J. Ritchie – yet another of the American millionaires who were trying to buy up Canada.[12] The *Empire* reporter no doubt would very much have wanted to be a fly on the wall at the Rossin House conference. However, the reporters had no more details on Farrer's movements that night. At some point he presumably wrote, or put finishing touches on, a column for the next day's *Globe* explaining that he had indeed written the wicked pamphlet, that he was indeed personally a supporter of political union with the United States, and that all of this had nothing whatever to do with the *Globe* or the Liberals. Willison, meanwhile, was also busy trying to control damage, insisting, as he would until his death, that neither he nor any other Liberal figure had known anything about the document.

When he did read the whole pamphlet, though, Willison might well have been relieved that the *Empire*, in excerpts it printed, did not include passages that made it seem to be a summary of the Liberal party position. And as the affair became more bitter, with embarrassing private letters appearing in print, he might also have recalled nervously a letter he had written to Laurier six weeks before. That letter had hinted clearly that the Liberals needed at least to *pretend* in Washington to be interested in political union, if they were to get any support there for the policy of unrestricted reciprocity.[13]

Happily for Willison his letter was never published during the campaign, but echoes of the pamphlet incident would long continue to haunt him. It was almost three decades later, and long after Farrer's death, that he received a letter from George Ham, Farrer's closest friend, stating baldly that Farrer had *not* in fact written the pamphlet, but had kept silent and protected others. Ham's 1919 letter, with frustrating brevity, said simply that Farrer 'did not write the famous annexation article and I cannot divulge the name of the person who did, but he took all responsibility for it and shielded some men whose names, if I told you, would surprise you very much.'[14] Willison replied four days later, with a crisp rejection and, curiously, no request for further amplification:

My Dear Ham: Your letter of the 9th I have found exceedingly interesting ... You say, 'he did not write the famous annexation article and I cannot divulge the name of the person who did.' If you mean the pamphlet from which Sir John Macdonald and Tupper quoted in Toronto and which was used so freely by the Conservatives in the election of 1891, there is no doubt that Farrer wrote it. My knowledge is direct and absolute. Indeed I have much more knowledge about Mr Farrer at that period than I shall ever put into print. Notwithstanding certain characteristics I had an affection for Farrer and an immense respect for his ability ...[15]

It was typical of Ned Farrer that even the most important single 'fact' about his career should be left shadowed in doubt.

2 The Partisans

The two *Globe* editors who walked together out of the Academy of Music were in every way in marked contrast. John Willison, now thirty-four, was a tall man with lean and strong features, a trim beard, and a prematurely receding hairline. Farrer, in his early forties, was, a contemporary said, a stocky, ruddy, and bearded man 'with a twinkling eye and a mind stored with state history that he had helped to make.'[1] Another colleague said Farrer had slightly protuberant eyes and could assume in moments of whimsy an expression very like an owl.[2] Cartoonists often concentrated on the eyes, making them surprised, ingenuous, puckish, as though Farrer found the world a constantly amusing and puzzling place. The cartoonists also made much of the generous belly, although one colleague noted that Farrer had a powerful physique until his later years.[3]

The background and personality of the two contrasted as much as their appearance. Willison, from a Scottish family in southwestern Ontario, was largely self-educated, groping upward from dime novels consumed in his farm home. In his mid-twenties he managed to break free of a dead-end job as a store clerk to rise rapidly in journalism on the strength of his energy and party loyalty. He saw nothing unusual (and his contemporaries would not have disagreed) in serving at the same time as the *Globe*'s parliamentary correspondent and as president of the Young Men's Liberal Club of Toronto. In 1889 he had organized a Toronto rally for Wilfrid Laurier, Edward Blake's still far from popular successor as Liberal leader. It was this sort of effort that brought him, in the summer of 1890, just months before the pamphlet affair, the surprise appointment as editor of the *Globe*.[4]

And the *Globe* editorship at the time was the best position open to a Liberal journalist – possibly the best job in the country for any journalist. He was inheriting the mantle of George Brown, the powerful journalist-politician who had started and shaped the *Globe*.

Everyone knew, though, that the *Globe* had gone downhill since the day a decade earlier when a printer had shot and fatally wounded Brown. Everyone knew Willison was short on experience and that some leading Liberals had opposed his selection. But he was sincere and dedicated (he would eventually be knighted), and he must have seen the appointment to direct the *Globe* as the high point of his career. It made him a figure not only in journalism but in politics, for the *Globe* was more than a newspaper and more than a party organ: it was the source and guide and director of a whole network of Liberal papers and Liberal politicians. And with Sir John A. surely nearing his end, the prospects for the Liberals were improving. At the time, it mattered a good deal to a newspaper whether the party it supported was in or out of office, or even whether it had prospects of gaining office.

Willison had thus come a long way in a short time. A journalist who had worked against him less than a decade before in London recalled that he had shown brains and energy, but was also 'raw and inept.'[5] Willison's biographer observes that when he arrived at the *Globe* editorship, he had proved his loyalty but 'had not demonstrated that he possessed the intellectual capacity to move beyond rhetoric and hero-worship to a subtle appreciation of the complexities of modern political and economic problems.'[6]

It was awareness of these failings that led party leaders to impose what Willison called the 'curious contract' – the flaw in his prospects that he learned of only a few days before his official appointment. Incredibly, Ned Farrer, by far his senior in years and experience and stature (if not in reliability), was coming over from the *Mail* to be the paper's real editor.[7] At best it was an unholy teaming of talent and responsibility. At worst Willison could have seen himself as a toothless watchdog for Liberal masters. It was humiliating that public comment on the appointments focused on Farrer. It was worse that he could not, under terms of his hiring, even overrule Farrer on policy matters. He could only hold back articles for judgment by a committee of directors. Willison realized the situation was impossible. If he actually did hold up a Farrer article for the directors' approval, he would be in trouble, whichever way the decision went. He decided, cautiously, to do nothing and let Farrer write what he chose. Neither of them ever spoke of the 'curious contract.'[8]

They even became friends – remarkable, considering not just the imposed working relationship but also the personality differences. Farrer was a wit and an intellectual and an iconoclast – as mercurial as Willison was staid. While Willison played by the rules, Farrer often ignored them. And while Willison's life was an open, rather dull, book, Farrer's was a mystery, a tale of contradictions – possibly a fabrication. He was described as gregarious and humorous, a delightful companion and raconteur, but he was also something of a remote philosopher, who kept his background and values hidden. He was a man of impressive intellect and yet something of a roguish troublemaker. There is a suggestion from one friend that he borrowed money, and from another that he was subject to depressions. He showed a classic pattern of alcoholism. Colleagues referred privately to his 'sprees' or his 'periodical toots,' while publicly they stressed only his good qualities: the grace and force of his writing, his prodigious output, and his unfailing congeniality. 'A strange and great man he was who found much zest in life, but I think was often lonely,' Willison wrote, long after Farrer's death. 'There was no window through which we could look into his soul.'[9]

Or into his past. Even during his lifetime friends knew little of Farrer's early years, and what they thought they knew is now suspect. Some things, of course, were more or less obvious. He was clearly Irish, clearly well educated, and widely read. Willison noted that he 'had French and the old languages' – presumably Latin and Greek. P.D. Ross said he once heard Farrer, then editor of the *Mail*, converse in a single day with visitors in four languages – English, French, Latin, and Gaelic.[10] He could also, Ross said, speak and write Italian. But it was far from clear how he had acquired this education.

Most contemporary accounts say Farrer was born in Ireland's County Mayo, near Castlebar, that he attended Stonyhurst, the famous Jesuit college in Lancashire, and then went on to train for the priesthood at the 'Jesuit College,' or the 'Irish College,' or the 'College of the Propaganda,' at Rome.[11] However, none of this can be confirmed. Neither the Mayo County library nor the National Library of Ireland has a record of any family named Farrer in the Castlebar area. It is possible, of course, that the name was changed for simplicity. An 1886 biographical sketch apparently based on an interview with

GRIP'S CRONY CLUB, *Grip*, 6 July 1889. This cartoon of Farrer was done for a satire in which he was portrayed as singing a ditty about his life, starting out:

'Twas in Ireland I was born,
   An' passed me youthful days, sirs,
'Twas there I got me wit,
   An' all me Irish ways, sirs

16 Secret Craft

Farrer said the name was usually spelled in Mayo as 'Farragher.'[12] In Canada even close friends often spelled it as 'Farrar.' However, none of these variants shows up at Stonyhurst or the other institutions he was supposed to have attended.[13]

While a name change is the simplest explanation for these gaps, there is reason to think the mystery runs deeper. For one thing, Farrer was notoriously secretive about his background. He once told Willison he had revealed nothing of his family background even to his wife.[14] George Ham claimed to know more, but his information is open to question. At one point after Farrer's death, Ham wrote: 'No one except his wife and myself knew that he was the Honorable Edward Farrer, and that he was a nephew of Archbishop O'Donnell of Cork.'[15] However, this promising lead to his early life also turns out to be illusory. Both the National Library of Ireland and the Irish College affirm there never was an Archbishop O'Donnell of Cork, although the library adds that bishops of that name were found in other parts of Ireland, usually Donegal.

Furthermore, these are not the only indications that Farrer fabricated a background. Other reports, published during his lifetime, offered a variety of birth and school backgrounds, none of which can be confirmed by the schools, or in English or Irish birth records. One said he had been born in Donegal,[16] not far from Mayo, in the coastal village of Bundoran, near 'Tullehan' (presumably Tullaghan, Leitrim), and educated at 'Coulnatoura.' Another said he had been educated at Maynooth, the famous seminary near Dublin.[17]

Since Farrer as a young man was clearly sympathetic to Irish nationalism, it is tempting to wonder if the mystery of his background is related. In his later writing, though, while he had frequent hostile words for British rulers and Irish landlords, he showed no support for extreme nationalists. (In fact, in Winnipeg he once stirred up a flaming exchange with Irish Catholics when he demeaned the new breed of Irish 'patriots' and suggested St Patrick's Day celebrators should break off their rhetoric and 'spend a few hours in asking the Almighty to cast the devil out of many of their countrymen.')[18] His work shows, however, intimate knowledge of both western Ireland and Rome – a pattern that supports the idea he merely changed his name, rather than fabricated a background. Strong evidence also appears of theological training, but there is little that bears on the question of why he broke with the church and became a devastating critic – at least of its ultramontane edge.

Two curious stories have been left on the record on the circumstances (but not the causes) of the break. One is from Ham and must be suspect, given his error on the archbishop, but it still deserves to be quoted, if only as evidence of Farrer's story-telling ability.

How [Farrer] happened to come to America is a queer story and has never before been told in print, for I promised not to tell it until he had passed away. While at college in Rome where he was studying for the priesthood, he, with a brother student, as remarkably clever as Ned, were taking a stroll the afternoon before the day of their ordination.

One asked the other: 'Do you want to be a priest?' and both agreed they didn't. Just then, a little breeze blew a piece of an Italian newspaper against Ned's leg and picking it up he read an advertisement for two interpreters – English and Italian – applications to be made to the captain of a ship, then in port. They hastened to the vessel, but the captain seeing their student's garb at first refused to engage them on the ground that the college authorities missing them would search and find them before they could get away. They, however, persuaded him that they could hide in the forecastle until the ship sailed, which they did. Shortly before the advertised time of departure, the captain saw the searching party heading for the ship, and although the tide was unfavorable, immediately cast off ropes and started – landing the two young men in New York almost penniless.

They, however, quickly procured employment, and later Ned became one of the most powerful newspaper writers in Canada, sought after by prominent politicians of both parties.[19]

A totally different account of Farrer's early life, admitted to be from second-hand sources and therefore probably no more reliable than Ham's version, was presented at the time of the pamphlet scandal by the Toronto *News*. Among other things, it said he was born in 1846 (his gravestone has it as 1850) and spent most of his early years in Rome (there was no mention of Stonyhurst). It quoted 'a gentleman who knows him' as saying Farrer was born in Mayo but had been sent at an early age to the College of the Propaganda in Rome. He had stayed there fourteen years and was about to take vows in the Jesuit order when, because of his ability as a linguist, the 'young lay priest' was assigned to serve as secretary to an Irish archbishop visiting Rome. 'After fourteen years absence he returned to Ireland, and he himself has often told how desolate was the scene, where he could scarce speak the language and where he scarce knew the inhabitants.

18 Secret Craft

Yet ... he could give a fine account of the riot in Cork in '68 and how the military suppressed it.' Farrer did not remain long as secretary to the archbishop, the *News* account said, but left to work as an interpreter on a steamer carrying immigrants from Le Havre. In New York he succumbed to ship fever, and on recovery went to work as an obituary writer for a New York newspaper.[20]

The conflicting versions thus leave Farrer's early life a matter of mystery and give no guidance on the larger question of why a brilliant young man, said to have a gift for friendship, would cut himself off from early ties, both spiritual and temporal. Farrer himself once wrote that North America had always been a refuge for 'the uneasy spirits of the world,' and he may have been thinking of himself.[21] But he told little, even to close colleagues. John Willison, more rigorous with facts than some of his colleagues, said he could not even confirm the Jesuit training. Writing in 1919, he said he could get no trace of Farrer before the spring of 1870, when he apparently emerged from an Ontario lumber camp, where he had been working as a bookkeeper, to offer the Lindsay *Expositor* a series of sketches of leaders in the British House of Commons. He broke off the series after one story was criticized, saying he had no wish to engage in controversy, but later he joined the Toronto *Telegraph* and, when it was founded in 1872, the *Daily Mail*.[22]

Again the *News* version is radically different. It said Farrer was brought into Toronto journalism not by the *Telegraph* but by Charles Belford and George Gregg of the *Leader*. And it added: 'He was on that paper in 1867 when Fenians invaded Eastern Canada, and he wrote those famous dispatches which threw all the correspondents at the front into the shade, and determined them never again to venture out of the city when they had an assignment, but to stay in the city and write it up.'

Since the Fenian raids in eastern Canada occurred in 1866 and 1870, it seems more likely that this story's basis, if it has any, relates to the second raid, from Vermont into Quebec in May 1870. A part of Farrer's later legend was his ability to 'annihilate space' as a rival put it, by writing magnificently of events taking place far from the newsroom.[23] That legend, though, was associated mainly with the Northwest Rebellion of 1885, when Farrer organized the *Mail*'s excellent war correspondence. The *News* writer may have confused this incident with the Fenian raids.

If, in fact, as seems likely, Farrer arrived in New York in 1869 and went on to Canada early the next year, the timing, plus his vague movements in the Ontario hinterland, raise inevitable questions on whether he served as a Fenian agent. His age, education, and republican leanings would have made him a natural target for recruitment, and there is no doubt that his talents would have made him an excellent agent. The failed Fenian rising in Ireland in 1867 had left much bitterness among young Irishmen, including those in the United States, and it is not impossible that Farrer, despite his later disillusionment, might have been drawn into the affair. John Willison hinted at one point, too, that Farrer's anti-British activities were more extensive than had been disclosed in his lifetime. 'He had the quality of a detective and that talent was exercised for various and curious causes,' Willison wrote. 'I had knowledge that I do not disclose and confidences which cannot be betrayed. In his outlook for Canada he was an incurable, mischievous, dangerous pessimist. For the British Empire he cared not at all.'[24]

The possibility that he worked for the Fenians is also supported by one other tenuous bit of evidence to the effect that Farrer lived for a time in Paris and associated with radical republicans there. The evidence is in the *News* account, which says Farrer's entry into Toronto journalism was aided by a story he wrote in 1870 concerning the slaying of Victor Noir, French republican journalist. While the *News* story has a number of errors, it could have a basis in fact. It told of how the shooting by Prince Pierre Bonaparte had caused a worldwide sensation and how Farrer, then 'in Belleville or thereabouts,' had written an interesting description of Noir, whom he had known at the College of the Propaganda. 'At that time Messers Belford and Gregg were editors of the Leader, and they were so struck by the excellence of the article that they entered into correspondence with Mr Farrer with the result that he joined the Leader staff ...' In fact, the only *Leader* story fitting this description was written in Oshawa, not Belleville, by a correspondent who claimed to have known Noir in Paris, not Rome. Nevertheless, the story raises the intriguing possibility that Farrer may have spent time in the brawling, pamphleteering demi-monde of Paris students and radicals.

The *Leader* story seemed, at least, to provide an authentic glimpse into that world. It began with a description of the men in the radical fringe – 'nightly frequenters of the gambling hells, far more scrupulous about their honour than about the sixth and seventh commandments, fond of absinthe and cordial haters of the government.' It then went on to tell how the writer had served as second in a duel pitting Noir, a member of this group and an outstanding swordsman, against a German named Carl Stuhlmann:

> Victor was in his twenty third year, standing six feet in his stockings, of gigantic build, with a handsome woman face, pale and haggard from midnight carousing ... One evening he entered a restaurant on the Rue Costiglione, where Stuhlmann was applying himself with great vigor to a mess of Bologna. 'Have I the honor of addressing Mr Stuhlmann?' said Noir, intent upon provoking a quarrel. Stuhlmann bowed. 'M. Stuhlmann, it is no wonder you defeated my Gascon friend if you are as clever with the sword as you are with a knife and fork' ... Stuhlmann demolished his last sausage and threw the empty plate at Noir, striking him in the face and covering him with grease. Cards were exchanged, seconds were selected, and a meeting was appointed for the next day at Lesurier's academy. The following morning the writer, as Stuhlmann's second, waited upon Noir at his brother's home on the Rue Louis Phillippe with the view of settling the matter peaceably, but Noir was irreconcilable. Accordingly they met in the academy, and after a few passes Noir received a severe flesh wound in the left shoulder, and was conveyed to his lodgings in a cab. This unexpected defeat cooled his impetuosity, and at his brother's earnest request he paid up what he owed to Lesurier, made friends with Stuhlmann, took an oath against duelling and turned over a new leaf. His wound confined him to his room for two months, during which time he wrote several violent articles for the *Gaulois* and the *Journal des Faubourg*, a scurrilous weekly ...[25]

If Farrer did indeed spend time in the Parisian radical fringe, it might account for some of his liberal and republican leanings, or for his hostility to the church hierarchy. But there is no confirmation of it, and in fact the record of his career remains vague and contradictory even in his early years in Canada, until he achieved national notoriety in the 1880s. It is certain, though, that he joined the *Mail* when it was set up in the spring of 1872, for its handwritten first roster lists him as 'leader writer' (he was still only twenty-one or twenty-two, if born in 1850),[26] and several letters and items of court testimony place him on the *Mail* until December 1873, when he received a seven-month appointment as a federal immigration agent in Ireland.[27] His movements in 1874 are uncertain. The *News* profile said he spent eighteen months back in Ireland; however, he returned to Toronto at least briefly in June 1874 to testify in a major libel case over a story he had edited. In any event, he was back on the *Mail* by 1875, first as night editor and editorial writer, and later as editor. He apparently left the *Mail* in 1881 to go to New York for a brief stint as foreign editor of the *World*, returning in 1882 to work for Macdonald in the spring election campaign and then taking the editorship of the Winnipeg *Times*. In Winnipeg the trail becomes plainer: firm evidence places him in that city from 1882 to 1884, first at the *Times* and then with the independent *Sun*.

While the general facts of Farrer's career at the *Mail* and the *Globe* in the late 1880s and early 1890s are not disputed, more confusion sets in thereafter, when his annexationist intrigues had sent him into partial obscurity. Some accounts say he went to the United States after leaving the *Globe*, returning only in 1905, when he settled in Ottawa. In fact, while he spent a good deal of time in New York and Washington, he lived mainly in Toronto and Montreal in those years, as correspondence and city directories make clear. And at first these years in exile may have been lean ones – possibly the years when he borrowed money. While he was at the *Mail* and the *Globe*, Farrer's earnings were the best the trade could provide. In the wake of the annexation imbroglio, he remained on the *Globe* for more than a year, until eventually he was forced out by Liberal loyalists alarmed over his continuing annexation efforts. For a time his name was too hot for public connections with newsrooms or party backrooms. Friends, notably Goldwin Smith, the famed and wealthy Toronto historian, helped him get freelance work, and he also worked for the Continental Union Association of Ontario, an organization that lived only briefly and was chronically short of funds, despite Smith's help. He also stayed close to the Liberal party, providing it with political ammunition or engaging in secret politicking. Before the 1896 election, for instance, he helped organize a curious three-way alliance among the Liberals, the agrarian Patrons of Industry, and the dissident Conservatives loyal to D'Alton McCarthy. When the Liberals took office, he engaged in a complex blend of activities. He worked regularly for Sir Wilfrid Laurier, as a confidential agent, investigator, writer, and general troubleshooter. Strangely, in view of his annexationist views, he was entrusted with a number of difficult diplomatic chores in Washington. More strangely, in view of his anti-Catholic reputation, he visited Winnipeg repeatedly to work on a compromise in the schools issue there. (At one point he even wrote Laurier about the 'clamour of the extremists in the Protestant population,' an irony that must have amused the prime minister.)²⁸ In this period he also investigated for the government an astonishing range of problems, from smuggling operations in Quebec to railway corruption or political intrigue. He also pursued – at times in a way that overlapped strangely with his government work – activities as a lobbyist or propagandist for various other interests, notably the Canadian Pacific Railway. He wrote regularly, as well, as a 'straight' journalist; he was a correspondent for the *Economist* and the *Manchester Guardian*, for instance, as well as for several U.S. papers. He also wrote what seemed to be independent, scholarly, articles for magazines such as the *Forum*, *Contemporary Review*, *Fortnightly Review*, and *Canadian Century*. He continued to be mildly annexationist in his writing until late years, when hints emerged that he had become somewhat reconciled to the prospect of Canadian independence. Even in his final years, though, he added to his reputation as a mercenary: just before the fall of the Laurier government in 1911 he reverted for a time to writing on behalf of the Conservatives, undermining Laurier's renewed effort for reciprocity with the United States.

His later years must have been relatively prosperous, for he broke a pattern of constant moves and for the last eleven years of his life he and his wife (their only child, a son named Henry, died in 1906) lived in a substantial area in Ottawa's Sandy Hill district. The home, at 488 Wilbrod, is a large, gracious, yellow-brick building, not far from Laurier House. Farrer never owned it but continued to live there until his death in 1916.²⁹

If the facts of Farrer's life present elements of mystery, so, too, do contemporary assessments of his personality and beliefs. Friends who tried to describe him assumed there was much in his thought and activities that would never be known, and his personal papers, in the National Archives at Ottawa, present a similarly enigmatic picture. His journals, written in precise, arcane script, suggest a man of wide philosophical and historical interests, but they are highly impersonal, giving little insight into his own experiences or thoughts. Some of the material is in shorthand,³⁰ and the remainder ranges from fairly routine notes, historical or statistical, for use in articles, to esoteric material on trade patterns in French Canada before the British conquest. Farrer had shown lifelong interest in the religious, literary, and social patterns of French Canada, but late in life he appeared to be collecting minutely detailed information on early trade and communications patterns there. There is no sign in the papers, though, of another reputed interest, in Indian languages.[31]

On three points about Farrer's life both friends and enemies agreed: his ability, his congeniality, and his care in never betraying a confidence. On most other points they disagreed. Even on Farrer's annexation sentiments, the issue on which his newspaper career foundered, there is doubt. Willison recalled that Goldwin Smith once asked him if he thought Farrer ever had a sincere conviction. 'I suggested that at least he was sincere in his desire to annex Canada to the United States. He said, "Oh, no, if Mr Farrer could get Canada into the United States tomorrow he would start next day to get her out."' Smith considered that Farrer was sincere only in his dislike and distrust of the Roman Catholic hierarchy, Willison reported. 'I could not agree for I think he had a liking for the cultivated priesthood of the church, however hostile he may have been to tenets of ultramontism and the absolutism of Roman Catholic teaching.'[32]

Walter Gregory had a different recollection on this point – a difference not important in itself, perhaps, but significant in showing how friends puzzled out the question of Farrer's convictions or lack of them. He quoted Smith as saying there were only two subjects on which Farrer had convictions – the Roman Catholic church, and trade relations with the United States.[33] The same fascination for Farrer's convictions was shown by O.D. Skelton, leading scholar and public servant, who within one paragraph referred to Farrer as a man of 'curious flexibility' and 'a man of real convictions.' Skelton would have known Farrer only in the latter's late years (if at all), but he went to Ottawa at a time when Farrer's reputation as an agent and fixer for the Laurier government was still fresh. He wrote:

Farrer was the most extraordinary figure in Canadian journalism ... He combined a keen interest in political and economic questions with unwearied zeal in investigation and most convincing powers of exposition. His curious flexibility, his powers of secretiveness, his loyalty after a fashion, made him capable on occasion of editing a morning paper of one political stripe and an evening newspaper of a contrary colour, in the same city, fulminating in turn against the futilities of his esteemed contemporary, and led in later years to his being entrusted by politicians on both sides with commissions of discreet inquiry without ever betraying a confidence. Yet he was man of real convictions of which hostility to the presumption of the hierarchy and a belief in the inevitableness of Canada's political union with the United States were foremost ...³⁴

The best testimony on Farrer's ability comes, however, not from his friends but his enemies – or at least from those who opposed him. The Toronto *News*, for instance, which throughout the 1891 election campaign lacerated him as a traitor or as Sir Richard Cartwright's 'little dog Neddy,' took time afterward to acknowledge his skill: 'There is no cleverer man in this country than Edward Farrer. He combines what is rarely met with in a man, great literary abilities with great aptitude for figures. In him mathematical exactitude and literary order dwell so harmoniously that they make a most formidable combination indeed. Add to this a most retentive memory, a thorough knowledge of Canadian affairs, and there is a man armed at every point for just such a contest as that through which the country has passed ...'³⁵ Others who opposed Farrer or felt betrayed in the pamphlet incident also acknowledged his genius. Ontario premier Oliver Mowat, who was influential in getting him dismissed from the *Globe*, commented: 'I don't know that there is an abler man, anywhere, than Mr Farrer.'³⁶ Joseph Pope, Macdonald's secretary, and W.T.R. Preston, Liberal organizer, who was hurt in the pamphlet incident, both described him as brilliant.

Willison, who knew him better than most colleagues, despaired of finding any simple way of summing him up. He marvelled at the breadth of Farrer's acquaintanceship and the breadth of his interests. He was fascinated by the way Farrer, in a faction-ridden country, could cross boundaries – could fight the hierarchy while having friendly relations with Catholic clergy, or could work for one party while maintaining intimate relations with leaders in the other. While Farrer had little real sympathy for any political party, Willison said, few men knew so much of the undercurrents of Canadian politics, and few received and protected so many confidences. Above all, Willison was impressed by the influence Farrer had on the people around him, and on the newspapers where he worked: 'It was inevitable that he should determine the character and temper of any page to which he contributed. He could not occupy a subordinate relation. Whether it was admitted or not he was at the head of the table. This was not because he strove to be first, but because his knowledge was so wide and his

The Partisans 25

experience so great that his authority was the natural result.' No newspaper on which Farrer worked could be dull or commonplace, Willison wrote:

He was bold at times and now and again greatly disturbed his political associates. One thinks of quotations from his pen which did service in various campaigns, and not always in behalf of the party with which he was allied. Such utterances, however, were generally in denunciation of abuses and were not dictated by any mere desire to create annoyance or friction. Behind the scenes he did much. He moved many men who perhaps hardly understood the influences to which they responded. He had perhaps more personal acquaintants than any other man in Canada, and more friends also. No one who ever worked at his side could forget his humour and his genius for comradeship, or ever cease to wonder at the ease with which he did his work, his familiarity with many books, his knowledge of the affairs of many countries, his prodigious memory and the numerous and varied channels through which he collected information on the subjects in which he was interested.37

Not everyone in the Liberal party, however, echoed Willison's fulsome praise for Farrer. Preston, for instance, mixed admiration with the disdain of the committed for the unbeliever. He also probably reflected party thinking in saying that Farrer's appointment to the *Globe* was a serious blunder, since the pamphlet incident was not the first time he had 'played the part of the stage villain.' His final verdict on Farrer, though, was sharply mixed: 'He was an extremely able man, exceptionally well informed on all political questions, and a brilliant writer. His pen was at the command of anyone who would pay for it. He never pretended to any principle in public matters, save that he never betrayed a confidence – never revealed information entrusted to him under the pledge of secrecy. Beyond that, he considered himself quite free to sell his services to either party.'38

For Preston and colleagues, of course, 'principle' meant above all loyalty to the party, and even among journalists there was debate on whether Farrer's switching of parties constituted unethical conduct. E.E. (Ned) Sheppard, another colourful editor, offered an explanation of his rival's philosophy on the point. Farrer, he said, 'belongs to a school of journalists who hold that, like a lawyer who will take a brief from either the plaintiff or the defendant, an editor has no more serious responsibility than to present the case for his employer as effectively as possible, and that having concluded the argument, it should excite no comment if tomorrow he appears for another client and demolishes everything he says to-day.'[39]

Sheppard thus admired Farrer's talent but deplored his ethics – a pattern unusual in an age when journalists seldom admitted to mixed feelings about friends or enemies. He was not alone, however, in making the distinction. When Farrer left the *Globe* in 1892, the Tory Ottawa *Citizen* devoted two long editorials to his career and showed a startling contrast in the way it spoke of his craftsmanship and his ethics. On the former, it analysed his record on the *Globe* in detail and saluted him as a master of his profession. On the latter, it condemned his 'odious and detestable' betrayal of the country and said his casual switching of party loyalty raised a question of professional ethics.[40]

No aspect of his career, in fact, so fascinated contemporaries as this flexibility in switching sides, or in working simultaneously for rival politicians or journals. And no part of the legend is more difficult to sort out. Certainly it is true that he wrote on both sides of various issues – on prohibition, free trade, even annexation, to name only a few. In so doing he did appear, as Sheppard suggested, to adopt the position of a lawyer taking a brief, and he probably enjoyed the intellectual challenge this presented.

There is, however, no clear evidence to back the myths that he worked for two newspapers at the same time, or that he would single-handedly sustain a public debate with anonymous articles in different journals. On the suggestions that he worked simultaneously for different parties, there is a little more evidence. It is certainly true, for instance, that he worked for the annexationist movement in the 1890s at the same time he worked for the Liberals (although on a quite different matter). In the 1896 election campaign he may have been paid by three separate parties – the Liberals, the Patrons, and the McCarthyites. The legend that he wrote the platforms for both major parties in another election is more doubtful. Paul Bilkey, another fellow journalist, said the story was probably apocryphal,[41] and Ham commented: 'While we were most intimate for more than forty years he never admitted it to me, but what he didn't tell of himself was monumental.'[42]

Preston offered some evidence in support of the legend, though he seemed to be speaking of something more akin to routine party publicity than the term 'party platform' would imply. Without making

[handwritten annotation: But the point is he wasn't in a partisan political culture where such an identity was at stake ? / dard.]

clear what election he was referring to, Preston said Farrer at one point when he was editor of the *Mail* came to him proposing to write the Liberal literature. '"But Ned," said I, "what about your editorial in the *Mail* this morning going for us all?" With the utmost insouciance he replied: "Well I prepared the literature for the other side, and I think I can answer my own composition." And he did so, in a very satisfactory manner.'[43]

Pope also provided some backing in his book *Public Servant*, in which he related that just before the 1882 election a friend who happened to be up about dawn on a beautiful May morning encountered Farrer – 'one of the most brilliant and versatile journalists of that or any other time' – taking a lonely walk on Parliament Hill:

'What are you doing up at this hour?' said my friend. 'Thinking over my paper in defence of the Government's railway policy,' replied he. 'Well,' said the other, 'are you satisfied with your work?' 'Satisfied, yes,' answered Farrer, 'I'm so d—d well satisfied that I don't see how I'm going to answer it, and that's what's keeping me up.' He had undertaken to write the railway campaign sheets for each side, and no doubt did both superlatively well.[44]

A somewhat firmer piece of evidence for Farrer's switch-hitting comes in a letter to Laurier from Sir Richard Cartwright in 1889, proposing that Farrer be hired, 'of course in strict secrecy,' to write a series of pro-reciprocity articles for Liberal papers. At the time Farrer, as editor of the *Mail*, had just dropped his support for the policy. The deal may not have been consummated, but Cartwright's tone seems to indicate neither he nor Laurier would find the arrangement extraordinary.[45]

George Ham, who worked with Farrer in Winnipeg in the 1880s and remained a lifelong friend, had an explanation for Farrer's capacity to argue issues from various directions. It was simply, he said, that 'his great mind could see both sides of a question, so that he could reply to his own arguments without any difficulty, and then controvert them to the Queen's taste.'[46] In general, though, Ham stressed Farrer's more easy-going and whimsical side, and it may be that Ham, himself an irrepressible extrovert and raconteur, brought out those facets of his friend's personality. Ham stressed, for instance, Farrer's fondness for sports and for card-playing, saying that he had been a good cricket player in earlier days, playing in matches in England against some noted players, and that later he would travel long distances to see a league baseball game in Canada or the United States. 'And he dearly loved a game of cards – Black Jack or Catch-the-Ten, an old Irish game, being his special favorite.'

At times, apparently, Farrer resorted to stratagems to get his friend to come to Ottawa from Montreal for a card game. In one instance Ham received a wire from Farrer on a Saturday saying Clifford Sifton wanted to see him:

When I reached his home in Ottawa that evening, I naturally asked what Sifton wanted to see me about. And he looked apparently amazed, and asked:
'What Sifton?'
'Why, the Minister of the Interior.'
'Never heard of him,' he replied.
'But,' I said, handing him his dispatch, 'here's your telegram.' He took it, scrutinized it carefully, and returning it casually remarked:
'Can't you see that's not my handwriting – it's a forgery.'[47]

P.D. Ross tells of another instance when Ham was the butt of a Farrer joke (or perhaps vice versa). This time they were travelling from Montreal to Winnipeg when Ham, feeling his responsibility as a CPR official, gave up his berth to a young woman who had not been able to get one. Next morning Farrer (as he told the story to Ross) went to Ham's berth, pulled the curtain, and, seeing his friend curled in blankets facing the wall, called 'Wake up, George,' and 'hit him a good hearty slap in a suitable location' before discovering the berth had a new occupant:

'The drawing room door was close by, fortunately,' continued Farrer, 'and I shot back into it undiscovered. When I looked out a minute later, the car was full of sobs and excitement. The porter was trying to quiet the lady, and I expressed my own sympathy warmly. I said I had seen a man in the car the night before who looked like a crazy man.'

Mr Farrer had large eyes, in a large face, eyes slightly protuberant, and he could assume an expression like an owl.

'In the confusion,' went on Farrer, looking at me like an owl, 'I'm afraid I gave a description of somebody like George.'[48]

Curiously (in a turnaround that says something of the embellishing talents of at least one of the two men), Ham also told this story but reversed the denouement to make *Farrer* the victim. As Ham told it, he had obtained another berth and was awake in the morning when Farrer came pattering down the aisle and administered the slap, saying at the same time, 'Get up, you old devil, you.' But Ham claimed it was he, not Farrer, who invented the story of the crazy man. He said he got the porter to tell the woman that a lunatic had escaped from the day coach, but had been recaptured and handcuffed. Then he told Farrer the woman had a description and was 'laying for him.' In a wrinkle that suggests the story is not to be taken literally, Ham also claimed that Farrer spent most of the day and part of the night in the baggage car, sending back occasionally to find out if the woman was still on the train and still vengeful.[49]

Another anecdote told by Willison displays both Farrer's humour and his reticence. While trying to find out something about Farrer's background, Willison related, he talked to a doctor who had attended him during an illness at Winnipeg. When Farrer's life was in danger, Mrs Farrer had asked the doctor to try to find out something about her husband's family. So when Farrer had a lucid moment, the doctor, leading up to the point gently, asked whether his relatives were noted for longevity. Farrer replied that most of them had died shortly after the court rose – although occasionally one had been lucky enough to pull through until the next assizes.

The same wryness comes through in a story Willison related of a time in the early 1890s when the future Edward VII was caught up in a gambling scandal. Willison was in Ottawa when he got a wire from Farrer. 'I am attacking the Prince of Wales tomorrow,' it said. 'Come home at once or you will not have a friend left.' Willison, in fact, kept a collection of Farrer's one-liners – on, for instance, the woman who had 'enough powder on her face to free Ireland,' or on the American farm expert who thought pig-growing would be profitable in Manitoba if every pig could be provided with a parlour stove and a buffalo overcoat. While they were enchanted by Farrer's stories, though, Ham and Willison both took them with a grain of salt. Said Ham: 'He was a brilliant writer, an interesting conversationalist with an unlimited fund of information and humour, and knew so many stories and told them so often that he actually believed them himself.' Said Willison: 'Mr Farrer often talked of his experiences as an immigration agent in Ireland, and on no subject was he more entertaining. But he was entertaining on all subjects. He had an amazing collection of stories. He saw humour in any and every situation. He was brilliant in conversation and he loved to talk ...'

Interestingly, Ham in connection with the Irish stories made further reference to the shadowy archbishop, said to be Farrer's uncle or employer or both. He said Farrer had many stories of how he had served as intermediary between the archbishop and the chief of the Irish constabulary, in dealing with Fenians. 'If the suspect was a pretty decent, harmless fellow the archbishop would arrange for him to be freed and sent home; if he was a dangerous character and an undesirable, he would be shipped to America, with passage paid and sufficient money to give him a fair start in the new world.'[50]

Some of the legendary stories about Farrer concerned his drinking. And while they were undoubtedly exaggerated in many press clubs, there was a firm basis in fact. In one case Farrer was dismissed, as editor of the Winnipeg *Times*, after what the publisher called a 'pretty extensive spree.'[51] Gregory told of attending a conference of annexationists in New York, where Farrer was so drunk he had difficulty getting on and off streetcars.[52] Willison related a story concerning Farrer and E.B. (Big Thunder) Wood, a politician who was also a notable tippler. Writing in 1919, Willison noted that Wood 'lived in a less arid time and was not always neglectful of its opportunities'; then added:

It is said that he and Mr Edward Farrer were once opposing speakers at a series of political meetings. At one of these meetings a voice shouted as Mr Wood was going in full sweep and majesty of deliverance that he had been 'drunk' the night before. Mr Wood paused and uttered a grave and feeling protest against the accusation. Turning to Mr Farrer he said: 'There sits the man who has been opposing me from many platforms. He cannot desire to shield me, but I have faith that he will not do me an injustice. After last night's meeting we spent the time together until we retired. We are opposed politically, but we respect each other and have friendly political relations. I ask Mr Farrer to answer my accuser.' Mr Farrer arose and declared with adequate emphasis that Mr Wood had been just as sober as he was.

Willison added that the story may have been apocryphal, but was 'supported by the probabilities.'[53]

Hector Charlesworth, writing in 1925, told of an incident at the Grange, Goldwin Smith's opulent Toronto home, that suggested both Farrer's weakness for the bottle and his ability as a storyteller. Farrer, he said, often helped Smith prepare articles when 'old age or ill health made him indolent,' and he would arrive to find the old scholar sitting wrapped in a blanket with his feet in a mustard bath, complaining that 'the inevitable dissolution' was at hand. 'Presently Farrer would tell him a lively bit of political gossip, or invent it if necessary, and the subject of dissolution would be forgotten.' On one occasion, apparently, Farrer brought to the Grange the noted character Joseph Haycock, a farmer and leader of the Patrons of Industry, who was rated by Farrer as the best company in the legislature. Goldwin Smith was intrigued – but startled and puzzled when Haycock, before each drink, seized the decanter of fine old whisky and gave it a rapid shake. He asked Farrer afterward if there had been anything wrong with the whisky. 'No,' explained Farrer, 'but you see Joe is used to drinking farmers' whiskey down in Frontenac County, and from force of habit he gives it a shake to bring up the tansy blossom from the bottom of the bottle, and make it bite!'[54]

Farrer's wife, Annie, seems to have shared her husband's sociable qualities, although little is known about her. She apparently married Farrer in the early 1870s (their son was born in 1873)[55] and may at times have provided fibre to stiffen her husband's easy-going temperament. Walter Gregory was with her on the night of Macdonald's denunciation of Farrer at the Academy of Music – in the crowd outside that failed to gain admission – and he recalled her saying that if she had managed to get in she would have got up and 'denounced' Macdonald.

As for Annie Farrer's sociable qualities, Gregory related that he became intimate with the household after meeting her at the home of a friend and receiving an invitation to her home, where 'I met her famous husband and we got along excellently.' Thereafter he often spent his Saturday evenings with the Farrers. 'Mrs Farrer was almost like a mother to me ... I was delighted to have an opportunity of meeting Mr Farrer and esteemed it a great privilege to be on such terms of intimacy with him.' Gregory found, however (long before the incident when he had to help Farrer on and off New York streetcars), that his hero was flawed: 'I used to believe, I think, at that time almost everything that he told me, but I did not continue to believe it, for Mr Farrer did not hesitate to embellish his stories with fiction, but he was never malicious.' Unfortunately, Gregory did not make clear whether Farrer embellished only his casual, amusing anecdotes, or expanded on more serious matters as well. But his final summation of Farrer is rather wistful. He had never known, he said, anyone who could explain economic matters as Farrer could. He had never known anyone who could tell a story better than Farrer. He had never known anyone with such a wonderful memory. 'If he had only had character, Farrer would have gone a long way.'[56]

As with his political views, and his character, Farrer's religious outlook was the subject of speculation among friends – speculation of a kind that shows they were not certain where he stood. George Ham, at least, considered him an essentially religious man, but neither he nor other friends provide insight into Farrer's reaction against the church. His personal religious views were sufficiently shielded, too, that Gregory, Ham, and Willison all considered it worth noting that at the time of his death he did not seek absolution. Gregory wrote that Farrer's wife, too, believed he had not entirely broken with the church, and had often predicted (wrongly, as it turned out) that when Ned was about to die, he would send for the priest. Ham, in a long letter to Willison covering many aspects of Farrer's last days, hinted that his ambiguous connections with the church continued until his late years:

The Catholic clergy endeavoured his adherence to the Church and a rest cure on St. Denis Street took care of him when he went on one of his periodical toots. He had no religion, as we speak of it denominationally. He worshipped the Creator in his own humble fashion and did his level best to do right as between man and man ... There was no person, not even his wife, who was closer to him than I was and there was scarcely a week during his residence in Toronto and Ottawa that he did not wire me to come down to see him. In fact I had to be with him in the latter days all week-ends and by doing so sometimes neglected other duties. At the end he professed no religion, but was buried in a Protestant cemetary [sic] and from a Protestant church but that was because his wife was Anglican and she directed the affair. He was very liberal with his money and gave generously to the members of his family dependent upon him ... All in all his was the greatest mind I have ever met and at the same time the most simple ... it was my proud privilege to be one of the chief mourners and to be able to do something to ease his last hours.[57]

As Ham's letter suggests, Farrer's final illness (cirrhosis of the liver, according to cemetery records) was somewhat prolonged. He died in Ottawa on 27 April 1916, and the funeral was conducted by Rev. T.J. Stiles of the Anglican Church of St Alban the Martyr. He was buried in Beechwood Cemetery, on a knoll shaded by beeches and maples, in a plot where Henry had been buried a decade earlier. Annie Farrer would be buried there the following year, and his granddaughter, Kathleen, after her death in 1978. The gravestone was sponsored by a group of friends, and inscribed simply:

Edward Farrer
1850–1916
'The Master Craftsman'
This monument was erected
as a tribute to his memory
by his confreres of the press
of Canada and other friends

Henry E. Farrer
1873–1906
Annie Farrer
1853–1917

3 'Scalps Must Be Taken'

The Toronto journalistic world that Ned Farrer entered in 1870, as a young man 'unwilling to engage in controversy,' was a bizarre blend of bombast and manipulation and chicanery. At the time of his arrival complex political intrigues were in motion to reorganize it, and while there is no sign he played a part in those intrigues, their result shaped his future. Their nature may also have had an effect: it is hard to imagine a young man entering a more fertile training ground for cynicism.

Dominating Toronto's journalistic horizon at the time was George Brown's *Globe*, the rock around which all other currents moved. The *Mail*, on which Farrer would spend much of his career, was still only an idea in the brain of John A. Macdonald. And the *Mail*, even in its great days, would never attain the unique status the *Globe* held in the 1870s. Unlike other journals that were subject to the pressure of political and corporate 'friends,' the *Globe* was itself a controlling influence. Or, rather, George Brown was a controlling influence in the Grit/Liberal/Reform party, and the newspaper was simply part of his machine. It set a standard for technical excellence and editorial cruelty that other papers felt required to copy. Brown's enemies, and they were many, considered him a vindictive bully, but certainly an able one.

Goldwin Smith was one of the enemies. That remarkable British intellectual took up residence in Toronto in 1871, a year after Farrer, and may have made the young Irishman something of a protégé. Certainly they were close associates later, and Farrer recalled that the relationship began in the 1870s. Smith was already a distinguished figure. A former history professor at Oxford, a confidante of the political and intellectual elite of both Britain and the United States, he would marry wealth (he was already well-to-do) and live in protected comfort at the Grange, using his wealth to start and support publications or to back various movements – such as the political union of Canada and United States.

Smith considered George Brown to be a blight on the country's political, cultural, and journalistic life. 'Of liberality of character and sentiment, of breadth of view or toleration of difference of opinion, no human being was ever more devoid,' he wrote. 'Master of *The Globe*, which then, unhappily for the country, was the only powerful paper, he used it without scruple or mercy to crush everybody who would not bow to his will ...'[1] Farrer came to share that view, possibly under Smith's influence, and it may have been a factor in keeping him loosely connected to Macdonald's Liberal-Conservative party, even though his instincts were reformist. In his periods of greatest independence he wrote in support of a variety of social causes, notably labour rights, prison reform, and protection of minorities. (The Catholic church, though, was never among these: he regarded that church not as a minority but as a tyranny of orthodoxy, whose influence on the state had to be resisted by all good liberals.) Farrer's early loyalty to Macdonald thus may have been partly a matter of chance, but he seems also to have sympathized with much of his policy. Late in life Farrer once wrote that Macdonald had not been a true Tory: 'In his private opinions there was nothing Tory in the technical sense; indeed, judged by what he did in public, he would have been regarded in the old country as a somewhat advanced Liberal.'[2] While he worked on Conservative papers, too, Farrer later rarely missed a chance to deplore Brown's influence. 'He was a good and, in his way, a great man; but Scotland never sent forth a more bigoted son,' he wrote at one point, not long after Brown's death. 'He made the party, and the party is what he made it – cold, narrow and Calvinistic.'[3]

Any natural hostility Farrer might have felt for George Brown was accentuated, perhaps, by the chance that brought him into the employ of John Ross Robertson, proprietor (with a succession of associates) of the *Daily Telegraph*. That paper had been set up in 1866, claiming to be independent but actually moving in and out of Tory influence. Robertson at this point was a boorish and bigoted young man, still in his late twenties and far from achieving the gloss he eventually acquired as one of Canada's great newspaper magnates. He hated George Brown ('the most notable charlatan the country has ever known')[4] as much as he hated Jesuit priests. One wonders if Farrer's alleged Jesuit training was revealed when he went to work for the *Telegraph*.

In the early 1870s Robertson was also the focus of frustration for Macdonald, who had been trying for years to organize in Toronto a government organ that would stand up to the *Globe*. In pre-Confederation times a number of publishers had failed him, and now he had a poor choice between James Beaty of the *Leader*, whom he considered incompetent, and Robertson of the *Telegraph*, who was unmanageable. During 1868–9 Macdonald had twice tried to solve the problem by engineering a move to Toronto of Thomas White and the Hamilton *Spectator*, but the plans had fallen through. In 1870 and 1871 the prime minister tried a couple of other schemes, either to take over and combine the *Leader* and *Telegraph*, or to start a new paper and drive the others into the ground.

In the process, Macdonald worked without scruple to subvert employees at both papers. On 16 October 1871, for instance, he wrote Charles Belford, chief editor of the *Leader*, saying a friendly journal at Toronto would be welcome, but adding: 'How is it to be done and especially how is it to be done so as to have an effect on the next elections?' The best plan, he said, would be to 'create a fusion of the *Telegraph* and *Leader* and then get possession of both ... I fear, however, that the thing is impractical. Beaty has an exaggerated idea of the value of his newspaper ...' Four days later Macdonald wrote the same kind of letter to George Kingsmill at the *Telegraph*, subtly undercutting Robertson and inviting Kingsmill to come aboard the new project. 'The proprietor of that paper [the *Telegraph*] will find that it has not been for his interest to take the course which he has pursued,' he said, adding: 'I shall be very much obliged to you if you would send me confidentially your views and opinions on press matters. Pray write without reserve. I shall treat your letters as confidential in every respect.'[5]

The machinations proceeded erratically, and Macdonald, in alliance with his provincial counterpart, John Sandfield Macdonald, was driven finally to the option of setting up a new newspaper. On 24 November 1871 he wrote to a colleague saying Beaty was refusing either to sell the *Leader* or to make it an efficient paper, while the *Telegraph* was 'a mere blackmail sheet, and the sooner it is crushed the better.'[6] Early in February 1872, with Beaty still holding out and Robertson repenting too late,[7] Macdonald and his associates hired Thomas

Charles Patteson, an aristocratic Englishman, pessimistic by nature and interested mainly in horses, to organize the new paper. The *Mail* appeared first on 30 March, with Belford and Kingsmill as editors, and Farrer as 'leader' writer. At the time he was still only a novice in his twenties, but he must have made some impact on the Toronto journalistic community. He would work for the *Mail* off and on over an eighteen-year period, rising twice to be editor-in-chief and pressing so hard on the weakened *Globe* that its directors finally decided to hire him, despite his reputation as a troublemaker.

Macdonald took the closest interest in every aspect of the fledgling *Mail* and probably approved personally Farrer's appointment as leader writer. Even before the paper was set up, he intervened to veto the appointment of one staff member, on the grounds he wanted to keep him back at the *Telegraph* – through its last few months of life – to act as a check on Robertson.[8] Again a few days later he wrote Patteson to complain that the paper had taken on a Halifax correspondent who worked for the Grits and advised: 'Please to drop him like a hot potato.'[9]

Patteson evidently entertained false hopes about his own authority to shape the paper. In an editorial-page manifesto on the first day of publication, he claimed that the *Mail* would be a 'bona fide' commercial operation, not a subsidized party organ (a clear lie, but a common one for the times), and another editorial the same day promised to elevate the level of political discussion above mere personalities.[10] The ink was barely dry on that issue, though, before Macdonald was demanding political blood. On 2 April he wrote Patteson:

I congratulate you on the appearance of the *Mail*. The first number is a good one – for a first number. You must assume an appearance of dignity at the outset.

The sooner, however, that you put *on* warpaint and Commence to scalp the better.

It must be done in first-rate style, with the skill of a Tecumseth [*sic*] or a Chingachook, but scalps *must* be taken.

Thems my sentiments.[11]

The *Mail* lived up to Macdonald's demands, and disappointed Goldwin Smith. 'Our hopes of emancipation and literary decency were excited when *The Mail* appeared announcing that it would be written by gentlemen and for gentlemen,' he recalled much later. 'But soon those hopes were dashed. *The Mail* had hardly run through a dozen numbers when it proved itself to be a counterpart of *The Globe* or worse.'¹²

And Smith was not alone: the disillusionment was shared even by Patteson. In the fall he wrote a striking letter to a correspondent who had evidently accused the *Mail* of sinking to the level of the *Globe*. Patteson accepted the truth of the charge but said it was not just the *Globe* – the same standard applied to all major North American newspapers. When he had written his prospectus, he said, he had fully believed in the possibility of changing the tone of political journalism. But he had found quickly that it was useless to swim against the tide. 'If I was respectable the people called me dull; if literary and argumentative I was heavy. A dish spiced with personalities, on the other hand, I was not slow in finding from the exchanges exactly suited the palates of the public ...'¹³

Ned Farrer presumably carried out the 'scalping,' under Patteson's direction, with amused cynicism and no great enthusiasm. (Later in his career he at one point refused to return to the *Mail*, it was said, until assured he would not have to 'scalp.')¹⁴ But he did the job effectively. In the summer of 1872, on the eve of the Pacific Scandal election, there was pressure on Macdonald to have Farrer take over the Tory paper in Stratford, despite his lack of experience. Patteson, however, evidently fought against losing him. On 13 July the prime minister wired Patteson: 'T.M. Daley is very pressing that Farrer should be allowed to take charge of Stratford Herald. He states it is important that Farrer should be the man sent. Try to do this.' Again on 16 July Macdonald wired: 'They cannot get on at Stratford without Farrer. Try to send him up.' But if Farrer went to Stratford at all, it must have been only briefly because he was still at the *Mail* in mid-August and mid-September. On 15 August, as the campaign heated up, Macdonald wrote:

My dear Patteson

Do let Farrer go up to attend two evening meetings in Bothwell – Things are not going right so we must spare no pains. He can then come back to work here.

Yours always
JA McD¹⁵

The note does not say whether Farrer was to speak at the Bothwell meetings (in the Chatham area) or to write about them. Nor is it clear what Macdonald meant by saying Farrer could 'come back to work here.' It may have been that Macdonald wanted him in Ottawa for various duties in connection with the campaign, in which the prime minister was lavishly spreading the American money that would lead to his downfall. In any event, the note indicates that Farrer was already a trusted member of the team, and that the borderline between journalistic and political work was almost non-existent.

The piece of evidence that places Farrer on the *Mail* in mid-September, after the campaign had been safely won, also provides an example of how Macdonald's ideas, even on minor matters, were worked into the paper. It is in the form of a 'pointer' from the prime minister – one of the celebrated notes in which he guided editors. Macdonald's letter has a handwritten note on the margin, from Patteson to Farrer, asking him to 'work up into shape' the prime minister's ideas. The subject was a routine bit of political knife-work on John O'Donohoe, a Roman Catholic politician who had allegedly sold out to the Grits, only to be meanly paid off. Farrer's editorial picked up the prime minister's thought without major change, even including Macdonald's reference to an incident in which Robert Burns had watched a sailor save a man from drowning, only to be rewarded with a sixpence.[16]

It is almost impossible, of course, to identify which of the *Mail*'s editorials in this period actually represent Farrer's early work. (In later years the task becomes easier, as his style and areas of interest emerge.) There are some articles, however, which seem from internal evidence to bear his stamp – especially those that show personal acquaintance with Ireland or with the Church of Rome. For instance, Farrer may have written a 'Gossip' column which appeared on the editorial page on the same day as the Donohoe editorial, and which drew the reader, after a pleasant ramble, to a surprisingly outspoken attack on British rule in Ireland. If Farrer did not write it, it is likely at least that it was he, and not the very British Patteson, who contrived to get the Irish case before Toronto Tories. In any event, the piece showed a pattern that would become a hallmark of Farrer's style: a soft, agreeable opening (this time on the art of euphemism) before building to a powerful point:

The present generation of Englishmen may wonder how its forefathers made such asses of themselves towards the end of the last century touching the American colonies and France. It may also be difficult to reconcile John Bull's ready sympathy and encouragement for 'national' and 'patriotic' risings abroad, with his decided disgust, and summary repression, of such things at home. The key to the mystery is that John is sadly humbugged by rulers and writers skilled in the way things ought to be 'put' ... I recollect once when those Fenian fellows were kicking up a fal-al in Ireland, and the botheration looked a little serious, the Marquis of Hartington made a speech, in which he didn't say the finest peasantry were struggling for independence ... The object of the Irish, he said, was nothing short of 'the establishment of the lowest form of socialism, the destruction of property, the levelling of all distinctions, and the overthrow of all order, and all religions!' Very neatly 'put,' my dear boy, because 'socialism' and the destruction of 'property' are fearful words for the English shopocracy. But did I believe it? Well, I didn't. Truth is truth, and humbug, humbug ...[17]

While the *Mail*'s major political editorials no doubt were shaped by the government or the publisher, the minor editorials presumably were Farrer's responsibility, and many of these show a catholic interest, touching on science and literature and religion and social patterns. Much of the job was unvarnished propagandizing, however, and that part became increasingly difficult during 1873 as the *Mail* fought a pathetic rearguard action in the Pacific Scandal wars. It is not surprising that Farrer looked for a way out. In December, a month after the Macdonald government fell, he received the seven-month appointment as a federal immigration agent in Ireland – a posting that may have been essentially a matter of getting free passage back to Ireland. It is not clear why the appointment was made by the new government of Alexander Mackenzie, but Farrer's Grit friend E.B. Wood may have been a factor. The questionable *News* profile of 1891 suggested as much and claimed that it was on this occasion that Farrer first showed his propensity for switching sides. Curiously, though, it had him defecting during the general election of 1874, a month *after* the actual appointment: 'He was standing on the steps of the old *Mail* building one day when the late E.B. Wood was passing along the south side of King Street. Wood hailed Farrer. "Ned," he cried, "come over with us and make money." That night Farrer went to the Walker House and he joined the Grit party. He went to Napanee and spoke for Richard Cartwright, and when the campaign ended and Mackenzie had won Farrer went to Ireland as an immigration agent as a reward for his services ...'[18]

Whether Farrer remained in Ireland seven months or eighteen, and whether his wife and newborn son accompanied him, are not known. It is clear that he returned from Ireland in June 1874 to testify in a major libel case[19] and was back on the *Mail* in 1875, taking an increasingly strong hand in editorial policy and gaining a reputation for mischief. A *Grip* article in mid-1875 included him in the Toronto press 'galaxy' and implied he was responsible for several stories embarrassing to the provincial Liberal government. These included the curious episode of 'Little Mrs Blank,' cartooned and described by *Grip* editor John Bengough as a mild joke that got out of hand. (Bengough explained later that an 'ingenious romancer' at the *Mail* had made up the story: he had implied that Archibald McKellar, a notoriously reclusive cabinet minister, had bought the portrait of a certain lady for his office, and opposition members had chosen to score political points by pretending to take the facetious remark seriously.)[20]

While he quickly made a reputation for satire, most of Farrer's work was basic Tory propaganda, this time with Sir John in vigilant touch. The Tories were now in opposition, and Macdonald was practising law in Toronto and sometimes contributing to the *Mail*. There is no sign, however, that relations between Macdonald and Farrer were harmed by the alleged defection during the Pacific Scandal. More than thirty years later, on one of the few occasions when he reminisced in print, Farrer recalled those years and stressed mainly Macdonald's kindness and congeniality, although noting that the leader could be 'severe' on occasion. 'Very frequently, in his Opposition days, he would write an article for the *Mail* and it was generally so harsh that we had to tone it down,' Farrer recalled. 'At first he used to protest in a good-humored way, saying that we were mere milk-and-water fighters, but in the end he came to see, with most men of journalism, that nothing is so unwise as to be extreme.'

Farrer also offered one small vignette that seems to indicate he looked back with pleasure at this era when he was engaged in some of the less edifying political games of the time:

On the night of September 17, 1878, when [Macdonald] was returned to office, he was in Kingston. Two or three days afterwards he came to Toronto, to the United Empire Club, 'in order, as he said, to divide the spoils.' He himself arranged the little party; there was no one there who had not worked to the best of his power, yet nobody was there who could be called well-to-do, by which I mean that Sir John purposely overlooked the rich men. It was a jolly gathering, for he was in good spirits, and at the proper time he said: 'Now, what am I going to give you fellows? You have fought without hope of reward.'

There was a poor fellow from the Maritime Provinces, long since dead, who had written letters for *The Mail*, which had helped matters no doubt, and Sir John there and then gave him a place, amid loud acclaim. And so it went, every one present being cheered, not by an office, perhaps, but by the kind words the 'Old Man' said. I think all are now dead, save myself, and O, dear, how sad one feels for loss of friends as one nears the common end.[21]

If Farrer the philosopher had small regard for party politics, Farrer the journalist clearly played the game with some zest.

It was in this period, during development of the protective National Policy which carried the 1878 election, that Farrer began to emerge as a significant figure in the exposition of economic policy. From this point on, at least, it was his clear and trenchant writing on economic issues that most impressed contemporaries. Ironically, the material is perhaps his least interesting from a later point of view, and is also the work that shows his most extreme mercenary tendencies. Over the years he switched sides repeatedly in the interminable debate over free trade versus protection. Starting as a protectionist, he switched to free trade at the Winnipeg *Sun*, then back again to protection at the *Mail*, and then to free trade when the paper broke with Macdonald. Finally, while not positively advocating protection, he switched one last time to oppose Laurier's reciprocity platform in 1911. While friends puzzled about his 'real' views, Farrer himself tended later to dismiss both sides with amused contempt: the Liberals, he liked to recall, had maintained a tariff of $17\,^{1}/_{2}$ per cent and called it free trade – whereas the Tory tariff of 20 per cent was protection and therefore abominable.[22]

In other ways Farrer in his first editorship, starting in the late 1870s,[23] showed some of the liberal tendencies that would firm up later. He advocated admission of women to universities,[24] condemned anti-Jewish pogroms in Europe,[25] and (more surprisingly) deplored the emphasis on 'race and religion' in Canadian politics. ('Let us have done with this cry about nationality and religion in Canadian politics.')[26] By the end of 1880, *Grip*, while it constantly sneered at Farrer's bosses, judged that the *Mail* 'in all that constitutes a newspaper of the present day' had clearly moved ahead of the *Globe* and was constantly increasing the distance.[27]

While Farrer's writing was thus attracting notice, it was presumably his skill as a defender of the National Policy that prompted Macdonald to bring him back from his brief stint in New York for election writing in the spring of 1882,[28] and then to send him on to Winnipeg. *Grip* cartooned him flying off to Winnipeg, watched apprehensively by Liberal leaders, and took it as a sign that the political wars were about to heat up: 'Mr Farrer is the most brilliant journalist available for the ministerial side, and he usually comes to the front on the eve of a general election.'[29] Similarly, the Toronto *World* a few years later quoted Sir John as having said (presumably before the 1882 election, although it did not make this clear): 'I may have some use for Farrer before the next general election. If I do I know how to fetch him.'[30]

Despite this reputation, Farrer seems to have been foisted on Winnipeg *Times* publisher Amos Rowe against his will, and the latter may already have had some inkling of Farrer's capacity for mischief. 'I suppose I must,' the publisher wired Macdonald on 2 May 1882, 'but want some help badly had you not better keep Farrar then and send me Johnson of the Mail answer.'[31] Another Rowe letter to Macdonald on 22 August makes clear that the publisher had cause for concern, since he was already apologizing for a Farrer article criticizing Ontario Tories.[32]

If the prime minister had been prescient, he might have seen in this small controversy warnings of the major problems Farrer would cause for him before the 1880s ended. Possibly because of his New York experience, or possibly because of maturity (he was now in his early thirties), Farrer would never again be an easily manageable editor.

4 Making Mischief

Ned Farrer's two-year stint in Winnipeg journalism, 1882–4, was significant for three things. First, it was during this period that his capacity for making trouble for his party emerged. At the Winnipeg *Times* he established a pattern, repeated later at the *Mail* and the *Globe*, of pushing journalistic independence as far as proprietors and political masters would allow – and sometimes farther. Second, his Winnipeg editorials showed clear hints of sympathy for political union. (At one point he was linked, unreliably, with a curious plot to take the whole of Canada's Northwest into the American union.) Finally, Farrer's own views on a number of topics, especially imperialism and militarism, emerged in his Winnipeg writing. His short term as editor of the Winnipeg *Sun*, from about April to September of 1884, gave him a good deal more editorial scope than he had ever enjoyed before. In this pattern there was one major exception: the *Sun* was the organ of the CPR and slavishly reflected its views on railway matters. But on the general run of issues Farrer may have had more latitude than he would have even as editor of the *Mail* during its great days of independence in the late 1880s. The *Mail* as an 'independent' was hedged about with political intrigues that have never been adequately explained.

In Winnipeg the freedom may have been partly a matter of isolation. The Manitoba capital at the time was a wide-open town, physically far removed from Eastern political controllers and responding in many ways to its own frontier dynamics. Farrer's arrival coincided with the end of the city's legendary boom period of 1880–1. After a decade-long influx of settlers and the excitement of the CPR's arrival, drought and depression nurtured discontent, much of it directed at Ottawa.

The city was full of disappointed 'boomsters' and their hangers-on, while the country was filling up with settlers resentful of the CPR monopoly.[1]

Winnipeg's newspapers more or less reflected the political spectrum, with the *Manitoba Free Press* supporting the Grits, the *Times* solidly Tory, supporting the quasi-Conservative government of John Norquay, and the *Sun* nominally independent, though leaning towards the Grits. But local issues – and the CPR – upset the political symmetry. The railway was a political force in the region, wielding power to an extent difficult to appreciate in a later age, and the effects showed up in various ways on all three papers. At the *Times* the connection was a simple one: Macdonald and the CPR were allies (at times the railway seemed to forget this, but later it would with justice be called 'the Conservative party on wheels'). The *Free Press* connection was less clear, but it was assumed that control of the paper was held by Donald A. Smith, a major figure in the railway syndicate and a one-time Tory, who had broken with Macdonald in the Pacific Scandal session of 1873.[2] As for the 'independent' *Sun*, it came under the control or influence of the CPR in 1884, before or during Farrer's tenure as editor, even though it had earlier been hostile to the railway's monopoly. Farrer thus defended the CPR at both the *Times* and the *Sun*, in a consistent pattern at odds with his rebelliousness on other matters.

At the *Times* that rebelliousness showed up on two levels: in direct (and heretical) criticism of the federal government; and in a broader tendency to undermine sacred Tory institutions of aristocracy or empire or military glory. Tory subscribers were puzzled by Farrer's editorials. One wrote to say he had subscribed on the understanding the *Times* was a good Conservative paper, maintaining the institutions of the Mother Country in King, Lords, and Commons, only to find that 'many of your articles of late have been as distinctly hostile to those institutions as the most radical paper would be.' The letter writer, a retired captain of the Royal Artillery, objected especially to the advocacy by the *Times* of votes for British farm labourers and of reform in the House of Lords, and to its 'sneering and disrespectful' attitude to the British army.

The newspaper's reply came in the best of Farrer's mature style, again starting gently and with courtesy for his opponent, then enlisting the support of all 'reasonable' readers, and carrying them along into territory they might not normally want to visit:

Elsewhere will be found a letter from Capt. Goodridge of Headingley, in which he takes the Times sharply to task for, as he alleges, attacking the institutions of the Mother Country, more especially the House of Peers. We plead guilty to having found fault with some British institutions, and to having expressed the belief that reform of the constitution of the Upper House is necessary, and will be brought about before long. And furthermore we say, without any disrespect to Capt. Goodridge, that on every fitting occasion the Times will reiterate these views.

Capt. Goodridge has, no doubt, heard of the Duke of Wellington's famous declaration that the British constitution was so absolutely perfect that mortal man could not a priori construct a better one ... Now with these views, which were the views of the orthodox Tory school at that day, Capt. Goodridge has probably little sympathy. He is far too intelligent a man to believe that Parliamentary reform has brought ruin upon the Empire; that the abolition of rotten boroughs and the open traffic in seats has dimmed Britain's glory; or that the manifold organic changes which have been silently wrought in the constitution since the beginning of the century, have been attended by disastrous results. So, too, The Times believes that further reforms are necessary; that such measures as the enfranchisement of the million and a half of small tenant farmers and agricultural laborers, who are now outside the pale of the constitution; the disestablishment of the State church, no longer, if the census figures are correct, the church of the large majority; the readjustment of the relations between landlord and tenant; and the destruction of those relics of feudalism, entail, primogeniture and tithes, would not impair England's strength but make her stronger as they would make her people freer. And for the accomplishment of these reforms it is necessary that the Upper House should be reformed ... The hereditary principle is a bad one. Does Capt. Goodridge seriously believe that blackguards like Lord Aylesford, or adulterers like Lord Shrewsbury, premier Earl of England, or common rogues like the Marquis of Huntly, or debauchees and gamblers like the Duke of Hamilton, or double-dyed scoundrels like the late Earl of Lonsdale, should be empowered to thwart the popular will simply because they are their noble fathers' sons?³

Such liberal reformist views seem unremarkable now, but at the time they stamped the writer as both an independent scholar and an enemy of high Tory principles, and this naturally caused uneasiness in the party. Worse was to come: early in 1883, the *Times* began to criticize specific party actions. At first these were minor matters. There was, for instance, a sniping engagement with the Hamilton *Spectator*, after the *Times*, ignoring warnings from Macdonald, described the Tory party in Ontario as lamentably weak, having no policy and few good men, and predicted a possible disaster in the next election. The *Spectator* sniffed that Conservative papers in Ontario were not in the habit of asking Manitoba Conservatives for advice on who should be entrusted with office. The *Times* replied that this was true enough – but that the Conservative press in Ontario was also not in the habit of consulting the Conservative *electors*. 'If it were, the humiliating defeat that overtook the party in 1879 would have been averted.'[4]

Farrer also satirized excesses of the chief party champions, the *Mail* and the *Globe*, in election campaigning, noting with amusement that the *Mail* had described delegates to Reform conventions as a 'semi-civilized crowd of dull-witted partisans,' while the *Globe* had replied in kind. Each paper, too, made a habit of claiming that its own speakers were received with unparalleled enthusiasm, while the other paper would report that half the audience left in disgust before the speech was over:

Rabid appeals are made on both sides to the Catholic vote, the temperance vote, the Methodist vote, the artisan vote, the colored vote, and to every other vote except the common-sense vote, each party accusing the other of being bitterly hostile to each and all of these interests.

It is safe to say that not one elector in fifty thousand is influenced by this sort of cannonading. The firing is altogether too wild to be effective, and the marksmen remind one of the stuttering man at a bird-shooting match, who loaded and fired at random with indomitable industry. On being asked for an explanation, he replied with a long drawn out stammer: 'F-a-c-t is I d-o-n-t e-x-p-e-c-t to k-i-l-l anything, but I'm t-r-y-i-n-g to k-e-e-p the air f-i-l-l-e-d with s-h-o-t.'[5]

This kind of needling of the party might have been forgiven, but the *Times*, late in the spring of 1883, moved well beyond the tolerable limit. The occasion was a federal budget brought in by Macdonald's finance minister, Sir Leonard Tilley, that maintained high duties on farm implements and hurt Manitoba in several other ways. The *Times*, despite its explicit claim to be the government's organ in the Northwest, reacted with sarcasm and outright opposition, at times hinting at Western separation or even defection to the United States. On 9 April, for instance, the paper responded angrily to a report that Sir Leonard had laughed off Western objections to his budget. Tilley's laugh, Farrer wrote, was ill-timed. 'This is probably a more serious business than he imagines. Nature, a more potent ruler than any New Brunswick statesman, has placed nearly a thousand miles of rock between us and Ontario. She has decreed, too, that our most convenient markets are St. Paul and Chicago.' The Eastern provinces, the editorial went on, should stop treating the West as a satrapy to be overrun by their carpet-baggers and start offering it a little decent respect.[6]

Over the next few weeks Farrer continued to lacerate the budget, while repeating that the U.S. border was not far away. The fundamental blunder underlying the policy of both political parties at Ottawa, he wrote, was the belief that the Northwest settlers were pampered people who ought to submit to little inconveniences like heavy taxation, unstable land regulation, and disregard for their rights as squatters. 'To make matters worse, the people at Ottawa forget that not too many miles from here a foreign flag offers the settler nearly all the advantages he can obtain here ...'[7]

Even tougher were the attacks by the *Times* on Ottawa's chief man on the Prairies, Lieutenant-Governor Edgar Dewdney of the Northwest Territories. In an astonishing display of party disunity, Farrer ridiculed the governor and accused him of committing an array of sins: of breaking faith with Indians, of favouring friendly contractors to the detriment of natives, and of engaging in blatant corruption in choosing and developing Regina (formerly 'Pile of Bones') as capital of the Territories. The full force of his contempt was perhaps not apparent until seven years later, when at the *Globe* he accused Dewdney of helping to cause the Riel Rebellion – of being *particeps criminis* with the interior minister, Sir David Macpherson, in 'goading the halfbreeds into rebellion by sheer callousness and neglect.'[8] But even at the *Times* in 1883, Farrer's ridicule was untypically harsh. In one caustic column, for instance, he regretted that the West had so few knights and suggested that Dewdney would be a fine candidate for that distinction:

That eminent official occupies probably the highest position under the Queen's sceptre. He is the Governor, the absentee Governor, of fifty thousand white men and some thousands of Indians, and likewise their Government, and also the fountain-head of their whiskey. They have no rights which he is bound to respect. He is empowered to form or join in speculative land syndicates, and at the same time to select the sites of future capitals and, of his own mere motion, to make appropriations of the people's money for works likely to injure their interests and build up his own. 'Sir Edgar Dewdney of Pile of Bones,' what a standing and peripatetic advertisement that would be for the Northwest! We must have some knights. If Her Gracious Majesty will not create them, Sir Leonard ought to be able to foster their growth by one of his skilful shuffles of the tariff.[9]

On another occasion, after a cutting review of Dewdney's treatment of Indians, Farrer wrote that the governor was entitled to some kind of testimonial, since he had proved himself such a grand friend of the Indians and a fine example to the Prairie whites:

He teaches the raw settler a new code of morals. He shows him by precept and example that in these degenerate days it is not necessary for a man holding a trust not to abuse it. He illustrates in his own walk and life the modern principle that every man should fight for his own wallet. He is, in this great country, the most signal exemplar of how to get along regardless of the means or methods of locomotion.

Mr Dewdney, therefore, deserves well at our hands and at the hands of the Indians of these territories. It would hardly be appropriate to present him with a homestead, for he has several, also pre-emptions in abundance. Money would also be out of place, inasmuch as while Sir Leonard has a surplus and Sir John remains in power, he will not want. Could anything be more appropriate than to present him with a petition to leave, to get out, to go elsewhere and teach other Indians and other white men the ethics of grab, greed and shamelessness he has introduced here?[10]

In Ottawa opposition MPs needled Macdonald for conspicuous failure to control his Winnipeg organ, especially its reaction to Dewdney and to the Tilley budget. Macdonald replied in the House on 7 May, in terms that were, ironically, almost identical to those he would use three years later as Farrer edged the Toronto *Mail* away from the party line. The government welcomed the support of newspapers, he said, but no newspaper could afford to be simply a servile tool of government. So, 'unless they tread very hard on our toes, we do not actually cut off newspapers from anything like Government patronage, because they choose to be independent and occasionally to disapprove of any course or act of the government.'[11] Understandably, Macdonald's forgiving comments sat ill with the true Tory journalists. His remark about servile papers was interpreted by both the Toronto

World and *Grip* as a slap at the Toronto *Mail*'s sycophancy; *Grip* cartooned the *Mail* as a snivelling cur being kicked by its master.[12]

Conservatives in Winnipeg were also miffed. 'A large number of our friends here are very unhappy with the course the Times is pursuing and talk of starting another Conservative paper,' Macdonald's son, Hugh John, wrote to his father on 31 May. Rowe and Farrer were making the paper unpopular, he added, 'and some of our strongest friends are giving it up and taking the Free Press.'[13] Pressure was undoubtedly brought to bear on Rowe, and the paper suddenly fell back into line, at least on the budget.

The reasons for this shift in focus are not known. Farrer may have been drinking, or may have run into the serious illness of which Willison wrote. He would certainly have been under party pressure, though, and may also have realized that Winnipeg in the grip of post-boom 'smash and crash' was not a good place to be out of work. Whatever the reason, the attacks on Ottawa faded, and for the rest of the year the paper's tone (except for an occasional slash at Dewdney) was mild. At times it even attacked the *Free Press* for despairing articles that injured the West and encouraged annexation. The *Free Press* replied with a long rebuttal quoting excerpts from a dozen *Times* editorials from April and May on the plight of the West.[14]

Farrer's mischief-making thus created a constant vexation for *Times* publisher Amos Rowe, and became something of a legend. Much later, John W. Dafoe, speaking on early journalism in Manitoba, told how Farrer on one occasion wrote an article criticizing the Orange order at the time when Rowe, an official of the order, was on a tour to promote it. When he got back, Rowe 'expostulated' with Farrer, saying people must be wondering why he spoke of the order in one way and wrote of it in another. ' "Don't worry, Amos," was the consoling reply ... "no one will ever accuse you of writing that article." '[15]

This mischief-making may have been in the background when, in April 1884, Rowe reported to Macdonald that he was parting company with his editor. The stated cause, though, was drinking: 'Farrer has been on a pretty extensive spree for the last few days,' Rowe wrote. 'I am afraid that I will have to let him go but the trouble is to obtain a person to fill his position. I must ask your assistance in that direction.'[16] Farrer apparently left the *Times* in the next few days. A letter to Macdonald on 23 April from Thomas Fahey reported that Farrer had resigned the *Times* editorship, and that he, Fahey, had been recommended as successor by Christopher Bunting of the *Mail*.

The letter respectfully solicited the prime minister's 'kind recollection of my humble services and unpurchased loyalty to the party.'[17]

Macdonald's view of Farrer's personal or professional qualities at this point is unknown, but it is unlikely he could have returned to the *Mail* later that year without the leader's sanction. Only one Farrer letter to Macdonald is known to exist, and none has been found to Farrer from the prime minister. The one known letter was written before the budget controversy and is respectful in tone. A wry comment at the end seems to indicate an easy relationship, possibly based on mutual liking for a good story or a good vintage. Aside from that, the letter is notable chiefly in showing that Farrer had succumbed to Winnipeg's pervasive fever of speculation. It also shows he was not above using his political connection, although the sin seems a borderline one, related to a technical point on timber limits in the area then disputed between Manitoba and Ontario. The letter said:

Private   Winnipeg, Feb. 19th, 1883
Dear Sir John

I hope you will pardon me for writing to ask you to interest yourself in a matter personal to myself. It is my first offence. I have paid out of a by no means bulky pocket for the survey of a timber limit – one on the mainland of the Lake of Woods, the other on the shores of Rainy Lake. I am, however, told that the department has ceased granting limits in those regions. This, of course, means loss to me, but I am quite ready to bear it if it cannot be helped. If any reasonable exception can be made, I can guarantee that an accurate description surveyed at our own cost shall be sent in ...

The complaints made here last spring against the Interior Department are rarely heard now. The people, although a generation of sharks, are becoming more reasonable.

We have had a hard fight defending the C.P.R., but I think the monopoly cry is exhausted and the cry about extortionate rates dead. Mr Norquay is not highly acceptable to old Ontario Conservatives here, but where to get a better man is a question not easily answered.

I hope you were satisfied with the result of our elections. We had two guinea-pigs of a sombre color in Winnipeg or we should have carried both ridings easily.

                                                             I remain, Dear Sir John,
                                                                       With great respect,
                                                                          Yours obediently,
                                                                                E. Farrer[18]

Macdonald was evidently sympathetic to the request, though there is no firm indication he acted on it, or that Farrer profited by the timber deal. A note handwritten by the prime minister on Farrer's letter says: 'So soon as the Ont. elections are over we must take up the question of dealing with the lands in the disputed territory.' It may be that the timber deal was part of a tacit payment for Farrer's journalistic services (such an arrangement was not unknown) and that he became a victim of 'Old Tomorrow.' It may also be significant that the problem with timber leases preceded Farrer's sharpest outburst against the party, in the budget issue.

In any event, Farrer's move from the *Times* to the *Sun* in the spring of 1884 gave him considerably more elbow room. The paper was not a distinguished one, but its editorial page after his arrival showed a good deal of verve and individuality, except where the CPR was concerned. On that subject its slant was all the more striking because of the sudden change. A few months earlier it had seen the railway as 'subsidized and petted' and had called for creation of a third party to fight the monopoly. Under Farrer's editorship (although the policy more likely came from its president, a prominent politician named Samuel Clarke Biggs), the *Sun* was as much a CPR mouthpiece as the *Times* had been. It worked assiduously to remove farmers' fears of the railway and urged the obstreperous Farmers' Union to make peace with it. 'It is impossible to regard the Canadian Pacific as the farmer's enemy,' it said at one point. 'If it does not encourage him it must go under ...' At another point it said the railway's twenty-year monopoly clause had given it almost unlimited power, but there were not ten men in the Northwest who would say it had abused that power.[19]

The *Sun*'s most notable feature that summer, though, was a consistent, subtle campaign to undermine Confederation and promote either Western independence or annexation – a campaign that should have amply warned Tories planning Farrer's return to the *Mail*. Indeed, some hints of the *Sun*'s machinations did show up in letters to the prime minister from Nicholas Flood Davin, another Irish journalist (later an MP) who had opened the Regina *Leader* in the interests of Macdonald and Dewdney. The *Sun* under Farrer, Davin said at one point, could now be classed as a consistent enemy of the prime minister, although allied with the CPR. On another occasion he hinted obscurely at links between Farrer and James G. Blaine, then running for the U.S. presidency and known to be an expansionist. Apparently

Making Mischief 53

attaching some items from the *Sun*, Davin said the views expressed in them were no novelty to him, but he had not heard them before from Farrer. 'When I was in Winnipeg F was talking about the road [CPR], Blaine's presidential schemes, and the government in a way that I would laugh at if his utterances were merely the utterances of Farrer.'[20]

Davin could have been referring to *Sun* comments a few days earlier that Blaine might encourage Northwest disaffection if elected: 'Sir John had better treat us decently, at least during Blaine's term.' Another comment on the same page added: 'It would not be an impossible task to annex Canada just now. She is particularly weak in the Northwest.'[21] Davin might also have sent along some of Farrer's repeated suggestions that the West should secede and either set up an independent state, or look to the south. In late May, for instance, the *Sun* had said that the all-but-universal opinion in the Northwest was that Confederation – that 'mongrel aggregation of colonies' – was a failure, and that the West was in a transitory phase, 'emerging from the chrysalis into a life that will begin heaven knows when and end heaven knows where.' The next day it endorsed Norquay's rejection of 'better terms' for Manitoba and called for a new ultimatum to Ottawa. 'We were brought into Confederation without our consent,' it said, 'and it can be no crime to leave it without ceremony.' Early in June it became more outspoken, after a warning from the *Times* that the province was extremely dependent on Eastern neighbours, and that Sir John might 'become aggressive' if Manitoba continued to resist the terms. The prime minister was mistaken in thinking the Northwest depended on the East, the *Sun* said. 'Our interests, it may be our destiny, lies to the South. If he wishes to test the matter, let him "become aggressive." He cannot strip us of much, for we are already naked. But he can succeed, if he tries ever so little, in precipitating secession; and if *he* desires that, it must be confessed that the ambition is mutual.' History had taught, the editorial went on, that loyalists to tyranny and injustice had always been a routed minority in North America.[22]

At the end of the summer the *Sun*'s anti-Confederation tone was if anything stronger. On 8 August it reviewed factors making for national disunity, said Macdonald would be hard-pressed to keep the country together for a decade, and observed that 'the ultimate collapse of the union and dispersion of the provinces is a foregone conclusion in the mind of every intelligent man ...' On 30 August it attacked the very basis of the country, in powerfully destructive terms very similar to those that would show up in Farrer's later editorials in the *Mail*:

It is manifestly impossible for the present system of government to endure. The thousand miles of rock and water dividing us from the East are arguments against it that cannot be overcome by tariffs, railroads or any other human contrivances. It is written on the face of nature that this region was not destined to be tied to the other provinces or ruled from a centre of authority so far remote as Ottawa; and what nature has decreed man cannot circumvent by acts of Parliament or even by such desperate enterprises as a transcontinental line. After seventeen years of Confederation, the Maritime provinces are in but not of Canada. The barriers that separate them from Quebec and Ontario are trifling compared with those that stand between the Northwest and British Columbia on the one hand and the rest of the Dominion on the other; while our connection with the United States is closer and more complete than theirs. Is the experiment that has conspicuously failed in their case likely to be crowned with success in ours? This is the paramount issue of the Northwest ...

A few days later the paper was back on the same theme. While the British connection was not in immediate danger, it said, 'it is as certain as anything can be in human affairs that independence or annexation is the ultimate destiny of Canada ... the birth of a Canadian nation or the bloodless absorption of these provinces by the Republic ... is written in the book of fate.'[23]

About the same time this was being written, Farrer's name was linked, privately, with a bizarre plot set in motion by one E.A.C. Pew, a promoter from Welland, Ontario, to annex the Northwest to the United States. In grandiose terms, Pew proposed not only to buy up the three Winnipeg newspapers, to pave the way for independence, but as well to buy Norquay and four of his ministers and to secure the support of the Roman Catholic church and Lous Riel, the Métis leader, then in exile in the United States. He planned to raise money for the scheme by issuing bonds in the new 'state,' these bonds to be redeemed later by the U.S. government at enormous profit to the plotters.

Pew implied to one government informant that Farrer would serve as a principal writer for the campaign. Nothing else ties Farrer to the plot, but the incident drew curious and shadowy connections between

Farrer and several people who would figure in the later annexation movement of 1891: S.J. Ritchie, the Ohio industrialist who apparently inspired Pew and helped finance the later effort; Erastus Wiman, who acted as *agent provocateur* in the Pew affair and would later be a sometime ally and enemy of Farrer; William McDougall, Wiman's cousin, a prominent but erratic politician, who acted as Macdonald's agent in the Pew affair and later, in the 1891 incident, informed on Farrer in return for the promise of a senatorship.[24]

Whether Farrer took part in Pew's extraordinary game is one of the most intriguing questions hanging over his career. The ultimate aim would have drawn his support, and it is easy to imagine him listening to Pew with enough sympathy to draw out the whole story. However, the *Sun* earlier in the summer had savaged Pew, repeatedly and brutally. This might be explained partly by the fact that the occasion was a clash between Pew and the CPR, the *Sun*'s backer, but the severity of the language seems to have gone well beyond what the connection would have demanded. The paper wrote off Pew's planned 'Manitoba Southwestern Railway' as a fraud and described the promoter himself as 'one of the cheap and noisy "boomsters" that have sprung up in the Northwest by the score.' Pew, it said, could not build a mile of streetcar track if given the material and the right of way. A week later the paper was more specific, going into Pew's shady background and bluntly challenging him to sue: 'He is a fraud. That is plain and no doubt actionable English,' it said. '... Mr Pew is simply a humbug with a pious turn and a marvellous stock of impudence. We don't want either him or his money, if he has any.'[25]

Farrer's alleged part in Pew's plot was reported to Macdonald by an informant who ran into Pew on a New York-to-Buffalo train. Pew was returning from an exploratory trip when he fell in with H.P. Dwight of Toronto, general manager of Wiman's Great North Western Telegraph Company, and confided, in the smoker, his great plan. Dwight promptly wrote to his boss in New York to tell him of the plot. Pew, he said, had just returned from Washington, where he had seen 'leading men' in his search for support for the plan, which involved first secession and then annexation – 'though of course the latter is to be left in the background.' The Americans, Dwight went on, had given assurance they would pay $25 to $30 million in one way or another for the country. 'Pew is now going to the Northwest to work the thing up. He has one of the Winnipeg newspapers already secured, and arrangements partially made for another, so that he will have two out of three of the best papers there with Farrer one of the principal writers ...'[26]

Wiman sent this letter on to McDougall, who passed most of it on to the prime minister. Macdonald saw no serious threat in the plot but nevertheless sent McDougall to Winnipeg and encouraged Wiman to go with Pew to Washington to test the waters there. While McDougall's work seems to have resulted in little beyond a dispute over expenses, Wiman's efforts brought striking results, including a long document written by Pew that set out the Great Plan. While there is no further reference to Farrer, it is interesting that Pew claimed support from the *Sun*. Some of the 'parties favorable' who had been consulted, he said, included S.C. Biggs, who was not only president of the *Sun* and former provincial secretary, but also a man of influence and position and one of the wealthiest men in the Northwest. 'Among parties controlling the press, Mr Roe [Rowe] of the "Times" would not be favorable to a United States connection, though strongly in favor of independence. Mr Luxton [W.F. Luxton] of the Free Press, would favor immediate connection with the United States ...'

Pew's plot faded without so much as a public whisper, and Farrer's reputation did not suffer in the episode. Macdonald must not have put much credence in the report of his involvement, given Farrer's reappointment at the *Mail* just weeks later. The *Mail*'s managers probably knew nothing of the incident, although they would have been well aware that Farrer at the *Sun* was expressing some decidedly unconventional views.

There were, for instance, in addition to the dark hints on the breakup of the country, his continuing attacks on the party press. 'It is no longer possible to believe the party journals,' said one editorial note. 'They cannot even give an honest report of a political meeting or present a faithful picture of the condition of trade and commerce.'[27]

Another consistent theme – a concern that would show up wherever Farrer worked – was a marked hostility for all things imperialistic and militaristic. On the Royal Military College, the paper wondered why Canada should support an institution for turning out officers for the British army. 'If Canadian lads thirst for the glory of butchering Arabs, sticking Zulus or shooting down Boer farmers, let them go to Sandhurst.' The United Empire Loyalists, an institution well-nigh sacrosanct in the colony, provided another target. At one point the *Sun* even opposed a UEL request for a public grant to finance centenary celebrations. The loyalists, it said, had 'abandoned the colonies because they could not distinguish the difference between a monarch and a tyrant'; there was no reason why Northwest settlers should be taxed to perpetuate the memory of such a cause. The same theme was sounded later in the summer: 'Altogether the Loyalists were a rather small-soulled mob ... It is true they suffered persecution at the hands of the patriots, but do men who have striven to perpetuate tyranny deserve to enjoy the hard-won blessings of freedom?'[28]

More particularly, the *Sun* ridiculed the family of Colonel George Taylor Denison, cavalry officer and police magistrate, who led Toronto's imperialist faction. The Denisons, the *Sun* said, were the 'very aristocracy' of the Loyalists, who had fled to Canada to avoid asserting their rights as men. 'Their object in rushing to Canada was not merely to evade service in the people's cause against a maniac despot but, apparently, to get office; and they have succeeded. One of the Denisons – they were all lieutenant-colonels – is a police magistrate, the other is a deputy adjutant-general in the pay of the Dominion and the rest, eight in all, who once held public offices of some sort, resigned only when they died. The remaining two will doubtless stand by the treasury and the old flag with the same desperate tenacity.'[29]

Curiously, this same George Taylor Denison would play a major part in the climactic episodes of Farrer's career. Six years later it would be Denison who, as police magistrate, decided against him in a libel case revolving on his 'traitorous' activities. Seven years later it would be Denison who helped to obtain the fatal annexation pamphlet for Sir John A. Macdonald. Eight years later it would be Denison who pressed hardest for Farrer's dismissal from the *Globe*. More curiously still, Farrer would write, in a bylined article twenty-six years later, that Denison was 'the kindest and best of men' despite a tendency to be fierce in the defence of the Loyalists.[30] (In that same article Farrer also took a much gentler view of Loyalists, saying history had proven them wrong, but that they could not really be judged by standards of a later day.)

While imperialism was considered a fair target, the *Sun* during that summer of 1884 consistently defended religious and racial underdogs. For instance, it reacted to attacks on the Salvation Army, then regarded as an hysterical fringe group, by reminding readers that Methodism had suffered the same kind of attacks in the previous century:

It is charged against them by an Eastern clergyman of some fame in the High

Church party, that their officers are illiterate. Probably they are, but then the Fishermen were not as learned as the Pharisees. It is said, too, that some of the officers are men of 'doubtful antecedents.' That is no doubt true also; but the same objection would have proved fatal to the employment of Saul ... The Salvationists are indeed humble and uncouth laborers, but they are intensely sincere; and religious sincerity, though it should take an exaggerated form, is sufficiently rare in these days to merit respect.[31]

The *Sun* also took issue with newspaper criticism of the establishment of a Jewish settlement in the Pipestone region. It described the Jewish settlers as a sober and industrious people and said there was among Christians a very unchristian prejudice against Jews. 'We want immigrants, and the Jew is as welcome as the Gentile.' When Chinese were stoned in Vancouver, the *Sun* deplored the incident and said missionaries being sent to China should be instructed to hold a revival *en route* among the Christians in British Columbia.[32]

More surprisingly, perhaps, in view of Farrer's later role as alleged satanic influence in the *Mail*'s 'race and creed' campaign, the *Sun* also strongly supported Métis land claims. It said Ottawa had long since promised Métis in the Prince Albert region land grants equal to those issued in Manitoba, but was now treating them the same as any other settlers. 'This is unjust. The half-breeds who made the great trails over the plains ... and who helped the Government to reach an amicable settlement of the Indian claims, are surely entitled to more consideration than the new arrival who shares in the fruit of their enterprise and loyalty ... a great wrong is being committed in the treatment of these people.'[33]

The *Sun* was also regularly critical of Dewdney's native policy, and as a result came under attack from Davin's Regina *Leader*. In June the *Leader* accused the *Sun* of persistently misrepresenting Dewdney and rejected its account of Indian problems at Battleford, where Dewdney was said to have ordered Indians back to the reserve and to have stopped their rations. Both points were wrong, the *Leader* said, and Farrer was surely entitled to a prize as the man who could tell the greatest number of whoppers in the fewest number of minutes. 'When it comes to heroic invention the agility of an antelope is nothing to that of the versatile and veracious Editor of the *Sun*.'[34]

This jab was only one incident in a long-running fight in which Farrer had mauled Dewdney and Davin in poems, satires, and serious prose – and sometimes a combination of all these. A typical Farrer sally (this one in the *Times*, aimed mainly at the Northwest Mounted Police) managed with one broad swipe to get at the governor, his editor, Regina's abysmal water supply, its exaggerated publicity, and its drinking habits:

Regina, happy in so many things, is supremely happy in her judicial system. Her magistrates, judges and chief justices are composed of boss policemen, who have left some civil employment, got dubbed by chance or design or favor, captains, majors and colonels, and by favor of Governor Dewdney, been endowed with judicial power ... Up to a short time ago this Mounted Police despotism was unqualified in the Northwest. Many a contraband keg of whiskey, many a furtive bottle of ale, many a flask of dark brandy, have had reason to know the promptness of their judicial administration and their peculiar views of the laws of evidence ... Since the Regina Leader sprang full-armed from the deforested front of Mr Davin, the despotism on the shores of the Pile of Bones, and by the flowing waters of the Saskatchewan, and under the shadow of the Rocky Mountains, has been a despotism qualified by criticism. But is the constitution safe? Is the criticism effective? Why no; it certainly is not ...[35]

This scrapping between the two Irish editors brought widespread enjoyment. In early 1884 *Grip* noted that the two, 'having exhausted their editorial resources in the way of strong language,' had turned to poetry. Farrer had opened the duel with a poem that looked ahead to Regina's inevitable collapse, which 'Explains these mounds of stones, / They mark the place where once stood Pile of Bones.' To which Davin had replied with a poem visualizing Regina in the future as a great city with parks and fountains – including a statue of Farrer with a unique function:

The lot of one wild scribbler stands alone
The gods in anger turned him into stone:
And by an irony Ned calls 'devilish quare,'
Him made a fountain in Regina's square;
And there he stands – no wonder you're amused
Spouting the water he so oft abused![36]

Farrer's Winnipeg writing thus foreshadowed some of his future issues, as well as the scrapping his satirical writing would provoke. At the same time it offered an occasional tantalizing hint about his past, in Ireland or Rome. At the *Times*, for instance, an editorial note implied personal knowledge of Ireland's chief prelate, Cardinal McCabe, raising the question of whether that senior churchman might have been the elusive archbishop in Farrer's background.[37] Similarly, a curious little item in the *Sun* suggested intimate familiarity with County Mayo. It criticized a *Free Press* report that a caretaker on Lord Cranmer's property in Mayo was dying after a beating by Fenians; then said the name was wrong – there was in fact no Lord Cranmer. 'There is a Lord Oranmore, however, who has been the curse of Mayo for forty years. The caretaker of his mansion and demesne at Castlemagarrett, near Claremorris, was beaten for assaulting a poor peasant woman. Give even the Fenians their due.'[38] The item prompts speculation, of course, that Farrer had personal knowledge of this 'curse of Mayo' and that the connection may have touched the mystery of his background.

Familiarity with County Mayo also showed in a delightful 1882 *Times* editorial – an editorial that reflected both Farrer's taste for whimsy and his mixed feelings on religion. The article reported that Toronto's Archbishop John Joseph Lynch, on a visit to Mayo, had expressed belief in an apparition of the Virgin said to appear on a church wall in the little village of Knock. The comment went on:

As a matter of fact, apparitions, but not of the Virgin Mary, have been seen at Knock for years. Knock is a hamlet of some forty houses, straggling on each side of a boreen [lane] and the boreen lies almost in the centre of a bog. If Archbishop Lynch had been born in that neighborhood he would know that the Will o' the Wisp often troubles the little graveyard that forms the background of the church where, according to his letter, he worshipped and wondered. Moreover, the people of Knock are a peculiarly practical people, that is for Ireland. It was there that Dr Fulton of New York, who visited Connaught in 1880 to distribute the food supplies sent from the United States, found Patriots making poteen out of the Relief meal.

But, assuming that the apparition and accompanying miracles are well attested, and the Archbishop says they are, who shall say that they are impossible? The evidence on their behalf is stronger and certainly more modern than that supporting the miracles wrought in the early days. If we believe the New Testament, and all Christians do, by what process of reasoning can we reject as spurious the testimony of Archdeacon Cavanagh of Knock and the thousand and one pilgrims who have visited the shrine, prayed at the ancient fane, gazed upon the luminous shadow of the Virgin cast by some strange agency upon the plaster wall, and experienced in their own person singular cures? The plea that the age of miracles is past is an insufficient one. It implies that God's right arm has been shortened. If miracles were a necessity when the Saviour came to earth, they are, humanly speaking, quite as necessary now when infidelity stalks abroad at noonday through Christendom, and when half the earth is still in pagan bondage.

The apparition at Knock is probably nothing more than the flickering of the Will-o'-the-Wisp; but if a thousand living Irishmen swear that it is the apparition of the Virgin Mary, why should be disbelieve them and yet believe, be it said with reverence, in the evidence of the four dead Jews who wrote the Gospels?[39]

Despite the whimsy, though, Farrer did not take religion lightly. At the *Times* an editorial comment, almost certainly his, raised furious controversy on the issue of salvation by criticizing two divinity students who claimed to be 'saved' by confession of sin. 'It is dreadful mockery, or perhaps it is only dismal ignorance, for these two raw youths to judge themselves and forestall the Day of Judgment and the Judge,' the editorial said. 'It is given to no man to know he is at peace with God ... it is nothing short of impious for modern man to assert that he has made his soul secure. The image, as the proverb says, cannot speak for the maker ...'[40]

On themes like these, Farrer *seems* to have written as he pleased, especially at the *Sun*. He certainly was constrained in some ways by the CPR alliance, though in other ways the railway patronage may actually have given him latitude. In any event the CPR connection was still strong when the time came for him to return to Toronto in the autumn of 1884. According to the *Free Press* social notes, Farrer and his wife spent the last week of September on a trip to the Rockies, presumably as guests of the railway. On the eve of their departure for Toronto, officials of the line entertained the couple and presented Farrer with a purse of $500 – a considerable sum, equal to a full year's salary for an ordinary reporter. Interestingly, the *Free Press* carried the story straight, with no suggestion that such a gift might represent conflict of interest. It said a number of Farrer's friends had gathered at the home of the CPR general superintendent, John M. Egan, for the presentation by J.H. McTavish, on behalf of the employees of the road, of the $500 purse and this address:

To E. Farrar, Esq., Journalist:
 Dear Sir, – On the eve of your and Mrs. Farrar's departure from our midst,

we take this opportunity to express to you our appreciation of your untiring efforts on behalf of this young country.

While we regret that we shall miss your familiar face, yet we cannot but rejoice that you are about to remove to a more extended field of professional activity, for which your many and varied talents so eminently qualify you – one in which you can with greater weight, and with more lasting results to us, advocate the cause of the Northwest ...

The *Free Press* also reported Farrer's reply in considerable flowery detail. He 'dwelt at some length' on the kindness of CPR employees to him and assured them that wherever he went, and 'beneath whatever sun the vicissitudes of fortune might cast him,' he would look back fondly on the hours spent with his warm-hearted friends on the railway. He would also, he said, be vigilant to defend the interests of the CPR whenever the slanderous pens of perverse and malignant men were wielded against the interests of the great corporation.

This little ceremony was followed by a social evening, the *Free Press* reported, and the next night, 2 October, the couple left for the East, 'carrying with them the hearty respect and esteem of very many citizens.'[41] If Farrer's CPR friends hoped he would promote their dream of unifying the young country, however, they were sorely in error. Over the next decade he would work steadily, first in secret and then in the open, to break up the country and encourage annexation.

5 Splendid Isolation

To modern readers the Toronto *Daily Mail*'s break with Sir John A. Macdonald in the 1880s may seem to be unexceptional, since a newspaper's decision to support or not to support a party is now of little moment. In the actual conditions of the time it was a startling move, executed with daring and a great deal of finesse. Before the break the paper's whole network of support, from the officials who fed it information to the readers who subscribed, had been made up of 'our friends' – the Tory party. The effort of establishing a new orientation for the paper was something like the challenge of turning an ocean liner in harbour – an exceedingly delicate task demanding opinion shifts spaced over time as well as deft enlistment of a variety of other forces. In retrospect the break may command little admiration since it was undertaken in questionable causes. It is true, too, that the independence was temporary. But it was important in Canadian newspaper history, coming as it did as one of the climactic episodes of the party press era and creating a model of what a great independent newspaper might be.

A.H.U. Colquhoun, a young newspaper man at the time, tried much later to explain the importance of the development, and the consternation it caused, by stressing the pervasiveness of political authority in journalism of that day, at least in the serious papers. The *Telegram* and the *News*, he recalled, had earlier claimed to be independent, 'but their views were never a source of danger to the "Old Man" ...' The *Mail*, by contrast, had taken great risk. 'Mowat, Macdonald and Blake were not leaders who could safely be challenged. The falterers [among newspapers] kept in view the fact that after Ajax stood on the rock and defied the immortal gods he was immediately drowned.'[1] In short, the *Mail* risked its life by declaring independence.

The paper's move, too, was inextricably linked with brilliance of technique. While modern analysts tend to see the paper as an irresponsible, almost irrational, maverick, it was as well a journal of outstanding craftsmanship, as even rivals acknowledged. John Willison, who never worked for the paper, was just one of those who admired it. 'I cannot think,' he wrote in 1919, 'that Canada has ever had a greater newspaper than was The Mail during [its] period of separation from the Conservative party.'[2]

The period Willison spoke of started in 1886 and continued at least until 1890, when the paper, after Ned Farrer's departure, became increasingly tame and manageable, finally slipping comfortably into bed with the Tory *Empire* in 1895. The intervening years, though, were important ones for the newspaper industry – years when Toronto journalists went through one of their roughest periods of competition and responded with a product that was often hilarious, often embarrassing, often imaginative.

Later, looking back, it would be clear enough that something had had to change. Newspaper technology was being transformed: the big, electric-driven rotary presses, the Linotype, the typewriter, the telephone, the half-tone photo-engraving process – all of this machinery and more was in place or was about to be, and it was obvious that Toronto could not afford to support six or seven daily newspapers.[3] It was also inevitable that the newspapers' political role would change, that as their complexity and mass audiences grew they would become less a link between politicians and a party elite, and more a link between advertisers and consumers. Politicians with the force and guile of a John A. Macdonald might retain their journalistic fiefdoms for a time, but the end was approaching.

In the period of change, though, Toronto readers had an impressive range of choices. On the lower end of the scale they had the *News*, specializing in gossip and scandal, and John Ross Robertson's *Telegram*, which stole news shamelessly from rivals to stay in the race.[4] Also aiming for the downscale market was the *World*, a racy, erratic morning sheet run by W.F. (Billy) Maclean, a sometime Tory with a reputation as shoddy as his paper. The two 'serious' morning papers, the *Globe* and the *Mail*, were joined at the end of 1887 by a third, the *Empire*, set up by the Tories as a direct result of the *Mail*'s defection. In 1892 a seventh paper, the *Star*, would join the crowded field. In addition there were a number of general and specialized magazines, including *Grip*, famous for its satires and for John W. Bengough's political cartoons, the *Week*, serious to the point of pedantry, and, after 1889, Ned Sheppard's *Saturday Night*, combining serious comment with toney social gossip.

In this crowded field the *Mail* found a unique place and earned competitors' respect. *Grip*, earlier a savage critic, in 1890 called it 'unquestionably the leading paper of the Dominion.'[5] Even the *Journalist* of New York gave it high rating. 'In order to keep posted on affairs in Canada one cannot find a better source of information than the columns of the *Toronto Mail*,' it said in 1889. 'This newspaper combines the energy and push of the Yankee with the dignity and conservatism of the best English journals.'[6] A later assessment from G.R. Tennant, who studied the *Mail*'s editorial shifts during 1882–92, noted a sharp change in quality after the paper declared its independence. 'The editorial standard rose and a whole new tone of political writing was introduced ... The *Mail*, free of its partisan tinge and prejudices, became a journal of good interesting reading, with editorials by Farrer that could not be surpassed by any other newspaper in Canada at the time.'[7]

The *Mail*'s reputation was based partly on its news coverage, extensive and well edited, partly on appearance (it had broken out of the traditional pattern of cramped columns and tiny type), and more particularly on the breadth of interest and writing quality shown on the editorial page, at that point still the heart of the paper. Since its founding in 1872 the paper had come under new ownership, falling in 1877 (when the Tories were in opposition) into the hands of its chief creditors, the Riordan paper-making family of St Catharines. T.C. Patteson, bitter over alleged trickery by the Riordans,[8] had gone on to his reward as postmaster of Toronto, and Christopher Bunting, a politician of murky reputation, had succeeded as managing director. In the late 1870s and early 1880s, about the time of Farrer's first editorship, the paper had moved ahead with vigour – booming the National Policy and in turn helped by the growth of Toronto that arose from it. In 1879 an impressive new building was begun, and new presses were ordered after a spurt of expansion in which, the paper claimed, daily circulation had doubled within eighteen months, while circulation of the *Weekly Mail* had increased fivefold.

John Riordan, the chief owner, was said to have been ambitious to follow the great New York publishers, and his new building at the corner of King and Bay seemed to reflect that dream. A five-storey red-brick structure that remained a Toronto landmark until the 1930s, it boasted a square tower topped by a cone, accounting for occasional references to the 'paper of the tall tower.' In the summer of 1880 the paper announced inauguration of its new Scott presses, capable of throwing off forty-five thousand copies an hour, and at the same time brought in the impressive new format with larger and clearer type. It also claimed considerable expansion in news-gathering facilities, boasting that it was not only the largest but by far the greatest newspaper in Canada. In politics, it added, the paper would continue to give 'cordial support' to the Conservatives, while acknowledging no master except the public interest.[9]

As the decade progressed, the *Mail* flourished, helped to some extent by political in-fighting at the *Globe* following the death of George Brown and by repeated electoral defeats for the Liberals. Gradually it came to rival the *Globe* in recruiting talent. It had an able staff of local reporters, hard-drinking and hard-living young men, who had learned to write their copy in longhand, in pencil, under the gaslight – although typewriters and electricity were on the way in. Writers who passed through its newsroom during Farrer's tenure included the energetic John Bayne Maclean, later founder of the Maclean-Hunter publishing empire (who came over from the *World* for a pay increase to $9 weekly from $5); P.D. Ross, later publisher of the Ottawa *Journal*; Katherine ('Kit') Blake Coleman, most famous of the early women's columnists; and Ned Sheppard, the rough-edged one-time cowboy and stagecoach driver, who would edit the *News*, *Saturday Night*, and the *Star*.[10]

Between Farrer's two stints as editor the *Mail* continued to be ably handled by Martin J. Griffin, a Newfoundlander who had worked in Halifax journalism. A slim, aesthetic lawyer who nourished social and political ambitions, Griffin was an able writer and was so loyal to Sir John A. that he sometimes sent him laudatory poetry.[11] (It was Griffin who, at least by report, had coined the much-repeated description of Grits as a 'semi-civilized crowd of dull-witted partisans.') The *Mail* was so thoroughly Tory, in fact, that rivals claimed it had a formal agreement to support the party. This the *Mail* denied, but until Farrer's last arrival its legendary mission, to 'stab the Grits under the fifth rib every morning,' seemed fixed and immutable. There was no detectable change when Charles Riordan succeeded to financial control, after his brother John became mentally ill in 1883, a year before his death.[12] Loyalty to the Tories continued unabated while the quality of the paper, if anything, seemed to improve even as the economy slid and competition increased.

Despite its quality, though, the *Mail*'s performance in the late 1880s, and Farrer's editorship in particular, have been remembered mainly for excesses in the so-called race and creed wars (misnamed, so far as the 'race' factor was concerned, although at the time the combatants certainly saw themselves as distinct races). Summaries of Farrer's role tend to fall into a conventional pattern, focusing on the Jesuits' Estates frenzy of 1889 and implying that the work of five years actually took place in five weeks. As early as 1912, for instance, an entry in *Canadian Men and Women of the Time* said that when Farrer was last employed by the *Mail*, the paper entered 'a crusade against Jesuitism, Cath. domination, the Federal ministry and the influence of the Hierarchy in Quebec, so skilfully conceived, so vigorously conducted, and so craftily fed, that in the course of 4 or 5 weeks the whole province of Ont. was worked into a fervid excitement.'[13] A 1938 summary in *Canadian Who Was Who, 1875-1937* showed a remarkably close parallel in wording. It said Farrer's knowledge of Roman Catholicism gave him the ammunition for articles that attracted national attention, and that the *Mail*'s attacks on Jesuitism, Catholic domination, the Federal ministry and the hierarchy in Quebec were 'so subtly conceived, so energetically launched, and so craftily nourished, that in the course of four or five weeks the whole province of Ontario was brought to a ferment.'[14]

Other historians take a longer view of the *Mail*'s course, but they tend to view the paper as something of a rogue elephant, inspired by Toronto's bigotry (or the fanaticism of its own managers) into a campaign to promote 'British ascendancy,' and afterward lurching on to the continental campaign when that issue seemed to be popular.[15] Basic questions thus remain open about the paper's true motivations – and about the relative influence and relative priorities of various executives.

From Farrer's view, certainly (and it is doubtful if the break could have been made without him), the 'race and creed' passion would not have been a prime motivation. While he seems to have been honest enough in his attacks on clerical influence, and in his pessimism for the future of a 'biracial' country, his record on religious and racial tolerance had been notably strong. And far from wanting to promote British ascendancy, his aim was the exact opposite – though he would have understood the futility of a frontal attack on imperialism. In the context of 1885–6, after Riel's hanging and French Canada's angry reaction, however, the race/religion campaign provided him with a tempting opportunity, allowing him to tap Toronto resentment to build a new support base replacing the party connection. It provided him, too, with the rationale for a subtle message: that Confederation was coming apart, and the only salvation for English Canada lay to the south.

That aspect was given some attention at the time, especially when Farrer's 'treason' emerged a few years later. 'A morbid desire to smash the Confederation into its original fragments has, we believe, possessed [the *Mail*] for five years,' the *Globe* declared in 1890.[16] A month earlier the Montreal *Gazette* had made the same charge in more specific terms: 'For three years past the *Mail* has devoted skill and energy towards creating dissatisfaction in Canada with the existing state of affairs,' the paper said, launching a measured and detailed attack. 'The race differences in this province [Quebec] have been exaggerated and embittered by its utterances, every weakness in the constitution has been magnified ... till any one reading and accepting all the paper's statements would be convinced that the federation was on the verge of dissolution and that the longer the collapse was delayed the greater would be the risk of violent disruption ...'[17]

Some politicians, too, saw this destructiveness as part of a carefully crafted plan. When the commercial union campaign was launched in the spring of 1887, for instance, Sam Hughes, later the controversial militia minister, wrote Macdonald saying he was certain Bunting, Farrer, and the *Mail* were 'body and bones' for annexation and were using both the race/religion issue and commercial union as stepping stones to it. Hughes implied that the plotters had confided in him because of his well-known anti-French, anti-Catholic views and went on to a detailed run-down on how they planned to manipulate various groups to encourage annexation:

They reason thus: – The scheme [commercial union] will be against Sir John's plans; therefore the Grits and their Irish and French Roman Catholic allies will endorse it. '*The 'Mail'* will come in as if spontaneously, which *undoubtedly* will carry over a lot of voters. The *Mail's* RC and Temperance stands have got nearly all the Protestant ministers on its side. It will in a *left*-hand way hold them to its general line, on those two specific points. Those are their sugar plums. Then the *Orangemen* are to be won from both *you* and the *Grits* to form a new party. The question of *Annexation*, mind you, is not broached to the preachers, the temperance men or the Orangemen ... Thus the *Mail*, having won from you your temperance followers, your Protestant clergymen and their influence, and the Orangemen, would have a strong party in itself.[18]

Ned Farrer's role in this intrigue must, of course, be seen in relation to the rest of the group dubbed by the *Globe* as 'the Bunters' (in honour of managing director Bunting). What, for instance, was the influence of Bunting himself on the paper? Or of chief owner Charles Riordan? Or Goldwin Smith, who wrote some of the paper's more violent editorials and seems to have had a behind-the-scenes role? Or of D'Alton McCarthy, maverick Tory politician who was instrumental in setting up the rival *Empire*, but late in the decade became the idol of the *Mail*? Obviously, none of the major changes, especially the break with Sir John, could have occurred without at least the acquiescence of Riordan and Bunting. Smith's influence undoubtedly supported Bunting's anti-French and anti-Catholic tendencies, and he would have been especially influential in persuading the *Mail* to take up commercial union. McCarthy would have strengthened the paper's stand against bilingualism, although the alliance between his followers and the *Mail* clique was limited.

The *Mail*'s course was thus shaped by some very contradictory forces. It is notable, though, that journalistic contemporaries gradually came to see Farrer as more than a tool of the Bunters. After his departure from the *Mail* in 1890 the Montreal *Gazette* editor, R.S. White, suggested the way was now clear for re-establishment of the *Mail*-Tory alliance.[19] A major 1891 article on Canadian journalism in the *New England Magazine*, by Walter Blackburn Harte, ignored Bunting's role and gave Farrer credit both for the paper's independence and for its anti-clerical and continental campaigns. The writer, who apparently had worked at the *Mail*,[20] showed mixed feelings about Farrer but was unstinting in assessing his impact:

It has to be admitted that Mr Farrer, though a most convincing writer, is not afflicted with a superabundance of literary conscience; but to him must belong the credit of having awakened a public sentiment against the insidious machinations of the ultramontane party to obtain complete control of the provincial and federal legislatures ... His articles, always moderate and dignified, with every statement enforced by its proper authority, created some-

THE UNRECONSTRUCTED REPORTER. Mr Bunting – 'Didn't I tell you to tie a piece of string around your finger so as to remind you that the *Mail* is INDEPENDENT now?' *Grip*, 25 December 1886. In the first months of the *Mail*'s independence cartoonist John Bengough was convinced that Farrer and Bunting were at odds, with Farrer favouring greater independence while Bunting continued to play the party game.

Splendid Isolation 71

thing more than a sensation; they aroused the whole country ... Mr Farrer also strenuously supported unrestricted commercial relations with the United States, and he made the *Mail* the greatest instrument in the hands of the free trade party ...[21]

At the time of Farrer's death the Ottawa *Journal*, in an editorial almost certainly written by P.D. Ross, said the *Mail* editor was 'popularly blamed' for the paper's break with Sir John, and for the resulting damage to the Conservative party.[22] There is also Willison's testimony that Farrer inevitably determined the character and temper of any page to which he contributed, and influenced others without appearing to do so.[23] After Farrer's death, too, Willison wrote an 'appreciation' of his career in which he gave Farrer the credit, or blame, for the *Mail*'s key policy shifts: 'More than any other man Mr Farrer produced the agitation in Ontario against the Jesuit Estates Act, as he was chiefly responsible for commercial union.'[24]

On the other hand, there were at the time some hints – especially in the early stages of his last editorship – that Farrer was simply writing to order, and was in fact unhappy with his paper's anti-French and anti-Catholic tone. The *Globe* in particular seemed convinced that Farrer was writing without conviction, in keeping with the 'pernicious' doctrine that an editorial writer had no responsibility for the paper's policy.[25] *Grip* also hinted that Farrer and Bunting did not agree, with Farrer wanting more independence for the paper and less of the 'No Popery' cry. Both *Grip* and the *Globe* painted Farrer as an amiable, malleable type, groaning under the demands of party masters. Even when the first hints of Farrer's annexationist activity emerged in 1890, the *Globe* considered him to be merely a tool for his paper (although that line may have better served the *Globe*'s interests).

The two versions of Farrer's role are so widely separated as to be mutually exclusive. He could hardly have been both the malleable, amusing mercenary and the subtle *éminence grise* who gradually turned a major newspaper to his own ends. The likelihood – given his eventual open commitment to annexation – is that he cultivated the agreeable, easy-going manner while joining his own sincere anti-clerical views to Bunting's more basic anti-Catholic, anti-French attitudes, with a view to damaging Confederation and encouraging political union.

If the *Mail* indeed nurtured black ambitions of destroying the country, it would seem likely that its principal owner had something to do with it. In fact, though, little is known about the influence on the paper of Charles Riordan. One assessment suggests that, in contrast to his brother, he was more interested in making money than in advancing the Conservative cause.[26] But he must also have had some pride in the *Mail*, especially after it began to be called the leading paper in the country. When the Tories in 1887 wanted to buy back the *Mail*, to return it to the path of rectitude, Riordan, according to D'Alton McCarthy, did not discuss price but simply said the paper was not for sale.[27] The image of Riordan as final decision-maker is also strengthened by the testimony of Martin Griffin, who in 1888 implied that his role in the defection was crucial. It was because Riordan was not 'looked after,' Griffin told Sir Charles Tupper, that the Conservatives had lost $200,000 in cash, and a good deal of their solidarity.[28]

As for Bunting, an Irish-born Protestant who had prospered as a sugar importer and had served as a Conservative MP, he was, in Martin Griffin's view, a kindly but vacillating man incapable of concentrated thinking.[29] The *Globe*, which respected Farrer's newspapering skills, derided Bunting as a man who had never written anything more important than a bill of lading for sugar. Other rivals liked to refer to him as 'Boss' Bunting, implying he wanted to be seen as head of the Tories' Toronto machine. Like Farrer, Bunting was over-fond of the bottle, but there is little to show that he shared Farrer's taste for independent journalism. Before the latter's arrival he had never been known to let convictions get in the way of party gain.[30] And shortly after the latter's departure he was indecently ready to abandon the paper's boasts of independence.[31] Politically, too, his principles were of doubtful quality: in 1884 he was implicated in an extraordinary Tory plot to buy up Liberal members of the Ontario legislature with crisp $100 bills. *Grip* repeatedly cartooned him as a rat (eventually as one of several rats escaping a cage, when he was acquitted on the scandal charges) or as a pig wallowing in Tory mire.[32] The *Globe* referred to him constantly as the 'sugar journalist' and lost no chance to link his name to the legislature scandal.

Bunting was consistent at least in his hostility to Catholicism, to the despair of Martin Griffin, whose letters give some picture of what Farrer faced when he resumed the editorship. A devout Catholic, Griffin worked to keep Bunting's bigotry in check, even though he himself opposed the local tyranny of Archbishop Lynch and deplored his influence on the Liberal provincial government. On one occasion

Griffin (who kept a regular flow of woeful correspondence crossing Macdonald's desk) complained to the prime minister that the archbishop's language in a particular incident had been 'scandalously partizan and insulting ... in fact, maniacal,' adding, 'I modestly think it was fortunate I was here at this time; as I have certainly kept the "Protestant Horse," which was very restive, from charging!'[33] In another revealing note Griffin explained an outburst in the paper by saying that Bunting had 'got excited' and 'listened to some Protestant idiot' who told him Grit votes could be captured by pushing the issue. 'My position is one of powerlessness. I am fighting the battle of your ministry and of the Conservative Catholics, and I have to bear the hostility of the Archbishop in public and private; and all his vile swaggering clique of followers here ...'[34]

Macdonald on this occasion evidently remonstrated with Bunting, for a few days later the manager promised 'in deference to your views' to 'let the old gentleman alone during the remainder of his days.'[35] But Griffin still considered his situation untenable. 'If I criticize the Archbishop I am called "a bad Catholic,"' he told Macdonald. 'If I don't scream for orangeism, I am "a Jesuit in disguise." Every idiot is at liberty to write me a bigot or a renegade; and I have no means of reply; can only do my duty as I can.'[36]

Bunting's anti-Catholicism was by no means Griffin's only problem. As Farrer had found during his earlier stint, the editor of the *Mail* sometimes had to handle the prime minister's requests with a certain diplomatic finesse. Much later Griffin related to his son an amusing anecdote that suggested the strain – and as well told something of the political role of the newspaper as a centre of the Tory party in Toronto. He had, he recalled, returned to the *Mail* building about three o'clock one afternoon to find the prime minister on the steps waiting for him:

He had been drinking. He told me to announce that Frank Smith was taken into the *Senate* and old [John] O'Donohoe into the *cabinet*. I said, yes of course if he wished that, I would go and write the article at once. I hurried upstairs, caught Bunting quite sober, told him the impending calamity; he got together a lot of stalwarts who interviewed 'the old man' and told him they could not stand O'Donohoe in the Cabinet!! The consequence was that it was Smith who went in and O'D went only to the Senate. Of course O'D did not know of the change til the morning paper told him. Imagine his surprise ...[37]

Ironically (in view of Griffin's agonies), Farrer apparently refused a first invitation to return to the *Mail* precisely to avoid partisan intrigues. Willison related that it was D'Alton McCarthy, rather than Bunting or Riordan, who pressed for his return. According to this account, Bunting had asked him to come back, but Farrer had declared that he was not willing to be a professional 'sandbagger.' McCarthy saw this as an additional reason to renew the offer: 'A man who will not stoop to party savagery is the man who will best serve the paper and the party.' Bunting had then given Farrer satisfactory assurances that he would not be required to 'sandbag, tomahawk, or scalp,' and so he had gone back to Toronto.[38]

Farrer did not (most later reports to the contrary) immediately resume the editorship, although there was some expectation he would quickly do so. *Grip* on 22 November 1884 ran a cartoon showing him eyeing the editor's chair in which Griffin was still ensconced, wearing a coat clearly much too large for him. The caption said simply, 'Ned Farrar waiting for his coat,' and a sign on the wall (presumably a compliment of sorts to Farrer) said: 'Notice: Semi-civilized Partizans Not Admitted Here.'[39] Farrer may well have been promised the editorship before his return, since Griffin for years had been pleading with Macdonald to relieve him of the *Mail* job and give him something less stressful. But while delighted to escape (in the summer of 1885, to become parliamentary librarian), Griffin was less than happy about his choice of successor. Farrer was his polar opposite in style and temperament, and Griffin had sometimes suffered because of his mischief. He was not likely to forget, for instance, that just a few months earlier he had been portrayed as a servile cur, in contrast to Farrer's independence at the Winnipeg *Times*.

Griffin also seems to have deplored Farrer's drinking and his irreverence. In 1883 he had written Macdonald at one point: 'Your fear about Davin is well founded I judge. I have no patience in speaking or writing about him and Farrer. Between these two and the ruffianly "Evening News" which is simply a scandal, they have made the position of a journalist almost untenable socially.'[40] The cause of Griffin's disdain on this occasion was probably liquor, since Davin that year had been involved in an unsavoury drinking incident that reached the public prints.[41] But Griffin, who prided himself on refined literary tastes, also disagreed with Farrer on what constituted fit material for the leading Conservative organ. And shortly after Farrer's arrival Griffin clearly lost editorial control, to the point where he wrote

NED FARRAR WAITING FOR HIS COAT. *Grip*, 22 November 1884. When Farrer returned to the Toronto *Mail* from Winnipeg in 1884, it was assumed he would go back to his old post as editor. Martin Griffin, in fact, remained as editor until the following summer, although he had (to his despair) little control over what Farrer wrote. *Grip* at the time despised the *Mail*, and the wall notice implied that Farrer, as a 'semi-civilized partizan,' was too good for it.

Macdonald plaintively appealing to him to get Bunting to curb Farrer – although the latter's name was not mentioned directly. In retrospect the issue that separated the two seems trivial to the point of absurdity, but Griffin considered it worthy of the prime minister's attention. In February 1885 he wrote:

Dear Sir John

Mr Bunting tells me you have written pointing out the impropriety of always saying Blake has no policy. You are very apt and correct. I think on looking into it you will write another letter pointing out the unwisdom of the comic articles about the North West, the funny references to 'unloading town lots on strangers' and so on. See the article for instance on 'a new city' in *Mail* of Wednesday Feby 11th. These articles are exquisitely funny but they are calculated to damage the North West by giving it the air of a broken down gamblers' paradise. You will see what I mean. The articles are sure to be continued and sure to be copied and sure to do damage. I have suggested it but have not cared to urge it for obvious reasons. The North West is too serious a matter for you, to have it joked about in the *Mail*.[42]

The article that so upset Griffin was actually rather gentle humour, well justified by the hysterical promotion of some Western towns. Typical of Farrer's satires, it began in deadpan style, so that readers became aware only gradually that they were reading a spoof:

The Portage La Prairie *Review* is satisfied that the Hudson's Bay route is navigable for twelve months a year, and urges the Winnipeg capitalists to begin the construction of docks at Churchill without further delay.

We regret to observe that the *Review* is inclined to go too fast. Things must be done orderly and in season. Before the docks are begun, the foundations of the city must be laid according to the established rites, or how shall it endure? First of all, a newspaper must be started at Churchill, the editor being subsidized with a couple of hundred town lots and the plant bought somewhere on credit. Forthwith coal, coal oil, salt, iron, silver, and gold must be discovered within the proposed limits of the city if possible or at all events in the immediate neighbourhood. Then it is advisable to strike a hot spring with a view to establishing the fame of the place as a resort for invalids. It will not in this case be necessary to make any extraordinary effort to build up the reputation of the dry atmosphere of the town in winter. These preliminaries having been adjusted, and the future metropolis thoroughly and scientifically boomed by the editor and newspaper aforesaid, it will then be the solemn duty of the projectors to sell the town site in Eastern Canada, in order to give people down here a chance to share in the prosperity that must inevitably follow. We need hardly tell the *Review* that selling the town site is absolutely essential to successful city building. Where to-day is Babylon? Why did she fall? The answer is obvious. The owners of the town plot omitted to take the rest of the world in with them on the ground-floor, the result being that after a few centuries of ups and downs she went under. Athens, Nineveh, Tyre, Sidon, Carthage, and Cork are all mute but eloquent monuments to the folly of trying to build a city without first disposing of the town site to strangers. Look, on the other hand, at Whitemouth, Moberley, Oak Lake City, and Wabigoon. They still live, and why? Simply because their founders enlisted outside support by loading up the people of older civilizations with town lots, and so compelling them to take a deep interest for all time in the fortunes of the place.

When the town plot of Churchill has been sold to advantage in Toronto, Hamilton, and London, and the auctioneer and the projectors have got safely across the line, then hurrah for docks and a municipal debt! But the *Review* must not force things with undue haste or there may be a crash.[43]

This satire was by no means an isolated case, and Farrer's growing reputation for such antics often got him into trouble. When the Riel Rebellion broke out in the spring of 1885, for instance, the *Mail* coverage was in fact massive, detailed, and well organized, but *Grip* suspected that some of the best of it was being put together in Toronto by the recent arrival from the West. It cartooned Farrer as an 'automatic' war correspondent, with Bunting turning the crank. 'It is alleged that some of the most interesting of the *Mail*'s special despatches from the seat of war are got up in the premises on King street,' *Grip* reported. 'It is felt that no absent member of the staff could possibly have invented the Indian chief "O'Soup," whereas a certain member of the home force is known to be capable of such acts of creation.'[44]

This jibe was unfair since a Saulteaux named Louis O'Soup was indeed prominent in the rising,[45] but the cartoon, along with the satires, probably nurtured Farrer's reputation for creativity. It was not just the satire, though, but also Farrer's increasing criticism of government handling of the Métis crisis that seemed to be troubling Griffin as he packed to leave Toronto. 'I am in a state of unhappiness about leaving the "Mail"; and to stay here with the probability of seeing such ridiculous episodes as the recent articles on the North

JOURNALISTIC ENTERPRISE. *Grip*, 11 April 1885. Because of his Western experience Farrer was the logical person to handle the *Mail*'s extensive coverage of the Riel Rebellion in 1885. But *Grip* suspected Farrer was overdoing one of the journalistic skills of the day: the 'working up' of brief telegraphic messages. In effect, *Grip* thought, C.W. Bunting had an automatic war correspondent in his office, inventing the rebellion coverage.

West occurring, would drive one mad,' he wrote Macdonald. 'I wrote you some months ago asking you to fire CWB [Bunting] a hint about the tone of the North West articles; they seem to me all wrong. If I live, in sanity, to see you soon I shall at least give you some reasons why I ventured on offering you some advice on a certain topic, which perhaps you deemed impudent.'[46]

Griffin may have been thinking still of the satires, but it is more likely that his concern arose as well from the Riel commentary. On 8 July, just a few days before Griffin's letter, the *Mail* printed a major editorial on causes of the outbreak – an editorial guaranteed to alarm the government and delight opponents. In blunt language, it said the Métis had indeed had cause for complaint, that despite the 'manifest and unanswerable logic' of their land claims, Ottawa had refused to move. It agreed with Edward Blake (an astonishing betrayal in itself) that the officials' negligence was 'gross and inexcusable, and contributed to bring about the insurrection,' and that the delay amounted to 'callous and cruel neglect.' Because they were only half-breeds, the editorial said, the Métis had been put off with eternal promises until patience had ceased to be a virtue.[47]

In the context of post-rebellion blame-dropping, such statements from an acknowledged government organ were explosive. True, the editorial directed its main attack at bureaucrats rather than party masters and insisted the Mackenzie Liberals were equally to blame with the Macdonald government. But the harsh phrases were there, and the opposition papers happily wrenched them out of context. Six months later the words were still reverberating. 'How poor Mr Bunting must suffer for having allowed that article in behalf of the poor ill-used half-breeds to appear in the *Mail* last July,' *Grip* observed. 'The *Globe* man, with fiendish malignity, has fastened that article up over the devoted head of John A., and is torturing him with it, drop by drop, day in and day out.'[48]

Griffin, in his total loyalty to party, would have been appalled by the Métis article and must have been thinking of it when he wrote of 'ridiculous' articles on the Northwest. But his concern was broader than a difference on one policy issue. After his arrival in Ottawa he again reported to Sir John on conditions at the *Mail*. Again he wrote in very guarded terms, but the intent seemed to be to warn that Bunting was not strong enough to keep the paper loyal. Circumstances at the *Mail*, he said, had made his own departure essential. 'I could not remain to see my own views quietly set aside for want of proper knowledge on the part of the manager, who is a very kind and friendly man but seems to have no strong hold on consistency and no power of consecutive thinking. I have not dared to write the state of affairs, but knowing that Mr Pope [presumably private secretary Joseph Pope] had your confidence I have told him much and asked him to tell you, but there are some things I must keep for you personally. Mr Bunting's own position is much more delicate than he imagines and it is *his* hands that will need to be strengthened by any move you can make to secure the allegiance of the others ...'[49]

While Griffin's exact meaning is obscure, it is interesting that he was concerned about the *Mail*'s loyalty from the very start of Farrer's second editorship. Griffin more than anyone else would have noticed how Farrer was changing the *Mail*'s policy lines – on the Métis issue, for instance, or on the Catholic hierarchy, or on imperial union, where Griffin's warm enthusiasm was dropped and the paper moved in cunning stages from damning by faint praise to outright opposition.[50] While the break with Sir John was more than a year off, there is no doubt the tensions between party and paper had already begun to appear.

As at the Winnipeg *Times*, the mischief-making was often subtle, of a kind difficult to censure. In the wake of Riel's hanging, especially, the *Mail* made trouble for the party by excess of zeal. On the surface the paper appeared to be simply joining, or leading, Ontario's reaction against the outburst of protest in Quebec. A few days after the hanging, for instance, there was a much-quoted editorial that wound up with a plea to Ontario Liberals to join in resisting attempts to impose 'the tyranny of a French minority upon a country consecrated by British blood to British freedom.' Repeatedly, the editorial said it would be better to destroy Confederation than to allow such a tyranny: '... after all our efforts to establish amicable relations with them, even at the sacrifice of prosperity, the French-Canadians are now seeking to compel us to recognize their right to suspend the operation of the law whenever a representative of their race is in the toils. But let us solemnly assure them again that rather than submit to such a yoke Ontario would smash Confederation into its original fragments, preferring that the dream of a united Canada should be shattered forever than that unity should be purchased at the expense of equality.'[51]

To some extent that sort of editorial could be considered as support for the Macdonald government's decision not to interfere with Riel's death sentence. But the attacks continued needlessly in the weeks after the hanging, bitterly condemning the *Bleus* who had deserted Macdonald, or the clerics who supported the 'Rielites,' and making reconciliation difficult. When some of the *Bleus* showed signs of returning to the Tory flag, the *Mail* was chillingly blunt: 'If they choose to return to their allegiance, well and good. But they shall receive no honeyed words from us, nor ever again be trusted by this journal as men of honour or stable resolve.'[52]

Gradually, the campaign broadened into an assault on the Roman Catholic hierarchy, going far beyond what Macdonald considered tolerable. In May the prime minister remonstrated sharply:

My Dear Bunting
  The Conservative Catholics all over the Dominion complain greatly, and I think with some justice, of the course of the *Mail*.
  You must remember that your paper is considered in all parts of the Dominion as the organ of the Government. Now you believe, rightly or wrongly, that the Conservative party has no chance of getting any support from the Irish Catholics in Ontario. I do not agree in that opinion, but you may be right. It is certain, however, that we get a strong support from the Catholics as a whole in the Dominion ...
  I enclose to you for your perusal a private paper signed by Conservative Catholics from Quebec, Nova Scotia, P.E. Island and New Brunswick remonstrating against the course of your paper. Please read and return. Our Conservative Catholic friends in Ontario are greatly distressed, depend upon it, and I am receiving letters from many of them asking what they have done to be abandoned in this fashion.
  Pray consider this well. I really think it would be highly expedient in you to come down and see our friends here, Catholic and Protestant, at once, before the House rises. You should come down at once ...
                                            Yours faithfully,
                                            John A. Macdonald[53]

During the summer of 1886 the newspaper's rebelliousness became more embarrassing as it demanded curbs on the political influence of the church and French Canada – through constitutional amendment if necessary. A gap opened between the two papers considered to be official government organs, the *Mail* and the *Gazette* of Montreal. The government was stung as observers interpreted this to mean the prime minister was hypocritically spreading one message in Ontario and another in Quebec. Especially hurtful was a *Grip* cartoon entitled

THE DISCORDANT ORGANS. *Grip*, 11 September 1886. The *Mail*'s first claims of independence were greeted by ridicule. *Grip* said the Tories must consider the voters fools to pretend that Sir John was not in fact controlling the strings of both the Montreal *Gazette* and the *Mail*, despite the conflicting messages shaped for the two provinces. The message on the *Mail* 'organ' calls for disestablishment of the church in Quebec, despite constitutional guarantees, while the *Gazette*'s conflicting message calls this dangerous nonsense.

'The Discordant Organs,' which showed Sir John as an organ-grinder simultaneously turning two organs and controlling two scrapping monkeys, the *Mail* editor demanding disestablishment of the Roman Catholic church in Quebec and the *Gazette* editor calling this dangerous nonsense. *Grip*'s editor observed that Macdonald had often found himself in ridiculous positions, but nothing could be more absurd than the way he was caught between his two accredited organs, both claiming to speak for the government.[54]

This comment – or comments of this kind – prompted Macdonald to distance himself from the *Mail*, though he did so in a way that would leave the path open to reconciliation. In a September speech at London, Ontario, he talked at some length about the role of the party press and insisted that the *Mail* did not speak for the government on Quebec matters. Conservative newspapers were free to write as they chose, he said. 'So with *The Toronto Mail*. *The Toronto Mail* is an able paper. (Loud cheers.) We are proud and glad to have its support. It is written with great ability, and its circulation is enormous – far more than that of the *Globe*. (Cheers.) I say that I do not feel, and I will not allow anyone to say that what is said in the paper is the language of Sir John Macdonald. (Cheers.)'[55]

For insiders this speech marked the real break between the Tories and the *Mail*. For the rest of the country, the significance was far from obvious. The ties between the party and the paper had been so close for so long that Sir John's 'repudiation' was met first with disbelief and even derision. 'If Sir John thinks the *Mail*'s course is doing him harm in the French province, all he has to do is to tell Mr Bunting to "let up,"' said *Grip*. 'The *Mail* is not so very independent that it would dream of refusing to do anything Sir John told it, and nobody knows this better than the Premier.'[56] The *Globe* said not one intelligent man in Canada would believe the prime minister. 'There never was a more dependent, a more servile press in any part of the world than the Tory press of Canada. Bismarck's "reptile" press was never more thoroughly under heel than are the papers named by Sir John Macdonald under his control.'[57]

The *Mail* itself meanwhile responded with a long editorial headed 'Our Position As a Public Journal,' and evidently designed to 'take the curve' to independence without alienating Conservatives. Although not a party organ, it said, the *Mail* had chosen to give general support to the Conservative party and its 'honoured leader,' but it was inevitable that differences would arise from time to time. It then

84 Secret Craft

went on to set out in detail its case against the Roman Catholic church:

As may be gathered from Sir John's remarks at London, we differ from him just now upon a question of very great moment. Though not conscious of being influenced in the remotest degree by religious bigotry, *The Mail* is nevertheless persuaded that a crisis in our affairs is at hand, in consequence of the overshadowing power possessed at Toronto, Quebec and Ottawa by the Roman Catholic Church. We would grant to every Church the utmost latitude of thought and action within legitimate bounds; but the vast organization of which we speak is everywhere invading the domain of civil government and undermining the authority of the State. In Quebec that Church is the State Church, licensed to invoke British law for the collection of tithes and of the onerous assessments she levies upon the people for the erection of her edifices. The temporal and spiritual privileges which she enjoys, enormous and exorbitant beyond any Old World parallel at present existing, enable her to control the Provincial Legislature as well as the great majority of the French members in the Dominion Parliament. The Riel agitation in Quebec has revealed the presence of a concealed imposthume more dangerous than an open wound. In Ontario, although she is here the Church of the minority, we see her holding the balance of power between the two parties, and wringing from the Government of the day concessions to which she has no sort of just claim ... we believe the time has come for compelling the Roman Catholic Church to keep within her proper sphere. She has no moral right to her extraordinary status in Quebec, her existence as a State Church being unjust alike to the *habitant* whom she crushes with her imposts, to the English-speaking settler whom she is eradicating from the soil to make room for tithe-payers, and to the people of the whole Dominion who are of necessity affected by the injury done to a component part. She has no right to interfere for her own aggrandizement or for the curtailment of the liberty of others in the public affairs of Ontario. She has no right to claim special representation in the Provincial and Federal Governments. She has no right to appear at all, as a Church, within the field of civil polity or secular administration. She is entitled like every other religious body the widest freedom of conscience and worship, but beyond that her claims are mere usurpations which must be met and overthrown, even though, in the case of Quebec, an alteration of the constitution should be found necessary ...[58]

Despite the strong rhetoric, though, the paper pledged to continue as an earnest advocate of Conservative policies on such basic matters as maintenance of the British connection, the encouragement of industry, or the building of railways – although it hinted it might be impelled to take a stronger stand on the developing temperance issue. The effect, therefore, was a furious public debate on whether the *Mail* had really broken with the party or was only engaging in a pressure play of some sort, perhaps on behalf of a party faction.

While the *Mail* itself kept silent (after the first declaration), its editors evidently put about the story that the break had resulted from government attempts to curb its independence. That line was taken, for instance, in a Montreal *Star* dispatch that amounted almost to a statement of the *Mail*'s case. (The *Globe* commented sourly that the story seemed to have come straight from the Bunters.) Date-lined Toronto and signed 'Native,' the *Star* dispatch claimed the first tensions had arisen over a bid by some whisky speculators (also government supporters) to launch a scheme in which they would store 'sour mash' in Canada and thereby escape American taxes. The *Mail* had editorially attacked the plan (along with the *Globe*), thus rousing the hostility of certain prominent Conservatives. They had appealed to Sir John to bring the journalists to heel, and 'certain remonstrances' against the *Mail*'s course had come from high ministerial quarters. The owners had 'backed their very able editor firmly,' and the paper had launched another assault on the whisky ring. 'The Powers of the *Mail* office distinctly informed the Powers at Ottawa that the paper owed nothing to the Ministry, but that the Ministry owed much to its powerful support which, in future, would be rendered independently if at all.'

The story said no further remonstrances had come from Ottawa until the fall of 1885, when the *Mail* began to attack the Riel agitators and the Roman Catholic church. Relations had become more strained when the paper refused to join in the whitewashing of a group of Tory 'Boodlers,' and eventually the administration had decided it was no longer worth while trying to maintain the link.[59]

The *Globe* found this explanation preposterous and tore it apart point by point, saying (with justice) that the 'chief Bunter himself' had been the leading spirit of the whisky ring, and adding that the *Mail* had in fact defended the 'boodlers' as ordered. And even if the explanation were true, it added, what kind of paper would go on supporting the government after this treatment?[60]

At the same time the *Globe* sought to divide the Bunters, claiming their chief writer did not share the anti-French and anti-Catholic venomousness of his chiefs. It detected an 'obvious and curious air of affectation' about the *Mail*'s alarm for Protestantism. No one could read its articles without perceiving that they were prepared with a humorous consciousness on the part of the writer that he was taking a wrong-headed course. 'Such being the effect, there is little reason to fear that serious evil will result from the organ's proceedings. They are none the less wicked, however, for its directing intention is to set race against race and creed against creed, to the destruction of public peace and the ruin of Confederation.'[61]

This comment was not the only hint that Farrer was less than happy at the *Mail*. In August 1886 Sir Richard Cartwright had written J.D. Edgar, another leading Liberal, indicating Farrer would be willing to come over to the *Globe*, which needed a 'vigorous, slashing' writer like Farrer or Ned Sheppard.[62] Some surmises about Farrer's position also emerged in a curious exchange between the *Mail* and *Globe* editorial writers – an exchange that violated the tradition of editorial anonymity and foreshadowed Farrer's emergence as a public figure.

The episode, a classic instance of the in-fighting that went on among the political journals, began with a triviality. The *Presbyterian Review* had said that all party journalists were liars, and a *Globe* writer named William Inglis, himself a retired Presbyterian minister, had taken umbrage. As the *Mail* told it, Inglis had appeared before the Toronto presbytery to demand that the *Review* be disciplined since he, as the *Globe*'s principal editorial writer, had been slandered by implication.[63] The *Mail*, with Farrer almost certainly wielding the pen, saw a chance to stir up trouble in the rival shop. The main target was not Inglis, however, but Timothy Warren Anglin, former Commons speaker and New Brunswick editor, who had been brought into Toronto journalism by the Liberals in an attempt to gain Irish Catholic support.[64]

Farrer's sparring with Anglin went back a long way. (At times, in recognition of the boodling that had cost Anglin the speakership, Farrer referred to him as 'Thoroughly Whitewashed Anglin.')[65] Now, tongue firmly in cheek, he wrote that Inglis's comments were puzzling: all competent authorities agreed that the *Globe* editorials were written not by Inglis but by Anglin, the 'incoherent champion of Race and Revenge.' So quite clearly Mr Inglis was mistaken – first in thinking that he *wrote* the *Globe*'s editorials, and second, in thinking they did not lie. And since Mr Inglis was a man of greatest respectability when in good health, the only explanation was that he was suffering from some minor mental disorder, 'brought on, in all probability, through steadfastly comparing the *Globe* of to-day with the *Globe* of the Brown dynasty.'

The shaft was a shrewd one, since Anglin's pro-Catholic editorials were raising difficulties at the *Globe*, the traditional champion of Protestantism. (He was dropped by the paper the following year.)[66] The sting was shown when the *Globe*, while insisting it would never break the impersonal rule and name a rival journalist, next day printed an elaborate and confusing string of 'suppositions' about a hypothetical newspaper, clearly the *Mail*, and its 'jolly, easy-tempered' editorial writer. The editorial called on readers to imagine a hypothetical newspaper manager (Bunting) who had 'contrived to persuade a rash capitalist' (Riordan) to degrade the paper to his personal uses, had been consumed by envy for a more successful rival (the *Globe*), and had been 'trapped in an attempt to place in power by bribery' a crew of politicians from whom he hoped to obtain plunder:

Failing these, suppose he had come to the conclusion that his sheet must try a new editorial role ... Suppose that he had then got rid of the very able but truculent writer [Griffin] who had lent himself largely to the purposes of his employer, but could not be prevailed on to assail the Church in which he had been suckled and bred. Suppose that that employer had made up his mind that the success of its rival was due to its steady adherence to the causes of Religion, Morality, Temperance, and Liberalism. Suppose he had concluded that his sheet must seem 'to purge and live cleanly as a gentleman should,' or put him to search for a new situation in sugar. Suppose he had then hired a jolly, easy-tempered writer, who had been Conservative and Reformer, moralist and immoralist by turns. Suppose this writer had been Macdonaldite and anti-Macdonaldite on two rival papers in one place within two years. Suppose he were a convivial fellow always ready to support any opinions yielding a fit salary – having deliberately adopted the pernicious and degrading doctrine that a press-writer is not morally responsible for setting forth his chief editor's opinions. Suppose this writer of easy virtue had yet never lent his talents to Orange enemies of the Roman Catholic Church to which he himself belonged. Suppose he had, on the contrary, often written, with a glow of self-approval all too strange in his career, in the praise of that Church, and particularly of the French-Canadians belonging to it. Suppose his delight had always been to ridicule Temperance men and Prohibitionists. Suppose he had not been told, when hired, that he would be required to appear in the role of the Orange fanatic, Francophobiac, and Prohibitionist; but suppose that he had gone to work on those lines as a matter of course when the sugar-journalist thought the time had come to declare an absolute reversal of all his sheet's previous opinions ...⁶⁷

The editorial went on to many more suppositions about how the *Mail*, over Farrer's objections, had singled out Anglin for attack as part of an effort to paint itself as the city's only truly Protestant paper.

A few weeks later the *Globe* dented the rule of impersonal journalism even more and made a telling argument that Farrer was out of sympathy with his paper's anti-French, anti-Catholic tone. With heavy irony the *Globe* contrasted the *Mail*'s campaign to a 'really charming' article written for the *Atlantic Monthly* in 1881 – 'by one whom The Mail will scarcely deny to be a gentleman, a scholar, a good judge of the *habitant*, and a writer of discretion, grace, force, and almost excessive versatility.' The article then went on to a long and detailed comparison of the *Mail*'s attacks with points Farrer had made in the *Atlantic* article, to the effect that French Canadians were admirable colonists, loyal and respectful to superiors – 'a great conservative force on a continent which has always been the refuge of the uneasy spirits of the world.' The article had also said that the Quebec people (far from being priest-ridden) had paramount control of affairs and that their education system, far from being steeped in ignorance and superstition, was equal to the best on the American continent.⁶⁸

The *Globe*'s excerpts were, in fact, a fair reflection of the tone of the *Atlantic* article and fairly defined a gap between the material Farrer wrote under his own byline and the material that appeared in the *Mail*. The *Atlantic* article revealed a writer with an intense and sympathetic interest in French-Canadian culture, although some portions sound patronizing to modern ears, and some underlined Farrer's belief that there was no future for a country that tried to embrace the two cultures.⁶⁹

Farrer's position among the Bunters, and the paper's relations with the party, were highlighted as well by the *Mail*'s decision, just after Sir John's repudiation, to join the prohibition movement, then becoming a significant political force. The move was astonishing to anyone who knew the drinking habits of Bunting and Farrer, not to mention Farrer's liberal views. And in its own declaration the *Mail* seemed notably apologetic. It conceded that prohibition had its defects, 'judging it by the strict philosophic interpretation of human rights,' and it added that the *Mail* would be happy to hear of a better solution to the problem. In the meantime, 'prohibition holds

GOOD BYE, OLD FELLOW; I'VE 'LISTED FOR THE WAR! *Grip*, 2 October 1886. *Grip* (the raven drummer in the background) was pleased and more than a little puzzled when Bunting and Farrer enlisted in the prohibition campaign. It wondered whether the *Mail* was really parting with Sir John ('The Girl He Left behind Him') or was actually charting out a possible campaign path for the Tories.

the field, and we intend to do what little we can for it – drumming up recruits, guarding the camp, keeping the weapons bright, and even carrying a banner in the fight if the leaders think fit to entrust us with one.'[70]

It may have been this martial note that prompted John Bengough to cartoon Bunting and Farrer as recruits enlisting in the prohibition forces, saying good-buy to Sir John and the 'Conservative liquor party.' *Grip* had long been an apostle of prohibition, and it was delighted by the conversion of the *Mail*. But its sense of humour was tickled by the thought of Farrer, with his well-known weakness for the bottle, sweating out the task of writing in favour of prohibition. It produced for the occasion one of its elaborate satires, a scene in which Farrer was coached in his odious writing task by 'Mr Aqua Pura.' Aside from the humour in that situation, the satire is notable for another hint that Farrer was fed up with writing anti-Rome articles. It also suggests a significant level of public awareness of the personalities fighting the usually anonymous journalistic wars:

THE 'MAIL' COACH – A FARCE

Scene – SANCTUM OF NEW PROHIBITION ORGAN

Dramatis Personae. – Mr F., editor-in-chief, and elderly gent in black, seated at table strewn with 'copy.' F. in shirt-sleeves – newly-opened bottle of whisky at elbow – face expressive of desperation – office water jug beside elderly gent – E.G.'s face expressive of apprehension.

F. loq. – Never mind, old chap, I think I can stand it, now that I've got something sustaining – fire away – won't try this sort of grind on blue-ribbon beer again, as long as my name's Ned.

(*Enter Mr B., the proprietor*). B. – Well, boys, how goes the coaching? Does he catch on to the racket, Mr Aqua Pura?

A. – Yes, brother, he has great receptivity for new ideas, and takes up the theory of prohibition –

F. (*interrupting*) – But, d— in the practice –

A. (*soothingly and drawing back his chair*). – There, there – don't excite yourself, brother. Rome wasn't built in a day.

F. (*rising wildly*). Come off, now. One thing at a time is all I can stand – Just leave the *Rome* racket to the Orange Coach, will you?

...

B. – Well, I'm off ... remember Saffron to-morrow to coach you on papal aggressiveness – ta! ta!. (*Exit*).

F. – I wish your Saffron and his Protestant horse were in Skibbereen – heigho, 'me party, what I suffer for ye!' Come along, now, old Aquarium, where were we? Oh, yes: 'The traffic is surely doomed since even *We* have turned against it. The *Globe* has been hammering away at the Accursed Thing for years, without effect. *We* will show the *Globe* how to put it down!' (*Pauses and puts some of it down.*) That's the stuff! ... Hooray for the three P.'s – Protestantism, Prohibition, and Plunder! (*Curtain*).[71]

In the wake of that satire Farrer must have faced a good deal of derision from fellow drinkers. And not only *Grip* was suspicious. The *Globe* warned that the *Mail* had 'just dropped out of the barroom' to join the movement and intended to use it to promote the Protestant cause – which in turn it was using to break up Confederation.[72] *Grip* became more impressed with the revolt, though, as the *Mail* distanced itself from Macdonald by backing labour rights, emigration reform, and franchise extension. By October *Grip* acknowledged the newspaper's move was a serious one, and it reacted with astonished confusion, offering a spread of six or seven cartoons, some contradictory, while admitting it was at a loss to interpret the phenomenon. The series included one cartoon of cabinet ministers reacting with horror as they read the *Mail*. Another showed Farrer painting moral spots on the tattered *Mail* tiger. The central cartoon, however, reflected John Bengough's continuing suspicion that Macdonald was still somewhere in the background. It showed Bunting and Macdonald, back to back, dipping fish nets into Ontario and Quebec, respectively, with the caption: 'It's all right – We put our fish in the one basket.'[73]

A more serious discussion of the meaning of the *Mail*'s move was launched in the Montreal *Star* by 'Native,' the same Toronto correspondent who had set out the *Mail*'s reasons for defection. In a series of dispatches this writer forecast far-reaching implications – for journalism, for the political parties, and even for the state. In the past, one column said, many of even the greatest Canadian journals, and nearly all the minor ones, had been dragged at the tail of party politicians, who had taken their journalistic echoes to reflect public opinion. 'From appearances here I am satisfied that one result of the *Mail*'s new departure will be to emancipate the whole daily press from party thraldom.' Since the *Mail*'s declaration of independence had

THE MAIL'S NEW DEPARTURE. *Grip*, 9 October 1886. After initial cynicism *Grip* acknowledged that the *Mail*'s 'coup d'état' was the sensation of the hour. But Bengough hedged his bets. While he showed Farrer painting moral spots on the old tiger, the cartoonist hinted in another sketch that Bunting and Macdonald were still working together.

Splendid Isolation 93

increased its subscription list, it said, the *Globe* would be likely to follow. 'With the two leading papers of Ontario free from party harness, it is reasonable to suppose that the minor ones will rapidly get outside the old traces ... Thus a great many able thinkers and writers, who have for years back represented any thought but their own, will be enlisted in sincere endeavour to bring about what they individually believe to be right. The effect on public education, thoughtfulness, temper and patriotism will be incalculably beneficial ...'[74]

In another column, however, 'Native' suggested the *Mail* had less honourable motives. Some people were saying that Bunting wanted to make himself leader of Orangeism and then strike a deal with some faction in Quebec, he wrote. 'On the other hand it is said that Mr Bunting means that the *Mail* shall keep on its present course, no matter who may gain or who may lose, and with the single design to break down the privileges of the Church of Quebec, even if that cannot be accomplished without destroying the Confederation. I have some reason to believe that this more fairly describes the intentions of the *Mail*'s managers ...' Such a course, 'Native' went on, would bring Ontario either into civil war with Britain and Quebec, or into peaceful secession and union with the United States – but he doubted Ontario would accept it.[75]

Despite analysis of this kind, there were many in Canada who remained unconvinced for months or years that the *Mail*'s separation from the Conservative party was genuine. Conservative insiders kept trying to bring personal influence to bear on Bunting and Riordan, and Bunting, at least, seems at times to have given them encouragement.[76] As late as the fall of 1887, Thomas P. Gorman, editor of the Liberal Ottawa *Free Press*, was uncertain about the *Mail*'s independence. 'For a long time and until very recently,' he wrote Laurier, 'I was of the opinion that the *Mail*'s independence was a sham and that the paper was playing the game of the Tories, but I am inclined to think that it is not so.' Whatever the motive, he added, the paper was certainly doing the Tories mischief, outstripping the *Globe* 'as a newspaper' and reaching a class of readers that did not normally see Reform papers.[77]

While the outside world puzzled out the problem, Tory leaders were well aware of the extent of the mischief. The *Mail*'s defection was particularly hurtful because both the provincial and federal parties were facing elections, the former on 28 December and the latter on 22 February 1887. On 22 December Macdonald reported to Sir Charles

Tupper on the damage: 'We have ... lost nearly the whole Catholic vote by the course of the 'Mail,' and this course has had a prejudicial effect not only in Ontario but in the whole of the Dominion, thus introducing a great element of uncertainty in a good many constituencies.'[78] Two days later the Conservative leader in Ontario, W.R. Meredith, made almost the same comment to Macdonald. 'The action of the Mail has, I think, practically detached the whole of the Catholic vote from us,' he wrote, and the result was likely to be a decided victory for Mowat.[79] Some analysts, though, including Bengough, felt Mowat had been clever to call an early election, avoiding the danger that 'four months more of Farrer's sledgehammer' would break away his Protestant support.[80]

The provincial voting showed the *Mail* had done more harm than good, and Macdonald felt he was being betrayed on the eve of his own battle, which turned out more successfully. 'You speak of the Mail,' he wrote to Viscount Melgund (later Lord Minto) several weeks after the federal election. 'We were deserted by it at the last moment, just before the fight[,] in the most treacherous manner – but I won't bore you with the reasons why.'[81] Macdonald's earlier correspondence with Bunting, though, makes clear that the *Mail*'s course had been apparent to him for some time. On 3 January, almost two months before the federal election, he had written:

Dear Bunting,

There is no use crying over spilt milk – the mischief is done, but I think you will admit now that the course taken by the *Mail* has not only resulted in Meredith's defeat, but prejudiced the Conservative party throughout the Dominion.

In don't wish to reproach you, but think you are bound, in justice to myself and the leaders of the Conservative party, to state that the course taken by you, was taken from conscientious motives and notwithstanding our strong and continued remonstrances. This should be done at once and in a leading article in the *Mail*.

The announcement is all the more necessary from the fact that the *Mail* is going to pursue the same course – be the consequences what they may!

The *Mail* having taken that stand, gives me, I think, a right to ask this avowal at your hands ...[82]

The *Mail* responded to this letter with what amounted to a full Declaration of Independence, without rancour. It had tried, it said,

Splendid Isolation 95

to live up to its pledge to break free of its fetters while still giving general support to the Conservatives but had found that to be absolutely free it had to be absolutely independent. As matters stood, the Conservative leaders were saddled with the paper's views, even though these views for nearly a year had been wholly at variance with their wishes. 'And whilst Sir John Macdonald and Mr Meredith are held responsible for our views, despite the fact that they have earnestly and even impatiently protested against them, we on our part have to shoulder responsibility for words and acts of theirs which we can neither justify nor excuse.' In sum, the paper said, the working partnership with the Conservative party had broken down, and nothing remained but to accept the logical step of complete independence.

While rejecting partyism, though, the *Mail* left itself open to the charge that it was a paper in search of a party. Its aim, it said, was to 'prepare the way for the birth of an independent organization that shall be British and Canadian and liberal in the highest and best sense.' The editorial also signalled, to a careful reader, the coming support for commercial union, and even hinted at annexation leanings. On the former, it supported maintenance of the protective tariff 'so long as our American neighbours deny us free entry into their markets *and no longer.*' On the latter it declared:

We do not believe it would be wise *at present* to demand the political independence of Canada, or to sue for annexation to the United States. The experiment of forming a great British State on this continent has *not yet* failed. It is evident, however, that we cannot always remain in the colonial stage of existence; and we do not count it treason, therefore, for Canadians to discuss their future. We would strenuously oppose any scheme of Imperial Federation that threatened to restrict the right of self-government or to embroil us in the quarrels of the Old World ... (italics added)

The editorial then went on to summarize the policy lines already struck by the *Mail*, above all for constitutional reform to abolish separate schools and place the civil power always above the ecclesiastical. Politicians had said that such a program would rupture Confederation, it noted. 'Our answer is that if Confederation cannot adapt itself to the principles of modern civilization, it is a house of sand.'[83]

Slowly, Farrer's true agenda was beginning to emerge.

6 The Hidden Message

In the spring of 1889 the Toronto *Mail* took note of accusations that its campaign against the Roman Catholic hierarchy was actually designed to serve the cause of annexation, and it politely rejected the theory. The charge, it said, was merely a red herring, a device used by politicians who found discussion of principle inconvenient. The way to bring on annexation, it said, was to let a company of 'alien conspirators' (the Jesuit order) become masters of Quebec and use the province as an engine against the religion and liberties of the British provinces.¹ Three days later the paper again insisted that it had come to bury annexation and not to praise it, but it shifted the argument slightly. The people of Ontario, it said, were watching the steady encroachment of Catholicism, the divisions and weakness among Protestants, and the untrustworthiness of politicians subjugated by the Catholic vote, and they were starting to use some very ominous language. '*They are beginning to say that the only hope of escape from French and Roman Catholic domination is union with the great mass of the English-speaking and Protestant race*' (italics added).²

The subtle pen of Ned Farrer was again at work, probably bringing nods of agreement from both those Protestants who supported political union and those who opposed it – and perhaps offering the germ of an idea to those without strong feelings either way. And the campaign had a powerful effect. In April 1889 D'Alton McCarthy wrote to the prime minister to say that the question of whether Canada would be English or French was 'driving people openly to talk of annexation as the only means of escape.' He suggested that Macdonald, 'living as you do in Ottawa,' could not realize how the idea had taken hold of the minds of even staunch loyalists.[3] A few months earlier Wilfrid Laurier had received the same message from a Toronto correspondent. 'There is an under-current of feeling in favor of annexation with the United States,' H.H. Cook had written. 'There is a strong outspoken sentiment on this question such as I never heard expressed before.'[4]

In a sense, these reactions were a tribute to Ned Farrer's skill. While the extent of his personal influence is impossible to determine, the *Mail* was clearly influential in provoking the extremes of Protestant fervour in Ontario in the late 1880s, and in linking that fervour with the idea of continental union.[5] Contemporaries agreed that, whatever the motivating force, it was Farrer who made the campaign. True, it was Bunting who showed the more fervent anti-Catholicism. True, it was Goldwin Smith who wrote the most inflammatory editorials on the Jesuits' Estates issue. But it was Farrer who carried the running, day after day and week after week, creating a clear change of opinion in Toronto on basic questions about whether the country could or should survive. The *Mail* campaign may have been cynical, irresponsible, even reprehensible, but it was unquestionably brilliant. It was not until a year or so later, when Farrer's commitment to annexation began to emerge, that Torontonians realized they had been had – although some, like the *Evening News*, claimed to have understood all along. 'We asserted from the first that the anti-Jesuit agitation, which Mr Farrer encouraged, was intended to dismember Canada, and that the men who were caught by it were merely playing into the hands of the annexationists,' it said in 1891. Those who had been inspired to join the campaign, it added, would find it pleasant to realize they had been played with.[6]

And indeed, if Farrer's day-to-day editorials are read in the light of later evidence of his hostility to empire and support for annexation, the destructive subtext is not difficult to find. On the surface, of course (and no Toronto editor could have done less), he paid due regard to the symbols of national unity or British 'connection.' Just below the surface, though, were hints that ran against the current of rhetoric – hints that the alien mass of French Canada was preventing the natural unity of the English-speaking peoples on the continent; that the secular power of the Church of Rome was forcing English Canada to contemplate radical solutions; that Canadians wanted to cast off 'Old World' evils and align themselves with fellow Anglo-Saxons in the United States.

Even a century later it is not possible to define his motivation (or the paper's) with certainty. No incriminating documents are known to exist that set out any deliberate blueprint for undermining Confederation in favour of political union. But analysis of Farrer's editorials over a five-year period yields considerable evidence of an organic link connecting the various stages of his last *Mail* editorship: the pre-independence period of 1885–6, when he laid the groundwork for separation from the party; the post-independence period of 1886–7, when he built a new constituency by nurturing Toronto's hostility to Quebec and the church; the commercial union campaign of 1887–8, when he brought the new constituency to an unprecedented level of interest in continentalism; the Jesuits' Estates / equal rights campaign of 1888–9, when, after the U.S. government rebuffed commercial union hopes, he rekindled the race/religion fires in an apparent effort to wreck the country and bring its fragments into the American union.

The strongest evidence of this is the apparent double levels of meaning in Farrer's writing. As the *Gazette* had astutely implied, Farrer's skill lay in creating a *climate of belief*. He was remarkably adept at making key points in a subtle or indirect way. He often gave attention to causes he favoured while seeming to criticize them. In various ways he suggested – without seeming to make the case himself – that patterns he was promoting were already accomplished fact. Canadians' growing reservations about the empire, their growing interest in continentalism, their disillusionment with Confederation – all were treated as patterns evident to any thoughtful person. It was self-evident (as Farrer described it) that Canadian farmers were in favour of commercial union. It was self-evident that French Canada, or the Maritimes, or the West, were discontented with Ottawa and sympathetic to free trade. Regularly, while seeming to be intent on a different point, he would portray these patterns as givens. At times he even left the impression he was deploring the patterns, when his real aim was probably to give them prominence.

Without directly advocating an end to British rule, for instance, Farrer managed in various ways to suggest that its ending would be a good thing. Only British rule was maintaining the special privileges of the Roman Catholic church: 'She [the church] upholds British connection because she knows that if it were severed the huge edifice of privileges which she has reared would at once be levelled to the ground.'7 The most potent force for political union was 'the desire of the English provinces to rid themselves and their institutions of the

MUCH ADO ABOUT NOTHING! *Grip*, 5 December 1885. After Riel's hanging *Grip* thought Farrer and the *Mail* were somewhat overwrought in their condemnation of Quebec's protests. Over the next few years *Grip* would gradually swing into line behind the *Mail*.

dead-weight of medievalism with which they are burdened.'[8] Church powers were certain to be curbed eventually – if not through political change, then through collapse of the divided country and its assimilation into the United States. 'For, let the clergy have no doubt about it, if the choice be forced upon them by further encroachments the English-speaking majority will prefer equal rights with their own kindred across the line to an unequal partition of power with an alien race and an alien church at home.'[9] Furthermore, frustrated English Canadians could look with hope to their stronger American brother: sooner or later, the French and ultramontane power would have to reckon not merely with the English-speaking population of Canada, but with 'the larger branch of our race in the United States.' And if required to intervene, the Americans would do so with a Yankee thoroughness that would flutter the birds of night.[10]

Subtly, too, Farrer implied that Confederation was not worth the saving. It had been constructed, after all, not so much by an act of consolidation as by one of dissolution, designed, unsuccessfully, to deliver the Protestants of Quebec and Ontario from French ascendancy in the united provinces of Upper and Lower Canada:

The French element having been set free for separate self-development, we have now a strong and growing French nation, interposed with its stubborn and impenetrable mass, between British Canada and the British of the maritime provinces, who on their part have not learned to call themselves Canadians. How such an obstacle to the consolidation of Canadian nationality is to be surmounted nobody has yet attempted to show. There is no doubt such a thing as undue pessimism, though the hope and desire of improvement can never deserve that name. But there is also such a thing as fatuous optimism which casts up the credit column of the ledger and shuts its eyes to half the truth. That optimism is surely fatuous which can warble about our national unity, and all the blessings and glories which it is to bring us in the future, without taking account of the fact that in the midst of our British confederation, and daily increasing in extent as well as in solidity and in tendency to isolation, lies New France, the people of which may be amiable, pious, and good workers in factories, but are not and never will be British.[11]

Curiously, Farrer played a parallel game in addressing French Canadians, implying that they, too, could escape oppressors through annexation. He regularly echoed the theme that a 'light from New England' – the modern views brought back to Quebec by French Canadians who had emigrated – was breaking down the myth of the contented habitant. At the same time he nurtured the idea that Anglo politicians were conspiring with Quebec clergy to exploit the ordinary people, who could escape only by looking south. 'Should they [English-speaking politicians] conspire with the clergy to keep the people down, the people may be expected to seek relief in annexation, and who could blame them?'[12]

In some instances, at least, Farrer seemed to take pleasure in crafting an editorial that made a disguised point diametrically opposite to the manifest argument. That seemed to be the case, for example, in his handling of an 1888 gaffe by a new governor general, Lord Stanley. Some French-Canadian commentators had attacked Stanley for his outspoken advocacy of imperial union, saying he was threatening to harm trade with the United States, so as to force Canada 'on the rebound' into the arms of the imperial federationists. Farrer, rather than supporting the critics (with whom he would certainly have agreed), pretended to defend Stanley. The critics, he observed judiciously, were probably unduly alarmed. Lord Stanley had been a colonial secretary, after all, and therefore understood that a governor general had no mandate to talk politics. 'The speeches complained of appear to have been made from the best of motives, though perhaps without sufficient reflection. The moral of the explosion is that the Canadian people are exceedingly jealous of any Imperial interference in their affairs.' Further, it was absurd to suppose Lord Stanley was seeking to harm relations with the United States. 'He could not hope to control the forces that would be let loose in Quebec and elsewhere in the event of such a calamity.'[13] The impact of the editorial was thus to suggest, first, that the Quebec comments amounted to an 'explosion'; second, that everyone accepted the importance of close trade relations with the United States; and third, that even Lord Stanley's natural allies were warning him – and the cabinet – not to promote imperialist plots. In Farrer's writing the second or third level of meaning was often the most significant one.

Ironically, while Farrer's work in this period is remembered as extremist, its brilliance lay at least partly in its understated tone. Farrer was by no means being facetious when he later wrote that in journalism, 'nothing is so unwise as to be extreme.'[14] Consistently, he wrote in a calm, rational, even judicious tone, building his argument logically on factual material and offering enough of the other side of a case to give the appearance, at least, of reasoned analysis. Consistently, he maintained that the *Mail* was in no way attacking the church itself, or its doctrines, but only its encroachment into secular matters, and by and large he held to that definition. Billy Maclean's *World*, certain that the *Mail* was going for annexation, was driven to fury by what it called the 'calm philosophical style' its rival had developed to cover its insidious disunion propaganda.[15]

The *World*'s vexation was well justified. Whether or not Farrer was Jesuit-trained, he had a fine understanding of the science of rhetoric. Consistently, he would start editorials, not with the point *he* wanted to make, but with the point his readers wanted to hear, before showing that their views logically supported his own. Consistently, he used Mark Antony's 'I have come to bury Caesar' approach, seeming at first to agree with his readers' biases, then working in point after point to turn their attitudes. Consistently, he left it to readers to make the obvious conclusion, rather than stating it himself. Opponents sought in vain for the decisive quote that would prove the *Mail* disloyal.

While the paper's 1889 campaign on the Jesuits' Estates issue provides the most interesting examples of Farrer's craft, his multi-layered messages can be traced through the various phases of his five-year tenure. Even in 1885, when he had just taken over the editorship and was ostensibly the leading journalistic champion of protection, some curious undertones appear. For instance, he gave what seemed to be inordinate attention to the advocacy of commercial union by a handful of young Liberals. On one level that might have seemed to be simply a desire to embarrass the opposition party, but the effect was also to put the topic firmly on the political agenda, and to attract the attention of young Liberals. And even at that early stage some of the messages were ambiguous. The paper equated commercial union with annexation, and attacked both – but it also seemed to concede reluctantly that Canadians would 'profit enormously' and that union 'would doubtless be followed by an extraordinary movement of American capital and energy to this part of the continent.'[16] And while attacking commercial union on the ground that it would devastate the protected Canadian manufacturers, the *Mail* also left a subtle impression that it would, and should, be popular in the East and the West. 'If the Maritime Provinces were annexed to the United States commercially for a period of ten or twenty years, how should we charm them back again to the old store? ... Commercial union would also deprive us of the North-West, for we should never be able to coax or compel the settler to deal with Toronto and Montreal again if he had the run of the St Paul and Chicago markets for any lengthened period.'17

While thus suggesting that commercial union, or annexation, might be profitable (even though undesirable), Farrer also created the impression that annexation sentiment was already widespread: 'The annexation spirit is rife among the Antis [anti-Confederationists] of the Maritime Provinces and the North-West, while the Cossacks of the Reform party in Quebec have long regarded British supremacy as baneful ... The forces making for annexation are much more formidable than they were in the abortive movement of 1849, and the task of overpowering them will call forth the best efforts of the loyalists.'18

Similarly, Farrer was already planting in a backhanded way the idea that Canadians were generally more disposed to an American than a British connection. While in the spring of 1885 the *Mail* had been enthusiastic about imperial federation, by fall Farrer had worked a clear turnaround. 'It is scarcely necessary to add,' he wrote in October, 'that no plan of federation tending to diminish that control over our own affairs which we now enjoy, or to interfere with the development of Canadian industries, or to involve us in the broils of the Old World, or to convert the United States into an angry and aggressive neighbour forever menacing us with war, would find favour here ...'19

In the Riel issue, too, Farrer's work reads in a later age much differently than it must have appeared at the time. To contemporaries, caught up in French Canada's anger over Riel's hanging, and English Canada's equally emotional reaction, the *Mail* comment could have been seen mainly as loyalty to the Macdonald government. Nothing could have been more loyal than the way the paper lacerated and ridiculed Liberal leaders for their failure to condemn the rebels. Scarcely a day went by without at least one mention of Laurier's famous statement that he himself would have carried a musket in the rebellion if he had been born on the banks of the Saskatchewan; equally popular were attacks on Edward Blake for refusing to approve Riel's hanging – even though he had, after the more defensible rebellion of 1869–70, called the Métis leader a murderer. Only in retrospect might one notice that the dominant thrust was not to condemn Liberals *en masse* but to appeal to the 'best' Liberal elements to curb, or disown, their leaders – apparently an attempt to establish a new constituency of disgruntled Reformers. In its treatment of Riel's hanging, too, the paper seemed to be thoroughly loyal, but it was already injecting the insidious idea that English Canadians could profit by turning away from French Canada and looking southward. The desire of the English provinces to 'do right' by French Canada, the *Mail* said, had undoubtedly hampered their material progress: 'The English-speaking majority in the United States would never have tolerated the demands which the British portion of Canada has cheerfully complied with.'[20]

In retrospect, too, one of the most striking features of the race/religion campaign is the way it was cleverly cast as a *defensive* action, nurturing English Canada's paranoia. The *Mail* might be on the rampage, but readers at the time would have had the impression the paper was simply defending, inch by inch, against assaults of the church or French Canada. From week to week Farrer built his best arguments on the more aggressive statements of his opponents. He quoted effectively from ultramontane writers who called for retention of church-state ties, for church control of education, and for extension of the parish system into Ontario. He skilfully used the tensions within the church to contend that the Jesuits and ultramontanes were intent on suppressing the church's more liberal elements, centring on Laval University. He quoted from papal documents to make the case that the church was indeed opposed to liberty of the press, liberty of conscience, and even to equality before the law. He argued that English settlers were being squeezed out of Quebec, and that their education rights were being curbed. He insisted that education and enlightenment had been blighted in those countries of Europe and Latin America where the church dominated, and said the battle for public education was a battle for the life or death of democracy. Without an educated people democracy would not exist for an hour. And wherever the church held sway it had damaged education. Repeatedly, though, came reassurance that the *Mail* was not attacking the church itself, or its beliefs, but only its interference in secular affairs.

An editorial of 5 January 1887, entitled 'Liberals and Liberals,' provides an example of the way Farrer both eluded charges that the *Mail* was persecuting the church and at the same time cast the newspaper as the inspiration for a new liberal constituency:

The accusation brought against *The Mail* by men calling themselves Liberals, that in resisting the overshadowing political power of the Roman Catholic

Church in Canada we are persecuting that Church, is a perversion of the truth with which the ordinary student of history is quite familiar. The Church has thrown herself across the path of progress, and in every free country in the world the men who are endeavouring to move her out of the way are described by her adherents as fanatics. Let any Canadian who entertains a doubt on this point procure a copy of the bulls, allocutions, letters and speeches of Pope Pius the Ninth. That famous Pontiff spent thirty years in cursing the Liberals and the Liberalism of Europe. In France, in Belgium, in Germany, in Spain and in Italy, whoso ventured to preach the supremacy of the State and the curtailment of the exorbitant prerogatives of ecclesiasticism, was a 'hostile' to God and man ... the long series of insurrections and revolutions by which the Church has been humbled in Europe were not the intemperate action of utopists or atheists, but simply the manifestation of the profound workings of the conscience and intellect of mankind. In every nation where it has prevailed, the Papacy has been arraigned on civil and political grounds as the very worst of rulers; and the fact that it has always relied upon the ignorant and superstitious multitude for support, and that it has as consistently condemned the free tendencies of the age as persecution, and the champions of enlightenment as persecutors, ought to make those Canadian Liberals who are echoing its cry against us think seriously of their own position in the great struggle impending here ...

Ironically, in view of Farrer's (and the *Mail*'s) long-standing antagonism for George Brown, this editorial wound up with a rousing reminder of Brown's role, after Confederation, in resisting church encroachment on the state:

We beseech those Reformers who followed him in that arduous campaign to tell us how they contrive, in their inmost conscience, to reconcile the Liberalism of that period with the Liberalism of this. Either Liberalism has ceased to be the aegis of liberty and enlightenment or the Liberalism of Mr Anglin and the *Globe* is a wholly bastard type ... ask where the party is today and the answer of every honest Reformer is the wail of Samson Agonistes:

> Promise was that I
> Should Israel from Philistian yoke deliver
> Ask for this great deliverer now, and find him
> Eyeless in Gaza at the mill with slaves,
> Himself in bonds under Philistian yoke.[21]

While Farrer's race/religion writing in the post-Riel era showed great cunning, later analysts agreed that the commercial union campaign of 1887–8 probably called forth his finest, and most influential, writing. O.D. Skelton, for instance, wrote in 1921 that the *Mail*'s influence was critical in the episode. The power of the press to select, shape, and force an issue, he wrote, had never been more clearly displayed in Canada than in the commercial union campaign, and 'Farrer's lucid, informing, businesslike editorials were the most important factor' in its growth.[22] Skelton's assessment may have been based partly on Sir John Willison's *Reminiscences*, published two years earlier, which pronounced even more strongly on this point. The idea had grown up, Willison wrote, that commercial union or unrestricted reciprocity had been imposed on the Liberal party by Sir Richard Cartwright, but in fact it was more likely the policy was conceived in the office of the *Mail*. 'Although Mr Erastus Wiman was the reputed father, one suspects that Mr Edward Farrer instructed Wiman, and by his persuasive and trenchant writing, made the proposal attractive to the Liberal leaders ... Between Sir Richard Cartwright and Mr Farrer there was a personal relation of long standing, although not an intimate friendship, and probably Mr Farrer persuaded Sir Richard to pronounce in favour of continental free trade before Laurier had committed himself.'[23] Both these writers may have been influenced by Walter Blackburn Harte's prominent 1891 article in the *New England Magazine*, which had given Farrer credit both for the *Mail*'s independence and for the anti-clerical and commercial union campaigns.

These assessments probably exaggerate Farrer's part, especially as an *originator* of the commercial union movement, though they may be an accurate index of his success in popularizing it. The idea was by no means new when the *Mail* took it up. Others, including Goldwin Smith and S.J. Ritchie, as well as Wiman, had been pressing it for some time. On 29 January 1886, for instance, Smith had written to the U.S. secretary of state, Thomas F. Bayard, that 'people on this side of the Line are about ready for the question of Commercial Union, if it can be brought before them in a definite and authoritative form.'[24] The *Mail*'s open espousal of 'C.U.' did not come until early 1887, and apparently followed a visit by Bunting to Bayard. The extent to which Bunting may have been primed by Smith, Farrer, Ritchie, or Wiman is not known, however. Neither is it known whether any money changed hands, although both Ritchie and Wiman had business interests in Canada that would have been advanced by commercial union.²⁵ Whatever the origin or the motivation, though, it is clear that the spread of interest in the idea was remarkably fast. It is also clear that the Liberal party took it up largely because it was seen to be a popular issue. Some scholars with justice argue that its support was never as great as newspapers of the day painted it, and they are probably right (although results of the 1891 election show it was not without substance). In its early days the campaign had a certain air of artificiality, with Smith and others busily organizing commercial union leagues or circulating pamphlets, while a group of newspapers led by the *Mail* gave exaggerated attention to every sign of interest. By the late spring of 1887, C.U. seemed to be the burning issue throughout the country.

In retrospect, the *Mail*'s move seemed well timed, coming as the country, still only two decades old, grumbled under Macdonald's aging regime. Nova Scotia the year before had elected a Liberal government pledged, in theory at least, to secession. Manitoba's weakening Conservative government gave Macdonald constant trouble as it demanded breakup of the CPR monopoly. Honoré Mercier's Liberal-Nationalists in Quebec were not only hostile but were rallying the other provinces for a fall meeting to coordinate anti-federal sentiment. Faced with this array of troubles, Macdonald considered the proper response to commercial union fervour was to ignore or ridicule it – to let it 'blaze, crackle and go out with a stink,' as he sometimes put it.²⁶

The Liberals were traditionally more sympathetic to free trade and so found the campaign more attractive. The party, adjusting to the leadership change from Blake to Laurier and trying to rally from its third straight election defeat, was also in need of fresh policies, and the continental idea was clearly taking hold among voters. In a letter to Laurier on 8 July Cartwright reported that 'matters have been moving very fast' in Ontario and that it was impossible to rise on a rural platform without pronouncing on commercial union. 'I am doubtful if we can fight any constituency without speaking plainly on this subject.' Laurier, after soliciting party views, wrote to Cartwright on 8 August agreeing with his assessment: 'I am afraid we are doomed to defeat following defeat unless we come out ... in favour of Commercial Union ...'²⁷

If Laurier seemed hesitant, other Liberals were even less enthusiastic, especially at the prospect of a full commercial union or *zollverein* in which the two countries would have common tariffs against the rest of the world. The problem was that the common tariff would have to be *set* somehow, and few doubted the clout in doing so would be with Washington. Late in the year, however, J.D. Edgar advanced a watered-down scheme designed to overcome that difficulty. His plan, called unrestricted reciprocity, was to leave these tariffs against the rest of the world in the hands of the respective governments and preserve custom-houses along the U.S.-Canadian border to deal with goods brought in from outside and then moved across the continental boundary. The plan would also be introduced over a period of years, to avoid disruption of trade patterns or sudden shocks for protected manufacturers. The Liberal leadership, with Blake conspicuously absent, found this a more congenial policy on which to unite, and early in 1888 they advanced 'U.R.' in Parliament as a concerted policy.

Much of the ammunition for debate came straight from Farrer's pen, as, day after day, week after week, he offered a brilliant marshalling of hard-headed business argument combined with subtle, almost subliminal, suggestions appealing to the deepest attitudes of his various readers. For nationalists, the message was that Canada would not come of age until it could control its own destiny and open up its natural trade channels. For Anglo-Saxons there were subtle reminders of the 'New World' bonds between English Canada and New England. Incredibly, even the imperialists came in for some stroking as they were told that Canada's maturation in a continental free trade area would be a crowning achievement of British policy, assuring maintenance of pro-British sentiment:

Every colony under the British system must gradually emerge from childhood into manhood, from government by a paternal despotism to autonomy, or else perish from arrested development. Each step in the journey implies a loosening of the original ties ... When we obtained responsible government; when we assumed control of our tariff, which had previously been adjusted for us in England; when we eliminated one by one the archaic prerogatives in the Governor-General's instructions; when the British troops were withdrawn and the protection of the colony thrown upon itself; above all, when we claimed the right in 1879 to levy heavy duties on British goods in order to benefit Canadian industry – in each of these instances it was said, and with unquestionable truth, that the connection was becoming more and more a matter of mere sentiment. Commercial Union is a fresh stage in the direction in which we have been travelling since Lord Durham's day. Its advocates, if *The Mail* may be permitted to speak on their behalf, are not actuated by the slightest desire to undermine British connection. On the contrary, they firmly

The Hidden Message 109

believe their scheme presents the only means of keeping the country together as a British dependency. If, as our opponents allege, it will weaken the connection, our reply is that persistence in the existing policy must inevitably destroy it ...²⁸

While thus paying lip service to British connection, Farrer also repeatedly showed that the status quo was intolerable – and then left it up to readers to consider what should be done:

No intelligent person can observe what is passing before his eyes without perceiving that we are on the eve of great events. The signs of transformation are visible on every hand. The presentiment of some change coming oppresses us all. Our enormous debt; the determination of the people in the North-West to break loose from trade and transportation restrictions in defiance of the federal authority; the exodus of population from the North-West and the far larger stream pouring out of the older provinces; the threats of secession heard in the three Maritime Provinces; the decline in our exports, which are less to-day by five dollars per head of the population than they were in 1873, although since then we have spent no less than $120,000,000 of borrowed money in developing our resources; the gathering of the Local Premiers at Quebec to devise ways and means for allaying provincial discontent and averting provincial bankruptcy – these, to go no further, are phenomena which, if they presented themselves in any other country, young or old, we should regard as the forerunners of dissolution. To what cause are they to be ascribed? In our opinion, two primary causes exist. In the first place, we are not a single community, but two communities, divided from each other by race, religion, language and sentiment; in short, by all those ethnical differences which mark out one people from another. Perhaps the nearest parallel to our case is that afforded by Bohemia, where two separate and distinct nationalities in the person of the Czechs and Germans are striving with doubtful success to preserve the stability of a house divided against itself. The other cause, in our judgment, is the failure of the attempt, undertaken by our politicians in good faith, to dissever us in matters of trade from the continent to which we belong. Nature has decreed that each of these scattered provinces should find its market, not with a sister province, but in the territory immediately to the south. All our efforts since Confederation have been directed to setting aside this natural order of things and erecting an artificial order. For this we have incurred the most tremendous liabilities borne by any people of our strength; yet, after all, what have we accomplished beyond bringing into play the forces of disintegration? Where is our Canadian spirit, our national comradeship, our interprovincial trade, our pride in our institutions, our hope for the future?

It was true, Farrer wrote, that commercial union would not relieve the rest of the country of the spectre of French Canada, which would 'remain to haunt us with ever-growing proportions to the end.' What that 'end' might be was not spelled out.[29]

As the campaign crested in the spring of 1888, Farrer continued to take his readers up to the very edge of political union, without ever crossing the line. Sometimes he would seem, in fact, to be heading the other way. In the following editorial, for instance, the first sentence seems to indicate that the column will *oppose* annexation. The article then takes a subtle curve, implying the country is only a makeshift, not worth preserving – and the original thrust is never resumed:

A Government journal in this city seeks to alarm the timid by asserting that the country is drifting towards disruption, and that there is a gigantic conspiracy on foot to bring about annexation. It is quite true that there exists a widespread feeling of uneasiness, that the old parties are breaking up, and that a new regime with an unknown mission is being born. So far as we can perceive, however, there is no disloyalty to the political institutions of Canada. Some of us may doubt whether it is within our power to construct a homogeneous country out of such heterogeneous material; and may be inclined to think that, in providing for the perpetuation of differences in race and language the fathers of Confederation exhibited a marvellous lack of foresight, although it may be said in their behalf that Confederation was simply a makeshift. But the question now agitating the people is one which concerns their present material condition rather than their political future. It is felt by most intelligent persons that our affairs are in a critical state ...

Farrer then went on to his usual budget of gloom, suggesting in various ways that Canada's colonial condition was cause for shame, while closer links with the Americans would provide cause for pride. When a critic argued that commercial union would degrade Canada, Farrer replied that the country's condition might already be described as degraded:

We are poor, but with vast natural wealth lying useless at our feet for want of a market. We are a young community, yet, in proportion to population, the emigration from our shores is as large every year as that from any Old

World country where overcrowding, militarism and other acute evils press upon the people and drive them forth. Lastly, under the existing fiscal system, we are taught to prefer the interests of the few to the welfare of the many; and led to believe that we are so wholly lacking in intelligence and self-reliance as to be unfit to meet the Americans in the field of industrial and commercial enterprise.[30]

While the impact of the campaign may have been exaggerated, there is no doubt Farrer's editorials won converts. *Grip*, which now praised almost everything the *Mail* did, cartooned him as the conscience of Sir John, reminding the prime minister that he, too, had once been a free-trader, before he had been captured by the manufacturers.[31] Even the governor general, Lord Lansdowne, might have been reading the *Mail* before he wrote a confidential dispatch on the subject in October 1887. In its strictly commercial aspect, he said, 'there appears to be no room for doubt that Commercial Union would be greatly to the advantage of the people of the Dominion' since the natural channels of trade lay north and south.[32]

The hopes of the free-traders were blighted, however, when in the fall of 1888 Americans elected a Republican administration headed by Benjamin Harrison, with James G. Blaine as secretary of state. The Republicans were traditional protectionists, and those among them who advocated commercial union over the next few years did so with a grave lack of credibility, made even more acute when they let down their guard and implied that the real aim was political union. Opponents were convinced that any American interest in commercial union came, not from liberal free-traders, but from business interests eyeing Canadian lumber or metals. Colonel Denison, for instance, was certain, although he could find no proof, that Wiman was working for 'great financial interests in the States, headed by Jay Gould.'[33] The strongest political supporters in Washington were known protectionists, more interested in annexation than free trade. One congressional resolution by Representative Benjamin Butterworth of Ohio even invited the president to open negotiations 'looking to the assimilation & unity of the people of the Dominion of Canada & the United States under one government.'[34] It was introduced in December 1888 at the very moment when Liberal MP John Charlton was in Washington to urge restraint on the party's American friends. (Charlton told Butterworth the move was worse than a mistake – that it would 'give point to the tory argument that Commercial Union

THEN AND NOW. *Grip*, 7 July 1888. A series of Farrer articles on Sir John A's past support for free trade led *Grip* to conclude that the prime minister had sold his birthright of moral and mental independence, becoming a chattel of the manufacturers.

meant annexation.')[35] Another key ally, Representative Robert R. Hitt of Illinois, was a close associate of Blaine, who had insisted during the election campaign that he would never give Canadians access to the American market while they retained their sovereignty.[36] Senators John Sherman and Henry Payne of Ohio also made little effort to conceal their view that commercial union should be only a device for bringing about political union. (Both had been linked, too, with E.A.C. Pew's annexation plot of 1884.)[37]

This kind of rhetoric was naturally hurtful to Canadian Liberals and pointed up fatal flaws in their campaign. Whereas Canadians might be fascinated by the benefits of reciprocity or commercial union (the two were almost indistinguishable in the public mind), Americans never saw them as more than a side issue. And those who sought to change American opinion tended either to exaggerate the benefits to the United States or to reduce the discussion to hints of an ultimate takeover. Even Erastus Wiman, who insisted at every stage that he was not advocating political union, was often an embarrassment because of his stress on commercial union's advantages to the Americans. In a long article in the *North American Review* summing up views he had offered from many platforms, he argued that Canada should be 'captured,' not through military conquest, which was unnecessary, or through bids for political union, which would be fruitless, but through commercial integration: 'If the enormous resources of this "Greater Half of the Continent" can be made tributary to the progress of the United States by legislation, by occupancy through individual purchase, by development, and by the creation of a mutuality of interests, it would seem to be the very best form of statesmanship to achieve that result,' he wrote. 'The time and the circumstances are extremely favorable to accomplish this purpose ...'[38]

Clearly, the Canadian continentalists were not getting much help from their 'friends' on the other side of the line. That factor may have been in the background when, to the dismay of the Liberals, the *Mail* in the spring of 1889 dropped its commercial union campaign. It was also in Farrer's mind when, about the same time, he met in Washington with George F. Hoar, chairman of a Senate committee on relations with Canada, to which Farrer was providing research materials. On 22 April Farrer wrote of his frustration to Wiman, in a document later to be famous as the 'two bites on the cherry' letter, when it was published during the 1891 election campaign. In it Farrer said there was a general belief in Canada that the Republicans would

A BREAK IN THE BAND. The 'Mail' – 'Let's move on, pard; what's the use of playing Free Trade music for people that have no ear for it?' The 'Globe' – 'Nonsense! You want to sneak out, that's what's the matter with you. If not, start her up and let's play 'till they order us off the premises!' *Grip*, 10 August 1889. While the *Globe*'s John Cameron accused the *Mail* of sneaking out of the commercial union campaign, Farrer insisted there was no point in continuing it.

DISGRACEFUL CASE OF CHILD-DESERTION. *Grip*, 28 September 1889. *Grip* was puzzled by the *Mail*'s abandonment of commercial union and blamed Farrer, while endorsing Goldwin Smith's chagrin over the defection.

not listen to any scheme of commercial union, and further that 'a very large number of people are inclined to think that we had better make for annexation at once, instead of making two bites on the cherry.' He had told Hoar, Farrer reported, that the 'smaller forces' favoured annexation and would favour it even more if commercial union were withheld. He had talked the thing over with Maritimes members and Manitobans, and it seemed that commercial union would only delay annexation. Among Liberals, he said, 'the truth is that every man who preaches C.U. would prefer annexation, so that the party is virtually wearing a mask.'[39]

The exact meaning of this 'two bites' letter is still a mystery. On one level it seems inexplicable because its basic thrust went against Farrer's approach at the *Mail*, and also later in his work for the *Globe* and as a freelance propagandist. In those roles he consistently promoted commercial union because (as he later made clear) he saw it as a natural stepping stone to political union. As well, the letter outrageously exaggerated Liberal support for annexation, and Farrer must have known this well. The letter *was* consistent, though, with a desire to get American leaders to back the Liberals while resisting any trade proposals from Macdonald. Wiman was notorious for an inability to keep anything to himself. Farrer may have calculated that he would pass his letter on to Washington (as, in fact, he did) and that it would work in the Liberal interest there. More likely, the letter was part of an attempt by Farrer to ingratiate himself with American hawks, including Blaine, Hoar, Charles Dana, and Andrew Carnegie, who were keen on annexation but had no interest in free trade. The *Mail* group may also have been disappointed in the level of tangible reward its C.U. campaign had drawn from Wiman and his associates. A hint to that effect emerged a few years later from Ottawa's spy in the U.S. annexation clique, who reported that the *Mail* had lost seriously in its continental campaign, and added: 'Mr B had been "hypnotized" it was said by Erastus Wiman. In the "Mail" office *they believed that he was a millionaire.*'[40]

In any event, the *Mail*'s new defection left the commercial union forces without their strongest artillery. For Cartwright that was by no means the end of the problem. Among some of his own Liberal colleagues, especially Blake, there was ominous silence. In the United States he had the wrong allies, many of them conditioned by Farrer's convincing claims that Canada was coming apart, and thus confident that if trade concessions were withheld, Canada would soon come pleading for admission. (The Hoar committee, for instance, would eventually publish voluminous background material on Canada made up almost entirely of *Mail* editorials, along with summaries very much in Farrer's style.)⁴¹

Amid these difficulties Cartwright soldiered on, and it may have been around this time that the idea resurfaced of bringing Farrer over to the *Globe*, to give the campaign new impetus. On 8 August 1889 Cartwright wrote to Laurier saying the *Mail* could no longer be relied on as an advocate of reciprocity, and that this seemed to result from 'the personal interest of Riordan' rather than any return to support for Macdonald. 'Still I think we must (if funds permit) subsidise Farrar to write a series of articles for the local press (of course in strict secrecy). I have written Preston and he may write you on this point.' Cartwright added, in a line that would prove prophetic, that the *Mail*'s defection 'makes it trebly inexpedient that Blake should in any way throw cold water on the movement for reciprocity.'⁴²

The *Mail*'s abandonment of commercial union more or less coincided with its belated plunge, early in 1889, into the bizarre Jesuits' Estates issue. While some later scholars would treat the two campaigns as unconnected, Farrer's 'two bites' letter made a clear, although carefully indirect, suggestion that they were indeed related. The Jesuit issue, he said, had 'brought home ... to thousands' the virtues of annexation. And indeed, given the *Mail*'s desire to show that Confederation was not working, the Jesuits' Estates issue provided splendid material for generating paranoia.

The actual cause of the issue, Quebec's Jesuits' Estates Act, would in time come to be seen as one of the more constructive acts of the Mercier government, and it provoked little reaction when it was introduced in the summer of 1888. Its purpose was to settle a long-standing difficulty on compensation for lands the Jesuits had held before the conquest, and which had remained in public hands after the period (1773–1814) when the order had been suppressed by the church. Mercier's solution was to offer the church $400,000 for educational purposes – the actual division of funds between Jesuits and other church components to be made by the pope – plus $60,000 for distribution by a Protestant education committee. The issue was enormously complicated, causing almost as much tension within the church as without, but for the *Mail* it came down to questions of papal interference in Canadian politics and a public subsidy for the wicked

Jesuits – in clear violation of principles of state-church separation. The paper, in alliance with D'Alton McCarthy, demanded disallowance by the federal Parliament, and when an attempt to achieve this was soundly beaten in the Commons in the spring of 1889, it turned to nourishing the emerging 'equal rights' alliance of Protestants.

While the paper's handling of the issue would come to be seen as brutally destructive, the actual day-to-day tone of comment conformed to Farrer's understated, reasoned style. It was Goldwin Smith, not Farrer, who wrote many of the extreme sentences that would be quoted later as evidence of the paper's fanaticism. Smith's contributions on this, and on the commercial union issue, have, fortunately, been identified from his files by historian Elisabeth Wallace,[43] and they show a clear difference in tone from the *Mail*'s day-to-day editorials. On a point of morality, the difference may be academic since Farrer as editor presumably had responsibility for the editorial page. On the question of damage, too, Farrer may carry an even greater weight of responsibility. But as a consideration of craft, at least, it is worth distinguishing between Smith's bludgeon and Farrer's rapier.

It was, for instance, Smith, not Farrer, who wrote that the Jesuit order 'stands arraigned in history as the head of that vast and cruel conspiracy against liberty, progress, science, and humanity of which the heart was Rome and the limbs were the Roman Catholic powers.' It was Smith, not Farrer, who portrayed Jesuitism as a miasma of darkness and evil, calling up in the minds of Toronto burghers images far more dreadful than anything one could put in print. Jesuitism was a 'new and portentous birth of evil in the world.' The system of training prescribed by founder Ignatius Loyola was a 'sensuous presentation of the bodily facts and personalities of the Gospel history by the imagination of the neophyte, superexcited by solitary seclusion in a darkened room.' To Jesuitism in particular belonged such 'sensuous stimulants of devotion as the adoration of the Holy Heart.' Smith combined these vague images of sensuality with tales of torture from the Inquisition and blended the two with pious concern for the salvation of the Jesuits themselves.

Mail readers who had heard the stories of Farrer's alleged Jesuit training must have considered this kind of material had the stamp of inside information. In fact, Farrer probably deplored the deluge of adjectives, if not the substance, in some of Smith's pieces. That would have been the case when Smith wrote of Jesuit education as an instrument of intrigue, designed primarily to get the youth of the higher classes into their hands, and added: 'The Jesuit curriculum was made up of effeminate classicism, of florid composition, turgid rhetoric, and an empty show of science which, combined with the general mental training of the Jesuit system, produced a polished and self-complacent cretinism.'[44]

More typical *Mail* editorials avoided this kind of thundering and made the case in low-key language, offering reasoned argument that the church had indeed limited free discussion and that Canada was lagging well behind Europe in escaping ecclesiastical tyranny. Farrer's approach also identified the writer – and by extension the reader – with underdogs, not just with the persecuted English but with the afflicted and repressed victims within the Catholic church and the French-Canadian community. Again, it subtly addressed Canadians' sense of colonial inferiority, implying that Canada was less progressive than Europe or the United States because it still suffered under a dark age of ecclesiastical control. At the height of the hysteria, however, even Farrer's editorials seem to have become extreme in content, if not in language. One editorial very much in his style even likened the issue to the freeing of the slaves in the U.S. Civil War. It was, the editorial said, the first gun fired in Canada in the battle between the priesthood and the society of the New World:

Another irrepressible conflict is impending, though it is to be hoped that it will not come to the same mortal arbitrament as the first, but be decided peacefully with the ballot ... Religious equality, liberty of opinion, freedom of the State and the actions of the citizens from ecclesiastical control are organic principles of society in the New World. To these the Roman Catholic priesthood opposes the principles ... that there are no limits to the powers of the Church, even in matters temporal ... A collision between this social system and the social system of New England or British Canada is just as inevitable as was the collision between freedom and slavery if the Roman Catholic Church possesses power enough to enter on the conflict ...[45]

Against this background, it is not surprising that some perceptive observers made good guesses at the nature of the game. 'The men to be dreaded at this time are the fanatical Protestants who talk nonsense and propose impossibilities,' wrote Principal George M. Grant of Queen's University. 'Such men, I sometimes think, are Jesuits in disguise. Certainly they play well the game of the order.'[46] But for a time, at least, the thundering was surprisingly successful. Both the

Conservative and Reform parties looked on with dismay in early 1889 at the fervour of independent journals, or the wavering of their own organs. The Ottawa *Evening Journal,* then a small independent, expressed the extreme limit of adulation, reporting that the *Mail*'s 'honest, noble and gallant' stand on behalf of Protestantism and civil liberty had enabled it to cut into the circulation of Toronto's party dailies. 'The *Mail* did risk a great deal by coming out frankly as it has done against priestly aggression. Now that it has started the fight and lost nothing by it, people perhaps underestimate the gigantic danger of the task it took up.'[47]

Many other small newspapers echoed that tone, and some of the larger organs came under pressure, as rallies proliferated and letters to the editor came in a flood. In February 1889 *Grip* formally joined the movement. The following month the *Globe* made an astonishing turnaround and came out for disallowance, adding to its reputation for vacillating. Clearly, the *Globe*'s directors were under pressure, watching their circulation decline and perhaps coming to share the anti-Catholic mood of Toronto. In January E.W. Thomson, *Globe* editorialist, had warned Laurier that the issue promised trouble. 'If McCarthy pursues his proposed programme this session,' he wrote, 'it will be no easy task for me to keep the *Globe* out of a new collision with the party.'[48] When the 'curve' was finally taken in March, the paper lost old friends while earning sneers from its new allies. *Grip* cartooned John Cameron, the *Globe* manager, as a contorted acrobat somersaulting from Mercier's arms into Farrer's.[49] When a Liberal complained of the paper's stand to Willison, who was then the *Globe*'s Ottawa correspondent, he replied wryly that the critic must be hard to satisfy since the paper had taken every possible position on the issue. At a Liberal party rally, a mention of the *Globe* was jeered and hissed.[50]

Grip's conversion, though not as abrupt as the *Globe*'s, was in some ways more striking, since the magazine probably felt less pressure on its circulation than did the *Globe*. Two years earlier *Grip* had been warning the *Mail* not to aggravate religious problems. Now it proclaimed wholehearted conversion, portraying its distinctive symbol, the *Grip* raven, as a latter-day Martin Luther, nailing on the church door a proclamation calling for, among other things, abolition of separate schools and disallowance of the Jesuits' Estates Act.[51] It also published a cartoon of Bunting garbed as a crusader (the Mail-ed warrior) magnanimously grasping the hand of 'Mother Church' and

THE MAIL-ED WARRIOR. *Grip*, 23 March 1889. The height of Ontario's hysteria – and of journalistic sanctimony – was reached when *Grip*, which earlier had warned the *Mail* against stirring racial and religious strife, joined the campaign against clerical influence. *Grip* proclaimed itself to be perfectly aligned with the *Mail*: it had no quarrel with the church itself but only with the Jesuits and with church interference in secular matters. But later it linked the campaign to achievement of 'the dream of a powerful nation on the British plan.'

assuring that the *Mail*'s quarrel was not with her, but with the mischievous Jesuit 'son' skulking behind her skirts. *Grip* said it wanted to stress this point because its own position was precisely that of the *Mail*. 'There is no attack being made on the Catholic Church or on any of her doctrines or practices as a religious institution ... The fight is against the *political* doctrines and ambitions of a single one of these Orders – the Society of Jesus.'[52] *Grip* also printed this effusive poem from an unidentified admirer of the *Mail*:

My Newspaper

What teaches me which way to go?
What toadies neither friend nor foe?
What would lay Jesuitism low?
   My *Mail*.

What, like the earth, turns round and round
So that each day some change is found,
And none can tell which way 'tis bound?
   My *Globe*.

What proves black white with wondrous skill?
What uses phrases fit to kill
And swallows many a bitter pill?
   My *Empire*.[53]

In the build-up to the 28 March parliamentary vote on disallowance it was clear that the *Mail* had also been dismayingly successful in generating excitement in Toronto. At a huge protest rally on 25 March at the Pavilion, a succession of Protestant clergymen praised 'equal rights,' prayed for suppression of an 'alien organization' that had been allowed to put its hands in the public money chest, and paid tribute to the *Mail*. A prominent Presbyterian, Rev. D.J. Macdonnell, declared (to loud applause and cheers, according to the *Mail*) that the newspaper deserved the thanks of every true Canadian for stepping into the breach at a time when it was dangerous to do so. The clergyman, however, went on to indicate a certain nervousness over the paper's motivation. 'I used to think *The Mail* had some tendency towards annexation,' he said, in what might have seemed a non-sequitur to some in his audience. '*The Mail* has, however, repudiated annexation, and I am glad of it. It has and does advocate a policy of Commercial Union with the United States, but I hope it will bye and bye come in line with us and assist in advocating Imperial federation ...'⁵⁴

Opponents, too, acknowledged the skill shown by the *Mail*. David Mills, a Liberal MP and editor of the London *Advertiser*, observed in the Commons that the agitation had been started by 'a journal conducted with more than ordinary ability,' which had 'gradually drawn to its side a large portion of the press of this country.'⁵⁵ Significantly, Wilfrid Laurier concluded his attack on disallowance by contending not with parliamentary opponents but with Farrer. Holding a copy of the *Mail* in his hand, he read a passage arguing that if the liberals of France or England were in the position of Laurier and his followers, they would not hesitate for a moment in 'killing this conspiracy in Quebec.' That might be true of French liberals, Laurier said, but not of those in England: 'They understood long ago that liberty is not only for the friends of liberty but for all.'⁵⁶

When the disallowance move was defeated in the Commons, the *Mail* praised the 'noble thirteen' who had voted for it (they were known elsewhere as the 'devil's dozen') and stepped up the effort to create a Protestant party. The two old parties had sacrificed the public interest, it said. If the people wanted to recover what had been lost, they would have to declare their independence of those parties and fill Parliament with men who were neither invertebrate nor corrupt. And again it raised the threat of breaking up the country: 'Ontario is prepared, before acknowledging herself beaten, which would be tantamount to confessing that she had ceased to be free, to insist on a revision of the constitution, even though the demand should put an end to Confederation.'⁵⁷

Thereafter, the paper gradually moved its focus from church to race. As McCarthy gained notoriety as a dissident Conservative championing the cause of British Protestantism, the *Mail* became more interested in encouraging a third party that would break up Confederation if necessary to ensure 'British' dominance. It was clear, the paper said, 'that in the course of time one of the two nationalities must strike its flag to the other and be content to surrender its language and institutions.'⁵⁸ Ontario, it said in another column, was waiting for the leadership of McCarthy and others like him to build a unified 'British column' that would shake free of the weak and corrupt old parties and beat back the encroachments of the ultramontanes.[59] Gradually, though, the paper dropped its specific demands for constitutional reform, suggesting this was not a realistic hope. Instead, it urged voters to place their trust in the emerging third party, even though its mission was not yet clear. This at any rate would be a step in the right direction, it said, and 'the logic of events must determine the next move.'[60]

As the summer of 1889 wore on and the Equal Rights Association began a short and inglorious career, Ontario journalists were reluctant to challenge it. Thomson of the *Globe* wrote to Laurier pleading that the paper not be required to print a major speech by Mills attacking the movement.[61] Incredibly, even the *Empire* had nervous yearnings about taking up the Protestant cause, as the paper's circulation and income languished. In a June letter to Macdonald, manager David Creighton raised the possibility hesitantly. Some party friends, he wrote, thought McCarthy ought to be urged to come into provincial politics. 'I have no doubt it would help us at the present juncture, but it would practically mean burning our boats behind us, and taking squarely to the Protestant programme.' That would mean a difficult role for the *Empire*, 'but while standing firmly by what was right I would endeavour to restrain anything like pitching into Roman Catholics or saying anything that might wound their feelings ...'[62]

Creighton presumably was squelched quickly, though by now Macdonald would have had no doubts about the mood of opinion in Ontario. Late in the summer a Port Hope Tory had even written to caution him 'as a true friend' to put off a planned visit to the town because feeling on the religious issue was running so high, even among the prime minister's old adherents. 'They have rented the upper flat of a building near the Post Office and removed several partitions to enlarge it for an Equal Rights committee room and they are pretty warm just now and I do not think your visit would allay it.'[63] By fall, *Saturday Night* was urging the Conservatives to adopt the equal rights platform, while *Grip* was pressing it on the Liberals. Bengough cartooned Farrer as a leprechaun urging Laurier, on horseback, to jump the hurdle of clerical privilege – and again as a groom urging Meredith, the provincial Tory leader, to mount the equal rights horse.[64]

Ironically, the first fruits of equal rights came not in Ontario but in the West. McCarthy, backed and cheered by the *Mail*, early in 1890 brought forward legislation to abolish the use of French in the courts and legislature of the Northwest Territories. And in the same year the Liberal Manitoba government, undoubtedly encouraged by

WILL HE GET OVER IT? *Grip*, 12 October 1889. As a young Rouge, Wilfrid Laurier had been a strong opponent of clerical interference in secular affairs; as party leader, he naturally found Farrer's program daunting.

A TICKLISH MOUNT. Ned Farrer (the groom) – 'Well, sir, why don't you get into the saddle?' Meredith – 'Er – are you quite sure he won't break my political neck?' *Grip*, 4 January 1890. The *Mail* was ready to enlist allies anywhere for the Protestant 'equal rights' movement, and for a time seemed close to getting the Ontario Conservative leader, W.R. Meredith, to climb on.

the Ontario agitation, introduced legislation cutting off support for separate schools. Both issues were to fester for years, and Farrer bears some responsibility for creating them,[65] both by the way he made race and creed paranoia respectable, and by the way he boomed McCarthy as 'the head of a new party whose formal appearance on the floor of the House as a separate and distinct entity is only a question of time.'[66]

Two days after that latter statement was written, however, an event occurred that would have major repercussions for Farrer, the *Mail*, and the equal rights movement. The first shots were fired, not in a battle for Protestant supremacy, but in the effort to prove that the *Mail* was a secret traitor, exploiting race and religion to break up the country and bring on annexation. Predictably, the paper tried to shield itself by waving the flag of McCarthy and equal rights. The fabricated charges of the party papers, it said, were the best possible proof of the fear and rage they directed towards anything that smacked of political independence. 'In like manner Mr McCarthy, having boldly adopted a patriotic and independent stand in the matter of North-West dualism [bilingualism], is evidently about to be assailed by both sides ... Like *The Mail*, however, he can not be intimidated, and will doubtless make a brave fight for the rights of the English population in the North-West.'[67]

This time, however, Farrer would not be able to hide in the race and creed smokescreen. It would soon be clear that he had been working for months, perhaps years, for political union. And the final irony of his exploitation of race and religion was that he himself summed up as well as anyone the damage done. In a much later piece of writing, left in his files at his death, partly in proof form and partly in his distinctive handwriting, he praised Quebec's record on religious toleration – and specifically *deplored* the waves of fanaticism that periodically swept through Ontario:

Whatever may be the cause, Ontario is behind the age in the matter of religious toleration, which, as Edmund Burke said, is almost as priceless a possession as religion itself. From time to time the province is swept by waves of fanaticism which keep the whole country in an uproar. There are no wars so sanguinary as holy wars; no persecutions so relentless as religious persecutions; no hatred so intense as theological hatred; and, one may add, nothing so dangerous to the peace and well-being of a composite country like Canada

128 Secret Craft

as these frenzied outbursts which occur from time to time in Toronto and spread like wildfire through Ontario at large.[68]

The actual evidence of the *Mail* campaign, of course, makes it almost incredible that these lines could have come from Farrer's pen. The handwriting, however, is his – and in fact the statement is entirely consistent with his views, *except* those of his last *Mail* editorship.[69] While some later historians would see the paper's course as erratic or even irrational, with no hard connection between its continentalism and its race/religion passions, it is clear that for Farrer, at least, the two were facets of the same campaign.[70]

7 Master Craftsman

If Ned Farrer had confined himself and the *Mail* solely to the issues of continentalism or race/religion, he would deserve to be remembered mainly as a crank. In fact, he and his editorial page ranged widely, opening up rich veins of social and political thought and presenting the results in reflective, often ironic, and often amusing style. At a time when Toronto was going through painful adolescence, marked by the immense distance between the immigrant labourers of Cabbagetown and the elite of Rosedale, by the raw scars of railways or factories, by muddy streets littered with manure and lined with taverns, by prostitution and violence and unaided destitution, by rigid forms of race and class and religion, Farrer steadily moved the *Mail*'s centre of political gravity to the left. While not as radical as Ned Sheppard's *News* (also owned by the Riordan family) or as vociferous in support of the 'people' as the *World* or *Telegram*, the *Mail* was quietly reformist: it seemed to assume that its enlightened readers were willing to deal with pressing evils of the city and the nation.

Over the five years of Farrer's last editorship the paper gradually became more radical on labour rights and a variety of other social issues, discarding traditional constituents as it gained new ones. By 1889 Farrer even felt free to abuse manufacturers, once the paper's core supporters. Now he showed them as crowding around the National Policy trough, demanding the right to combine while denying that same right to labour.[1] He pressed as well for federal legislation on factory inspection (partly on the grounds that it would be unfair for Ontario to ban factory employment of children under fourteen while Quebec continued to permit it) and saluted the unions' constructive work in this area.[2] As in Winnipeg, he also felt free to chip away at imperialism or aristocracy, while supporting British liberal tradition.

Again, though, he pressed for reform in a calm, reasonable tone, designed to persuade rather than alienate, and it was this quality more than any other that drew the respect of colleagues, even of rivals. The tone was a distinct change, for Torontonians had become used to the strident voices of George Brown or John Ross Robertson. Farrer, as one rival put it, helped to bring in a style that was 'moderate but telling, restrained in expression but candid.'³ It was this quality that led G.R. Tennant to write in 1946 that the *Mail*'s post-independence work 'remains as some of the ablest journalistic writing that has been produced in Canadian history.'⁴ Even at the time, despite editorial anonymity, readers were well aware of Farrer's special imprint. A Farrer editorial, one journalist of the day observed, was to an ordinary editorial as a diamond to a pebble.⁵ Even writers who could not themselves escape Victorian prolixity were impressed by the simplicity and grace of his style. One such admirer, apparently quite unaware of the irony, wrote this effusive assessment in 1886:

It would not be a sketch of Mr Farrer which failed to make mention of his ability as a writer, and the individualities of his style. We may at once get at the main point of the matter by saying that he is, beyond question, the ablest writer connected with the political press of Canada ... Although his writing is by no means devoid of passion and fire, these are so admirably tempered, and held within check, that the skill of the man never loses its sway. As for his literary style, there is no exaggeration in saying that it is admirable ... The chief characteristics of Mr Farrer's sentences are their sheer directness, their absence of wordy adornment, the fitness and nicely judged aptness of the epithets used, and with all these qualities there is an exquisite lightness of touch, which brings the most overwhelming sentences to you upon tip-toe ...⁶

Farrer himself would have been amused by this baroque tribute, but the admirer did in fact show discernment when he stressed the simplicity and directness of his idol's style, combined with compelling rhythm and imagery. He might also have fastened on Farrer's skill as a polemicist – the arguments so carefully understated that readers hardly realized how radical his viewpoints sometimes were.

An 1888 *Mail* editorial on jail reform, for instance, started out with soothing words that gave no hint of the punch lurking deeper in the article. It said the provincial secretary had reacted to the *Mail*'s campaign for reform by speaking of a feeling in society that criminals should be 'coddled and nursed.' But surely, the editorial went on, that could not be said of a desire for the removal of abuses against which even jailers themselves had protested: 'Those of us who consider it a crying shame that lunatics, whose loss of reason is their only offence, should be consigned to prison with malefactors, that boys accused or convicted of comparatively trivial offences should be associated for months with hardened criminals, and that young girls should be forced to consort with the most abandoned of their sex, can scarcely be accused of wishing to have the inmates of the gaols "coddled and nursed." Humanity cries out against evils such as those ...'[7]

As he had done in Winnipeg, Farrer also continued to show sympathy for religious minorities – aside from the Catholics. One editorial, almost certainly his work, even defended settlement in the West of the Mormons, who at the time were considered to be not just crackpots, like the Salvation Army, but profoundly evil. The editorial went into the history and theology of the church in sympathetic detail and concluded:

Their polygamy aside, the Mormons appear to be a tolerant, thrifty and industrious people. They have certainly brought prosperity to Utah, and will no doubt make good settlers in the North-West. In the United States the anti-polygamy law was passed despite the protests of those who held that, under the spirit of the constitution, every form of religious belief should be tolerated; but so far it has failed to accomplish its purpose. Those who favour the passage of a similar measure by the Dominion Parliament ought to bear in mind that with these people polygamy is an affair of the conscience; and that, in the abstract, we have no more right to compel them to give it up than a Mohammedan Government would have to forbid celibacy and monogamy in Christian residents or missionaries. A French Canadian journal says 'force should be used if necessary to uproot this vile weed from Canadian soil' and to 'bring the Mormons into an orthodox way of living.' But the employment of force in such matters is always attended with danger. He who is absolutely convinced that the only way of serving God and winning Heaven is his own way is probably warranted, *ex hypothesi*, in invoking force against those who are pursuing a different and therefore a wrong way. Yet we know that this doctrine has led to indescribable evils, and is at variance with the modern spirit of toleration ...[8]

On other bitter theological issues of the day, like Darwinism, Farrer took remarkably advanced ground, but did so in a carefully conciliatory way. Abandoning literal belief in some parts of the Scriptures, he wrote, would surely not be fatal to the prime dogmas:

John Wesley, who believed in witches, declared that if witches were given up, the Bible, which treats them as existent and provides for their punishment by death, would be destroyed. We know that a somewhat similar view was held by all Christendom concerning the probable effect of the great discoveries of Galileo and Copernicus, which decentralized the earth and reduced it to the proportions of a speck of dust in infinite space. Yet the Bible and Christianity with it have survived these shocks, and we are sure that, if it were admitted to-morrow that the Book is not a manual of science nor even a strictly accurate account of all God's workings from the beginning of time, no harm would be done to the religion of God or to the cause of God, which is truth and morality. Theology might suffer, but theology is not the vine of God's planting so much as a trellis made by weak human hands.[9]

On matters of aristocratic pretension the *Mail* was more outspoken – as, for instance, on an occasion when it deplored the attempts to fasten on Canada the court etiquette and court practices of the Old World. Discussing a fuss over precedence at a vice-regal ball at Ottawa, Farrer (or perhaps Goldwin Smith) wrote that Canada had no genuine aristocracy beyond that of muscle and brains:

The social idea as understood at the capital is of course an importation from England. It is a weak imitation of that relic of mediaeval times, the system which frequently retains poverty of intellect in the front circles while it condemns commercial men, who have been the foundation of the nation's glory, to rank with peanut-vendors and organ-grinders. The presence of this excrescence in Canada is not gratefully recognized. We live under a monarchical form of government; but at heart the people are democratic. They dislike caste; they abhor titular distinctions; they object to the introduction of class discriminations, patterned after the English plan. Were the populace permitted to peep behind the scenes to witness, for example, a vice-regal reception, at which the manners and customs of the Court of St. James [*sic*] are reproduced on gingerbread scale, a feeling of indignation, coupled with pity, would no doubt be awakened ...[10]

Imperialism also came in for occasional jabs, although the language, for Canada's most imperialist audience, was muted. On one occasion in 1885, for instance, the *Mail* deplored demands from Anglo-Indians for a 'vigorous' foreign policy. All the English in India – the civil servants, the military, even the merchants – profited by war, it said. 'Therefore an English minister must be on his guard against their solicitations to slaughter.'[11]

Farrer also wrote movingly of the native problem, although he accepted, with seeming harshness, conventional wisdom that predicted the inevitable extinction of the race. In January 1886 the *Mail* dispatched George Ham to explore Indian problems on the plains, and in his editorial columns Farrer argued that the tribes were being driven to violent reaction:

Darwinian

From first to last the struggle for the survival of the fittest which took place in Old Canada between the savage and the white pioneer was atrociously cruel, though probably not more so than the conflict now going on in Africa, where, next to Stanley's explosive bullets, the rum keg is the most potent agency of civilization ... The preaching of the Gospel has undoubtedly helped to prepare [the Indian] for his exit, but it is no reflection upon the intrepid missionaries who have devoted their lives to him to say that the work of evangelization has been terribly handicapped by the presence of those unpleasant specimens of Christianity who, in all new countries, constitute the advance guard of civilization. The missionary asks the savage to look to Christ, and the savage retorts by asking if the whites around him, who are engaged in debauching his family, are the products of the new cult that is to comfort him whilst meeting his doom ...[12]

A few weeks later, commenting on one of Ham's dispatches, Farrer was even more outspoken:

The crimes perpetrated upon the savages of this continent, and perpetrated, too, in the name of Christianity and light, cry to heaven. We shot the Indian in Newfoundland like a seal, for the sake of the fur he wore. In Florida we hunted him to death with imported blood-hounds. In New France and New England we dosed him with drugged rum and brandy that we might rob him of his peltries and of his women. And now in the North-West the remnant of this people is dying a miserable death from whiskey and disease brought in by those who, with ghastly irony, are called the pioneers of civilization, but who to the Indian are known as the heralds of his physical and moral ruin.[13]

The same blend of sympathy and harsh Darwinism comes through in a *Mail* editorial written in January 1886 on a famine in Connaught, the western Ireland province that includes Mayo:

Beyond doubt a heavy responsibility attaches to the landlord class. In times past men like Lord Lucan and Lord Sligo, acting on the principle that it was easier to feed cattle than to collect small rents, evicted their tenants by wholesale, and converted the holdings into pasture land, the animals being shipped to the English market and the proceeds spent in maintaining the absentee proprietor. In this part of Ireland the landlord is seldom one of the people. The old Irish families of Connaught – the Martins, Lynches, O'Flahertys and Blakes – were broken up years ago by the unromantic agency of the sheriff's office in consequence of their own desperate recklessness; and when their mortgaged estates were flung on the market retired manufacturers from Ulster and Scotland stepped in and bought them up, hoping to found a new order of landed gentry in that wild region. The result has been constant warfare between landlords and tenants, the alien proprietor bending all his energies to get rid of the troublesome aborigine, who looks upon him as a shoneen or upstart thrust by the accident of wealth into a position he was not made to adorn ...

In the heart of these mountains and moors, the police barrack, with its angular, stern walls, is a ghastly object. The police are there to protect the landlord. From the peasant's point of view the Government is thus constantly engaged in depriving him of his rights. Hunger is an evil counsellor, and when the potato fails or the yield of kelp or fish is diminished, the eternal enmity between the peasant and the landowner finds expression through the mouth of the blunderbuss ...[14]

Alongside his general flow of serious work, Farrer regularly offered a leavening of satire, always written in a form that started in serious, deadpan language and eased without warning over the line to whimsy or exaggeration. Usually gentle in tone, it sometimes built to formidable impact. Shortly after his arrival from Winnipeg, for instance, Farrer savaged Manitoba legislators in a piece that grew out of a controversial prison flogging that had caused disturbances in Winnipeg:

McCormick, the prisoner who was flogged for attempting to escape from the Winnipeg gaol, has been interviewed. He declares that he 'did not feel the flogging,' owing, no doubt, to that peculiar dryness of the atmosphere which prevents the Manitoban from feeling cold while the mercury is lost in the abysses of the thermometer.

All the same, Attorney-General Miller had better not order that sort of punishment again. The cat may be used upon the bare backs of criminals guilty of assaults on women, greatly to the good of society. But to strip a lad in the open air, to tie him up to a triangle during a Manitoba snow storm, and to administer twelve lashes, all for taking advantage of a turnkey's carelessness and trying to escape, was an abuse of authority that is utterly indefensible. If McCormick had lost somebody else's money in a land boom, or got ahead of creditors in Toronto or Montreal, or carried off a portion of the sinking account of Winnipeg, or made an inroad upon trust funds, or sold bogus town sites, or swindled half-breeds out of their land scrip – if he had done any one of these things he would not have been flogged; if he had done them all, he would probably have been elected to the Provincial Legislature ...[15]

A lighter Farrer satire, this one aimed at Regina, was the subject of a complaint to the prime minister from Nicholas Flood Davin, in the letter wherein he warned that Farrer should not be allowed at the *Mail* to 'play the tricks' that had shown up in his work in Winnipeg.[16] The satire in question took issue with an Englishman from Yarmouth who had written to his home paper reporting that Regina was a fraud – that he had set out to a meeting at the town hall only to find that in fact there *was* no town hall, and that furthermore this sort of exaggeration prevailed in every town in the Northwest:

This Englishman has evidently failed to grasp the first principles of North-West economy. The town hall in Regina is not always the town hall. It was originally the modest and circumspect storeroom of an implement agent, but since his sudden and lamented departure it has been in a measure compelled to lead a dissipated life. When a transient Methodist minister preaches in it it is Wesley Hall; when Bishop Anson holds services in it it is St. Alban's Cathedral; in winter it is the skating rink; when a permit reaches town it is the Wascana Assembly Rooms; on Mondays, Wednesdays, and Saturdays, and also on Fridays, Thursdays, and Tuesdays, it is devoted to sheriff's sales; yet through all these mutations it is also known as the Rolling Mills, a tinsmith of some distinction occupying one end of it. The indignant correspondent will at once perceive that this building has not time to attend regularly to the duties of a town hall; indeed, it is only known as such about once a

The *Mail* building, King and Bay streets

The *Globe* building, 1890

month, when the City Council meets to endorse Imperial federation or to pledge its credit in behalf of the Hudson's Bay railroad. The Yarmouth man evidently struck Regina when the versatile shed was engaged in some of its other occupations. His letter being thus founded on a misconception, he will no doubt apologize. If he refuses to do so after this explanation, we commend the foul slanderer to the indignant attention of an outraged populace, merely suggesting that if there is water enough in Pile of Bones Creek, a loyal coroner's jury should have no difficulty in reaching a verdict of 'found drowned.'[17]

While this sort of thing delighted Toronto readers, Nicholas Flood Davin, his old rival in Regina, was not amused. He insisted straight-faced to Macdonald that Farrer's description of Regina was inaccurate: in fact, Bishop Anson preached in a 'well-built and pretty' church, while the Methodists also had a nice church. 'Poor Regina is sufficiently handicapped without having the leading Conservative organ send broadcast misrepresentations regarding it.'

Another *Mail* spoof of the same period, again almost certainly Farrer's work, had more serious repercussions, leading to a libel award of $10,000 to former justice minister Rodolphe Laflamme. The column told of a Napanee incident in which local Grits had tried to block an election inquiry by reporting smallpox in the area. It went on:

Age cannot wither nor custom stale the infinite variety of Reform statesmanship. Year by year, nay, day by day, the grand old party is improving its electioneering devices with a fertility of resource that is truly amazing ... In [1878], it will be remembered, Mr Laflamme, the Minister of Justice, patented an invention which promised to meet to the fullest the demand for a safe and reliable method of electing the party's candidates. It was a cheap process, a false bottom to each ballot box being all the machinery required ... Mr Laflamme's boast that the party could by this means carry any given province, provided it had the making of the boxes, was undoubtedly well-founded. But it is a matter of history that his brilliant scheme was burked by an intoxicated Liberal at the Ste Anne's booth in Jacques Cartier, who at the very first trial of the apparatus stuffed over twice as many ballots into the box as there were electors in the whole of that division. It was a frightful instance of the injury done to public morality by the use of strong drink ...

When the libel suit resulting from this story came to trial at Montreal in January 1886, the *Mail* lawyers argued in vain that it was really just a humorous article, not meant to be taken seriously – and that, anyway, Mr Laflamme had clearly known of the ballot box fraud, even if he had not 'patented' the device. (In one instance, a lawyer pointed out, forty-eight electors had made statutory declarations saying they had voted Tory, while only fourteen Tory ballots emerged from the magic box.) The jury was not convinced, however, and found against the *Mail* people, who went away protesting that the paper's stand on Quebec had affected the decision.[18]

Another of Farrer's targets was a man who would later be his close ally, J.D. Edgar, later Sir James Edgar and speaker of the Commons, who was not only a leading Liberal but a well-known amateur poet. Farrer accused him facetiously (at the start of a controversy that would stretch on for several days) of writing some of the grosser Grit campaign songs, including the famous 'Ontario, Ontario!' an anti-French, anti-Catholic song that had severely embarrassed the Liberals in the 1882 election, and which included the lines: 'The traitor's hand is at thy throat, / Ontario, Ontario! / Then kill the tyrant with thy vote, / Ontario, Ontario!' Worse, Farrer accused Edgar of writing the following horror, concerning Sir John A. Macdonald's tendency to fawn on the 'hideous *Bleus*': 'You'd kiss their feet, you poor old sinner / And think it sweet, like the master's dogs did after dinner.' Edgar, unwisely, replied with a poem in the *Globe* clearly directed at Farrer:

SAD PLIGHT OF AN EDITOR
(By a Tory Journalist)

I am an able journalist,
I'm ready to discuss
Most any question one may name
Except the Halfbreed muss;
When that is on the carpet brought,
I'd rather be away, –
It kind o' sort o' doesn't seem
To glorify John A.!

Farrer replied with delicious irony, saying Conservative papers, in the interests of encouraging a Canadian poet, had given Mr Edgar's poems handsome treatment, perhaps jeopardizing their own reputation for literary taste in so doing:

We warn him, however, that when he seeks to attribute the authorship of any of his works to 'Tory journalists' he commits an outrage upon the latter to which they will not meekly submit. They may overlook his ingratitude, but they will never father his poetry. He may as well learn now that he has chosen a peculiarly unfortunate time for his outrageous act. A poetess has recently come into notice in the United States whose work is superior to his, and a very little 'booming' of her effusions by Conservative papers will effectually extinguish his rushlight. The lady, whose name is Mrs Sarah A. Ulrich Kelly, calls herself 'The Bard of Shanty Hill,' and she has applied to Congress to be appointed the National Bard of the United States. Her poetry is not quite so original as Mr Edgar's, but its rhythmical grace is quite on a par with that of any of the lines he has ever worked up. Moreover, her verse is far less laboured than anything from his pen. Of her facility in this direction she has sweetly sung as follows: –

'I thank the Lord that I can write,
Without Sav'ral Days' seclusion quite;
Ten to Thirty minutes is all I ask,
To write from Three to Seven Verse Task

'A European poet in his time
Did suffer much composing rhyme;
So hard for him 'twas to compose,
For several Days with blinds aclose,
And then wrote but a line or two,
Ere to seclusion bade Adieu.'

And that, Farrer concluded, was certainly superior stuff to Edgar's poetry.

Next day, Edgar ventured a humorous prose reply, taking issue particularly with Farrer's attribution to him of 'Ontario, Ontario!' He was pained, he said, that the *Mail* so often robbed the modest authors of Canadian political ballads of their proper laurels by attributing this poem and others of the kind to his pen. Farrer in turn treated this letter as a literary development of first magnitude, as one that would leave readers 'consumedly thunderstruck.' He wondered if Edgar really meant it, or was only indulging in excessive modesty:

If Mr Edgar should persist in disowning the ballads of modern Canada, the literary world hereabouts will be indeed bereaved. All that is good, all that is

Master Craftsman 141

beautiful, all that is aesthetic and transcendent in the production of home talent, the united acclaim of his countrymen has ascribed to his graceful muse ... But there are one or two poems which Mr Edgar shall not repudiate. Canada will not permit him to cast adrift upon a cold world all the sweet and stirring lines that have hitherto been regarded by her as the progeny of his inspired swan. He may disown 'Ontay-ree-o.' He may give the go-by to 'By bad laws condemned to die,' and proclaim no connection with 'Rise against the Bleus.' Mr Edgar may go as far as this; he may even tear from our lacerated hearts the fond belief that he is the author of 'E. Blake is the Man for the People.' But he shall not rob us of the long-cherished conviction that he is the architect of the grand epic, beginning:

July the First in Oldbridge Town
There was a grievous battle,
And many a man lay on the ground,
And the cannons they did rattle;
A bullet from the Irish came
And grazed our monarch's arum,
The enemy swore that he was kilt,
But it didn't do him any ha-rum.

Mr Edgar knows he wrote this great historical masterpiece. Many unterrified braggarts, in Ireland as well as in Canada, have claimed it for their own; but we know and he knows that he threw it off in a moment of rapture whilst discharging the duties of fourth committeeman of L.O.L. [Loyal Orange Lodge] 24, Woodbridge; and that he sang it for the first time one night in 1863, when the lodge, exhausted by labour, was engaged in the cheerful process of refreshment. Let all true Canadians, therefore, cherish this bold and striking drama of July in memory of Mr Edgar, and resolutely refuse to permit him to disown it. It is the only thing we now have to remember him by, except the Public Accounts.[19]

That seemed to be enough for Edgar, and the controversy disappeared from the *Mail* and the *Globe*. But it was not quite over. John Bengough kept the issue alive in *Grip* with a cartoon that seemed to imply 'Ontay-ree-o' had actually been written by *Farrer*. It pictured a puzzled Farrer listening to Edgar's repudiation and commenting: 'Not his? Who the divil else's?'[20] The matter was thus left in doubt. Curiously, though, almost forty years later Hector Charlesworth claimed certain knowledge about the origin of the song. It had been written, he said, on a certain rainy afternoon, at a committee meeting of Toronto Liberals – by John Bengough.[21]

While humour of the kind shown by the Edgar episode was no more than a sidelight on the *Mail*'s rich editorial page, something of Farrer's delightful irreverence also infected the news pages and helped Toronto journalism escape a kind of George Brown lugubriousness that had afflicted the 'serious' political journals. Now, the *Mail* – while still treating serious matters seriously – started to react to bizarre happenings with a verve echoing New York's racier journalism.

There was, for instance, the 1889 incident of the clergyman and the marvellous 'scoopograph,' a story that kept Toronto entertained for weeks. The scoopograph was a mythical listening device which (the *Mail* claimed with mock seriousness) had enabled its reporters to crack a secret Methodist conclave as it considered charges against one of its preachers. The inquiry in question had extended over seven weeks – considering, among other things, the delicate question of whether Rev. Thomas W. Jeffery had used alcohol for spiritual solace, or only as liniment for his sore joints. The evidence was taken in closest secrecy while Toronto buzzed over the scandal. And it was naturally a sensation when, after Mr Jeffery had been cleared, the *Mail* began to run, in daily instalments, the full hearing transcript. Some thought the *Mail* reporters must have camped by a listening hole in an adjoining room. Others – in an age entranced by Edison's magic – thought the paper had used some new and mysterious electrical snooping device.

The *Mail* responded by drawing from the situation every possible ounce of fun and profit. It soberly reprinted various theories about its magical 'scoopograph' and mused about them, alternately encouraging the myth and knocking it down. The crowning touch came when the paper claimed to have solved the mystery. It printed ponderous statements from a doctor and a clergyman (Drs Galen and Wycliffe) who had attended the tragic deathbed of the *Mail*'s scoopograph operator and had heard his confessions:

Upon entering the room ['Dr Galen' wrote] on the bed I found one of the most unique cases it had ever been my fortune in a quarter of a century's practice to meet, a case of sinistral unilateral auricular hypertrophy, with a protrusion of a flat glassy surface, the diameter of about two inches, which I took to be the drum of the poor fellow's ear, extended over three inches from the side of his head, the lobes of the ear themselves being so large as to reach from the curve of the skull above to his shoulder below. The patient was evidently in a state of intense mental excitement, and was wild and starting every few moments, then he would assume a listening attitude and pass into a state of absolute quiescence, though every muscle in his body would be as rigid as to resemble catalepsy ...

The doctor immediately deduced the cause of the malady and confirmed it by putting the poor fellow in a trance, during which he revealed that the scoopograph had been operated through the telephone system. Before dying he had also stated his regret that he would not live to enjoy the quarter-box of Partaga cigars with which the *Mail* had rewarded his exploit.[22]

Twelve days after the original break – while the *Mail* was still running several pages of transcript each day – there was also a mock-serious summary of comment on the issue. 'The mystery regarding the "scoopograph" is as far from being solved as ever,' the paper said. 'Each day's report of the evidence increases the wonder and perplexity of all, and shows the importance of the discovery, which belongs exclusively to the *Mail*.' The Woodstock *Sentinel*, for instance, had pronounced the coup a great feat, but had worried about its implications: since there seemed to be no limit to the capabilities of the scoopograph, reporters using it could report even 'the most private transactions in the most private apartments.' The *Mail* also reported, however, on a meeting of the Canadian Shorthand Association where a more prosaic explanation of the scoopograph was advanced, one member claiming he had seen two perpetrators of the scam in the vicinity of the hearing room.[23]

Whether Ned Farrer had a direct role in the work of the scoopograph is not certain, but his tendency to 'see humour in anything and everything' certainly had an effect on the paper. And his special touch seemed to show at least in the heading of the first exposé. It declared the material to have been 'reported for The Mail exclusively by our own apparitions,' and followed that credit with a Biblical reminder: 'Therefore whatsoever ye have spoken in darkness shall be heard in the light, and that which ye have spoken in the ear in closets shall be proclaimed upon the house tops.'[24]

Farrer might well have taken that warning to heart himself as he worked secretly in the late 1880s to bring about the union of Canada and the United States. Not everything that he 'spoke in darkness' would reach the light, but in time a great deal of it would be proclaimed from the housetops.

8 The *Globe*, the *Mail*, and the *Empire*

While the *Mail* during 1887 confirmed its independence and developed its dream of commercial union, Sir John A. Macdonald was again turning over plans to set up another newspaper. In so doing, he was setting the stage for the climactic episodes both of Ned Farrer's career and of the annexation affair. He was also, perhaps, marking the end of an era, in launching the last significant attempt by a Canadian government to set up a fully controlled newspaper organ. For Macdonald, however, the effort probably seemed to be no more than a tedious repeat of the *Mail*'s conception and birth fifteen years earlier. Again, there was the difficulty of finding reliable backers. Again – more acutely now – there was the problem of shaping something that would be both a commercial and a political success. Again, there was the dilemma of whether it was wiser to start something new or to manipulate existing papers.

In early stages of discussion Macdonald was keen on the idea of a new paper (it was known tentatively as the *Standard*, later as the *Empire*) but determined to keep it firmly under party control. 'We must not make the mistake we did in regard to "The Mail,"' he wrote to one ally. 'There we began with a large project and insufficient Means, and the paper in consequence was Eventually removed from our control ...'[1]

At that point D'Alton McCarthy, still Macdonald's chief man in Toronto, though becoming increasingly independent, looked more favourably on the idea of buying an interest in the *Mail* and bringing it back into line. That, of course, would have meant enduring a certain amount of public ridicule. There were limits to a paper's ability to bend its spinal column. But the only practical alternative seemed to be Billy Maclean's *World*. Macdonald had been advised that Maclean's loyalty could be bought for as little as $10,000,² but for a number of other reasons, bearing on the quality of both Maclean and his paper, the option was unattractive. So in February 1887 McCarthy found it reasonable to suggest another assault on the *Mail* – or at least a reconnoitre. From a purely business standpoint, he told Macdonald, he was very doubtful about the success of a new paper. '... I think the *Mail* can be got – that Bunting is much alarmed. Perhaps we might [buy?] a controlling interest in the Mail and get rid of Bunting and Farrer?' A week later McCarthy reported that he had been in to see Charles Riordan and had asked bluntly whether the *Mail* was for sale. Riordan had replied that he 'thought he might say it was not.' He had also gone on to say, gratuitously, that he doubted the *Mail* would be much hurt if the party started up a new organ; so, McCarthy concluded, there was 'nothing for it' but to go on with the new paper.

During the summer and fall the need for a new organ became more pressing as other newspapers followed the *Mail*'s lead in taking up commercial union. The problem, as Macdonald well knew, was not just Toronto, pivotal though the city might be. It was rather that the *Globe* and the *Mail* were the two influential morning papers that were spread by train into the hinterland – to Kingston and Barrie and St Catharines and scores of other towns, where editors read them carefully before setting up their own pages. Even outside Ontario their influence was felt. Aside from the major Toronto papers, there was no reliable channel to the politically committed of the country.

Despite the clear need for a new organ, party response to the fund-raising effort was not strong, and as late as September Macdonald was pondering another effort to bring the *Mail* to heel. McCarthy, however, was by now not interested. In September he wrote: 'There is no use in my seeing Bunting ... for unless Riordan is propitiated no arrangement can be made – even if any that could be made with the *Mail* was desirable – which I more than doubt. No, we must start the Empire or prepare for defeat at the next general election if not before that.'³

McCarthy was unhappy about delays in organizing the paper, but Macdonald's efforts to raise money for it were at least sporadically forceful, passing the level of arm-twisting and coming close to blackmail. 'I want you to take ever so much stock in the Empire Newspaper,' he wrote in October to Sir Alexander Campbell, his one-time law partner and cabinet colleague who was now lieutenant-governor of Ontario. 'The future existence of the party depends on our having an exponent of our policy. – You have now arrived at the Summit of political position thro' the party and must now come to the rescue.'[4]

Macdonald reported that the paper would be under the prudent direction of David Creighton, a Scotsman who had run a Conservative paper at Owen Sound and had been a minor figure in the Ontario legislature. Other party people, however, did not share the prime minister's confidence in Creighton. During the *Empire*'s life of less than eight years he was subjected to more or less constant criticism from party leaders, from his staff, and from the party at large, and he was frequently reduced to pleading for more government ads, or for better treatment from the CPR and other corporations allied with the government.

Creighton and his first city editor, Louis P. (Pica) Kribs, were to become over the next four years Farrer's bitterest enemies, in public at least, and it is ironic that both, like Farrer, would be described by contemporaries as kindly and amiable men, suffering under the party yoke. Hector Charlesworth, who worked briefly on the *Empire*, gave a graphic picture of life on a confirmed party organ, saying no one on the paper, not even Creighton, felt safe from incurring the dislike of some politician with a personal axe to grind. 'There was a tendency among the younger men on staff to regard David Creighton as weak, but in the light of experience I now see how helpless he was ... Mr Creighton was a most kindly and lovable man who wanted to do right by everybody, and I wonder that the politicians did not hound him into his grave ...'[5] Creighton himself would later write, plaintively and with no sign that he saw the irony, that the *Empire* had 'never hesitated to sacrifice itself from a newspaper point of view for the benefit of the party.'[6] The line might have served as an epitaph for the paper, or even for the era: the tough Toronto market would not put up much longer with a committed party organ.

The heat of competition, in fact, probably had much to do with lapses of taste and perspective during the period when Farrer emerged as a point of controversy. The *Mail*'s popularity in the Jesuits' Estates issue of 1889 had put both the *Globe* and the year-old *Empire* into serious straits. As the 1890s opened, and Farrer's career moved from the relative seclusion of the editorial room to become public property, the in-fighting sometimes reached bizarre levels. It was typical of the period that the *Globe* was accusing Farrer of plotting at Washington as an agent *for* Macdonald at the same time the *Empire* was accusing him of plotting *against* the prime minister – not to mention the rest of the country. It was typical that the *Globe* accused Farrer of traitorous conduct just months before hiring him. It was typical that the bitterness would spill over into court, and that both the *Mail* and the *Empire* would fly into a frenzy when Farrer, at the *Globe*, scored a major personal beat on the big murder story of the day. Other journals on the sidelines found the struggle funny or deplorable or outrageous, depending on the stage of the action or their own moods or biases.

Ironically, the *Empire*, which worked ferociously to destroy Farrer, was scooped on the first firm evidence of his annexation plotting, though it made up for its lateness by enthusiasm. It was the *Globe* that, on 7 January 1890, gave major front-page attention to a Washington dispatch saying Farrer was campaigning in Washington to get the Americans to force annexation on Canada by withholding reciprocity concessions. The story said Senator George Hoar's committee on relations with Canada was relying heavily on information given to it by Farrer, who had been on a 'prolonged' visit to Washington the previous spring, and had returned on a 'special mission' in December, when he had interviewed Blaine and spent a large part of his time with Hoar. As a result, the committee was ignoring Erastus Wiman's plea for commercial union and thinking only of annexation.

The dispatch was headed:

STARTLING
The Hoar Committee Loaded
Up the Other Way
THE MAIL'S EDITOR AT WORK
False Representations as to the
Feeling in Canada
ANNEXATIONISTS AGAINST RECIPROCITY
Secret Information Supplied to Senator Hoar – Ottawa Dictation Suspected – A Scheme to Force
Annexation

The story, based on a letter from an anonymous man who had attended the committee's New York hearings, said it was clear the committee was interested in promoting relations only on lines that would tend towards annexation:

> Throughout the examination of witnesses Mr Hoar's questions tended constantly towards the disclosure of his possession of secret information from Canada that the growth of the Annexation sentiment had increased so greatly that it was only a question of time when the 'ripe plum' would fall into the hands of the United States. It was in vain that Mr Erastus Wiman, in his three hours' examination, explained how impossible it was ... Throughout the entire sessions of the committee Mr Hoar, every now and again, called upon Mr Wight, the Secretary, for information which he said had been furnished by a Mr Farrer, the editor of The Toronto Mail, of which paper, by the way, Mr Wight turns out to be the Washington correspondent ... It was clear from the figures, which were frequently referred to and which had been collated by Mr Farrer, that the Committee were relying for information as to the state of feeling in Canada upon representations from The Mail office.7

Strangely, the Washington story then went on to a long interpretation of Farrer's efforts as a Tory ploy, designed to undermine the Liberal policy of unrestricted reciprocity. That line may well have been inspired by 'Ras Wiman. A few days earlier he had written to Laurier on the same matter, saying the reciprocity cause had suffered 'because the Hoar committee are pledged to annexation through the influences of Mr Farrer and Mr Bunting who, I fairly believe, are acting as "cat's paws" for Sir John.'8 In any event, the *Globe* blindly seized on the theory, to explain what it called 'one of the most astounding disclosures ever made in connection with Canadian politics.' Clearly, it said, the Liberals' enemies had devised the scheme to undermine, without publicly opposing it, a reciprocity bill by Congressman Butterworth. 'After this perhaps nobody in Canada will be gullible enough to give any credit to the *Mail*'s professions of independence.'9

The *Mail* next day jeered at the *Globe* 'revelation,' said Farrer had gone to the United States only for his health, both in the previous year and in the previous month, and ridiculed the notion that anyone on the *Mail* staff would be plotting annexation. The only fact that the *Globe* had got right was that Mr Wight was the *Mail*'s Washington correspondent – as he had been for years. 'Those capable of believing that a member of the *Mail* staff is secretly leagued with Sir John Macdonald in operating against the Canadian Liberals, in directing the trade policy of the Republican party at Washington, and in hastening the annexation of the Dominion are, we fancy, few in number and confined to the *Globe* office and the lunatic asylum.'[10]

In fact, the *Globe*'s wild surmise of a conspiracy with Sir John helped Farrer and the *Mail* elude the more pointed charge of promoting annexation. As was shown later by the 'two bites on the cherry' letter and the Hoar committee's report, Farrer was indeed pushing (for reasons still obscure) the line that annexationism was on the rise in Canada, and that a tough U.S. policy would encourage it. *Mail* editorials included in the Hoar committee's background papers were almost all of the kind that hinted at the breakup of Confederation or spoke of the kindred spirit between English Canada and New England.

Given this flow of material, and matter of the same kind that Farrer would later write for the New York *Sun*, it is not surprising that Washington politicians, and some business leaders like Dana or Carnegie, would develop unrealistic estimates of the prospects for annexation. Nor is it surprising that some American newspapers assumed the country was ripe for plucking – if only marginally worth eating. The contempt would show up in comments like that of the Buffalo *Courier*, that Canada was swiftly hastening to dissolution through a combination of moral and material leprosy. Or from the New York *World*, which thought Canada could easily be bought up with five or six million dollars 'judiciously expended.' Or from the Cleveland *Leader*, which assured its readers the Canadian Liberals were on 'a straight road to complete absorption [of Canada] in the great nation to the southward.'[11]

While Farrer's work encouraged those attitudes in the United States, they also brought dismay to Canadian friends of commercial union who had convinced themselves the policy would actually *strengthen* the country rather than make it vulnerable to absorption. *Grip*, for instance, reacted with consternation to the annexation charges against Farrer, declaring itself disappointed with the *Mail*'s defence. The explanation that Farrer had gone to the United States by his doctor's orders was so weak that it went a long way to prove the story well founded, it said. 'Is Mr Farrer too ill to hold conferences with Senator Hoar? Has he ever held any? Let the *Mail* answer these questions squarely.' *Grip* also mused about the connection between the charges and the *Mail*'s sudden abandonment of commercial union a year earlier, around the time of Farrer's first Washington visit. In view of the sinister new developments, those anxious to retain faith in the *Mail*'s

CONSPIRATORS AT WASHINGTON!!! Ed. of Mail to Uncle Sam – 'Don't make any offer of Reciprocity, and before long you will have Canada asking for Annexation!' *Grip*, 25 January 1890. By 1890 Bengough had become a warm admirer of Farrer and the *Mail*, but he was uneasy at reports that Farrer was engaged in an annexation plot. Normally he portrayed Farrer as an amused, rather harmless leprechaun, but he now became a more tense and ominous figure.

honesty were entitled to a reasonable explanation of the sudden switch. The following week *Grip* was still uneasy. It ran a cover cartoon of Farrer leaning over the shoulder of Uncle Sam, advising how to go about annexing Canada. And it commented stiffly that the *Mail*'s defence was 'not satisfactory to those who would fain continue to have faith in the honesty and independence of that journal, which is unquestionably the leading paper of the Dominion.'[12]

Saturday Night's writer, presumably Ned Sheppard, rejected as ludicrous the idea that the *Mail* was still working for Macdonald, but hinted at knowledge that Farrer was indeed an annexationist: 'The Globe's story is a tissue of absurdities, though no doubt built upon a sub-stratum of fact. Nothing is more likely than that Mr Edward Farrar, who is a gentleman of very pronounced opinion and marked individuality, while at Washington spoke very much in the strain attributed to him by the Globe.' But no one could be so stupid as to think that Macdonald had deliberately engineered the seeming antagonism of the *Mail*, or that Farrer in Washington had been part of a plot led by the prime minister. 'The Globe has always been virulent and unscrupulous in dealing with political opponents, but only of late years has it been weak and puerile.'[13]

Meanwhile the *Empire*, chagrined by the *Globe*'s scoop and enraged by the canard that Farrer was working for Macdonald, decided on the unusual move of sending its own man to Washington to follow Farrer's footsteps and discover his machinations. The man selected for the task, the kindly Louis Kribs, in fact discovered little that the *Globe* had not already reported, but it was enough to send the *Empire* into a frenzy. On 21 January a gloating Creighton wired Macdonald: 'In order to ascertain definitely what Farrer has done in Washington I sent Kribs down to investigate. He has returned and the Empire in the morning will make a sensation. We have the most conclusive evidence by interviews with Senator Dolph and others that Farrer was in secret communication with the Republican members of Hoar's committee and furnished them with information that they had but to hold off a little and they could coerce Canada into annexation as the feeling in favor of it is growing. This will be a startling dose for those who have stood by the Mail to swallow.'[14]

The *Empire* next day reflected Creighton's excitement, giving the story extraordinary play under no fewer than seven headline banks. The first four read:

THE PLOT EXPOSED

A Desperate and Unholy Annexation Alliance

THE 'MAIL' DEEP IN THE PLOT

A Commissioner of 'The Empire' Fully Investigates the Case.

After the hysterical headline the story went on to a pompous and detailed report of how the plotting was uncovered by the *Empire* 'commissioner,' concluding:

The 'Mail' is a Traitor

The result of *The Empire* commissioner's investigations establishes beyond the shadow of a doubt or the possibility of contradiction that the *Mail*, through its chief editor, not only secretly furnished the Senatorial Committee with information on Canadian affairs, and garbled information at that, but that Mr Farrer, the *Mail*'s editor, appeared before the Republican section of the committee at Washington, arranged for furnishing this information, and did it; assuring the committee that if reciprocity of all kinds were refused, Canada could be coerced into annexation in a very short time.

The story then told how Kribs followed the trail of the traitor through New York and Washington. The investigation in New York was difficult, it said, because it was hard to find people with 'positive' information — and those who did have information had pledged secrecy to the *Mail*. However, an unidentified New York reporter told of how the committee hearings had been 'loaded up' against Wiman's plea for commercial but not political union. This had been so apparent that Wiman had been asked afterward who had 'primed' the committee against him, and had named Farrer. Another unidentified 'gentleman' had confirmed the story that Hoar frequently referred to Farrer's material. 'When Mr Wiman would make a particularly strong point Senator Hoar would lean over to the secretary of the commission, Mr Wight (the Mail's Washington correspondent) and say, "Now, what does Farrer say about that?" or "Where is that evidence that

Farrer gave us on this point?" ... This occurred at least half a dozen times.'

From New York the *Empire* commissioner went on to Washington, 'headquarters of the conspiracy,' where he first interviewed Senator Hoar, who suspiciously refused to say anything, and Senator Joseph Dolph of Oregon, who was slightly more open, confirming that Farrer had indeed told the committee that if the United States did not accept reciprocity, Canada would before long be very willing to be annexed.

Kribs later came up with one more piece of firm information. After his Washington sleuthing, he went back to New York and spent two hours with Wiman – a man not normally considered by the *Empire* to be an impressive source. Mr Wiman 'knows all about the conspiracy,' the *Empire* reported, but his information was in the main confidential. However, he had gone on record at the end of the interview with one significant statement, saying he was satisfied that Farrer, representing the *Mail*, had furnished the committee secretly with 'a mass of information all tending to strengthen the annexation theory.'

The *Empire*'s editorial writers next day reached for their richest adjectives to attack the *Mail*, describing it as perfidious, traitorous, treacherous, and flagitious, then concluding it was no wonder the 'sneaking traitor' was being execrated and spurned from one end of the country to the other. It also sent reporters into the highways and byways to find any notable citizen who would say something critical of the *Mail*. Its lead story on the day after the exposé seemed calculated to persuade all right-thinking people to drop the rival:

THAT UNHOLY CONSPIRACY
THE 'MAIL' CONDEMNED ON
ALL HANDS [sic] ...

The exposure of the *Mail*'s annexation plot in yesterday's *Empire* struck like a thunderbolt from one end of Canada to the other. On the streets in Toronto, and on the streets in other cities it superseded all other topics of conversation. The consensus of feeling was one of astonishment that a Canadian journal should have descended to such dastardly plotting against its own country ...[15]

The *Empire* assault launched an episode that would rank as one of the most extreme outbursts of partisan journalism in Canadian history – an outburst that perhaps marked the last bright flareup before the era ended. The *Mail* in response naturally tried to cool out the issue. It specifically denied that Farrer had talked of annexation with the Washington figures. ('As a matter of fact that subject excites but a feeble interest in Washington.') It made capital of the fact that the *Globe*'s story had Farrer plotting *for* Sir John while the *Empire* painted him as operating against the government. And it suggested it was being attacked because the other papers found its independence intolerable. ('The *Mail* has the very best of reasons for knowing that it is crowding these party journals to the wall, that one or the other must shortly give up the fight ...') The *Empire* replied to this with almost a full front page of condemnation, under a curious headline proclaiming that the *Mail*, 'hunted to earth,' had admitted itself a traitor. The *Mail* in turn fought back by reprinting a Washington dispatch to the New York *World*, Farrer's old paper, featuring denials from all Republican senators on the committee that Farrer had held a private meeting with them. Senator Dolph, for instance, conceded he had met casually with Farrer but that his visitor had said nothing that would be seen as treasonable by even the most loyal of Queen Victoria's subjects. He also specifically disowned his *Empire* quotes, saying he had in fact never even met with an *Empire* reporter. Congressman Hitt had similar (perhaps somewhat more ambiguous) quotes:

'Mr Farrer,' said Mr Hitt, 'is an old friend of mine, and one of the ablest newspaper writers on the American continent. I saw a good deal of him when he was in Washington, and we talked about art and literature, politics and commerce, about international relations and perhaps the weather ... Mr Farrer is an enthusiast in all his work, and he is a vigorous opponent of the Tory government. He did tell me that if he were in my place he would not favor making any more overtures to the Tory government until they showed a better disposition to entertain our propositions. Mr Farrer is a Canadian to the backbone, and anyone who intimates that he was in Washington to say or do what a Canadian need be ashamed of either lies deliberately or speaks without knowing the man.'[16]

Grip was somewhat reassured by the Dolph denial, saying the *Mail* had at last taken hold of the charges in a businesslike manner.[17] The *Globe*, however, added another piece of incriminating evidence. It published a 'private letter from a very prominent congressman,' saying Farrer had indeed promoted annexation among a good many Washington people, especially Democrats, that Blaine had heard him at considerable length, and that Farrer had 'produced some impression on him, as to the advisability of our doing nothing on this side, as the annexation movement was going on in a very substantial way on the Canadian side.' The *Globe* quickly pulled back from the bizarre charge that Farrer was working for Sir John but continued to insist that he could only have been acting as a tool for his paper. (This, ironically, was the precise opposite to the case it would make a year later when the 'traitor' was in its own camp.)[18]

Meantime, a flood of newspaper condemnation poured in, largely from the Tory papers, on Farrer and the *Mail*. The Toronto *World*, for instance, charged that the *Mail* wanted to set itself up as a major newspaper in a united North America. (Curiously, it also tried to tie the *Globe* in with the plot.) Other newspapers focused on the *Mail*'s surprise abandonment of commercial union the year before. The Montreal *Witness* echoed common opinion when it said the *Mail* was quite at liberty to advocate annexation openly if it wanted to do so. 'But for Mr Farrer and the *Mail* who have with great ability advocated commercial union and unrestricted reciprocity as a great boon to both countries, secretly to advise a committee of a foreign nation to withhold reciprocity on the ground that such action would compel Canada to accept annexation, cannot but be regarded as a betrayal of his country.' The Lindsay *Post* pushed that thought one step farther, making a link between the *Mail*'s annexationism and its exploitation of the race/religion issue. It thought the intelligent reader would wonder, in view of the *Mail*'s sincerity on the commercial union issue, whether its race and religion campaign was aimed to bring about reform – or disintegration.[19]

While the *Mail*'s motives thus commanded most of the attention, the issue also prompted *Saturday Night* to offer an essay on the sins of party journalism, and on changes taking place in the press. The main thrust was an argument that the public was not taking the *Mail-Empire* affair very seriously, and that there was a profound and growing disbelief in the sincerity of newspapers, in contrast to the 'almost superstitious veneration' they had once commanded. But the column also perceptively defined a major trend in the press that was at this point just barely begun:

Formerly, the mainspring of daily journalism was partyism. Today it is business modified in most cases by party considerations. The increased amount of capital necessary to establish and conduct successfully a metropolitan daily newspaper brings the commercial element into increasing prominence. In old

The *Globe*, the *Mail*, and the *Empire* 157

THE QUEEN CITY JOURNALISTIC ORCHESTRA. *Grip*, 22 March 1890. On a local issue Bengough pictured the *Grip* raven orchestrating the leading Toronto media figures: Farrer, John Cameron (*Globe*), John Ross Robertson (*Telegram*), Ned Sheppard (*Saturday Night*), Billy Maclean (*World*), and Thomas A. Gregg (*News*).

times the leading dailies were started and controlled by some one prominent man of strong individuality and decided political views who made his newspaper a vehicle to advance party objects. But personal organship is rapidly becoming extinct. If the modern newspaper is partisan it is simply on commercial grounds, because there is more money in being so than in assuming an independent role. Where the two interests clash it is the political and not the commercial object that usually goes to the wall ...[20]

These commercial considerations may have been a factor when the *Mail* decided, unwisely, to take the brawl to court. On the evening of 24 January 1890 Creighton received a writ charging him with 'malicious and defamatory libels' against the *Mail* and Bunting, and on the following day Farrer brought charges against Creighton and Kribs. The *Mail*, with a hint of relief, observed that the issues were now *sub judice*, so that 'we are no longer in a position to discuss them.'[21] The *Empire* vowed that it would not be muzzled and launched yet another tirade against the traitors.

Privately, Creighton was again gloating as he wrote the prime minister on 26 January: 'I am still out of gaol, although summonses were issued in a second criminal case last evening, at the instance of Farrar, in which they have joined Kribs and me. The Mail crowd are hit hard. The whole press of the country is shouting "Traitor" at them, and unable to make reply they have in desperation taken this method to shut off further comment ... We are not going to be gagged by any threats, and before we are through with this business we are going to make it so hot for traitors and traitorous papers that there will be no room for them in Canada ...'[22]

The *Mail*'s first charges came up in court on Saturday, 25 January – before Colonel George Taylor Denison, the arch-imperialist, hater of annexationists, and the man whom Farrer, or Farrer's editorial columns, had personally ridiculed. While the *Mail* tried to play down the case, the *Empire* carried the testimony in astonishing detail, and with a tone so frankly partisan it would, in modern times, draw a contempt citation. The Monday paper, after Saturday's first hearing, carried what seemed to be every word of the appearance, under a six-bank headline:

INTIMIDATION

The 'Mail's' Latest

Plan of Defence

BEATEN BEFORE THE PUBLIC

It Appeals to the Courts
of Law

to silence the Empire

Its Counsel Threatens in Police Court –
But the Threat is Laughed at – The 'Empire'
Will Stand at the Post of Duty Against
All Traitors ...

The actual story was reasonably straightforward, reporting on Creighton's not guilty plea and on a discussion of when the case would proceed. But on Monday the second case, Farrer's charges against Creighton and Kribs, descended into Gilbert and Sullivan farce as Farrer's lawyer, A.H. Marsh, tried to establish the seemingly simple fact that the exposé actually had been written by Pica Kribs. Everyone in Toronto newspaper circles knew that Kribs was indeed the man, the famous 'commissioner,' yet Marsh called one *Empire* employee after another, from the chairman of the board to the proofreaders, without being able to pin this fact down. The witnesses, with only a little coaching from the magistrate, created bafflement: no, they couldn't swear Kribs had written such-and-such a story; no, they weren't able to identify his handwriting, although he had been city editor since the paper's founding in 1887; no, they couldn't swear Kribs had been in Washington.

The *Empire*'s coverage on 28 January filled no fewer than seven columns with this sort of fencing:

Mr W.R. Brock was then called by Mr Marsh and examined as follows:
I believe you are president of *The Empire* Printing Company? No, I am chairman of the board of directors ...
Do you remember the occasion within the last few weeks when Mr Kribs made a trip to Washington? I don't understand you.
The magistrate – Do you know that he went to Washington? I have heard since that he has been there.
Mr Marsh – Are you aware of that in connection with the business in the regular way? No.

Have you heard Mr Kribs admit being there? Well, I really don't think I have ...

Wm. J. McMicking deposed: I am engaged by The *Empire* Publishing Company.
What is your position? Proof-reader.
Have you, as proof-reader, read proof of these articles that have appeared in the four numbers of *The Empire* referred to in the information? (Copies produced.) I cannot swear to it.
They are not a very usual kind of articles are they? Could you have helped noticing them? I could not swear next day to an article I read the previous night.
Answer my question, sir. Do you mean to tell me, in the case of a startling article like that, that you cannot tell inside a week whether you proof-read it or not?
The Magistrate – You would be surprised, Mr Marsh, at the mechanical kind of way in which such a thing might be done ...[23]

There was much, much more of the same – so much, in fact, that a humourist at *Grip* developed an elaborate satire showing how the mysteriously unknown Kribs had received and carried out his assignment:

THE 'EMPIRE' AND THE 'PLOT'
(The actual facts just as they transpired – if the evidence given before the Police Magistrate is to be believed.)
SCENE I. – *Empire Sanctum*
Editor-in-Chief. – 'There's a good chance to get a drive at the *Mail* over this Washington business. We ought to send somebody to Washington to get at the facts and write the case up. Why not send Kribs?'
Manager. – 'Who is Kribs?'
Ed.-in-Chief. – 'I don't know, but somebody told me he is our city editor.'
Manager. – 'He may be. I wouldn't swear he isn't. Well, if anybody is sent, Kribs (providing there really is such a person) would be the right man to send. I'll see if I can arrange it.'[24]

Again, there was much more of the same – but no clear indication of why it was so difficult to prove in court what everyone in Toronto seemed to know well enough. In any event, the ploy worked, and on

Tuesday Denison threw out the case against Kribs. The *Empire* exulted that one of the *Mail*'s cases had been 'laughed out of court' and indulged in an orgy of self-congratulation. The *Empire*, it said, would not have been worthy of the proud position it occupied in Canadian journalism if it had allowed itself to be intimidated. And when duty was fearlessly entered upon, the press could be a terror to evil-doers.[25]

While the case started with massive coverage, it eventually faded away, possibly in an out-of-court settlement. (It is notable, at least, that the *Empire* did not refer to any victory in the case when Farrer's annexation pamphlet emerged a year later.) The main case actually came to trial on 10 June 1890, but was quickly adjourned after Mr Justice William Falconbridge (another noted imperialist) granted a defence motion to send a commission to the United States to take testimony from various politicians to prove the truth of the *Empire*'s charges. Again, the *Empire* seemed to have the support of authority. The *Mail*'s lawyer noted that the commission had been granted under a law that had received royal assent less than a month earlier, and said it seemed to be a statute born for the occasion.[26] The ploy, however, apparently failed, because the American congressmen refused to testify for the commission. The *News* reported in July that the progress of 'the big suit' had been stayed because of a U.S. law that protected congressmen from being examined on state matters outside Congress.[27] Creighton confirmed this defeat in a letter a few days later to the prime minister, promising that the paper would fight to the end and 'make the most of the fact that the Washington politicians being all in league with Farrer and the Mail are endeavouring to thwart us getting at the facts of their annexation plottings.'[28] The *Empire*, however, then became curiously muted on the issue, and what had started as a *cause célèbre* faded away, probably in the hands of lawyers with cooler heads than the journalistic foes.

On its editorial page the *Empire* had made a more sober and cogent case that the *Mail* had been working for years towards a disguised goal, ever since it had betrayed its party and reversed all its old principles:

With a skill, which employed in honest attempts to better our national condition would have been worthy of praise, and with an ingenuity that may justly be termed devilish, the abandoned journal began to advocate commercial union as the only relief from what it described as an intolerable state of things. The Dominion was pictured as being absolutely dependent upon United

States trade for existence, and day after day it was darkly hinted that the prospects of the country were growing dimmer the longer commercial union was delayed. There was annexation in every line of those arguments because, though it was never specifically mentioned, the natural conclusion ... was that Canada had no hope apart from intimate political and commercial association with the republic. Then the controversy over the Jesuit question arose, and the *Mail* ... began to rouse discontent on a fresh tack ... Why? The aim is clearly seen now in the light of the Washington tactics, because the burden of every article was that the difficulties of Canadians were insuperable, that we were controlled by priestcraft ... The political conditions in the United States were always referred to as free from these evils, and if the statement was made once it was made fifty times that Confederation on its present basis could not last. Will any thinking man say that the paper had not annexation in view all this time ...?[29]

Given this conviction, the *Empire* managers considered it worthwhile to track Farrer's movements, passing them on to Macdonald with all the keenness of a manic spy agency. On 29 March Creighton wrote Macdonald: 'One of our men today telegraphed me that Ned Farrer is on the train going east, presumably for Washington. I have had our Washington man instructed to look out for him, telegraph his arrival if he reaches there, and keep an eye on him. Nothing may come of it, but it is well to be on the watch. I am *convinced* that the annexationist traitors are all in league, and if we convince the public that they are intriguing at Washington, we will not only kill the *Mail*, but also smash Sir Richard and the wing of the Grits which follows him.'[30]

Creighton's paranoia by this point seems to have been out of control, but he was by no means the only Canadian taking the threat seriously. In March Goldwin Smith had stirred anxiety with a comment in *Bystander* that nothing but a bold organ and a resolute leader seemed wanting to turn a vague tendency towards annexation into a pronounced movement, or to turn whispered heresy into an avowed creed. Ned Sheppard noted this 'plain manifesto' and mused about who might become the movement's leader. Perhaps Smith himself? And which paper would be the organ? Either the *Mail* or the *Globe* would do, he concluded. Neither would have to make any radical change. And it would be much more decent, he said, for the whole outfit to drop the 'whispered heresies' and come boldly out from under the barn.[31]

9 The Mercenary

The *Globe*'s attacks on the *Mail* at the start of 1890 added a certain piquancy to the news, in the summer of that same year, that Ned Farrer would join the leading Liberal organ. But even aside from that factor the event caused a considerable stir, explainable only in terms of the complex ties between national politics and Toronto journalism. It provoked speculation, public and private, on what it would mean for the *Mail* (Would it now be brought back into the Tory fold?), for the *Globe* (Would it be making another of its notorious policy switches?), and for the future of the continental movement or of the party press.

Several commentators joined Ned Sheppard in agreeing that Farrer was worth stealing. Sheppard also implied, though, that the move was somehow discreditable:

A great deal of newspaper comment has been excited by the announcement that Mr Edward Farrer, who has for the past four or five years been recognized as the editorial brains of the *Mail*, has made an arrangement whereby the said brains are to direct the editorial policy of the *Globe*. There is no doubt that Mr Farrer is mentally better equipped for editorial work than any other man on the daily press. Indeed he has few peers in America, and not only in Canada is his ability recognized, but in New York his pen would find ready employment on the best journals of that great city. Fortunately, perhaps, for him, he is not encumbered with strong personal opinions, and is quite as ready to write on one side of a question as on the other ...[1]

Sheppard evidently had forgotten his magazine's comment, just six months earlier, that Farrer was a 'gentleman of very pronounced opinion.' If he had remembered, he might have reflected that the move could have more than mercenary implications. Unionists, commercial or political, saw greater importance in it. 'Mr Farrer I see is to go to the "Globe" staff,' Congressman Hitt wrote to Goldwin Smith on 30 June. 'I hope his pen, which is a really powerful one, will be there efficient for the good cause.'[2] On the other hand, loyalists saw reason for alarm. 'When money can buy the most powerful pens,' Principal George Grant observed in a Toronto speech, 'a free people will not surrender its judgment and its destiny to the thunder of double-leaded editorials.'[3]

Grip got much amusement from the switch, publishing an elaborate cover cartoon showing Farrer as a pudgy, bearded child being kidnapped by the *Globe* controllers, while grasping a 'Grit' pen in one hand and a 'Tory' pen in the other. 'The cartoon sets forth with a good deal of realism the business-like hustle which was displayed by the *Globe* people in this matter; but it falls far short in depicting the frenzy and wrath of Bunting,' *Grip* said. '*That* was beyond the scope of any pencil.' *Grip* also had an elaborate satire purporting to show how *Globe* president Robert Jaffray had recruited his new editor, with Farrer gravely assuring him that he was not at all in favour of such nasty things as crushing Confederation or promoting equal rights or annexation. At the same time *Grip* could not resist the temptation to poke fun at the party papers, especially the frantic attempts of the *Globe* and the *Empire* to locate the *Mail* in each other's camp: 'These cross-theories as they stand furnish the comedy element in our local politics. 'Twere a thousand pities to have them smashed.'[4]

Billy Maclean's *World* also made much of the switch, telling in detail of the departure, the affecting leave-taking from Boss Bunting (after which the two left 'Pulptower' and dropped over to Hooper's for a glass of Saratoga and phosphate). It also dwelt on Farrer's mercenary qualities, likening him to Sir John Hawkwood and other medieval soldiers of fortune: 'He has been in all camps and in all sorts of warfare. But if he preaches many things he believes nothing.'

Other commentators took a more serious view of what the move would mean for the three-cornered fight among the three serious papers. 'I am not surprised at Farrer's shift: nothing he could do would surprise me,' wrote R.S. White, editor of the Tory Montreal *Gazette*, to Willison of the Liberal *Globe*. 'He will be a great accession of strength to you and if our friends [the Tories] are wise they will endeavour to bring about a fusion of the *Mail* and *Empire*.'[5] The clear

THE KIDNAPPERS. *Grip*, 5 July 1890. The *Globe*'s theft of Farrer in 1890 prompted Bengough to show Farrer with a Grit pen in one hand and a Tory pen in the other, as a reminder of his mercenary background. The magazine claimed the cartoon showed with a good deal of realism the hustle displayed by the Liberal kidnappers, Robert Jaffray, J.D. Edgar, and Joseph Tait. But it fell short in displaying the 'frenzy and wrath' of *Mail* manager Christopher Bunting.

implication was that with Farrer gone, the *Mail* could more easily be brought back into the Tory fold – either because it would be commercially weaker, or because Farrer's influence had sustained its independence. The *World* story struck the same note, quoting party insiders as saying that Bunting was ready to quit, and that consolidation of the two papers would 'settle the newspaper situation.' (In fact, these comments foretold the actual fate of the two papers, though the merger was more than four years off.)

A crucial aspect of the switch, as some players noted, was that Farrer had upset the symmetry of the party press, attracting to the *Mail* young Liberals who would now go back to the official Grit organ. A.H.U. Colquhoun, at that time assistant editor on the *Empire*, wrote later of the uneasiness that had shown up on the *Globe* 'when the persuasive pen of Farrer, combined with the independent tone of *The Mail*, began to attract more and more Liberal readers.'[6] Walter Gregory also made the point, saying he himself had been first attracted to Farrer through his *Mail* articles on commercial union, and adding: 'The independence of the *Mail* in this matter appealed strongly to many of the young Liberals.'[7]

A newspaper's circulation, of course, was an index to both political and commercial success, and the *Globe* was suffering badly, under the combined impact of the *Mail*'s independence and the arrival of the *Empire*. From a peak of more than 31,000 at the time of the *Mail*'s declaration of independence early in 1887, it had fallen to 24,500 by 1890.[8] 'I don't think you can be aware of the desperate struggle the *Globe* is having to maintain its Protestant and Liberal readers,' President Robert Jaffray had told Edward Blake in 1889.[9]

These factors were no doubt in the air when the *Globe* syndicate was restructured early in 1890, with the Nelson publishing family of Edinburgh withdrawing, and Cartwright apparently taking a stronger hand.[10] Farrer's recruitment evidently was a key part of the reorganization plan. As Willison reported it, Cartwright and other Liberal leaders had been hoping for some time to entice him to the *Globe*:

Mr Farrer stood foremost among Canadian journalists and was better equipped than any other writer to expound the fiscal policy to which the Liberal party had committed itself. It was true that in *The Mail* he had thundered against Rome, the Bishops, the Obscurantists, the black Militia, and the Jesuits, lay and clerical, domestic and imported, while *The Globe*, through the Mowat government, as Conservative Oppositionists contended, was in practical political alliance with all these interests and agencies. But it was believed that Mr Farrer could safely become an editorial writer for *The Globe* if he was not available as its official editor. When I was told that Mr Farrer was engaged I acquiesced, but did not reveal the extent of my understanding. I knew that Hon. Edward Blake, Sir Richard Cartwright and Sir Oliver Mowat were not very favorable to my appointment. They doubted, as I did myself, if I had the necessary experience. But they did not agree upon any other candidate. Sir Richard was eager to have Mr Farrer associated with the *Globe* ...[11]

Cartwright's need for an advocate of reciprocity evidently blinded him to the danger of hiring Farrer, whose annexationist views were well enough known in Toronto journalism. If so, he might well have been disconcerted by the *World*'s flat assumption that the hiring of Farrer placed his patron among the annexationists as well. 'Sir Richard Cartwright is now the inspiration and the political beacon of [the *Globe*] and Mr Ned Farrer is to reflect his light,' the *World* claimed. The *Globe* was to be run ostensibly as a free-trade paper, but practically as an annexation advocate. '"If we can't get free trade out-and-out then let us have annexation," is to be the catch phrase of the movement.' Instead of galvanizing a dead party by sending a 'Farrer current through its rattling bones,' the *World* said, the party was actually splitting, into patriotic and disloyal factions.[12]

In fact, the *World* probably exaggerated the degree of Cartwright's continentalism; no proof was ever advanced that he went beyond support for commercial union. His alliance with Farrer seemed to be a matter of expedience, rather than reflecting any identity of view or personal rapport. Cartwright would soon grow impatient with his editor, and after Cartwright's death Farrer would write what was for him a rare personal criticism, saying Cartwright was 'inordinately vain, and could not bear those who would not accept him at his own valuation.'[13]

Cartwright was recognized, however, as leader of the party's Ontario wing, and Willison had this factor very much in mind as, shortly after his appointment, he wrote his own patron, Laurier. 'How does Mr Farrer's engagement with the *Globe* strike you?' he asked cautiously. 'I have little fear but I can work amicably with him.'[14] Laurier replied in a way that could be taken both as a warning and as a reassurance: 'He [Farrer] is a splendid writer, but he has the reputation, I think not undeserved, of being erratic in his opinions, and this may to some extent impair his usefulness.' Good writing, Laurier added, 'is doubly effective when it is known in the general public that good writing is the work of men of high character and firm opinions.'[15] All this, of course, can be read as a sop to Willison's ego, or a hint that loyalty to the party line would be rewarded. It is doubtful whether Laurier or any other politician worried about an editor's views being *erratic* as long as they stayed with the party line. In fact, an editor's ability to take the curve when the party changed policy or to stay with the right faction in party wars were crucial qualities.

For Willison and Farrer both these tasks were extraordinarily complex. They faced not just the problem of separate patrons but also tensions generated by Mowat's strong provincial group and by broader problems arising from the groundswell of change in both society and in the party press. In that context Willison's letters to his leader show interesting pressures flowing both from the *Globe*'s corporate directors and from Toronto's Waspish predilections. They also seem to imply that Farrer and McCarthy were moving apart, each resisting the other's wiles. Willison insisted that neither he nor Farrer was interested in supporting the equal rights movement, though they shared at least some of its aims. He was not satisfied that the movement was dead, he said, but hoped to be able to force other issues to the fore – 'and I have some of Mr Farrer's faith that McCarthy will bungle it.' (McCarthy, he said, was already concerned that his movement would mean the destruction of Confederation, and was getting afraid of it.) Willison said he also disagreed with Cartwright's desire to keep on beating Macdonald with the Jesuits' Estates issue, since a campaign of that kind would simply build up a separate equal rights party at the expense of the Liberals. 'In proportion as we deal with that question we will build up Equal Rights at the expense of ourselves ... We must force material issues on the attention of the people and with Farrer on hand I believe we can do it.'

Willison also correctly identified a problem for the *Globe* in differences between Mowat and the federal leaders, but made Laurier uneasy by implying that the party leader shared the now conventional Toronto views on bringing into check French Canada and the Roman Catholics. 'Where I see most danger for the *Globe* is in a conflict of policy between the Dominion leaders and the Ontario Govt,' Willison wrote. 'Mr Mowat is not ready to admit the possibility of a revision of the constitution. He would stand unflinchingly by his separate schools and the constitutional settlement ...'[16]

In fact, Willison had misread Laurier's stance on this issue, and

The issue, the implications of righteousness

his own 'firm views' on it pointed ahead to the rock on which he and Laurier would eventually split. In the short run, though, Laurier may have been reassured by Willison's declarations of personal loyalty, his explicit recognition that he owed his job to the leader, and his assurance that he was 'going slow' until Farrer arrived and policy lines were clarified. In the long run Willison's appearance of docility would prove to be misleading. Within two years he would be stiffly reminding Laurier of the financial facts – that, for instance, Cartwright's share of the paper's stock amounted to only $1,400 while Robert Jaffray, the president, had $20,000.[17] Within ten years he would be complaining that even though the *Globe* spent large sums spreading Liberal information to smaller papers, party men 'with incredible insolence and presumption' attempted to discipline him like a servant.[18]

Those problems lay over the horizon, but a more immediate issue discussed among Toronto journalists was the question of controlling the individual writer, within the party-newspaper apparatus. Farrer by this point, despite the anonymity of his editorials, had gained more fame or notoriety than any other working newspaperman in the country. The question naturally arose as to who was to take responsibility for his actions – the party, the paper, or the man himself. Ned Sheppard wrestled with the question in *Saturday Night* and ended up arguing both sides against the middle: on the one hand, he wanted newspapermen to sign their work and take responsibility for it; on the other hand, every newspaper man had to 'sink his preferences,' so that the paper could remain consistent. He could not agree, though, Sheppard wrote, with Farrer's philosophy that a journalist was like a lawyer, free to take a brief from either side in a controversy. Newspapers would lose some of their power if they hired men who did not have to worry about the righteousness of their arguments so long as they drew a good salary. 'As things stand the many able and stinging things which Mr Farrer has written concerning the aggression of the Catholic Church cannot be made to bear witness against him when he next endeavors to prove that Roman Catholics are really badly treated ...'[19]

This rush of comment about Farrer's move naturally created a vexation for Willison, especially when writers assumed that Farrer would direct the *Globe*'s policy line. Willison was, after all, officially listed as editor-in-chief, even though people perversely insisted on describing him as manager, and Farrer as editor. Willison was especially irked when comment started to appear saying Farrer had made a sharp improvement in the paper – even *before* he had actually started work. (He confessed that one premature comment prompted him to write an angry private letter of rebuttal, and he wished afterwards that he could recall it.)[20] *Grip*, in early August, also noted this pattern, saying some of the 'knowing ones' who with great discrimination had spotted Farrer articles as early as 1 July were disgusted to find that he had not in fact joined the *Globe* until about 15 July. Then *Grip* itself joined the knowing ones, with a cartoon of 23 August showing Farrer as an acrobat, the Star of the Arena, negotiating the 'Globe' up a teeter-totter. The caption reported a noticeable brightening of the *Globe* editorial page: its old-time glory was steadily returning as it found live and interesting topics, and discussed them with incisive force. 'In the popular mind this is all due to the masterly pen of Mr Edward Farrer. It is certainly a noticeable coincidence that the improvement began about the time that gentleman joined the staff, and he is entitled to enjoy the benefit of any doubt there may be on the subject.'[21]

At the *Empire* David Creighton was also keeping a close eye on the *Globe*'s progress and boasting to Macdonald that his own writers were holding their own against Farrer – again, perhaps, before Farrer had arrived. On 21 July he wrote:

Farrer's leaving the *Mail* having been so prominently noticed will doubtless hurt it somewhat, though from present appearances it is not going to strengthen the *Globe* much. Having been educated at Jesuit colleges gave him a vantage ground in discussing the Jesuit question which nobody else in Canada possessed, while the subject being one on which the public were roused, it gained him a great reputation which he will not keep up when, on the *Globe*, he has to drop that and go to other topics. His articles so far have been of a pessimistic pattern which will not carry the public with them, and our fellows are quite able to hold their own with him, and have been doing it, on the subjects he has now struck. Our cue is to stand up for our country – to preach up patriotism and hopefulness for the future, and to impress the people that the Grit party are the party of despair, who in their desperation are working to sell the country to the United States. I am credibly informed that Farrer has been put on the *Globe* by Sir Richard Cartwright and is responsible to him rather than to the Manager. It is perhaps as well, for it means that 'blue ruin' will be the pervading element, and I hope before the elections come we will get the people thoroughly saturated with the idea that this country cannot afford to place itself in the hands of the apostles of despair ...[22]

Creighton had reason to keep an eye on the *Globe*, for Farrer's arrival – or other causes – had brought an astonishing leap of several thousand in the paper's circulation. 'You were good enough to ask me about the Globe,' Willison wrote Laurier on 22 October, 'and we are doing very well, better than I ever expected. Since Sept. 1 the Globe's circulation has increased by 3,000 daily and the returns are still coming in, as they say, in the townships.' Willison was also pleased to report that the 'curious contract' was working out, and his directors were happy. 'I am getting along absolutely without friction with both staff and directors. My relations with Mr Farrer are very pleasant. I am learning to think a great deal of him. Of course there is no fear of trouble with the directors if the concern continues to advance towards a good financial basis.'²³

The *Globe*'s booming circulation was probably caused, not by Farrer's political writing, but by a quite different phenomenon – a uniquely sensational crime story. The occasion was the Birchall murder at Woodstock, a case that gripped Canadian (and foreign) attention in a way that has probably never occurred before or since, and displayed what Willison called Farrer's 'qualities of a detective.' It was only in the context of near-hysterical coverage, in fact, that Farrer's scoop in the case could have caused such a stir, bringing harsh and envious criticism down on him. Rivals of the *Globe*, stung at being beaten, insisted Farrer's story had to be a fraud, or at least an exaggeration. They dragged out the old cases, probably based on his own press club anecdotes, when Farrer had embellished or invented news.

These charges had a heavy coating of self-righteousness. Newspapering was still in an era when its great figures boasted of times when they had taken a fifty-word cable, about a fire or flood or earthquake, and turned it into two thousand words of magnificent copy. Such stories were rarely about politics, which was taken seriously, and they never hurt a journalist's reputation so long as they were told privately. In Farrer's case they were already part of the legend, as witness the 1885 Bengough cartoon of the mechanical war correspondent writing of 'Chief O'Soup.' The Birchall coup, though, coming at a time when competition in Toronto newspapering had never been tougher, had a special sting that made rivals abandon the press club code of discretion.

In retrospect it is hard to fathom why the case made such an extraordinary impact. It may have been because Reginald Birchall was not just a rogue, but a suave, upper-class British rogue, who had even attended Oxford. Thereafter he had, possibly with his wife's help, set out to swindle gullible young English 'remittance men' in deals for imaginary Canadian farmland. The case broke when one of the victims, Fred Benwell, was shot and his body left in a swamp near Woodstock. Birchall was arrested, convicted – on circumstantial evidence – and sentenced to be hanged. In the interval before the actual hanging, carried out on 14 November, newspapers in the United States and Britain, as well as Canada, continued to give the case garish coverage, even extending to the food the condemned man was getting in prison. No reporters, however, were allowed to interview him.

Murder cases were apparently yet another of Farrer's many areas of interest and expertise. 'He would talk for hours of great historical trials for murder, with exact knowledge of the evidence and the pieces of testimony which brought conviction or acquittal,' said Willison.[24] He recalled as well that he had never seen Farrer so utterly absorbed as he was at the time of the Birchall trial.

In view of that reputation, press people covering the case in Woodstock were naturally nervous when Farrer showed up in town on Saturday, 4 October, blandly assuring them that his visit had nothing to do with Birchall. They were appalled when the *Globe* on Monday came out with a remarkable story, of more than seven thousand words, that appeared to be based not only on an interview with Birchall himself but on a great deal of inside information from both the Crown and defence sides. The *Globe* treated the story as a *tour de force*, running it over five front-page columns, plus another inside, with a headline saying Birchall had made a partial confession and had admitted (not in the interview with Farrer, but to some of his sources) that he had been an accessory before and after the killing.[25]

The impact of the 'rockets' sent off by editors in the wake of this coup can be imagined only by reporters who have been beaten on a big story. The journalistic code called for the story to be matched or discredited, and in this case there was only one choice. The reporters in Woodstock scrambled to find officials who would deny that Birchall had confessed (which was not what Farrer's story had claimed) or who would state that *they themselves* had not told Farrer of a partial confession (this would allow the reporters to write that the *Globe* piece had been 'denied'). Back in the newsrooms, meanwhile, editors sharpened their pens to write attacks on the provincial authorities for permitting Farrer to see the prisoner (clearly a case of Grit favouritism for a Grit journal) or on Farrer himself for yet another irresponsible invention.

Even the *Mail*, so recently Farrer's own paper, called the exposé a pure fabrication. The paper's Woodstock correspondent said the *Globe*'s alleged 'partial confession' had created considerable talk, but was transparently false. 'Birchall denies ever having made any confession, and those who know him well are of the opinion that he is not the man to do anything of the kind as long as there is any hope for a commutation of his sentence.'[26] Woodstock papers also came up with statements that Birchall had denied confessing, and had in fact exclaimed, 'What a lot of rubbish!' when he read the *Globe* article. (These reporters did not, however, claim to have seen Birchall, nor did they indicate how they had come by the 'rubbish' quote.) The *Sentinel-Review*, in fairness, followed that quote with recognition that the *Globe* had not actually claimed the partial confession came directly from Birchall, though a 'careless reading of the report' might lead one to think so. But where, the paper wondered, had the *Globe* got the information?

Mr Edward Farrer, chief editorial writer on the *Globe*, was in Woodstock on Saturday, and though he vowed that his visit here had no connection with the Birchall case he did have an interview with the prisoner. During that interview the 'partial confession' was not mentioned; it was simply with reference to Mrs. Birchall's alleged connection with the farm fraud. Mr Farrer was allowed to ask the prisoner whether or not Mrs. Birchall was cognizant of the swindle, and he was allowed to interview the prisoner on that point with the understanding that it was to be used only in a certain London, Eng., paper, which was said to have made inquiries on the subject. Both Mr Cameron, the gaoler, and Mr Forbes, the turnkey, deny very emphatically that the information came from them. Not having come from the prisoner and not having come from the gaol officials, where did it come from? There are still left the counsel for the defence and the detective who worked up the defence, but professional honour would prevent them revealing the secrets of their client if they had any secrets.[27]

While others were content to denigrate the *Globe* story, the *Empire*, Farrer's special enemy, decided to go directly for the writer, producing a story on Farrer's past sins and implying that the details on those sins had come from Farrer himself. The *Empire* story, better written than the paper's usual shrill polemics and possibly from 'Pica' Kribs's pen, started out thus:

There is a story told of a certain kind of journalistic enterprise that, whether true or not, is retailed with considerable gusto by people who believe in that kind of thing. Mr Edward Farrer at the time of the last English campaign in Egypt was the editor of the Winnipeg *Times*. By a singular coincidence the *Times* came out one day with a magnificent account of the battle of Tel-el-Kebir, several columns in length, purporting to have been specially cabled from Egypt to that paper. The battle as it appeared in *Times* [sic] was quite a different affair from the battle as it actually occurred – when it did occur – but everything went.

There is another incident related by the same people. These people say that when Sitting Bull made his emeute into Canadian territory the New York *World* one morning published a splendid account of that celebrated Indian's doings while on Canadian soil. The most minute details were given. The despatch was dated from Cypress Hills, but there are those – the people before mentioned – who aver that it was written in Toronto in the *Mail* office. By another singular coincidence Mr Edward Farrer was at that time editor of the *Mail*.

In fact, there are several such stories told – one about the Countess of Dufferin's trip to the Gulf, one about the French-Canadians dated from Quebec, when the writer was actually in New York – all of which goes to show, whether true or not, that a good imagination can sometimes be depended upon to annihilate space – in a newspaper and otherwise – and beat electricity itself in swiftness.

Mr Edward Farrer is now editor of the *Globe*. He was in Woodstock on Saturday and yesterday's *Globe* contained a six-column report under the following head-lines: 'Birchall,' 'Statements Made by the Doomed Man,' 'A Partial Confession,' ... Taken by itself the article is one of the most wonderful that ever appeared in a Canadian or any other newspaper. It is a greater mass of contradictions than even Birchall's stories about himself ...

The *Empire* then went on, at some length, to define the alleged contradictions, although it did not in fact manage to directly disprove any of Farrer's assertions. It made a stronger case, though, in attacking some shadowy attribution in the story ('It is understood ... Birchall admits by not denying') and also in condemning the *Globe*'s

The Mercenary 175

decision to print Birchall's statements incriminating another young Englishman named Graham, not charged in the case, as the actual killer.[28]

Elsewhere on the same day the *Empire* complained sourly about the way the interview had been obtained, suggesting it must have been because of the *Globe*'s influence with the provincial Liberals. Farrer himself gave no clue on how he got the interview, but he did admit – or half admit – in the original story that he had deceived Birchall with the pretense that his comments were for publication in England. The section in question went as follows:

I spoke to Birchall yesterday concerning the impression prevailing here and in England that his wife was privy to the swindle if to nothing else. He was told that what he said would be cabled to England. He declared, and the tears filled his eyes as he rose and grasped the bars of the cell door, that his wife was innocent both of the fraud and of the more heinous crime. 'My wife,' he said, with much warmth, 'is a perfectly honorable woman. She knew nothing of what was going on. I deceived her. I lied to her. She believed all I said. If she found me out, or thought she had found me out in one lie, I told her another. My word is of no weight now, but I tell you she is as innocent as a child of any participation in the affair. I mean that she had no hand in or no knowledge of the swindling ...' He was considerably moved as he spoke. It was early in the morning. He had not been long out of bed, and looked as if he had passed a hard night. He repeated over and over again that he had deceived his wife about everything, and expressed the hope that the public would do her the justice to believe she was absolutely without blame.[29]

While the tone of Birchall's quotes seems artificial – at least to modern ears – no proof ever was advanced that the story had been faked. Even the statements about Graham brought no libel suit, although the *Globe* was apparently vulnerable. The attacks continued, though, with the *Mail* later in the week publishing (in clear imitation of the *Empire*) an editorial about great newspaper hoaxes of the past. The column led up to the topic by remarking that the people of Woodstock found the newest hoax as heartless as it was immoral. It then went on to say that most of the great hoaxes in newspaper history had been designed to stand up for at least a few days. In that category were the New York *Sun*'s famous stories about a three-day Atlantic balloon trip, or about the group of astronomers in Africa who had allegedly found life on the moon. The Birchall story, the *Mail* added, was also consistent with the tradition of invented confessions published by London's 'halfpenny dreadfuls' on the eve of executions.[30]

The *Globe* itself meanwhile brushed aside the attacks, saying the story had been carefully double-checked, that the paper had no intention of revealing its sources, and that the fuss was simply a case of annoyance by rivals at being scooped. 'Our brethren should learn to bear the ups and downs of journalistic competition with greater equanimity. In the slang of the day it is absurd for them to "do the baby act" whenever a rival manages to outstrip them.'[31]

For the *Empire* this was entirely too much – especially, perhaps, the reference to a 'baby act.' It dropped its earlier tone of lofty remonstrance and slipped back to its normal fits of sputtering rage, accusing Farrer of having a 'depraved and unscrupulous imagination,' recalling his traitorous activities, and saying his disgraceful invention of a sham confession was made even more disreputable by the wicked trick of connecting innocent individuals with the criminal deed. 'This system of falsifications would be bad enough in itself, even without the further taint of being designed to injure innocent individuals or to strike a blow at our country.'[32]

The *Empire* at that point was clearly lusting for revenge on Farrer. It had just four more months to wait.

10 The Plot

Shortly after New Year's 1891, Colonel George Taylor Denison received at his Toronto office a caller – a fellow officer – who went some way towards confirming his suspicions that Toronto was infiltrated by traitors. Major Percy Sherwood, a somewhat shadowy figure, was head of Sir John A. Macdonald's Dominion Police. He explained that he had come on the orders of the prime minister, on a matter of secrecy affecting national security. Denison must have felt his cavalryman's adrenalin flow.

The matter, Sherwood explained, had to do with a treasonous document written by the editor of the *Globe* – the same editor who had appeared before Magistrate Denison just a year earlier in the libel action against the *Empire*. As Denison later described the meeting, Sherwood told him that a printer at Hunter, Rose & Co. had reported the existence of the suspect document. The printer, one Christopher Clark (the name was not used in Denison's account), had given the word to C. Hibbert Tupper, son of Sir Charles Tupper and a member of Macdonald's cabinet. Hibbert Tupper had in turn reported to the prime minister, who had ordered Sherwood to Toronto to pin down evidence of the offence. Denison was to be brought into the case to prepare affidavits, in his role as magistrate, certifying the printer's statements that the work was indeed that of Edward Farrer.[1]

As a magistrate, of course, Denison might well have considered calling in the local police, to seize the offending pamphlet and find out whether it contained anything justifying a charge of treason. If he suggested that course, though, he did not tell of it in his account of the affair. It apparently did not occur to him he might have been prostituting his magistrate's office to serve Macdonald's need for a mystery that would give maximum impact to the later revelations.

Soon after the first visit Sherwood returned with the printer and two or three pages of the pamphlet. It was arranged that any more sheets the printer could get would be brought to Denison, who would prepare the affidavits and forward them to Sherwood. But getting the copies was difficult: the proof sheets were watched so closely and taken back so carefully after corrections that the printer had to work fast during the dinner hour, inking the type and taking 'rough and primitive' copies of only some parts of the pamphlet before the type was broken up.

These portions, however, were quite enough, as Denison observed. (In fact the last few pages would have been enough; the main part of the pamphlet was a detailed review of the fisheries feud, and it was only the final pages that contained advice on how the United States could coerce Canada into union.) Denison, in any event, played his part in the intrigue with delight, and he may have had a personal animus. Later, the Toronto *Telegram* reflected with amusement on how much regret Denison would suffer if Farrer managed to leave police court jurisdiction 'without doing something to justify the court in sending him down without the option of a fine.'[2]

While Denison's account is highly circumstantial, it is only one version of how the pamphlet came into Sir John's hands. A second version has it that William McDougall (who had served as Macdonald's agent in the 1884 plot to annex the Northwest) procured a copy and passed it on to Sir Charles Tupper, who gave it to Macdonald and passed back to McDougall the promise of a senatorship as a reward. There are strong indications, however, that this promised reward was not for provision of the pamphlet, but for Farrer's 'two bites on the cherry' letter.

At any rate, Denison was deeply engaged in the events leading up to the election and the 'terrible indictment' at the Academy of Music. Though not always a Macdonald supporter, Denison had already supplied the prime minister with secret information about Cartwright and Farrer and their visits to Washington. At least some of this information came (although Denison did not tell of it in his memoirs) from E.W. Thomson, Farrer's predecessor at the *Globe*. Thomson had obtained from Wiman and others information that convinced him Farrer and Cartwright were selling out to the Americans, and it was perhaps natural that he would share his fears with the city's most fanatical imperialist. Denison's files contain several items from Thomson. There is, for instance, a document ostensibly from Wiman headed 'Concluding portion of letter to E.W. Thomson, undated, apparently about Jan. 5, 1890,' which reported on the 'very important influence' of a recent Farrer trip to Washington. 'He has seen Blaine and had a long talk with Hitt, and he has tried to make them all believe that the annexation sentiment is growing so rapidly in Canada that it is useless to talk about commercial union ... Perhaps he is right, but the liberal party cannot afford to allow that impression to exist ...'

The same Denison documents indicate Wiman kept Thomson informed of Cartwright's movements in Washington in February 1890, and that Thomson eventually resigned from the *Globe* because he was convinced the paper was heading into a continentalist adventure. In his 22 March resignation letter to Jaffray, Thomson said he had learned that Cartwright 'has been recently engaged in a political intrigue which, in my opinion, is of an extremely discreditable and dangerous nature.'[3]

Denison delighted in sniffing out this kind of scheme. (He would be described by a later scholar as a man who saw the world through a haze of conspiratorial fantasies.)[4] He passed some of the information on to Macdonald at an encounter early in the new year. On that occasion, he recalled, the prime minister asked for advice on whether to call an immediate election, and Denison's reply was forceful. 'I jumped up from my chair at the suggestion that he was in doubt, and said, "What, Sir John; in the face of all you know and all I know, can you hesitate an instant? You must bring the elections on at once. If you wait till your enemies are ready, and the pipes are laid to distribute the money which will in time be given from the States, you will incur great danger, and no one can tell where the trouble will end."' Macdonald apparently replied only with an enigmatic smile and a warning to be ready for sudden developments.

Denison claimed the affair was handled with great discretion, only David Creighton being brought into the secret. However, he himself did not keep entirely silent. He went to two particular friends in the Ontario Liberal cabinet, Premier Mowat and G.W. Ross, to warn them that 'unpleasant matters' would be divulged, and that they should keep as far away from the election as they could. Macdonald, too, was not as secretive as Denison assumed. He sought advice on the wisdom of making the pamphlet a central campaign issue, and not all of it was positive. The governor general, Lord Stanley, was notably unimpressed, writing to Macdonald:

My dear Sir John.
   I return by safe hand the papers you gave me today.
   I have only been able to read them through rather quickly, but the impression which is left on my mind is that, apart from the circumstances connected with their origin and printing, Art. 15 is the only one in which there is anything even approaching to treasonable language. There can be no doubt of the general drift of the whole paper – but were I engaged in the election contest, I must say that I should not like to depend on this, as evidence of the annexationists being identical with the unrestricted reciprocity men.
   The one passage cited does appear to be over the line.
   Of course, however, you know best. I don't venture to express an opinion one way or the other, as to the policy of using this unpublished paper as a weapon of political war.
   The circumstances of course are suspicious.

Yours very truly
Stanley of Preston[5]

Macdonald himself must have been aware that the pamphlet provided only a thin connection between the annexationists and the Liberal leaders. However, he had few other weapons to hand (a situation for which Farrer was partly to blame) and was facing the campaign of 1891 with a formidable array of troubles before him. At home there was the looming McGreevy scandal, concerning contract kickbacks to government members. Abroad there was the ancient problem of Atlantic fisheries – terribly tangled, but centring on Canadian determination to restrict U.S. fishing vessels from using Canadian ports or inshore waters until Canada could obtain free access for her own fish into the U.S. market. Serious trouble was also brewing with the United States over sealing rights in the Bering Sea. And there were broader problems on general trade relations. It was in the latter area that Farrer had played a small but irritating role, although the real damage had been done by the Republican administration at Washington.

During the previous autumn the Americans had confronted Macdonald with a double problem. In October they had brought in a highly restrictive tariff policy, the so-called McKinley tariff, seriously affecting Canadian exports and giving credence to the Liberals' claims that only they could achieve a reasonable trade arrangement with the United States through the avenue of unrestricted reciprocity. Immediately after that blow, word had come that the Americans were negotiating through the British a fisheries and trade deal with Newfoundland – a clear attempt to undermine Canada. At Macdonald's demand the British agreed to delay negotiations until Canada could be included. At that point Blaine came through with a tantalizing offer – one that Macdonald distrusted but could not ignore – for private discussions on a possible reciprocity agreement. In December, through the British, Macdonald's government proposed a formal commission to cover a wide range of problems, including trade. Blaine replied offering a 'full but private' conference, and making a particular demand for secrecy. 'If an agreement is reached all [is] well,' he said. 'If not, no official mention is to be made of the effort. Above all things it is important to avoid all public reference to the matter. This the President insists upon.'[6]

The wording of that message was crucial, for misunderstanding, deliberate or accidental, arose on the question of whether secrecy was to apply only to what *transpired* at the discussions, or to the very fact that discussions were to be held. Macdonald later claimed that he did not know until January that the Americans held to the latter interpretation. On 16 January the *Empire* ran a story (presumably provided by the government, though there is no evidence of this)[7] saying negotiations were in progress, at the instigation of the Americans. Later in January the British, on Canada's behalf, asked Blaine if he would object to making public the U.S. willingness to meet, and Blaine replied with a curt rejection.

That made the situation bad enough, preventing Macdonald from campaigning on his own platform of partial reciprocity. But what made it worse was that Farrer on 29 January had a well-publicized meeting with Blaine, followed almost immediately by a denial from the secretary of state that any negotiations for reciprocity were going on. Macdonald biographer Donald Creighton notes that Blaine was able to receive Farrer even though he had found it impossible to meet Canadian representatives until 4 March, and that news of the Farrer visit was 'instantly given to the press' even though the official negotiations were to have been strictly private. 'The [Canadian] government was in an appalling position. It had been led up the garden path, double-crossed with cool efficiency, and then effectively prevented from uttering a word of explanation or protest.'[8] From the

American point of view, of course, Macdonald had only got what he deserved for trying to make political points out of what were to have been very secret and tentative discussions. (Two years later, a visitor found Congressman Hitt still bitter about this incident, saying the U.S. government was 'stung to the quick' over the way it had been manipulated to 'forward the political interests of a lot of Canadian tricksters.')[9]

In any event, the contretemps made clear to Macdonald that he could expect no aid and comfort from Blaine in his effort to make reciprocity prospects a campaign plank. Worse, it was possible that Farrer had talked Blaine into leaning towards the Liberal version of unrestricted reciprocity. Macdonald was left with no option but to fall back on the Farrer pamphlet, and to try to paint the Grits as secret annexationists. On 2 February the order for the general election was signed, and on the same day the prime minister received a discouraging response from Washington on queries about the secrecy issue and about 'the gentleman from Toronto' – presumably Farrer. The response, passed on by Lord Stanley from Sir Julian Pauncefote, the British ambassador in Washington, said:

Cypher
  Secret and personal, your telegram of yesterday. I have not yet been able to obtain any information respecting the gentleman from Toronto but will telegraph again should I discover anything. Blaine certainly holds as to secrecy in regard to his proposal for private negotiations here ...[10]

While Macdonald was disappointed, David Creighton had no doubt that Farrer's machinations could only help the Tories. 'The Lord hath delivered the enemy into our hands,' he wrote the prime minister on 30 January. 'The traitor is again at Washington, and you see we are after him sharply.'[11] Creighton followed that up with an *Empire* front page reminiscent of the broadside delivered a year earlier when Farrer's traitorous activities at the *Mail* had been revealed:

PLOTTING AT WASHINGTON

A GRIT EMISSARY DOWN SOUTH

Holding informal conferences with Secretary

Blaine – Under the Wing of Representative Hitt –
The 'Peculiar Significance' of His Visit – As
'One of the Laymen Leaders of the Liberal Party
in Canada' – He Wants 'Assurances' from
Headquarters ...

New York, Jan. 29 – The *Herald*'s Washington special says: A highly important, although informal conference, was held this morning at the residence of Secretary Blaine between the secretary of state, Chairman Hitt, of the House committee on foreign relations, Mr Blaine's supporter and right hand man in Congress, and the Hon. Edward Farrar, editor of the Toronto *Globe* and one of the laymen leaders of the Liberal party in Canada.

It is 'important'

The conference was important as being the first of a series of informal talks with Secretary Blaine upon the question of Canadian reciprocity, which Mr Farrar has come to Washington to obtain ... Mr Farrer's visit is believed to be for the purpose of obtaining assurances from party leaders in this country of the possibility of reciprocity being acceptable to the United States at this time, which assurances he wishes to communicate to his colleagues in the Liberal Party of Canada ...[12]

This story, with its bizarre suggestion that the 'Hon.' Edward Farrer, 'one of the laymen leaders of the Liberal party,' had 'come to obtain' reciprocity, must have raised snorts of disbelief in both Tory and Grit ranks. With the embroidery set aside, though, Canadian readers probably would have seen it as a coup of sorts for the Liberals, implying (though by no means stating) that Washington would be more favourable to the Liberals' kind of reciprocity. Whether this was Farrer's sole aim, though, is still unclear. He may indeed have been acting as a Liberal, or Cartwright, emissary, doing what the *Herald* story implied in trying to find out whether Washington actually would respond to the Liberal version of reciprocity. He may also have been seeking financial support for the Liberals. Or he may have been continuing quietly to push the line he had advocated to Blaine two years before, when he urged the Americans to hold off concessions so as to force Canada into annexation. Variations on these themes are also possible: he may have urged Blaine to take a soft line towards the Liberals until they were elected; then tighten the screws.

It seems likely, though, that he favoured the hard line only as a device for getting the Liberals into office, or as a way of gaining points

184 Secret Craft

LAYING OUT THE GRIT CAMPAIGN (Conservative campaign poster). One of the most striking Farrer cartoons of the 1891 election was this Tory poster showing him plotting the sell-out of Canada to President Benjamin Harrison and Secretary of State James G. Blaine. Cartwright and Laurier are across the table, and Erastus Wiman is at Farrer's left.

in the United States by telling American leaders what they wanted to hear. In later, signed writing Farrer consistently rejected the idea that Canada could be starved or bludgeoned into political union. In a long and thoughtful article on Canadian-American relations in the *Contemporary Review* in 1906, for instance, Farrer said some Americans imagined that onerous taxes on Canadians' exports would starve them into annexation. 'If, however, they would have us join them, they should throw down their tariff wall against us in order that we might realize to the full the advantage of belonging to so rich a country and such a vast free-trading area.'[13] Writing of this kind indicates Farrer had either abandoned the view set out in the pamphlet and the 'two bites on the cherry' letter, or he had never genuinely held it. The latter seems most likely, especially since both documents exaggerate outrageously the extent of Liberal interest in annexation.

As for Blaine and Hitt, it is clear that they were interested in commercial union or 'U.R.' only as a stage on the road to political union, although they were willing to make some slight concession to the Liberals. On 14 February the *Empire* noticed what it considered to be a significant shift in opinion on the part of Blaine's 'mouthpiece,' the New York *Tribune*. In October and November, it said, the *Tribune* had ridiculed the idea of unrestricted reciprocity, while saying there could be no objection to a limited experiment with the principle – a position in line with Macdonald's hopes. The Canadian government on that basis had accepted Blaine's invitation to talk. In reaction to this the Canadian 'traitors' – Farrer and Cartwright and Laurier – had quickly gone to the United States. 'The result of these visits was such as to convince Mr Blaine, that valuable as a limited and fair reciprocity might be to both countries, Mr Hitt's desire for a complete monopoly of Canadian trade was within the bounds of possibility, and to secure that it would be necessary for the American people to absolutely refuse limited reciprocity to Canada!' Blaine's organ, which in November had ridiculed unrestricted reciprocity, in January had been sympathetic.

The *Empire* also reprinted a remarkable article from the Detroit *Tribune* that bore the clear imprint of an administration plant and set out Blaine's thinking in detail:

Mr Blaine's purpose as to reciprocity with Canada, and some of his recent utterances concerning issues prominent in Canadian politics, are likely to be misunderstood by those who do not appreciate the delicacy of diplomatic responsibilities ... Secretary Blaine is a far-seeing diplomat and too courageous and patient a statesman to jeopardize ultimate results by a hasty declaration of purposes, and for these reasons his countrymen might remain long in ignorance of his real hope as to Canadian-American union. But we believe that the plans of the secretary of state affecting our relations with Canada comprise vastly more than appears on the surface, and we are convinced that the time has come when the American people should begin to think seriously about the future of the large British territory to the north of us. More than that, the proper destiny of this continent seems so plain that it is already the duty of the Republican party, which has led in every great movement for the national advantage, to examine the question of commercial union with Canada and afterwards of its actual annexation, with a view of placing the attainment of these results among the definite purposes of Republicanism ...[14]

It appears, therefore, that Blaine was throwing out hints to Canada that he would respond to the Liberal initiative, while reassuring Americans that he would be satisfied with nothing less than political union. As for Farrer's role, even Willison, who was close to the action, had trouble sorting it out. The following year he privately expressed the view that Farrer had been working all along *against* the Liberal policy of reciprocity.[15] In his later memoirs, though, Willison portrayed him as Cartwright's agent. He said there was no doubt that Farrer in this episode was trying to induce Blaine 'to give public assurances that unrestricted reciprocity would be established if the Liberal party succeeded in the election ...' And he added: 'Of Mr Farrer's activity at Washington Mr Blake had no knowledge, nor had Mr Laurier any direct responsibility for his movements. Sir Richard Cartwright had full knowledge ...' At another point Willison said that despite Cartwright's efforts to forge a Washington alliance, and despite Farrer's pilgrimages, 'there was no ground for the suspicion that any compact was entered into affecting the political status of Canada, nor was there any understanding that commercial union should be regarded as a deliberate and conscious step towards political union.' The truth was, he said, that the Liberals simply could not get any assurance of U.S. support for their policy.[16] In that quandary, of course, the Liberals were prepared to go some distance to get even a sympathetic nod from Blaine – or, indeed, even to buy his neutrality. It was natural that in dealing with the Americans they would hint at stronger leanings towards political union than they actually felt. It was natural that Liberals known to be continental-minded, like J.W. Longley of Nova Scotia or John Charlton of Ontario, would be chosen for New York and Washington lobbying. Willison himself said almost as much in his letter to Laurier of 5 January 1891, when he suggested Erastus Wiman was undermining the Liberals at Washington by talking *against* political union:

Dear Mr Laurier.
  You ask me what I mean by saying that Mr Wiman hurts us at Washington. I mean that he has no tact, no judgment, no discretion, that although a good fellow, he is vile with egotism ... In his mania for advertising himself *he overthrows the best plans that are laid at Washington* and hurts the movement in the House and Senate. Such men as Blaine and Hitt and Carlisle and Mills will not be led by Wiman. These men resent his posturing and assumptions to leadership. He goes to Washington and rants against political union. *Do you think these men at Washington are favoring Reciprocity because they want to build up a great British or a great rival power on this continent?* (italics added)[17]

In short, Willison seemed to be saying that only by convincing the Americans of an interest in political union could the Liberals hope to make progress in Washington. And in that game Farrer was a natural player – a man who, while unable to commit the party, could leave an impression in Washington of Liberal sympathy to annexation. If that were actually the case, Farrer would have been playing a role similar to Blaine's New York *Tribune*, in holding out vague promises that might get results without locking the party in on future actions.

  That interpretation is also supported by some of the wording in the stolen Farrer pamphlet – wording that implies the document was designed to sum up the Liberal point of view, and especially to show that Liberal policy was in line with Republican views. Among the lines leaving that impression were these:

The Liberal party favors a settlement of the fishery and all the other questions at issue between the two countries on the basis of full and absolute reciprocity in manufactures as well as natural products ...

... a precis of the views of the Liberal leaders and of the principal Liberal newspapers would read somewhat as follows ...

Other points, in addition to those cited, are sometimes urged by Canadian Liberals ...

In short, the Liberals of Canada virtually adopt the line taken by the Republican leaders in the controversy over the Bayard-Chamberlain treaty ...[18]

The thrust of the pamphlet thus seemed to be to convince the Americans a Liberal government would be easy to deal with. So if the pamphlet was in fact paid for by 'an American friend, not in politics,' as Farrer claimed, the ironic possibility is that the 'friend' actually paid to hear Liberal propaganda. If the real sponsor was Blaine, as a Farrer associate later implied,[19] the irony is sharpened. If Farrer was used by the party, though, it would appear that the manipulation cut both ways: Farrer's specific suggestions on how the United States could put pressure on Canada went well beyond anything the party would have endorsed, although they could have been seen by Liberals as directed not so much against the country as against its Conservative government. The clear implication was that with Liberals in office, no such pressure would be needed.

It is just possible, then, that Cartwright or Laurier, or both leaders, encouraged Farrer to go beyond the party's public stance to enlist sympathy in Washington. Such a role would help explain why Farrer was able to stay on at the *Globe* for seventeen months after the crisis – until, in fact, Laurier came under strong pressure from within the party because of Farrer's continuing annexationist efforts. It would help explain why he was entrusted with a succession of confidential missions for Laurier, both before and after he left the *Globe*. It would help explain the conflict between Farrer's view in both the pamphlet and the 'two bites' letter, recommending that the Americans bludgeon Canada into union, and his more usual (and more sane) efforts to build from commercial to political integration. It would also help explain Ham's later statement that Farrer had not in fact written the pamphlet, and had 'shielded some men whose names, if I told you, would surprise you very much.' It would also, perhaps, be consistent with Willison's seeming lack of interest in finding who the 'shielded' men were.

Whatever his motivation, Farrer's efforts backfired spectacularly in the election furore. If he had actually been working directly for Sir John A. Macdonald, he could not have better contrived to serve the 'old man' in his final campaign. From the night of the great rally in the Academy of Music the election battle was stripped of all subtleties of trade or other policy differences. The issue became simply one of loyalty, of choosing between the United States and Britain. The well-developed idea of an independent Canada, detached from both countries and allied with both, fell in a crossfire of rhetoric. The idea of some kind of free-trade area – an idea that clearly had considerable support across the Dominion – was tainted beyond repair with the stain of annexation. An era of imperial fervour was launched.

In the midst of the campaign the *Globe* did its best to treat the annexation issue as a miserable sidelight, but it was thrown decidedly on the defensive. On the morning after the Academy of Music rally it chose to treat Macdonald's charges not with anger but with yawning indifference, saying the Tories had had a 'fine meeting' at the Academy, and adding: 'Sir John, who, we regret to say, does not appear to be in strong health, devoted himself almost altogether to levelling charges of treason at Sir Richard Cartwright, Mr Charlton and other Liberal leaders. His accusations against a member of the editorial staff of the *Globe* are dealt with in a letter, printed elsewhere, from the person accused.' Even this small item was tucked inside the paper. No mention of the rally appeared on the front page, which featured a two-column spread on a Liberal meeting in Montreal ('When Mr Laurier rose to speak in English it seemed as if the applause would never cease').

Farrer's own reply to the prime minister's charge, covering almost a full column on the editorial page, insisted there was nothing secret about the pamphlet and that it was merely a piece of journalistic contract work, with no connection to the Liberal party. Headlined in small type, the statement read:

A Reply from Mr Farrer
What There is to the Charges Made by
Sir John Macdonald

To the Editor of The *Globe*:

Sir, Sir John Macdonald saw fit to devote a portion of his speech at the Academy last night to charging me with writing and with circulating in Washington a pamphlet which he pronounces treasonable. He added, I am told, that the police were tracing the evidence of my handiwork, leaving the impression that I had committed some grave offence at law.

The facts are briefly these: last summer an American friend of mine, not in politics, asked me for certain information regarding the North Atlantic fishery question ... Shortly afterward my American friend asked me to give him my own views of the case as it related to the refusal of commercial privileges in Canadian ports to American vessels, and to put myself in his place, as it were, and say what line I should take if I were an American ...

The police need not trouble themselves about looking for evidence. I admit that I was the writer and sole author of the brochure, and I should not hesitate, under like circumstances, to write another, or a dozen more, on that or any other subject ...

All or nearly all this took place before I had any connection with *The Globe*, good, bad or indifferent. But the accident that I was on another journal does not affect the case at all. I should do the same thing if I saw fit tomorrow without reference to *The Globe*, just as I did it without reference to *The Mail*, for surely a writer on a newspaper conducted, as all Canadian papers are, on the impersonal system is entitled to his private opinions and his personal liberty of action ... I wrote freely and privately about what I regard as the illogical, unfair and wholly out-of-date policy which the Government of the Dominion has pursued towards the vessels of a friendly neighbour, and, having been asked, proffered my view of the mode which I should favour, were I an American, of bringing about a more rational state of affairs for both countries. The references to Sir John are not, I hope, in bad taste; I certainly did not vilipend him. The statement that I believed his methods of government would not outlast him, and that I thought political union with the United States was the manifest destiny of Canada and that in the fulness of time we should see it, may be a mistaken one; but I believed it and believe it now and shall continue to do so until I am shown satisfactory evidence to the contrary.

This is the whole story. I deny the assumption that *The Globe* or the Liberal party is bound or affected by anything written, said or done by a mere writer for *The Globe* in his private hours or private capacity ... If there is treason in what I wrote under the conditions described let me be put on trial and tried for it. My own view, but I am no judge, is that intelligent men will feel sorry that Sir John should have been driven by the stress of the battle he has on his hands to resort to so poor a subterfuge.

Toronto, Feb. 17.   E. Farrer[20]

The *Empire*, predictably, also carried Farrer's letter in full, under a shrill headline:

Treason Confessed
Traitor Farrer Unblushingly
Admits His Guilt
Tells a Very Weak Story
A Transparent Effort to Screen His
Masters[21]

Willison, evidently under pressure, replied with a signed editorial detaching the *Globe* both from Farrer's views and from the Liberal party. It said no journal could be expected to control the private opinions of staff members: 'Mr Farrer is a newspaper writer; by unanimous consent, we believe, the ablest writer in the Canadian press. He was engaged by *The Globe* to write for *The Globe*, and his work has been most faithfully and efficiently performed.' And while the *Globe* advocated the cause of the Liberal party, it was not the subsidized organ of that party. 'It is not responsible to the Liberal leaders nor are the Liberal leaders responsible for its opinions ...'[22]

The *Globe* did not share with its readers what was actually *in* the pamphlet, although the *Empire* editors printed a considerable excerpt from the conclusion, so that, they said, the treasonable character might be clearly seen. They must have done so with mixed feelings, though, because in exposing Farrer's treason the excerpt (following a long historical treatment of the fisheries issue) also offered some home truths about Macdonald's patronage system on the east coast:

A word in conclusion about the situation in the maritime provinces. Outside of Halifax, the people as a body are well disposed towards the United States. The fishermen's phrase, that they should like 'to see Gloucester moved east,' in order that they might enjoy higher wages, commends itself to the majority. Sir John Macdonald secures the election of a Tory majority from Nova Scotia only by a system of largesse and corruption carried on without attempt at concealment ... It is felt by all that Sir John's methods of reconciling these provinces to the vast economic loss they sustain from being severed from their natural market in New England, cannot survive the man himself. No one else could employ them with equal skill or success. He is now 75 years old. The fishery question owes its existence not to the people but to the fish merchants and vessel owners. The traders in other lines would be glad to see the widest privileges extended to the Americans, whose custom was once, and might be again, an important factor in the business of the provinces ... *The imposition by the United States of a tonnage tax on all Nova Scotia vessels laden whole or in part with fish would speedily put an end to seizures and indeed to the whole controversy. Another ready way of bringing the government and all concerned to their senses would be to suspend the bonding privilege, or to cut the connection of the Canadian Pacific with United States territory at Sault Ste. Marie.* Either of these methods would rouse the full force of western Canada influence against the Government. *It would be better still to oblige Britain to withdraw her countenance and support from the Canadian contention as she did in 1871.* That would secure the end desired without leaving the United States open to the charge of being animated by hatred of Canada, on which Sir John Macdonald trades. Whatever course the United States may see fit to adopt, *it is plain that Sir John's disappearance from the stage is to be the signal for a movement towards annexation.* The enormous debt of the Dominion ($50 per head), the virtual bankruptcy of all the provinces except Ontario, the pressure of the American tariff upon trade and industry, the incurable issue of race, and the action of the natural forces making for the consolidation of the lesser country with the greater have already prepared the minds of most intelligent Canadians for the destiny that awaits them; and *a leader will be forthcoming when the hour arrives.* (*Empire*'s italics)[23]

Macdonald, on the hustings, enjoyed making sport of this suggestion that his impending death would mean the breakup of the country. At a rally in London, Ontario, for instance, he noted that Farrer had urged the Americans to harass Canada – 'like Rehoboam with scorpions' – and that when he died the country would be ripe for annexation:

'Well, perhaps, to tease Mr Farrer I will live a little longer.' (Cheers)
A voice: 'You'll never die.'[24]

Prominent Liberals, of course, scrambled to detach themselves from the whole affair, stressing that Farrer was in fact a long-time tool of the Tories. Cartwright was quoted in a Kingston speech as saying Farrer's private views on annexation were perfectly well known to Macdonald and his friends long before they selected him to write their campaign sheets in 1882, and afterwards to be editor-in-chief of the *Mail*.[25] In a story sent to the *Standard* in Britain he went ever farther, saying Farrer was only a 'paid contributor' to the *Globe*, and that he had contributed as much to the Conservatives as to the Liberal press.[26] The *Empire* also reported with considerable glee on a speech by Premier Mowat in which he argued, laboriously, that Farrer had learned his annexationism from the Tories and might well reform now that he was among better influences. It was, the *Empire* said, 'a sight for gods and men ... to see the old loyalist, standing on a public platform and apologizing to a Reform gathering because George Brown's paper is edited by an avowed Annexationist. And Mr Mowat did not do it well.' Excerpts from Mowat's speech reported by the *Empire* backed up the suggestion that the 'little premier' – considered to have one of the shrewdest political minds in the country – was not at ease on this occasion. After arguing that Farrer had written the pamphlet before he joined the *Globe*, Mowat expressed annoyance that he was constantly being referred to as the paper's editor, when in fact the real editor was as true a Briton as ever breathed the air of Canada:

Mr Farrer occupies a different position altogether from this editor. He is a contributor to the Globe. He is a very able man. I don't know that there is an abler man, anywhere[,] than Mr Farrer, but Mr Farrer has been most of his life at all events a Tory ... Therefore, how does he happen to be an annexationist? Why, he has learned to be an annexationist in the Tory camp ... I am sorry to say that the evil so clings to him that he appears to be an annexationist yet. I am glad the *Globe* got his services. I was not a party to getting them; I did not like the idea, but he has been of great service on the *Globe* in showing the people the advantage of free trade ... I don't know how long his relations with the *Globe* are to continue such as they are, but this I would say, I have no doubt the editor of the *Globe* will not permit any use of its columns that will be unfavorable to the continuance of what we all desire, and that now that Mr Farrer is no longer with Tory associates, that now he is surrounded by the far better influences of Liberal leaders and liberal politicians, he will learn to abandon this absurd annexationism of his and will become an anti-annexationist, as we all are ...

In a follow-up story the same day the *Empire* ran no fewer than three editorials attacking Farrer in its most brutal language. It even suggested that he deserved hanging – though it did not actually recommend that action:

If in time of public trial any person within the camp gives information to the enemy revealing the weak points of the defence and suggesting means of

Sir Richard — "Neddy, I repudiate you; do you understand? I repudiate you. Now beg."

I REPUDIATE YOU! Toronto *News*, 25 February 1891. Through most of the campaign the *News* ran daily cartoons of Sir Richard Cartwright and his 'little dog Neddy.' At the end of the campaign, though, it saluted Farrer as a formidable rival, saying there was 'no cleverer man in this country than Edward Farrer.'

breaking down the fortifications, he would be strung up without mercy as the cowardly betrayer of his fellows, and who would be so weak as to interpose and save such a wretch from his fate? The stern tribunal of prompt and ready justice is felt by all men at those times to be at once the only effectual protection to the state, and the only righteous punishment for the traitor. Of course, in a case like this, where the contest is not one of arms, no one thinks of such vigorous treatment, but ... does it materially reduce the offence, does it affect the moral aspects in the eyes of right thinking persons, when the enemy is advised not to attack by force of arms, but by those almost as powerful weapons which the necessities of trade and the development of international communications have placed in their hands? ... Or is it not, as we hold, conduct so base and treacherous as to excite wonderment that a man could have been found with conscience so deadened, and moral principles so confused, that a Canadian so black hearted and lost to self-respect should have stooped to do this unworthy thing?

The *Empire* also reprinted – although it must have known it be false – a report by the Halifax *Herald* that Farrer had fled the country to escape arrest. The *Herald* said Farrer's pamphlet must have been prepared and circulated with Cartwright's full knowledge, and added: 'If so, there is only one thing left for him [Cartwright] to do. Mr Farrer, we hear, skipped across the United States line to avoid arrest, when he found that the Government was on his tracks. The best thing for Sir Richard Cartwright to do is to follow him ... This "region behind" has an ugly habit of hanging traitors.'

In ensuing days the *Empire* became, if possible, even more shrill, mainly in condemning the Liberals for not condemning Farrer severely enough. It also carried columns of criticism from other papers – from the London *Times*, for instance, which fastidiously regretted Farrer's treason could not be dealt with by Elizabethan methods, or from *La Minerve*, which brooded over the connections between Farrer's treasonous plotting and his scandalous wars of race and creed ('His Yankee pen furnishes at all times embarrassment and discord, out of which the Liberals expect to see developed a strong feeling of disloyalty and annexation').[27]

The Tory press, meanwhile, indulged in rhetoric that set a highwater mark in the history of campaign billingsgate. The Toronto *World* (whose proprietor, Billy Maclean, was contesting East York for the Tories) said Farrer had been 'caught red-handed in an attempt to overthrow the Canadian government and force Canada into annexation.'[28] Both the Toronto *News* and the Halifax *Herald* offered suspiciously close echoes of the *Empire*'s views on rebels and traitors, the *News* observing that 'to Edward Farrer and the Wimanite leaders belongs the odium of conduct that has no parallel in history.'[29]

The Tory papers also served up for their readers campaign songs like this one (sung, ironically, to the tune of 'Marching through Georgia'):

Come all ye true Conservatives and join the
   patriot throng
We'll teach the Grits a lesson they've been
   wanting now for long
...
Let Sir Richard go to Boston for instruction
   from Mr Blaine
And Farrer down to Washington – their errands
   are in vain
For loyal men we all were born, and loyal will
   remain –
While we scout the crew who whisper
   'Annexation.'[30]

The *Empire*'s first attempt to follow up the pamphlet coup with another exposé – an attempt based once again on the detective work of 'Pica' Kribs – backfired badly. On 19 February, two days after the Academy rally, Kribs wired Macdonald a triumphant message saying he had just received indubitable proof that a pamphlet of Goldwin Smith's, printed at Hunter Rose under sponsorship of Toronto Liberals, had carried printing instructions showing that as early as 4 or 5 February other Grit leaders knew of and had seen Farrer's pamphlet.[31] Next morning the *Empire* again made a sensation, but Smith wrote a furious letter of denial and the *Empire* backed off, grumbling that Smith's rage was the strongest proof of the outrageous character of Farrer's work.[32]

In the face of the *Empire*'s frenzy, Farrer fought back with long and closely reasoned editorials, maintaining that the Tories were appealing to blind patriotic emotion to obscure the real advantages of free trade:

Samuel Johnson described patriotism as the last refuge of the scoundrel. It was a harsh dictum. A French philosopher expresses the same meaning in the smoother phrase that a privileged class always uses the flag as our first parents used the fig leaves ... But the world has been moving of late. The schoolmaster is abroad in the person of hard times. The electors want to know what our Tory rulers can do to rescue this country from its present plight. Have they anything better or half so good to offer as free trade with the American nation? The question is not whether a *Globe* writer wrote a private pamphlet, or thinks this, that or the other thing; but how the farmer is to save the vanishing equity in his land and by what means he is to escape from the grasp of the combines on the one side of the line and of the McKinley tariff on the other. The people are not going to fill their bellies with the east wind of a loyalty which is only a fine name for injustice and fraud.33

If the pamphlet had been the only evidence against Farrer, he might have been able to convince his readers that it did not signify all that much – that it was simply the personal view of an editorial writer. But on the morning of 24 February, a week after the Academy rally, the *Empire* hammered in the second nail, with documentary proof that Farrer was not just expressing an opinion but had actually been working with American leaders to promote annexation. The proof was in the revelation of Farrer's 'two bites on the cherry' letter to Wiman that William McDougall (in promise of a senatorship) had passed to Sir Charles Tupper, along with a letter to Wiman from Congressman Hitt. Tupper had unveiled the two letters at a rally in the Windsor Opera House the night before, in what clearly was a pre-set plan to reinforce Sir John's pamphlet attack.

The *Empire*, mindful of the trouble it had suffered a year earlier in the libel trials, brought out its biggest type for the disclosure and put special stress on Farrer's own statement linking the Jesuits' Estates campaign with the promotion of annexation. It printed the two letters on its front page not once but twice – once in ordinary type and again in large type, spread over three columns and sprinkled with crucial sections in capital letters. It was headed:

PEOPLE OF CANADA READ THIS!
Toronto, April 22nd, 1889

My Dear Wiman:
  Our Ottawa man will send a good summary of your speech, so that on our

account you need not go to the trouble of preparation. At present the C.U. movement is at a standstill. First of all, the Jesuit agitation, which is here to stay, has to some extent supplanted it. Secondly, the general belief is that the Republicans would not listen to any such scheme. Thirdly, a very large number of people are inclined to think that we had better MAKE FOR ANNEXATION AT ONCE, INSTEAD OF MAKING TWO BITES ON THE CHERRY. Lastly, the old parties here are rapidly breaking up, and WHEN SIR JOHN GOES we shall be adrift without a port in sight, SAVE ANNEXATION. Moreover, although the Liberals have taken up C.U. they are not pushing it with any vigor. For these reasons the 'Mail' has, in the slang of the day, given the subject a rest. There is really no use talking it up to a people whose politics are in a state of flux, and whose future is wrapped in doubt. I saw Mr Hoar, while at Washington, and told him just what he says I did, namely, that THE SMALLER FORCES FAVOR ANNEXATION AND WILL FAVOR IT ALL THE MORE IF C.U. BE WITHHELD. It seems to me, and I have talked the thing over lately with Maritime members as well as with Manitobans, that C.U. would only delay the coming of the event those people most desire. Hence, in the provinces referred to, C.U. does not take hold, while annexation will always demand a hearing. In Ontario, the Jesuit campaign has brought that aspect of things home to thousands who would not look at C.U. The littleness and half-heartedness of the Liberals is also very disheartening. Then again, THE TRUTH IS THAT EVERY MAN WHO PREACHES C.U. WOULD PREFER ANNEXATION. SO THAT THE PARTY IS VIRTUALLY WEARING A MASK. Can't you come round this way and have a talk?

Yours very truly,
Signed, E. Farrer.

The accompanying letter from Hitt to Wiman made clear that Hitt assumed Wiman, too, was a secret annexationist, and said he was surprised that Farrer had given up on commercial union as a stage in that effort, since Republicans were in fact supporting it:

THERE IS SOME LOGIC IN WHAT F. SAYS OF NOT MAKING TWO BITES OF A CHERRY, BUT GOING FOR ANNEXATION AT ONCE, but I think he is misled ... WE MUST BE VERY PATIENT WITH THE SLOW-MOVING POPULAR MIND. If the Canadian public of farmers, artisans, lumbermen, miners and fishermen can be in three years ARGUED UP TO THE POINT OF VOTING COMMERCIAL UNION and giving sanction to the movement in Parliament, IT WILL BE GREAT PROGRESS ... (*Empire*'s emphasis)

The *Empire* said Tupper's astonishing disclosure of these two letters completed the chain of evidence against the miscreant. It showed why Farrer had used all his influence to keep alive the Jesuit controversy, so that annexation should be forced on. It showed how Farrer had worked in Washington to rouse hostility against Canada and hasten unfriendly legislation. 'We find there, in short, a cynical confession of the most unprincipled rascality that a responsible individual has ever had the brazen impudence to avow.'[34]

The *Globe*, under increasing pressure, also condemned Farrer's letter, while continuing to insist it had no relationship to the paper. 'In Mr Farrer we have the best writer on the Canadian press, and he has done his work to the *Globe*'s satisfaction. With his private views or with the letters he may have written two years ago we have nothing to do. The *Globe* has been thoroughly loyal; the *Globe* has not engaged in any movement for the promotion of treason ... It does not hesitate to condemn the sentiments expressed in Mr Farrer's correspondence ...'[35]

Throughout the rest of the campaign the *Empire* continued to taunt the Grits with Farrer's words, especially the statements that the party was wearing a mask and that every advocate of commercial union was actually an annexationist. Other journals, however, were disposed to doubt the complicity of the Liberal leaders. *Grip*, for instance, found the whole issue overblown. And the *Week*, a ponderously independent sheet, was ponderously content with the 'explicit and unequivocal' disavowals of Laurier and Cartwright and the other Liberal leaders. It was also especially pleased that Goldwin Smith, a man whose 'personal courage and manliness' it much admired, had been cleared. And since there was no evidence of complicity, the *Week* thought it hardly dignified for the prime minister to spend so much time proving the personal disloyalty of a mere journalistic writer, even one whose consummate baseness had been so clearly shown. The whole issue also prompted the *Week* to reflect on the question of freedom of speech, and it seemed to find Farrer's actions preciously close to the line of toleration: 'One shudders at the thought of the awful consequences to which the machinations of one clever but unprincipled writer, were his influence on a par with his literary ability, might conceivably lead ...'[36]

If the *Week* seemed somewhat carried away by the rhetoric of loyalty, it was not alone. Throughout the Dominion there was a rush to

EXALTING FARRER INTO AN ISSUE. *Grip*, 7 March 1891. As the 1891 election campaign reached its climax, *Grip* concluded, with justice, that Sir John had vastly overblown the Farrer issue.

join the crusade, especially by the Establishment – by the CPR and other corporations, and by church leaders. 'It is a rather significant fact,' wrote the *Mail*'s Montreal correspondent, 'that few attempts are made in any of the public meetings here to deal with the great question at issue on its merits. Amidst the cries of "Treason!" "Rebels!" and "Traitors!," the fulminations of the Church and the interested workings of the combines, the real question of whether it would be beneficial to have unrestricted reciprocity or not seems to be utterly lost sight of.'[37]

This fever of reaction had its effect. With only a few days left before the 5 March vote, Ned Sheppard noted with satisfaction that the mood of the campaign had been transformed, that 'Sir John's supporters are stiffening up all along the line,' and that there seemed to be no doubt they would carry the country. Sheppard also noticed the fulminations of the church, but was not impressed. The Quebec Catholic hierarchy, he said, seemed to have espoused Sir John's cause at the last moment, while in Toronto a Protestant clergyman had suggested that traitorous Grits should be immured in a dungeon cell. Parsons, Sheppard observed tartly, should confine themselves to topics they understood.[38]

Despite the surge of loyalty, though, the actual vote-counting showed Sir John's edge to be far from impressive. In Ontario it was especially thin: 183,326 votes to 182,141 for the Grits, or an edge in popular vote percentage of only 49.4 to 49.1. Nationally, the Conservatives had 52 per cent of the popular vote and 122 seats, compared with 46.4 per cent and 91 seats for the Liberals.[39]

In the aftermath both sides reflected on the damage done by Farrer's pamphlet. A New Brunswick journalist-MP, J.V. Ellis, wrote to Laurier that the loyalty cry had been the main factor in defeat. 'It really surprised me in the end we had any votes left.'[40] Joseph Pope, who travelled during the campaign with Sir John A., observed later that the extent of damage was difficult to determine, in view of the 'undoubted loyalty' of such Liberals as Laurier and Mowat. 'Farrer's declaration, however, that Sir John Macdonald's disappearance from the stage would be the signal for a movement in Canada towards annexation, proved, in what was generally recognized as Macdonald's last fight, of immense assistance to the old chief.'[41] Macdonald himself, in a slightly cynical tone, wrote George Stephen that 'the movements of Cartwright, Farrer & Wiman enabled us to raise the loyalty cry, which had considerable effect.' But he added that the defection of farm voters, and large sums undoubtedly sent from the United States, had left a diminished majority and an uncertain future.[42]

An uncertain future indeed. Macdonald at that point was in fact less than two months away from the stroke that would end his life. Edward Farrer would continue to write for another quarter-century, but his future was also very much in doubt.

The pamphlet debacle left several curious footnotes, aside from the major question raised by George Ham on whether Farrer was shielding someone else when he took responsibility for it. One was that the two key informants who brought on the exposures failed to profit by their acts.

The printer, Christopher Clark, did in fact get a government job as promised, but lost it and complained about ill-usage. One account says he lost the job because of malfeasance, having been found (by none other than Major Sherwood) to have stolen a batch of government correspondence.[43] Ironically, those to whom Clark complained included both Laurier and Goldwin Smith. In 1895, Clark wrote Laurier offering to prepare campaign literature on the whole history of the Farrer intrigue – 'the correspondence and interview with ministers, and the lying promises that were made by the government.' The exposure, he said, would 'show the Canadian public how they were duped in 1891, myself amongst others, Sir John Macdonald having stated to me that it was his ability to identify the Liberal party with an Annexation movement which carried the election for him.'[44]

William McDougall, meanwhile, failed to receive the Senate sinecure promised for delivery of the two letters to Wiman. The circumstances of that promise were spelled out by Sir Charles Tupper in an 1892 letter to Macdonald's successor, Sir John Abbott:

I have been awaiting the reconstruction of the Cabinet to bring before you a pledge that I gave to the Hon. W. McDougall with the authority of the late Premier that he should be made Senator.

When Sir J. A. Macdonald and I were both apprehensive of the result of the general election we decided that it was very important that the attack he made on Farrer and his associates should be *backed up and confirmed* by the papers that Mr. McDougall had confidentially placed in my hands. Sir John then authorized me to assure Mr. McDougall that he would shortly be made a Senator and I gave him Sir John's assurance to that effect. Mr. McDougall is one of the fathers of confederation & did all he could, in the face of great difficulty, to support us at a most important crisis, the last general election. I sincerely hope you will take an early opportunity of redressing the pledge given to him. (italics added)45

At least two historians have inferred that this letter meant McDougall supplied the pamphlet to Tupper.46 The indications, though, especially in Denison's detailed account, point to the 'two bites' letter as the item for which a Senate seat was promised. That interpretation is backed by Tupper's comment that McDougall's contribution 'backed up and confirmed' the charges against Farrer. It is also supported by two letters in Tupper's papers, one from Wiman to McDougall and the other from McDougall to Tupper. On 25 April 1889, three days after the 'two bites' letter was written, Wiman promised to bring McDougall 'an important letter from Farrer.' On 11 May McDougall promised to let Tupper 'peruse confidential [sic] some correspondence in my hands re the movement for closer trade relations with the U.S.' – information that would 'supply you with more reliable data on the nature and force of the movement than the newspapers, or even the British Embassy at Washington.'47

This version of events was also backed, less reliably, by a report in 1894 from the Canadian agent in the annexation movement at New York. The agent said that Wiman, who had just been charged with forgery, fraud, and embezzlement, had been ruined by certain powerful business interests backing annexation: 'What decided their action against Wiman I understand was that some years ago when Farrer was editor of the "Globe" he had some confidential correspondence with Congressman R.R. Hitt [sic] ... Two of these letters came into Wiman's hands and were given by him to an uncle [sic] named McDougal [sic] ... who gave them in turn to Sir Charles Tupper.' Later the agent spoke to Wiman himself about the letters and said Wiman claimed to have lost them – 'and that somebody found them and conveyed them to Sir Charles Tupper'.48 Tupper biographer E.M. Saunders also indicates McDougall supplied the Wiman letters, although the reference has the direction backwards, describing them as Wiman letters *to* Farrer and Hitt.49

The exact details of these intrigues are probably not important – except, perhaps, in suggesting the complexity of the web of relationships that surrounded Farrer. It is not surprising that John Willison later despaired of ever untangling them.

11 A Wicked and Ungovernable Force

The election campaign left the Grits not only bleeding but also badly divided. There were in fact two camps in the party: the continentalists led by Cartwright and the loyalists led by Mowat, with Edward Blake a sporadic ally. Laurier was whipsawed between the two factions, scarcely able to pick up a newspaper without reading about the division or about the party's folly in allowing its chief organ to be edited by an annexationist. During the campaign the young leader had, with Willison's help, been able to keep Blake in check, but immediately afterwards came release of the former leader's famous letter to West Durham electors, warning that flirtation with the Americans could only lead to rape or wedlock. That made it more difficult to argue that unrestricted reciprocity would actually *protect* against political union. It opened a gap between those who were, and those who were not, alarmed about that ultimate destiny. The true loyalists, led by Denison and Mowat, saw the *Globe* as the heart of the radical camp. Mowat gradually came to the view that Farrer had made 'lively annexationists' of the whole *Globe* staff and directorate, and that Cartwright, too, had sold out to the Americans. Denison saw Cartwright and Farrer directing the paper, in alliance with Wiman, with a clear aim of annexation.

In fact, the continentalist camp was never as united as its enemies feared, though it managed for a time to make a show of significance. As a flurry of annexation meetings broke out in western Ontario, Willison and Cartwright were already getting ready to move back out of the line of fire, and Wiman, suffering business reverses, was scouting an alliance with the Tories. Farrer was left exposed, although he continued throughout 1891 to mount a subtle annexation campaign.

A Wicked and Ungovernable Force 205

That work, combined with the annexation meetings, was enough to alarm the Toronto imperialist community, which brought pressure on Mowat to do something about it.

The loyalist view of events was set out in detail in a report by Colonel Denison to Lord Salisbury, covering the 'momentous events' of the autumn of 1891. There had been a lull after the election, Denison reported, 'but when the fall set in the movement for open annexation commenced, as I anticipated.' There had been meetings in Essex, 'our most disloyal county,' and in Oxford, a close second. Mowat had finally taken alarm and had written letters condemning the movement – letters which created a sensation not so much on account of the expressions of loyalty as on account of the dumb silence of the *Globe*, which was directly under the control of Cartwright and Farrer. 'This proves,' Denison concluded, 'that the Globe is more anxious to stir up a spirit of annexation in Canada than to see Reciprocity carried out or even the Liberal Party immediately in power if pledged to loyalty to the British connection.' Denison said he had had several long conversations with Mowat, who was clearly anxious about the party's Cartwright wing. 'He has done however a grand service to Canada and the influence of his letters has been excellent ...'¹

Denison's concern over the *Globe* had some basis, for Farrer again, as at the *Mail*, was busily praising annexation while pretending to bury it. In September, for instance, he observed that the Tory government had no solution to the country's economic problems; then added: 'The Liberals propose absolute free trade with the States, *whilst a third set of men, becoming more numerous every day, believe that political union with the Americans affords the only practicable solution.* At the approaching by-elections the whole case must be laid before the people. They were not allowed to pass upon the Confederation measure when it came from the anvil. But the politicians must needs consult them now that hopes and prayers have come to nought, and we find ourselves in the fearful plight of a young community stricken with decay' (italics added). The same kind of two-edged message showed up in a November editorial: 'The Globe is wholly opposed to the annexation movement which is *bursting forth* in Ontario and Quebec,' the paper said. 'But all who agree with us that British Connection should be maintained at any cost must allow that *the present economic conditions are well calculated to breed political unrest ...'* (italics added).

Mowat, a much cleverer man than Denison, had no trouble deciphering the message. The premier publicly criticized the paper for annexationist leanings, and the *Globe* in December took the radical (and dangerous) step of challenging him directly. The long article, a fine example of Farrer's craft, seemed on the face of it to be mainly a reflective discussion on the value of the British connection. On a subtler level it clearly undermined the imperial tie and promoted continental union. In its early stages the article brushed aside, without quite denying, Mowat's charge that some articles in the paper had appeared to advocate political union. It then discussed drawbacks of the British connection and built to a climax in a way that suggested the logic of political union:

Lastly, we are inclined to believe that Mr Mowat underestimates the number of political unionists in this and other Provinces, and is mistaken in supposing that the movement is caused by the temporary depression in trade. A long line of politicians from 1841 to the present have spent their time in predicting wonderful things for the country. The panorama of our future greatness and grandeur has been unfolded on every stage – in Parliament, in the churches, on the stump, in the school-house; but ... men are asking when the beatific vision is to be realized ... *It is the fear of public opinion that keeps many who are annexationists at heart from saying so on the street.* Yet the number who openly avow that they have lost confidence in the status quo is large and getting larger ...

Where the *Globe* differs from Mr Mowat is in his conception of the fundamental duty of this colony. He seems to think that where measures are laid before us affecting the welfare of Canada we are bound to ask whether they are likely to make for British connection or not and to be governed accordingly ... Of late years we in Canada have invariably acted upon the understanding that Canadian interests are supreme in this community ... while sentiment is a potent force, it would be no match for the storm that would sweep over this country if its well-being were sacrificed to the venerable superstition that we exist to serve others rather than to serve ourselves. We know not what our ultimate political destiny is to be. That is a problem in the 'dark forward and abysm of time.' But this much may safely be predicted, that to whatever goal we may be tending it is only by being true to Canada and by being loyal to her above all other lands that we can walk surefootedly and without fear. (italics added)[2]

This editorial perhaps marked a peak both in Farrer's career and

A Wicked and Ungovernable Force 207

in the *Globe*'s efforts to establish itself as a distinctive and independent liberal (and continentalist) voice. Oliver Mowat recognized the challenge and met it head-on, more effectively than Macdonald had coped with the rebelliousness of the *Mail* five years earlier. The premier wrote Laurier a pair of crisp letters, warning of the machinations of the *Globe* and Farrer and setting out the federal leader's path of duty:

Toronto, 26th December, 1891

My dear Mr Laurier,

The Globe is creating an annexation party out of members of the Reform party ... I find that at meetings in the rural parts, in even my own constituency, the Globe is being cited to old Reformers as going for annexation, and that this is bearing fruit amongst them. I presume you disapprove of this and might do something to prevent further harm in that direction. I shall be glad to join in any practical movement having that object. If nothing can be done, an open division of the party is inevitable, and its consequent destruction. Whether a strong annexation party can be created from its ruins I do not know, but I should hope not.

Five days later, on New Year's Eve, Mowat pinned the blame directly on Farrer:

My dear Mr Laurier

I have your letter of the 26th. One thing to be done if you can see your way to it would be a very distinct declaration, so clear and emphatic that there could be no cavil as to its meaning, against political union as a price too great to pay for unrestricted reciprocity. In the absence of such a declaration, the *Globe* and some minor journals which have followed it would make the United States believe we would go for political union if we could not otherwise get unrestricted reciprocity and in that event the United States would of course refuse reciprocity on any other terms.

Farrer seems to have made lively annexationists of the whole *Globe* staff and directorate, and the amount of harm done, – harm from my standpoint – is much greater than I was aware of ... Such a declaration from you as I have mentioned would be of service, but would not alone undo the past, or prevent future propagandism against our nationality. I make no further suggestion however until I hear from Sir Richard, and know exactly where we stand ... I have this morning read in the *Globe* a sketch of his Almonte speech yesterday, in which he says a good deal about loyalty, but I should gather from it that he is contemplating and desiring political union. If that is to be the policy of the Dominion Liberal party I cease to be a member of it.³

Mowat had clearly thrown off the confusion that beset him ten months earlier when he had tried to cope with the pamphlet revelations by offering plaintive hopes that Farrer might be cured of annexationism by associating with Liberals. But whether the *Globe* actually had become the nest of annexationists the premier saw in his nightmares is still an open question. Cartwright was never shown to be an annexationist. The Almonte statement that so alarmed Mowat was (as the *Globe* reported it) simply a plea to the audience to support reciprocity and thereby 'undo the evil of 100 years ago and aid in bringing together the two severed parts of the British race.'⁴ The *Globe* itself, despite Denison's more or less constant alarums, never came close to open advocacy of annexation. Hints did emerge, however, that both Willison and President Robert Jaffray had developed more sympathy for the movement than they later cared to admit. In 1889 Jaffray had been quoted as saying in a speech at St Paul that it would be greatly to Canada's benefit to be annexed to the United States. He had said (according to the *Empire*) that 'thinking men' were all siding with the commercial union movement and that 'I quite agree with Professor Goldwin Smith who says that this is the first step towards political union.'⁵ Walter Gregory later wrote that Jaffray had repudiated this statement when he came back to Canada, but that Willison had told him there was no doubt whatsoever it was correct. Jaffray was 'in full sympathy' with the movement, Gregory said, and even Willison had sometimes observed that every four out of six or seven Liberals were supporters of political union. 'Willison and I used to discuss the matter [of political union] a good deal and I remember telling him that I felt "in my bones" that it was right and must some day prevail. Willison, I think, thought much the same as I did.'⁶

Gregory, writing forty years after the fact, may not be the best witness. But undoubtedly the continental idea had gained currency among Liberals. 'The sentiment in favor of political union with the United States has made great progress beyond all question,' John Charlton wrote in his diary year-end review for 1891. 'Politicians and newspaper editors fear to pronounce publicly for it, but great numbers secretly favor the movement.'⁷ As for Laurier himself, he does not seem to have shared Mowat's concern over the annexationists, but his position was ambiguous. In the wake of the election it would have been natural if he had moved to excommunicate Farrer, but in fact he apparently remained at least privately cordial. A few weeks after the election when Farrer went to Montreal to meet with Laurier, he seems to have been *briefing* the leader, rather than hearing a lecture. ('I have no doubt,' Willison wrote to Laurier, 'that through your talk with my associate you are in pretty full possession of our views as to policy and the political situation.')[8] There were later indications as well that Laurier's relations with Farrer remained cordial, although Cartwright may have grown exasperated with him. Other tensions, besides annexation, complicated relations between party and paper. During the summer of 1891, after Macdonald's death, the continuing McGreevy scandal had exposed massive boodling in the party he left behind. The scandals also touched some of Laurier's Quebec allies, however, and the *Globe* refused to soft-pedal these sensitive areas, to the annoyance of Cartwright. *Grip* approvingly cartooned Farrer as opposed to the party, in a way that recalled his mutiny against Macdonald five years earlier.[9] Late in the year Cartwright wrote Laurier implying that he was having difficulty controlling the *Globe*, and adding what may have been a hint of Farrer's intransigence. He warned that a *Globe* campaign against Quebec might be in the offing, and added: '... knowing how sensitive your Quebec followers are to any attacks from the Globe I am uneasy lest some foolish editorial may come out before I can stop it as you know has happened more than once – The truth is, I fear, that there are occult and dangerous influences at work from a quarter you can guess at and as I have already mentioned the entire surroundings at Toronto are unfavorable to a calm consideration of this difficult question.'[10]

Despite his anomalous position in the party, Farrer went on another visit to Washington in the fall. His reports to Laurier indicate that the continental idea was by no means dead among Liberals, despite discouraging by-election results, and that he himself still had both standing in the party and good contacts in Washington. At that point Macdonald's successor, Sir John Abbott, was still pursuing the Tory aim of limited reciprocity, and Farrer's efforts were directed at undermining the attempt while maintaining the American leaning towards the Liberals. Strangely, in view of Blaine's earlier emphasis on secrecy, Farrer obtained assurances that Abbott's emissaries would be required to make their basic proposals public, so that the Liberals

STICKING TO MERCIER. Rouge Partizans – 'Cartwright, if you don't call off that dog and muzzle him at once, we'll – we'll – do something terrible!!' *Grip*, 29 August 1891. The McGreevy scandal hurt mainly Conservatives, but the fallout also caught the Quebec Liberal-nationalist premier, Honoré Mercier, and Laurier lieutenant Ernest Pacaud. *Grip* was pleased that Farrer and the *Globe* did not refrain from attacking corruption among their own party allies, despite pressure on Cartwright to curb the paper. (The count's hat and cross reminded readers that Mercier had recently been honoured by the Vatican.)

could snipe at them. Farrer reported that he had received this assurance from J.W. Foster, acting in Blaine's absence, and went on:

I undertook to tell him that you were going to make an important speech at Boston on Nov. 17 – I gathered this from a letter of yours which Mr Edgar showed me – & that they ought not to meet the Ottawa men until you had spoken. He promised to tell the President & I am to see him tomorrow (Monday). Mr Blaine arrived last night and I communicated the same thing to him today. I shall see him on Tuesday.

Mr Foster as much as said that much would depend on what line you took at Boston. You are of course aware that the men here are disposed to think that the Liberals have not gone quite far enough – that they have not differentiated their position with sufficient clearness and boldness ... I ventured to tell Mr Foster that you would, at Boston, clear up everything. They are particularly anxious that Liberals should show that they are not afraid of discriminating against Britain, and that they take no stock in imperial federation but believe that their future lies on this continent. I said you would no doubt say something on that point, that I thought I knew your views and that you certainly had no fear of speaking out on the discrimination matter, still less on imperial federation. Of course I had no authority from you, but it was important that they should be assured, and I hope you will not think I went too far.

There are other matters about which I shall write you on my return to Toronto ... I am writing this on a railroad train & it is not very legible or coherent ...[11]

In a follow-up letter a few days later Farrer stressed again the need for a 'clear statement' differentiating the Liberals from the Tories on the discrimination question. 'Such a statement is deemed necessary to silence those who urge that the Liberals differ in no way from the Tories. It is not asked by anyone that you would go out of your way or injure yourself or the cause in the slightest; but simply that a clear, straightforward definition of Liberal aims should be made ...'[12]

Cartwright and Goldwin Smith were pressing the same line on Laurier, and the Liberal leader complied to some extent in Boston, while failing to go far enough to satisfy the continentalist group. Smith apparently reacted by urging his American friends to take a tough line. In the spring of 1892, when the much-delayed trade talks with Blaine finally began, Laurier advised Charlton that Smith was in Washington telling the Americans to insist that reciprocity could be had only on the basis of political union. Laurier asked Charlton to go to Washington to counteract Smith's effort. But again the Liberals seemed willing to ingratiate themselves with the Americans by pretending sympathy to *eventual* union. After a 16 March meeting with Laurier, Charlton recorded in his diary the substance of their discussion, aimed at finding ways to prevent the Americans from insisting that free trade should be conditional on political union. 'Reciprocity is what we want, the declaration for Political Union would fire the tory heart, and solidify prejudices,' Charlton wrote. 'We want free commercial intercourse, Commercial Union in fact, and the Political Union question may be left to take care of itself.'[13] In diary entries after he met several Washington politicians Charlton reinforced the impression that he had been making sympathetic sounds about eventual political union. 'I urged more intimate commercial and social relations as the true pathway to Political Union if it were ever reached,' he wrote, 'and said that the only Canadian political party having affinity for the American system was the Liberal party.'[14] This effort may by this point have become somewhat academic, though. Blaine and other Republicans were again stressing that Canadians would taste the benefits of the American market only if they came all the way into political union.[15]

By the spring of 1892 several other issues were irritating U.S.-Canadian relations, and these, together with the pressure from Blake and Mowat, combined to discourage both Laurier and the *Globe* in their continentalist leanings. By that point, too, Laurier, was coming under renewed pressure over the *Globe*'s performance. He was embarrassed, for instance, by a carefully worded attack in the Commons on 7 April from the finance minister, George Foster. 'I make the assertion here tonight,' Foster had said, 'that an unprejudiced person may read through the columns of the Toronto Globe for the last three years, and he will find, in almost every edition, argument, insinuation, open assertion and appeal, all with the purpose of undermining the feeling of this country in favour [of] British connection. And the Globe has to-day for its brains and its inspiration, Farrer, the self confessed traitor, and Sir Richard Cartwright, the financial leader of the Opposition in Parliament ...' Laurier found this charge impossible to refute, and so confined himself to setting up and demolishing a straw man, by insisting that he himself was not an annexationist. In a wry turn Laurier also managed to remind the Commons that Prime Minister Abbott had once been an annexationist, having signed the manifesto of 1849. 'At one time, when I saw that Mr Farrer was an annexationist, I thought of writing to the Globe, requesting his removal from the office; but it occurred to me that perhaps he was destined to become the Premier of Canada and the leader of the Conservative party ...'[16]

While brushing aside this charge, Laurier was undoubtedly stung by yet another *Grip* cartoon showing the *Globe* in conflict with the party on the schools and language issues. (Farrer was again shown as an organ-grinder's monkey, as he had been in the 1886 cartoon about the *Mail*'s rebellion against Macdonald; this time the organ-grinder was Willison.) Within the *Globe* meanwhile Farrer's reputation for mischief had been furthered by another *Grip* cartoon showing him as a fighting cock besting his own president, Jaffray, on a matter of local politics.[17]

Any Liberal hopes that Farrer would lose his notoriety as the pamphlet episode faded were thus disappearing. Across the country journalists watched his work with fascination. The major article on Canadian journalists in the *New England Magazine* in December not only had placed him first among the country's journalists but had made much of his role in promoting fusion of the two countries.[18] Such comment helped to provoke the loyalists to action, and by spring pressure on the *Globe* was building up. The paper carried fewer of Farrer's insinuations, and fewer of his powerful arguments on why a radical solution to the country's problems was necessary. It seemed, in fact, to be ready to give the continental topic a rest. An editorial of 18 March, commenting on annexation meetings at Woodstock and Paris, insisted that Canada's task was to get its own house in order, not to worry about political union. In the 1891 election many people had been frightened by the annexation cry into forgetting that the protected manufacturer had his hand in their pocket: 'The most ardent advocate of political union with the United States would probably agree that it would be a melancholy fate for Canada, out of mere helplessness, to drift into that union upon any terms that the United States might impose. Strength, self-reliance and the ability of this country to meet its own obligations would be the necessary conditions of an honorable union.'[19]

The *Globe* seemed to be taking the curve, and the Toronto newspaper community assumed it was because Farrer – or the party's continentalist faction – had lost an internal struggle. They also assumed that Sir Oliver Mowat, recently knighted in recognition of his

DISCORD IN THE PAIRTY. Laurier – 'Stop! Stop! This tune will get us into no end of trouble with the French vote!' Willison – 'Very probably. But, most respected Sir, don't forget to remember that this is not your organ!' *Grip*, 9 April 1892. Before his departure from the *Globe* Farrer was repeatedly cartooned by John Bengough as challenging the paper's Liberal masters. In this instance, with less justice, John Willison was also portrayed as a rebel. (Ironically, the image of mischievous monkey was the same one that Bengough had given Farrer six years earlier as he rebelled against the *Mail*'s Tory masters.)

A Wicked and Ungovernable Force 215

loyalty campaign, was somewhere not far in the background when the following short notice appeared in the *Globe* on 27 July 1892:

We are sorry to have to announce that Mr Farrer, who for the past two years has been the principal editorial writer of the *Globe*, has decided to retire from active journalism for a time and will sever his connection with the *Globe* on August 1st. The *Globe* has found Mr Farrer to be a man of unusual ability and of the strictest integrity, a master of his profession, conducting public discussions upon a high level, and scrupulously avoiding the meaner and coarser habits of political controversy, and the *Globe* parts from him with regret.[20]

This announcement set off a flurry of rumour and speculation, much like that raised by Farrer's arrival at the *Globe* two years earlier. 'All day long the clubs, the streets, the counting houses, and even the shops, have canvassed the possibilities of Mr Farrer's future,' said the *News*. It observed that the *Globe* announcement was a nice tribute to Farrer, 'but nobody in the world believes there is not something else behind it.'[21] The *World* agreed, saying Farrer had made himself too important a personality in the Canadian political world to let his comings and goings be unheralded or unnoted. 'His connection with The Globe has actually become embodied in the warp and woof of our politics, and therefore when it was announced that he was no longer chief leader writer of the Liberal organ the quidnuncs cried with one accord, Why is this thus!'[22]

Both the *News* and the *World* gave the resignation front-page treatment, the *News* awarding it six headline banks:

NED FARRER OUT.

The Globe and Its Chief Writer
Part Company.

The Organ Pays a Neat Tribute to
the Dear Departed,

And he Says Sir Oliver
Mowat Forced Him Out.

A Sensation To-day in Local
Journalistic Circles.

> What the Globe Has to Say and
> What Farrer Has to Say – He Re-
> signed a $5,000-a-year Position.

In fact, Farrer did not, even by the testimony of the *News* (below its headline), say directly that Mowat had forced him out. Most papers, however, treated the point as almost self-evident. 'We do not say that Sir Oliver came down to The Globe office, thumped the counter and told the directors to bounce Mr Farrer,' said the *World*. 'But all the same the directors agreed to accept Mr Farrer's resignation and they did it in order to remove the anomaly of Mr Farrer's professed and declared annexation principles and Sir Oliver's avowed and declared anti-annexation position.' The *Telegram* thought that Mowat 'has done a kind turn by relieving a great journal of a burden too heavy for it to carry.'[23] Some papers linked Farrer's exit with Mowat's dismissal of another prominent annexationist, Elgin Myers, as Crown attorney of Dufferin County and thought it meant, in the words of the Halifax *Herald*, 'the return of the grit party to a broad Canadian platform.'[24] Mowat's role, though, was only one element in the rich variety of rumour sniffed out by reporters of the *News* and the *World*. Among other things, they reported speculation:

– That Farrer would become 'head' of the New York *Tribune*.

– That a company had been established to set up a new annexationist daily. The *World* said only that it could not confirm this, but the *News* offered some shadowy details – that the capital stock had been set at $100,000 and that a number of prominent local politicians were said to be subscribers.

– That Christopher Bunting would resign from the *Mail* to allow a consolidation of the *Mail* and the *Empire* into a Conservative organ. (This perennial rumour was still two and a half years away from reality, and when the merger finally happened, Bunting was the victor rather than the victim.)

– That the *World* and the *Empire* would be merged. (The *World* commented that the reporter who came up with this angle had been 'withdrawn from the local staff and put on the romance department.')

– That (most amazing of all) David Creighton was 'looking all over town for Mr Farrer to offer him a job on The Empire.' Only the *World* reported this one, the *News* perhaps deciding that credibility had limits.

Both the *News* and the *World* interviewed Farrer, the *News* reporter arriving first and, according to Farrer's comments in the later interview, constructing his story more from his own questions than from Farrer's answers. Said the *News*:

Mr Farrer admitted a reporter to his study in his home on Grenville street this morning. He was in characteristically good spirits, apparently undisturbed by the circumstances which had led to the announcement in the Globe and untroubled by the heat, which he met in his shirtsleeves and with open waistcoat. He talked freely of his resignation.

'You know,' said he, 'Sir Oliver Mowat is riding the loyalty horse and I'm not. He has been worried about me ever since the morning after Sir John Macdonald's meeting at the Academy when I published that letter in which I avowed myself an annexationist. They tell me that I have haunted him ever since that. I don't blame him for his principles. He seems to be conscientious enough in his loyalty.

'But he was badgered so much about it, he had to go through so much with Elgin Myers and those [political unionist] fellows, that he began to urge the directors of the Globe to get rid of me. He saw annexation in everything I wrote, but everybody knows that you can't touch the trade question from that stand-point without seeming to advocate annexation. Sir Oliver himself couldn't do it.

'Well, he has stock in the paper, of course, but his position counts for more than the stock. The directors always listened to him, but he never got any satisfaction from them. Jaffray, [Joseph] Tait, and the rest of them stuck to me nobly. I owe Mr Willison also a debt of gratitude for his stand. About six weeks ago the directors and Sir Oliver had a battle royal, and they finally refused to get rid of me.

'As a matter of fact they couldn't have done it unless I had wanted. Under my agreement they had to keep me. But the news of that battle came to my ears, and after some consideration I decided that it was not fair to the directors who had defended me so stoutly that my presence in the editorial staff should embarrass them in their relations to the only man who has anything in the shape of patronage to give. So I handed in my resignation. They objected at first, but I made it imperative and they finally accepted it.

'Now, don't misunderstand me. I have no grievance against anybody ... I don't want to abuse Sir Oliver either. He is entitled to his convictions.'

So far Mr Farrer had talked without prompting. A hint as to the future set him off again.

'The "traitors" are underneath now,' he said. 'I am a free man again and may be able to give them a hand. I shall write a little for the American magazines and other magazines. I have no definite plan ...'

This interview by the *News* – like its earlier profile of Farrer – left a number of questions in conflict or confusion. For one thing, the *News* reported, without attribution, that Farrer had just signed a new contract with the *Globe*, 'for three years from this past 1st of July at $4,800 a year.' This conflicted directly with a later statement from Willison, who said: 'He had a two-years' agreement, and at its termination his resignation was accepted.'25 The question of Mowat's formal relationship with the *Globe* also remained in doubt, the newspaper later denying that the premier owned any of its stock. It was also notable that Farrer, in his later interview with the *World*, criticized the *News* account and avoided any mention of a 'battle royal,' or of direct attempts by Mowat to oust him. In other ways, though, the *World*'s quotes from Farrer were consistent with the earlier story, focusing on the discrepancy between Mowat's views and his own, and saying he had wanted more than once to resign, but had been dissuaded from doing so. 'Mr Farrer was very frank, as cheerful and entertaining as usual and had nothing but kindly feelings towards all men,' the *World* concluded. 'Indeed, the sense of relief from responsibility was quite apparent in his blithesome talk.'

While most of the press comment followed this kindly tone, *Saturday Night* was harsh, in a column signed not by Ned Sheppard's pen-name ('Don') but by that of his assistant, Joseph T. Clark ('Mack'):

... the history of this clever editorial writer's connection with the Liberal organ has been so dramatic, his views so offensive and his personality so aggressive that his retirement is regarded as more like that of a public man than of an anonymous editorial contributor. Whatever Mr Farrer's abilities may be, it was thought by many that his engagement by the *Globe* directors was a piece of bad policy, unless, indeed, they were prepared to give him free rein and endorse his Annexation, anti-French and anti-Catholic crusades. The man had so many and such conspicuous antagonisms that it was impossible to dissociate the paper from the bad odors thrown off by its chief writer. He was one of the biggest and most vindictive bees in every hornets' nest that menaced the security and harmony of the household of Confederation. As such he proved a source of wicked and ungovernable strength to a paper that had been traditionally hum drum but sure footed. Every dip of his pen in the editorial ink sent out ripples of disquietude over the placid surface of deep, unchangeable Liberalism ...[26]

Saturday Night's transformation of Farrer from an amiable writer of no strong conviction to a 'wicked and ungovernable' force was exactly paralleled in *Grip*, which two years earlier had seen him as a precocious child being kidnapped by the *Globe*. Now it portrayed him as a powerful, ominous Lucifer, being driven from the 'globe' by Sir Oliver Mowat. Following up the Miltonian theme, *Grip* claimed to have discovered in the Ontario parliamentary library a 'prophetic' extract from a rare early edition of *Paradise Lost*:

> And now the heavenly host in conclave meet
> In high deliberation grave to wrest
> Once more from the destroyer's deadly grasp
> This Globe – this World, this Empire that for long
> Has quailed beneath the crushing iron heel
> Of one great power, who erstwhile clad in Mail,
> On eagle wing outspread e'en to the stars
> ...
> Whose mighty scream strikes terror Far-'er near
> In truly loyal breasts.
>   So the Convention great called 'Liberal,'
> Descending, armed with sword of lambent flame
> And broad impenetrable shield of brass,
> Led by Ithuriel of the dreaded spear,
> That doughty champion – great Protector high –
> Drave off this Globe that arch conspirator,
> Hurled his unwieldy bulk to nether worlds

On a less lofty note *Grip* also poetically warned Sir Oliver that alienation of the continentalist wing could be costly to the Grits:

THE PARTY HEELER EXPOSTULATES.

> Sir Oliver! Sir Oliver! I very greatly fear,
> There is danger to the party in the future drawing near.
> Your Loyalty I much admire, and yet I somehow feel
> You are injuring our interests with all this over-zeal.

SCENE FROM A RARE EDITION OF 'PARADISE LOST.' *Grip*, 31 August 1892. Two short years earlier, *Grip* had seen Farrer as a precocious infant, grasping a Grit pen in one hand and a Tory pen in the other. But in 1892 he had become a figure of Satanic aura, being driven from the 'globe' by the newly knighted Sir Oliver Mowat.

On wicked annexationists it may be right to sit,
But the wicked annexationist is usually Grit.
While from a moral point of view your conduct wins applause,
You are turning friends to enemies and injuring our cause
...
The Farrers and the Myerses, with dozens more of such,
Have an influence in the country that may hurt us very much.
So please call off your boycott on the annexation Grits,
Or at the next election you may bet they'll give us fits.

In serious prose *Grip* was inclined to see the issue as one affecting the journalist's freedom from party, as well as one of political unwisdom. Newspapers that tried to regulate the personal opinions of their staff, it said, were likely to lose the services of men of superior talent – men who would not efface themselves at the bidding of a board of directors and become mere literary automatons. 'The political sensation of the week has been the retirement of Mr Edward Farrer from the *Globe*, which is understood to be the result of pressure on the part of Sir Oliver Mowat, on account of Mr Farrer's well-known annexationist views. The latter is a writer who can at any time command a good position, and the general verdict is that he can stand it, if the Globe and the alleged Liberal party can.' *Grip* also underlined in more serious terms the poem's suggestion that annexationism had become a significant force among Liberals. Party members were wondering how far the premier's 'inquisitor-like zeal for the extirpation of political heresy' would go. If Mowat carried out his program thoroughly there would be a good many high official heads in the basket; so it was no wonder the Tories had nothing but approval for his course. 'If deprived of the voting strength of those annexationists who are also Grits, Sir Mowat [sic] could not hold office for a week.'[27]

The Ottawa *Citizen*, a Tory paper, shared the harshness of *Saturday Night*, reviewing Farrer's 'odious and detestable' act of perfidy, but balanced that with surprisingly generous words for his craftsmanship:

The conspicuous ability with which the *Globe* has been edited during the past two years will be acknowledged by every reader of that journal, and sufficiently vindicates the truthfulness of the assertion that Mr Farrer is a master of his profession. The excellent qualities of his writing have been fulness of information, controversial power, a vigorous and finished style and good tone. As a rule the Globe under his management has been free from objectionable personalities, – although its references to Sir John Macdonald both before and after his death were an exception, – and in discussing public questions it has applied itself vigorously to handling them in the way of legitimate argument. This, of course, is quite consistent with our belief that the general strain of the journal's utterances have [sic] been most dangerous to the best interests of the country, especially in everything that concerned our relations with the United States.

In the same issue the *Citizen* argued that Washington was following 'pretty faithfully' the advice of Farrer's pamphlet as it developed hostile action against Canada: on proposed higher duties on fish, on the possible closure of the Sault Ste Marie Canal to Canadian vessels, or on the threatened withdrawal of the bonding privilege.[28] Other commentators echoed that thought. 'Mack' in *Saturday Night* assumed, for instance, that the hostility of the Americans had tipped the decision of the *Globe* directors to abandon Farrer. If a commercial war with the United States actually developed, he said, the Liberal party would be hampered by the presence on its chief organ of the man who had supplied the Americans with plans for 'bringing Canada to her senses.'[29]

While most journalists thus made a fine issue of Farrer's resignation, the *Mail* studiously ignored it, and the *Empire*, to its credit, refrained from gloating over the victory it had so avidly sought. It ran a single short paragraph and even included a grudging word of praise, saying that Farrer, 'who, though he has misused his talents, is undoubtedly an able writer,' had retired from the *Globe*.[30]

That paragraph must have brought a wry smile from Farrer. But he was, despite the 'blithesome' appearance put on for the reporters, apparently in one of his darker moods. In early August Goldwin Smith wrote Laurier suggesting that the resignation had been brought on partly by depression. 'The Tory papers are chanting hymns of praise to Mowat for turning Farrer out of the *Globe*,' Smith wrote. 'I fancy they overstate the case. But I think it probable that the Mowat pressure had gradually rendered Farrer's position untenable. Physical depression may have helped to make him throw up at last. He is a loss, and there is no other place for him on the Canadian press.'[31] Two days later Willison also wrote Laurier, implying there was more to the resignation than met the eye, but declining to be specific. 'There are some things I want to tell you about Mr Farrer's resignation in strict confidence but I do not care to commit them to paper,' he wrote.

'Of course he left on the best of terms with us all. Mr Mowat is not at all responsible for his resignation. He only is responsible.'[32] Later, too, Willison continued to insist that there never was any quarrel between Farrer and the paper.[33]

Laurier evidently wrote a sympathetic letter to Farrer, but it is not, unfortunately, among Farrer's papers. Farrer himself replied in terms that indicated his personal relations with the leader were still warm:

Dear Mr Laurier

I am much obliged to you for your very kind letter. It cheers me to know that you think that amid many imperfections, I was of some use to you. Believe me that whenever and wherever I can I shall not be slow to serve you to the best of my limited ability and opportunities in the future ...

I know quite well that the course of the *Globe* must often be exceedingly embarrassing to you. There are ugly questions looming up. But, now that I am an impartial witness, let me say that Mr Jaffray and Mr Willison are as loyal to you as any two men could be. When they run counter to your wishes or known desires it is only because stern necessity, in one form or another, compels them to do so. The Globe's position is a difficult, almost a perilous one on several issues – rendered all the more so of late by Sir Oliver's strong stand and reactionary associations. I suppose such things always occur when political parties are in a state of flux and transition.

I beg once more to thank you for your unvarying kindness and to wish you health, strength and good fortune.

with great regard
yours truly
E. Farrer[34]

As for the *Globe*, after Farrer's departure it rapidly moved away from its reputation as a nest of annexationists. For Willison it was a time of many troubles. He sorely missed Farrer, and was stung by criticism that the *Globe* was declining with Farrer gone – just as he had been stung two years earlier by talk that the paper was improving because Farrer had joined it. He was also hurt by a conviction, recently developed, that Farrer had indeed been working all along *against* reciprocity, not for it. Some of these thoughts Willison passed on to Laurier. In a September letter devoted mainly to assurances of loyalty to the leader by himself and Jaffray he wrote:

I notice in your local paper an attack on the Globe in consequence of Mr Farrer's departure. It may be that the Globe cannot be maintained at the old standard, but you should remember that during the last few weeks, since Mr Farrer left, we were struggling with new men. It was not easy at once to give proper consideration to questions which Mr Farrer alone had been handling for two years. However, I do not assume to have any right to complain of any legitimate criticism by any of the Globe's contemporaries. Of course I do not blame you for the attack.

While my relations with Mr Farrer are as cordial as ever, you may depend on this that any influence he has, as I have lately learned, has been exercised throughout and will still be exercised against us securing any trade arrangement at Washington. I shall be glad to go into this more fully when I see you.[35]

The 'local paper' attack that hurt Willison came from Ernest Pacaud, Laurier disciple and sometime victim of Farrer, who edited *L'Electeur*. That paper had deplored the direction of the Liberal party in Ontario, saying the *Globe* after Farrer's departure had lost its originality and vigour and become no more than a shadow of its former self.[36] And in one area, at least, the *Globe* was not at all like its old self, as Willison rowed back from extreme depths of unrestricted reciprocity, keeping aloft the U.R. flag but explaining that it really meant only a desire to get the best possible trade deal with the Americans. A year earlier, with Farrer at his elbow, he had been eager to see a policy discriminating against British manufacturers. 'As to discrimination against England,' he had written to Laurier, 'it has always been my view that we should boldly assert its necessity and justify it in the interests of Canada.'[37] With Farrer gone, he wrote Laurier that the general line of the party ought to remain the same, but 'I am convinced that little can be said about discrimination against Great Britain and that we must not admit the idea of a common tariff ... We want Reciprocity if we can get an arrangement on terms that will not infringe on our national integrity ...'[38]

Beyond question Willison was moving to safer territory, impelled not just by Blake and Mowat but by the cold attitude of the United States government. And he was not alone. While the *World* continued to rant of the dangers of annexationism, saying the biggest Ontario office-holders in Toronto were unionists and that the real struggle still lay ahead,[39] the actual developments proved that assessment to be well off the mark.

The struggle ahead, in fact, turned out to be mostly farce.

12 The Forlorn Hope

In the wake of the 1891 election the leaders of the annexationist movement 'came out from under the barn' (in Ned Sheppard's memorable phrase). As Walter Gregory recalled it much later, the movement leaders had been cautioned by Goldwin Smith to do nothing during the campaign lest they damage the Liberal chances. But after the defeat it was 'not unnatural' that supporters of commercial union would become supporters of political union. The depression of the 1890s had put country people in a mood to back almost anything that might improve their situation, so that when the Liberals were defeated, the movement for continental union 'took definite form.'[1]

Starting in the autumn of 1891, and peaking during the winter of 1892–3, a significant annexation lobby was mounted by Smith, Gregory, Farrer, and a handful of others – bolstered by a parallel group in New York. As in the commercial union bubble, its significance was often exaggerated, especially when Charles Dana hired Farrer late in 1892 to orchestrate an 'echo chamber' campaign in the New York *Sun*.[2] In signed columns by Farrer, in overblown interviews with annexation sympathizers, in strident editorials, and in carefully selected quotes from every Canadian newspaper that noticed the phenomenon, the *Sun* treated the movement as one of the great developments of the day. Canadian newspapers (and some in the United States) took notice and commented – and were in turn quoted, creating the echo effect.

Meanwhile, behind the rhetoric, annexation groups were set up on both sides of the line, for earnest and often unrealistic discussions – some of them reported to Ottawa by the spy maintained near the New York organization. For a time Honoré Mercier, now discredited ex-premier of Quebec, was a sympathizer, along with some of his associates who were apparently willing to sup with the devil to repair wasted fortunes. (They were greeted with mixed feelings by the Ontario campaigners.) For a time 'traitor' counties in southwestern Ontario seemed to harbour a critical mass of annexationists, while significant numbers of Montrealers also supported the movement. In a matter of months the fever passed, and in time the whole business was remembered by some with a touch of shame. But for a short period it had significance, if only as a sign of the country's despair.

The intellectual foundation of the movement was supplied by Smith's book, *Canada and the Canadian Question*, which came out after the election and may have been written in collaboration with Farrer. (In turn, some of Farrer's columns and pamphlets were undoubtedly done in collaboration with Smith.)3 The book echoed much of the *Mail*'s line in explaining why Canada could not be held together and went beyond it to paint the rewards of union. While he refused to call it annexation – an ugly word that conveyed the idea of force or pressure – Smith insisted an honourable and equal union would bring Canada great advantages. It would give inhabitants of the whole continent 'as complete a security for peace and immunity from war taxation as is likely to be attained by any community or group of communities on this side of the Millennium.' It would join Canadians to a kindred people, whose immense prosperity they were prevented from sharing only by a political line.4

Smith was also the moving force when the continentalists formally emerged to public status in the fall of 1892. As Gregory told it, some twelve people met at a Toronto office in September or October of that year to form the Continental Union Association of Ontario, as a parallel to the similar group in the United States. One of its first acts was to engage Farrer to write a pamphlet entitled *Continental Union – a Short Study of Its Economic Side*. It was, Gregory said, extremely well done and was widely circulated. 'Goldwin Smith, I think, paid Farrer for writing the pamphlet.'5 Smith, Gregory said, was not at the first meeting but was kept fully informed and was the movement's principal backer.

Farrer, too, implied later that Smith was the driving, and faithful, force behind the movement. In 1910 he reminisced about forty years' acquaintance with Smith and praised his courage and persistence. 'I have been a follower of his in some rather keen campaigns, and can vouch that as the leader of a forlorn hope, of a despised and impotent minority, he was splendid,' Farrer wrote. 'His tranquil spirit never quailed when persecution was rife, his sole concern was for the brethren.'⁶

While the movement did indeed decline quickly into a forlorn hope, it could claim in its early days to be taken seriously. At a Montreal meeting late in 1892 that packed the seven-thousand-seat Sohmer Auditorium, Elgin Myers engaged in a debate on Canada's future and must have been gratified by the response. The meeting's final vote, as reported by the *Globe*, was: independence, 1,614; American union, 992; colonial system, 364; imperial federation, 29.⁷ The credibility of the movement was also heightened when the *Globe* sent out two 'commissioners,' one Liberal and one Conservative, to explore Ontario together and assess the mood of its people. Their findings sometimes clashed, but in general they reported a sullen, discontented electorate, in which many were unenthusiastic about annexation but ready to accept it if it were the necessary price of prosperity. (The Liberal commissioner was Joseph Atkinson, later publisher of the Toronto *Star*.)⁸

Interestingly, Farrer's propaganda material changed very little from the sort of thing he had written at the *Mail* and the *Globe*. The *Empire*, with justice, said he was simply rehashing his *Globe* work, adding his byline and also 'that plain advocacy of annexation which was only hinted at in the organ.'⁹ It is true that at the *Sun* Farrer followed, in more muted language, the paper's policy line of insisting on no trade deals without full union, but in general there was no dramatic shift in his tone of argument. In both his pamphlets and his *Sun* columns he took care not to offend readers, but instead stroked and directed their prejudices. A pamphlet called *Our Best Policy* (unsigned but attributed to Farrer by Gregory) even started off with an appeal to British sentiment, before subtly listing Britain's failings:

Nearly 150 years have elapsed since Canada was acquired by Britain. During all that time Britain has done her best for us. Her treasury has paid millions of pounds for our military protection, and her investors have supplied loans for the development of the country with so free a hand that to-day, on public and private account, we owe them a thousand million dollars. It is sometimes said that she has sacrificed Canadian interests in diplomatic squabbles with the United States; that she gave away invaluable seaboards rather than fight, pooh-poohed the Fenian raid claims, and let the Americans get hold of Alaska. The answer is, briefly, that she could not help it. Her own interests are worldwide, and if she is to continue to bear on her shoulders the 'too vast orb of her fate,' it is obvious that she cannot afford to plunge into war every time a colony considers itself aggrieved. Taking everything into account, she has been a truly generous parent to Canada. None acknowledge this more cordially than the advocates of the Political Union of Canada and the United States. Paradoxical as it may appear to some, they take their stand on that measure because they believe it would redound to her well-being no less than to the well-being of Canada.[10]

In his New York *Sun* articles, too, Farrer's themes were familiar: that Canada's natural trade lines lay north and south, and therefore the country's great potential wealth lay unexploited; that the racial division made the prospect of a separate nation unlikely; that colonial status was unenviable; and that Canada's population exodus had strengthened cross-border ties. He also sought (in a tone that would sometimes be patronizing to Canadian ears) to persuade Americans of the advantages of union with Canada. 'The people are law-abiding, thrifty, intelligent, and, within the limits of their narrower horizons, just as enterprising as the people of the United States,' he wrote in one column, 'but their efforts to foster trade between scattered provinces lying within the same high latitude have not come to much, and they are being drained of their best blood by the enormous flow of population into the United States, which their commercial isolation entails.'

Again, too, Farrer played on the fears of both sides in the race/religion dispute: 'The French say that if they are to be stripped of their constitutional rights by the Orangemen, the sooner they join the United States the better, to which Orangemen retort that if dualism is to be imposed upon the virgin regions of the Northwest at the instance of an arrogant hierarchy the annexation of the whole country cannot come too quickly.'

One major change in Farrer's New York *Sun* work, though, was abandonment of the idea of building from commercial to political union. It would be unreasonable, Farrer argued tactfully, to expect that Congress would let Canada sit at the American table until she joined the American family. The *Sun* editorials were much more outspoken on the same point, insisting that the new administration of Democrat Grover Cleveland would never lower trade barriers and thus let the lion's whelp fatten on the eagle. It warned 'the anti-American party' in Canada that while the Democratic government would treat its neighbour with decent consideration, it would leave her to seclusion and starvation so long as she chose to remain a part of Europe rather than of America. 'Let the United States extend from the Gulf of Mexico to the Arctic circle.'

With exaggerated headlines and selective reporting, the *Sun* also gave the impression that Canadians were eager for annexation. One typical report started out thus:

CANADA WANTS TO COME IN
THE PRESS EAST AND WEST CLAMOR-
ING FOR ANNEXATION.

Outspoken Opinions Favoring Political Union
with the United States – No Half Measures
are Satisfying to the Present Agitators

OTTAWA, Dec. 4 – The Annexation movement in Canada has reached beyond the few more daring ones who had the courage of their convictions and spoke out, and is now openly advocated as the inevitable destiny of the country. All along the line the press of the Dominion see trouble ahead ...

The story quoted such distinguished organs as the Tillsonburg *Liberal* ('Political union is fast becoming something more than a plaything') or the *Irish Canadian* ('that the annexation fever is spreading cannot be denied') and combined this with heavy coverage of the annexation meetings in Montreal and in southwestern Ontario. At the same time the *Sun* appealed fairly directly to the natural greed of its American readers. It reminded them of the 'incalculable though as yet undeveloped' wealth of Canadian minerals, forests, fisheries, and lands. It warned that American wheat land was almost all occupied, while 'immense areas of virgin soil suited to wheat culture await us' in the Canadian West. It said union would 'give us command' of the St Lawrence / Great Lakes system and would 'bring ... under our control' the CPR, ending its piratical and unregulated competition with U.S. lines. But above all, continental union would mean national power, making the United States the richest, strongest, and most progressive nation in the world: 'No foreign power would dare provoke it to war or could successfully assail any of its essential interests.'[11]

Farrer's own material avoided this kind of aggressiveness, although it echoed (less blatantly) the *Sun*'s exaggerations on the extent of unionist support in Canada. While much of that analysis had a quality of wishful thinking, it is true that a number of Canadian newspapers were tolerant or even sympathetic, and for a time efforts were made (with American support) to launch or obtain a major Toronto paper. According to Gregory, Elgin Myers made an approach on this point to Christopher Bunting, who was 'in general sympathy' with the movement.[12] At one point, too, the New York *Sun* actually claimed that a Toronto annexationist paper had been launched, also called the *Sun*. It quoted repeatedly from the new journal and called it the most important step towards annexation that had yet been taken, though the paper apparently lasted for only one issue.[13] Goldwin Smith, in letters and articles and interviews, was similarly hyperbolic. 'Political unionism unquestionably gains ground,' he wrote to Laurier, towards the end of 1892. 'I have intimations of its development in the very heart of the Conservative party. It wants nothing but a leader and an organ.'[14]

Neither the leader nor the organ emerged, however, and the Canadian movement declined quickly, to a despised and impotent minority. The parallel group in the United States, the National Continental Union League, lasted longer, drawing on members more solidly respectable and more solidly wealthy than the Canadian recruits, and backed by a dozen or more major newspapers.[15] Indeed, the Canadians who stayed in the movement were something of an embarrassment, especially Francis Wayland Glen, a one-time Canadian MP who lived in Brooklyn, scrounged from friends, cheated secretaries, and built castles in the air, and E.A. Macdonald, a city politician in Toronto and a confidence man of stupendous gall. Farrer seems to have been one of the more respectable members of the team, although Gregory recalled with some chagrin his contribution to one New York session. Attending the meeting on the American side were luminaries like Dana and Carnegie, while from Ontario there were only Gregory, who had to borrow money to make the trip, and Farrer, who was drunk. The other Canadians present, along with Glen, were Mercier and a few of his associates:

We had [Gregory wrote] a general and most interesting talk, the principal spokesmen being Mercier, Dana and Carnegie. The whole situation was generally discussed, but no definite plan for promoting continental union was outlined. Farrer though at the meeting was somewhat the worse for wear and I took him home to a place in Brooklyn where he was stopping, having some difficulty in getting him on and off the cars, by which we were travelling. I did not expect to see him again, but in the evening, when a further conference was held, he was back.[16]

Neither Carnegie nor Dana attended the evening meeting (perhaps not surprisingly), and Goldwin Smith, who was staying in a nearby hotel, refused to attend when he found that Mercier would be present.

While the correspondence of the two associations for a time showed a certain level of credibility, later material suggests a rather pathetic movement, hurt as much by friends as by enemies and living more on hopes than cash. The part of Farrer that saw humour in every situation must have responded to the wonderful absurdities (like his amazing alliance with Mercier), while the part of him driven to drink and depression might also have found raw material for despair. Letters to Farrer from Macdonald and Glen in April 1893 illustrate the more bizarre side of the movement. Macdonald complained that Glen was trying to steal his glory as the true founder of the annexation movement, while Glen in turn complained that Macdonald – 'the great lieutenant-colonel' – was trying to claim all the glory and at the same time bilk everyone he met. Glen's letter, especially, presented an astonishing mixture of fantasy and paranoia:

My Dear Farrer
Yours came to hand yesterday and contents are noted. I will raise the $150 and remit at the earliest possible moment. I find it difficult to raise money purely from *one* cause, not being organized. No one has any authority to act, or assets. I had 190 names last night, and this week will add many. My Brother got Governors of NY., NJ, Conn & R.I. Pres of Brown University and Harvard ... [a list of names follows] I wish our friends in Canada had your courage pluck energy and good judgement they would do some things themselves. Mr Lowry a soninlaw of Justin Armour, is dead buried tomorrow. I will try and see him before he goes home from the funeral. I have tested my strength *daily* and two days last week it simply poured down rain and at the same time blew a gale. My son will leave for the west tomorrow with 150 letters from Mr Dana. Mr D is a *grand man* to work with. The more you know him the *better* you will *like him*. He has an *unlimited* supply of pluck.

The Great Lieut. Col from Toronto they say at the Prep Club left for home or elsewhere friday. Mr Harman introduced him to three men before I could go out. He borrow [sic] from all ... Is he sane[?] You would suppose he gave me the idea of political union. He tells men to whom I have talked it ever since I came here in 1886 so. Of course it doesn't hurt anyone but himself ... If he attempts to blackmail anyone someone here will fix him ...

Ironically, Farrer was simultaneously warning movement members about *Glen*. Sometime in 1893 Farrer wrote Gregory telling him that Glen had tried to borrow from everyone in the supporters' list, adding: 'The whole business has been gravely discredited by G and a strong effort will be necessary to revive it ...' A letter from a prominent Chicago backer indicated Farrer had warned him as well, and asked for more detail about Glen's performance.[17]

The farcical side of the movement also showed clearly in reports of the spy who infiltrated the New York movement, and who, in another irony, reported to Ottawa through Farrer's old enemy, David Creighton of the *Empire*. The spy, an erratic, often paranoid Irish-American journalist named T. Burke Grant, set up the contact with Ottawa in November 1893 after learning accidentally about what he took to be a massive and powerful conspiracy to take over Canada. By the following spring he had to admit, even at risk of losing his espionage pay, that the conspiracy was mostly illusion. But in the meantime he was able to obtain (through a sympathetic secretary) a good deal of Glen's correspondence to Farrer, and to provide through it an uncertain glimpse into the extraordinary operation.

Grant had evidently corresponded with Creighton on other subjects, but the first letter on the conspiracy that shows up in Ottawa files is dated 24 November 1893. It has a breathless quality, a suggestion that dreadful things so far only suspected were now becoming concrete facts: 'I have actually been confided in by one of the conspirators and let into the facts to an extent which is perfectly surprising. I have been shown the prospectus of the new organization, the object of which is to unite Canada and this country "under one flag" and which has been signed and approved of by over 120 of the leading Americans of Boston, New York and Philadelphia ...' The whole business, Grant went on, was so vitally important to Canada, so extensive in its ramifications, and so powerfully backed – even by men of the stature of Andrew Carnegie – that a story about it would raise a sensation in England and Canada. But for the moment, there was an almost desperate need for secrecy: the mere writing of the letter to Creighton might be 'a matter of the greatest consequence to me,' and it was therefore to be shown only to the governor general or Prime Minister Sir John Thompson.

Creighton passed the information on to the prime minister but warned that the spy's material was slightly exaggerated, although 'there can be no doubt from the other perfectly independent material we have that he is on the track of a large conspiracy.' He also recommended a payment to the spy of $30 a week and gradually got caught up in the espionage game, relying more and more on code words and on elliptical references.[18]

Over the next ten months Grant's letters, and those written by Glen that he was able to pilfer, provide an erratic record of the movement's collapse. Neither source was particularly reliable (as Creighton must have quickly realized). Both were hazy on developments in Canada, and Glen was hopelessly unrealistic about the strength of the movement there – either because he adopted a salesman's optimism or because he was genuinely deluded, or both. A number of points on which Glen had personal knowledge do show a degree of credibility, however. For instance, the letters support the stories that a unionist Toronto newspaper, perhaps with Farrer as editor, was seriously considered. In a letter to Mercier Glen told in some detail how the Ontario group in 1893 had asked their New York patrons for a $100,000 fund to set up such a paper. Carnegie had pledged $10,000 on condition the rest could be subscribed quickly, but that goal had not been achieved. It is also clear that the Toronto and New York operations often squabbled. It is evident, too, that Canadian Liberals on the fringe of the continental movement kept in touch with the New York group, and probably sought money from it.

Despite the in-fighting Glen's letters indicate he had great faith in Farrer and considered him the brains of the Toronto operation. Goldwin Smith he considered too theoretical, while the nominal Toronto leader, insurance executive John Morison, was a disaster. In January 1894, for instance, Glen wrote:

Confidential
My dear Farrer,
  I was delighted to receive yours of the 19th tonight. First, because I have great confidence in your practical political judgment: Second, because I have great confidence in the sincerity of your advocacy of continental union. You had nothing to gain personally and much to lose by your outspoken demand for continental union and I very much appreciate your support.
  Little Johnny Morrison [sic] is sound at heart but a *boke* in practical politics, like our friend Wiman. Wiman has a brain, however, and Johnny

has not ... The Prof. don't pretend to be a practical politician but there is more brains in his slippers than in little Johnny's head ... I want to see you very much and Mercier. Want to send Mercier $500. Want to send you at least $207 ... You stand well at Sun Office, Paul Dana said he would be glad to make a place on Sun for you ...

Glen's perception of Farrer's role is also shown in a letter to Mercier, designed to convince the Canadian plotters that the New York operation should go public with a fund-raising drive. Glen said he was deeply sorry about Mercier's financial position, but was not any better situated himself. 'I want you to urge Farrar to persuade Prof. Smith to tell us to organize here. Then we will do it at once, and then fuel to get up steam can be had abundantly ... Farrar is sound and true and level headed: urge him in a confidential note to press for our organization here.'

As for the movement as a whole, the thrust of Glen's letters early in 1894 was that a serious mistake had been made in preventing him the previous year from organizing a big Carnegie Hall rally to launch a public campaign. He also blew hot and cold on the Liberal party connection. At times he seemed convinced that Laurier could be forced to join the movement. At others he doubted the loyalty of even Mercier and feared (correctly, for once) that if the Liberals gained office they would quickly lose interest in continentalism. In one January letter, for instance, he reported on a December meeting hosted by Carnegie and attended by Smith at which the decision had been: '*No help for Laurier, plenty for Mercier and independence.*'[19]

As for the spy's reports, one sub-theme was his efforts to meet Creighton's particular interest in the sins of his old rivals, Farrer and the *Mail*. In February Grant wrote that he had tried to pump his contact in the movement about Farrer, but had failed to find out anything definite. 'My idea is that he has not been here this year; but they have a high opinion of him and say he has done good service for which during a period when he was engaged travelling through the Dominion he was paid $100. a week and expenses. I did not dwell further on that subject or learn more.' A few days later Grant added some tenuous information on the *Mail*, phrased in a way that suggested Creighton had told him of a 'syndicate' planning to turn that paper into an annexationist organ. He knew nothing of the syndicate, Grant said, but the *Mail* was apparently still sympathetic to the movement – although unwilling to help it unless guaranteed against possible losses. In March Grant added that the unionists were still anxious to have an organ in Toronto, but they had not opened any direct negotiations.

In his search for information Grant decided to ingratiate himself with Wiman, who by this time had encountered his financial and legal difficulties, and was in fact incarcerated in 'the Tombs,' on charges brought by R.G. Dun & Co., of which he had been manager. Grant sent a sympathetic note and flowers to his cell, and later, apparently, was welcomed in Wiman's home, after the latter was released on bail. Wiman, he related, told him all about an offer that had been at one point made by a group of American capitalists to buy the *Mail*. 'The price for which the paper was offered was $100,000. and it is still for sale.'[20]

As Grant burrowed deeper into the movement, his tone for a time became more conspiratorial. He set up a direct link with Ottawa using a fake name, 'Marcus Robinson,' while his Ottawa control was identified as McM. He asked for money to buy a camera and take a photography course, and for a time planned to get at the traitors' correspondence by suborning a postman. He proposed at one point that a phoney annexationist group should be set up near Toronto as a means of tapping into the movement's literature. At another point he suggested a legal gimmick under which Farrer's debts in Toronto would be bought up, and his papers seized.

More desperate devices were abandoned, though, when Grant was lucky enough to gain the sympathy of Glen's typist, Angela Barnard, who was angry with her boss over unpaid salary.[21] As Glen's health failed in the spring of 1894, along with his financial and political schemes, the spy was able to get Barnard to turn over a bundle of letters. He also seems to have gained the confidence of Glen himself, and of others in the movement. At one point he reported that he had been used by the plotters to plant a news story discrediting Wiman. The special irony was that the plotters were angry with Wiman because they assumed he had given a list of movement backers to Ottawa; in fact, the list had been supplied by Grant.

Eventually, the spy's view of the movement became contemptuous. 'The closer range at which I view Glen the more convinced I am that the man's judgment is not good, and that he is a visionary enthusiast inspired for the most part by feelings of hate against the C.P.R.,' he wrote in March 1894. 'But he is a resourceful sort of conspirator, and for the life of me ... I am at a loss to know how he succeeded in obtaining such a list [of backers].' In May Grant wrote that Glen was not prospering, that he had utterly failed in raising money 'and was compelled to ask me for the loan of a "V" yesterday which I cheerfully gave him.' During the summer he reported that Glen had disappeared from his Brooklyn home without a trace; he managed to search the home and found nothing of importance. Later he traced Glen to a new apartment and reported him as saying that his brain and nervous system had given out. Grant then inveigled Barnard into an unsuccessful attempt to buy more papers from Glen's wife.

By this time Farrer may already have detached himself from the movement. On 7 April Grant had reported there was to be a New York conference of annexationists, including Farrer, in the following week. On 11 April he wrote that the Ontario men had not arrived, and also that Glen was worried because he had sent three letters to Farrer without response. On 19 April Grant reported that J. Israel Tarte appeared to be taking Farrer's place as *Sun* correspondent – 'but they do not desire to give much confidence to his views which are favorable to Laurier and the Liberals.[22]

Glen's view of Canadian politics had by this time passed the unrealistic stage and reached the level of fantasy, and this may have had something to do with Farrer's defection. On 20 March Glen (in an exuberant mood because Farrer had reported that Myers would succeed Morison as Toronto leader) had seemed to think that Laurier could be pressed into joining the movement. He suggested J.A. Chapleau, long a leading Quebec figure, would come in, and that Laurier would have to follow:

Chapleau is getting ready to make a break and land on his feet. Laurier must come then or lose his hold upon his own Province ... Meantime our policy is to *disintegrate* both parties. *Smash* Sir Oliver if we can and so disintegrate the Grits in Ontario. If the Governments delay going to the country this year, we can, if Mr Meyers [sic] is made Pres'dt in Toronto, get seats enough to hold the balance of power in the next Parliament. This should be our game. Meantime *get firm hold on Quebec* ...

Farrer apparently did not answer this letter and ensuing ones. On 30 April Glen wrote Myers to say he had heard nothing since Farrer had written six weeks earlier about plans for the New York meeting. The final dissolution appeared to be setting in.[23]

By fall, at least, it was clear that the movement had imploded.

Mercier's early death on 30 October closed off one avenue of hope (although his motives and reliability had always been suspect), and no other leader emerged. The government felt it safe to drop the services of 'Marcus Robinson,' and it did so with a piece of sloppy tradecraft that fittingly symbolized the comic opera quality of the whole episode. Grant received a letter indicating his services had *already* been dropped; he was puzzled and confused until he received an earlier dated letter that had been circulating among the M. Robinsons of New York. The bumbling spymasters had apparently neglected to put his post office box number on the letter of dismissal.[24]

By that point continentalists on both sides of the border had little to cheer them. 'The flag has not been hauled down, though it has been necessary to keep in port,' Smith wrote to an American sympathizer.[25] Smith, however, was now the leader of only an impotent remnant, and he must have known it well enough, even within the sheltering walls of the Grange. The movement would end with a whimper, Gregory plaintively wondering how to cover rental arrears on the Toronto office. Goldwin Smith, as usual, signed the cheque.[26]

13 Remarkable Connections

Throughout the annexation farce Ned Farrer was never far removed from the Liberal party, though the connection was carefully shielded. In 1893–4, for instance, he mediated between the party and the main villains of the McGreevy scandal, trying to entice from them revelations damaging to the government. In 1895–6 he managed an elaborate three-way alliance among the Liberals, the McCarthyites, and the burgeoning agrarian party, the Patrons of Industry – an alliance exceedingly profitable to the Liberals and wellnigh fatal to the Patrons. In both instances he operated with great discretion. In at least one case he apparently used a false name, and in another he insisted on direct cash payment rather than a cheque. While the second affair became public at the time, it was not because of Farrer's actions but because of sloppy security on the part of the Patrons. Farrer's obsessive secrecy in both matters, in fact, leaves questions about what other political fixing he may have done in this period.

In the McGreevy affair Farrer built on sleuthing he had already done while at the *Globe*. That scandal, exposing an elaborate kickback system, had been unfolding for years. By the fall of 1893 Thomas McGreevy, sometime Tory MP and bagman, and an associate, Nicholas Connolly, had been convicted and jailed in Ottawa. This development gave hope to Liberal leaders that the two men, with nothing more left to lose, might disclose details of their boodling in a way that would bring down some leading ministers, especially Sir Hector Langevin and Sir Adolphe Caron. On 24 November 1893 (ironically, the same day on which T. Burke Grant was advising Creighton he had cracked the annexation conspiracy) J.D. Edgar wrote to Laurier as follows:

Private and Confidential
My dear Laurier,

I lost no time in seeing Farrer after McGreevy's conviction with a view to seeing what the prisoners would now do in the way of making a clean breast of it. He is very confident they will do so now. Indeed he has been with them and discussed their whole position in these 2 or 3 weeks. They were going as far as possible to make the political feature of their work a defence so far as they could by examining Langevin, Caron, etc., and hoping to prevent a jury from agreeing to convict. It was only by the strongest kind of promises that, if they would keep quiet, this trial would amount to nothing, that they were induced to keep quiet. In fact their wives were seen and assured of the same result. F. believes that they will be ready and anxious to give the whole story in its political aspect to the public to show that they are the lesser culprits ... He advises them that it should be published simultaneously in the *Globe* & *Mail*. He says he is sure the *Mail* will do it. I have seen Willison and they will of course be ready. The original documents necessary to defend in libel actions I have advised should be put in someone's hands, and he thinks they would be put in mine ... I think Farrer is right from every point of view in not putting his new exposures into the hands of any of us to father politically. They will be more effective coming direct from those who know all about it and who are not grits – and who have ample grounds for such action ...

A few days later Edgar reported that all was going well, that Farrer expected the failure of an attempt to overturn the verdict, and that the defendants, resentful because the government had refused them clemency, would 'bring everything out.'[1] For unknown reasons Laurier in January turned not to Edgar but to another leading Toronto Liberal, William Mulock, to check a rumour that McGreevy had given his papers to Farrer for publication. Mulock replied that he attached little importance to the rumour, although he had talked to Bunting about an item to that effect in the *Mail,* and had been told it was probably correct. 'Yesterday I saw a friend who did not wish me to make use of his name who told me that Mr Farrer was in Ottawa a short time ago and under the name of Fair secured an interview with the Ottawa prisoners who had refused to allow newspapermen to interview them,' Mulock wrote. 'My informant, a sensible careful person, thought there was very little yet to be told and though he did not say so I drew the conclusion that he had formed this opinion from conversations with the gentleman in question ...'[2]

As the plot developed, the government moved to block the disclosures by launching a civil suit against the prisoners – a warning, in effect, that anything they disclosed might boomerang on them and increase the civil damages. Thereafter tensions arose between Farrer and his Liberal party contacts, possibly because the latter thought the prisoners were holding out. On 3 February there was a cryptic note from Cartwright to Laurier saying only: 'Read enclosed and return it. My own impression is that it is best to leave Farrar severely alone and not to do anything to antagonize him ...'[3]

Two letters to Laurier from Thomas P. Gorman, editor of the Liberal Ottawa *Free Press*, on 4 and 7 February indicated the plot was still bubbling but with less spirit. The first note simply confirmed Farrer's possession of the papers and said he was on his way to Montreal to prepare the exposé. The second passed on a note from Peter Ryan, another Toronto Liberal and sometime political unionist, who had also been dealing with Farrer. In essence the note reported that the government's civil action had closed the prisoners' mouths, that they had been advised strongly to do nothing to 'afford the government any aid' in the suit, but that, nevertheless, incriminating documents would soon be in Cartwright's hands. 'They include many of very great importance not dreamed of by the public.'[4]

While the prisoners', or Farrer's, hold-out made sense to Gorman and Ryan, Cartwright was growing cynical. 'I much fear,' he wrote Laurier on 8 February, 'that all this procrastination means that these papers are for sale in which case we will not get them.'[5] On 20 February, too, Edgar reported that 'some very curious features' had arisen in the case, but added: 'I am kept well informed and believe that my advice is being taken in such a way as to bring things out as we wish – more I cannot let you know until I see you. Depend upon me keeping it in hand as well as I can.'[6] The next month, after the prisoners had been released, Edgar was still hopeful: 'So far as I am informed the release of the state prisoners has not secured their silence,' he wrote Laurier, 'but I have a strong suspicion that the Connollys are influenced in holding back by the civil action against them in the Exchequer Court. It is expected that Mr Connolly will be here in a day or two, and I will then probably learn the latest. However, we have splendid material as it is ...'[7]

The material was indeed enough to gravely discredit both Langevin and Caron. But it was never quite clear whether the most damaging of Farrer's information was ever released.

If the Liberals were unhappy about Farrer's handling of the scandal documents, the relationship with Laurier seemed unaffected. There is no sign of strain, for instance, in a Farrer letter early in 1895 passing on some information received from D'Alton McCarthy. Farrer may, indeed, have played a subtle mediating role between the party and McCarthy, who was by this time moving closer to the Liberals and would eventually, before his accidental death in 1898, be considered for a Liberal cabinet post. The substance of Farrer's letter reported on federal and Manitoba government intentions on the schools controversy, then the dominant national topic, and signalled that the maverick Tory was open to communication: he had a long talk with McCarthy, he said, and was passing on the substance because McCarthy 'did not seem averse to your knowing certain things of which he has knowledge ...'[8]

The indications that Farrer provided a link between McCarthy and the Liberals were strengthened as news of the secret three-way alliance among the Liberals, Patrons, and McCarthyites emerged in the run-up to the 1896 election.[9] That story broke in June, just weeks before Laurier's triumphal victory, and was predictably exaggerated by the Tory press, which leapt on Farrer's role and sought to paint it as another Cartwright-Farrer attempt to sell out the country. In this case, though, Farrer's secret work provided not just embarrassment for the party but also dramatic gains. Not only did he help to set up a deal with the Patrons, under which Liberals and Patrons withdrew candidates in key ridings to avoid splitting the anti-government vote, but he also wrote propaganda promoting the alliance – for both the *Globe* and the Patrons' organ, the *Canada Farmers' Sun*. In fact, he also contrived, through Gregory and Smith, to keep the *Sun* alive, to work in the Liberal/Patron interest – without telling Patron readers that control of the paper had passed to Smith.

While Farrer's part in these latter activities was not disclosed at the time, the Tory papers were able to offer detailed documentary evidence showing how he had worked to set up the three-way alliance. Most specific was a letter from the Patrons' grand president, C.A. Mallory of Warkworth, Ontario, to the movement's grand secretary, L.A. Welch, who resented the deal and leaked the correspondence. Dated 1 January 1896 Mallory's letter gave a detailed account of how Farrer and Liberal organizer Alex Smith had made their first approach to him:

Some days ago I received a letter from Farrer urging me to come to Toronto on Dec. 24th on important business such as he could not write about, but of supreme importance to the order.

I accordingly went up and was met by him, and went with him to his house, when Smith came in as representing the Reform Executive. He said he was commissioned by the Executive to see if something could be done to prevent three-cornered contests in the various constituencies. I said that if I had known that I would not have gone up, as we were not in the habit of holding conferences with the representatives of other parties; but, being there, I would be glad to hear his propositions ...

Mallory then went on to offer details that suggested he was not in fact particularly reluctant to talk. He had told Smith that the Patrons would not be dictated to, had demanded better treatment in the *Globe*, and had asked for a list of constituencies the Liberals would be willing to vacate. His letter then went on to tell of a subsequent meeting that gave a fuller picture of Farrer's role in the intrigue:

Now follows a new chapter of events. On my return home from municipal nomination on Monday night I found Farrer at my house, representing McCarthy (for whom he is working), as well as the Reform Executive. He had with him the Reform and McCarthy proposals. McCarthy would like a general convention of all opposed to the government policy. I objected to this, saying, that while we opposed protection we could not oppose the government until they had an opportunity to accept or refuse our demands on the floor of the House. He said he had already raised this objection for me, and McCarthy saw its force. The next thing was to furnish me a list of constituencies that McCarthy wanted, Reformers wanted, and both were willing to leave to Patrons. The list is too long to copy. McCarthy will do all in his power quietly to help us, and there will be no conflict between us ...

The letter went on to name thirteen constituencies the Liberals were prepared to vacate, along with detailed analysis of how other ridings were to be handled – then warned that the letter must be 'destroyed or kept secret.'

The same set of revelations also offered entries from Welch's diary, including reference to a meeting of Farrer, Alex Smith, Mallory, and a couple of other Patrons, to arrange 'matters of reconciliation' between the Patrons and the Grits – 'the outcome of which was the articles that appeared in the *Globe*, written by Farrer, saying that

Patrons and Grits can conscientiously vote or support each other ...'
The same entry said Farrer had also prepared an article for the *Farmers' Sun* along this line and had revised it at the instance of the board, but that it had not yet been published.[10]

After the revelations the *Farmers' Sun* downplayed the significance of the arrangements, saying they were six months old and had never actually been put into effect – although they might quite properly have been used. It also insisted that Farrer had never worked for it and had not 'for a long time' been a contributor to its columns. Some of the party propaganda inserted in the paper seemed, however, to be Farrer's work.[11]

Tory papers naturally made much of Farrer's role, especially of a statement by Mallory saying a $100 payment to him was to be made in cash rather than by cheque – in the interests of both parties. (This payment apparently was for a service that predated the three-way negotiations – possibly the writing of a party handbook.) A typical headline in the Ottawa *Citizen* read:

THE CONSPIRACY.

Complete Expose
of the Plot.

ENGINEERED BY FARRER.

The Arch-Traitor Acts
for McCarthy.

Along with other Tory papers the *Citizen* revived the rhetoric of 1891: it recalled that Farrer in the 'two bites' letter had promised that Macdonald's going would leave the country adrift with no port in sight except annexation and said he was now trying to make use of discordant elements opposing the government to bring about his darling scheme.[12] Several Tory papers also made much of a quote in Mallory's letters that implied Cartwright and Farrer were still working for commercial union, despite its lack of popularity in the party at this stage. The quote in question, part of a discussion on how the Grits were adjusting to Patron demands, reported: 'Farrer says: – (1) Cartwright is going to advocate Canadian commercial independence, Canada to have the right to make trade arrangements for herself; (2)

the Republican Committee at Washington is going to offer reciprocity in various lines, but must include more than natural products between U.S. and Canada. Republicans expect to be in power in the fall.' The Toronto *News* said Cartwright had been muzzled in early stages of the campaign, but that the correspondence made clear that, aided by Farrer, he was 'cooking a scheme with Washington that will entail the virtual handing over of Canadian interests to the United States.'[13] In the absence any hard evidence, though, the Tory papers reluctantly gave up this theme.

As for Farrer's part in keeping the *Farmers' Sun* alive, Gregory, later the paper's editor, told how Farrer approached him for help in persuading a reluctant Smith to buy control at a time when the paper was on the edge of collapse. 'We were all interested in the approaching election and as the Patrons' organization was opposed to the Government of the day, we naturally did not wish its organ to suspend publication,' Gregory wrote. It was thought best, he added, to make no announcement of the change in ownership until the election was over.[14] Significantly, too, Mallory apparently thought the paper remained under Patron control. The Tory 'revelations' included a letter from him saying he had secured control of the paper, and that those who furnished the money 'put it up without any security and without anything to show for it except our honor, and do not wish to be known.'[15]

Ironically, Smith himself later wrote a singularly apt epitaph for the Patrons. They had, he said, been caught between the two parties like a flock of sheep between two packs of wolves.[16]

Smith's reluctance to invest in the *Farmers' Sun* was understandable, for by the mid-1890s, depression had laid a very cold hand on Toronto journalism. All three of the 'serious' papers were losing money in alarming fashion, and the fire of their animosity burned low as corporate and political backers looked for a way out of the difficulties. In 1894 there was even a serious suggestion to Prime Minister Thompson that the *Globe* might be secretly taken over by the Tory party.[17] While there is no sign that such an arrangement was ever consummated, the tone of the papers in mid-decade was much more bland, as though editors were walking cautiously. When the *Globe* was burned out in January 1895, David Creighton courteously offered use of the *Empire*'s facilities, and for a month the two rival sheets rolled off the same presses.[18] At the *Mail*, meanwhile, the rumours were all black. The paper was said to be on the verge of bankruptcy, and Bunting was playing a dangerous game, alternately courting the Conservative government and threatening to stay independent (or worse) in the coming elections. Almost since Farrer's departure, Bunting had been hinting to party people about possibilities of renewed alliance,[19] and rumours of a *Mail-Empire* merger kept recurring. As early as 1892 the *Empire* felt constrained to deny that the *Mail* – that shameless 'consorter with annexationists' – would again become the official Tory organ.[20] At the end of 1894 Bunting was still blustering about his independence. In November Edgar wrote Laurier to express amazement that Bunting was still talking an anti-government line. 'He says the Tory party is broken up in Ontario – the ministers are no good – the press is dissatisfied – no pap going. This certainly looks as if he has no hope of coming to terms with the *Empire* and the Govt.'[21]

As late as 17 January 1895, in fact, the *Mail* was denouncing rumours of the merger as malicious and without foundation. But on the morning of 7 February, with no warning, subscribers of both papers found on their doorsteps a paper headed *Mail and Empire*, saying nothing about political implications and blandly explaining that the merger was needed to put Toronto newspapering on a healthier basis. Hector Charlesworth, who was covering the story for the *World*, saw it as a triumph of diplomacy for Bunting. As he told it, Bunting had escaped disaster by outbluffing the new and 'weakling' prime minister, Sir Mackenzie Bowell – and as a result had left the *Empire* reporters rather than the *Mail* people on the streets in the midst of a cruel depression winter.[22] Billy Maclean, in a fury after he lost his Commons seat a year later, said the party's return to the 'out-and-out annexation organ' was the most disgraceful episode in Canadian political history, and that nothing had been more damaging to the already tottering Tory government. He said the act had been carried out by two or three ministers who, without Bowell's knowledge, had smothered the *Empire* in a single night and turned its lists over to the renegade.[23]

Whatever the details, the episode was not a proud one for Toronto journalism. And for Farrer, too, the period was evidently not an easy one. The political union movement was dead, and journalism across the continent was comatose. Goldwin Smith, ever loyal, did his best to generate freelance assignments for him in American magazines, but the pickings seem to have been thin.[24] Clearly, the mid-1890s represented a low point both for the nation and for Farrer's career. The great days of Laurier-era prosperity still lay over the horizon. The great days of Macdonald's nation-building were irrevocably behind. Politics seemed fretful and mean-spirited. The economy sagged and the Tory leadership disintegrated. And in journalism, too, some of the vivacity seemed to have gone.

14 Backstairs Agent

In the summer of 1896 Wilfrid Laurier's Liberals finally took office, and Ned Farrer's prospects improved. Over the next fifteen years he carried out an extraordinary range of assignments for Laurier, all demanding the highest degree of trust and discretion. At times he seems to have lived on the train, with pen and notebook in hand. From hotels in a dozen cities came back terse, clear reports on a multitude of issues, ending often with the comment that there was much to say that could not be written. He was, for instance, often in Washington, dealing with officials up to the rank of secretary of state, and sending back to Ottawa suggestions on how to deal with tariffs, or boundaries, or immigration. He was in Winnipeg, repeatedly, working out a compromise in the tangled schools issue (an astonishing assignment for the *bête noire* of the Jesuits' Estates affair). He was in Toronto, setting up a meeting between Laurier and the distillers. He was in Montreal, helping to confound an elaborate plot to divorce *La Presse* from the Liberal party. He was in Quebec City, investigating a major smuggling operation. He was in Vancouver, reporting on railways, on pulpwood, on nickel. He was in Michigan, assessing the strength of the lumber lobby, or in Buffalo studying the alien labour law, or in Boston, again on railway matters. He was in Edmonton, assessing the impact of the planned new transcontinental railway. He was in the Maritimes, looking into 'boodling' on the Intercolonial line, or in Newfoundland, exploring its fishing problems with Canada. He was in Ottawa, organizing a party propaganda campaign. He was in the press gallery, sending down a note to Laurier reminding him of an earlier position taken by someone in opposition.

At the same time he was writing journalistic copy, seemingly for anyone who would pay. Some of the material was bylined and carried no suggestion of hidden purpose. On annexation, for instance, he still advocated it, but without great conviction, as though the issue belonged to the past. On imperial federation he was more outspoken. That idea was much in Canadian minds, and Farrer cut it apart forcefully. (For a time in 1910 he wrote a signed column for the magazine *Canadian Century*, but the contributions ended abruptly, possibly because the owners were more keen on imperial unity than their columnist.) As in his early years, much of Farrer's material in this period was unsigned, and was written to support one cause or another, usually that of the Liberal party or the CPR.

Throughout the period there was no sign that he was drinking, although he may still have been subject to the 'periodical toots' George Ham mentioned. His handwriting remained crisp and impeccable, his language a model of clarity and conciseness. Even when he wrote on a moving train there was never an illegible word, never a loose or ambiguous phrase. Throughout this period, too, there was little sign of the old mischievousness, although one writer told of an embellishment in a Commons speech prepared for Laurier that apparently brought the prime minister a bad moment. In general, though, Farrer caused the government no embarrassment and in fact often got it out of trouble. 'Mr Farrer played a busier part in Ottawa party politics than would appear on the surface,' the Winnipeg *Tribune* wrote, at the time of his death. As the 'keep-us-out-of-trouble' agent of some of Laurier's ministers he had been able to recount to friends many amusing and stirring incidents in his work of saving some politician's hide.[1]

Very frequently it was not clear just whose interest was being promoted by Farrer's writing. In 1897, for instance, he submitted a long report entitled 'The Bonding Privilege' to the chairman of the Committee on Interstate Commerce of the U.S. Senate. The report appears for the most part to be straightforward research for American readers, and it is interesting mainly for the contrast it shows to the 1891 pamphlet, and because of a concluding reference to Laurier that seemed designed to ingratiate the new prime minister with U.S. leaders. The reference said leading Canadian Liberals, including Laurier, had all along condemned the restrictions imposed on American fishermen in Canadian ports. No doubt steps would soon be taken to remove the grievance, and when it was out of the way the bonding system would be fairly administered from one end of the international frontier to the other. 'The maintenance of the system is as advantageous, I venture to think, to the interests of the upper tier of States between the Atlantic and the Pacific as to those of Canada; and its impairment or abolition whether east of the Great Lakes or west of them would look like a blow at civilization.'[2]

Here, as in other pieces of Farrer's public and private writing of the time, there was not the slightest suggestion that the United States could or should bludgeon Canada into union. On the contrary, the accent (with the Liberals now in office) was consistently on cooperation and compromise. While Farrer made no secret of his personal preference for political union, he also acknowledged there was little support for the idea. At least one leading Liberal assumed he had dropped it as a practical goal.

Farrer's relationship with Laurier, however, is more ambiguous. At times his writing was clearly designed to promote or explain Laurier's views, while at other times he diverged from the party line, so that it was difficult for observers to tell when a Farrer piece actually reflected Laurier's thinking. In one instance even the governor general, Lord Minto, puzzled about whether a Farrer article had been inspired by Laurier. That occasion came after the Alaska boundary dispute, in which Farrer had played a role as Laurier's agent in Washington, where in effect he short-circuited British diplomats who were losing the confidence of Ottawa. Shortly after a joint British-American tribunal in 1903 produced a decision on the boundary that angered Canada, Farrer wrote a long article for *Contemporary Review* attacking schemes of imperial centralization. Lord Minto considered it worth bringing to the attention of the Marquess of Lansdowne, Britain's secretary of state for foreign affairs, describing Farrer as 'the backstairs go-between employed by Sir Wilfrid, during the Alaska Tribunal negotiations to carry on communications with the U.S. Govt.' Because of Farrer's meetings with U.S. Secretary of State John Hay, he said, the British embassy had occasionally felt indirect influence at work:

Sir Wilfrid himself told me of his employment of Farrer, and tho' I did not like it ... a positive objection on my part would not have stopped the intercourse, and it seemed best to keep the knowledge of it in my pocket. Sir Wilfrid assured me he had the highest opinion of Farrer, in which from what I had heard I was not inclined to share – now comes this article in the 'Contemporary,' and I hear that Farrer is at present employed in Sir Wilfrid's office – this may not be strictly true, but there is no doubt he is in close connection with the Govt. and that the article is inspired by someone of high standing ... I am afraid the article indicates a good deal of what is going on here. I am not at all satisfied with the political position here – I can't quite make out what is going on ... No doubt Canadian public feeling is strongly adverse to the U.S. almost dangerously so – yet at the same time I am suspicious of an inclination in high quarters towards the doctrine of the Contemporary article. Things are very ticklish here just now ...³

The article Lord Minto spoke of was actually very similar to other Farrer attacks on schemes of imperial trade or defence unity. If there was an 'inspired' dimension, it may have been in the argument that Laurier's resistance to imperial centralization was backed in English as well as French Canada. Imperialist journals in England blamed Laurier for not contributing to the imperial army and navy, Farrer wrote. And while it was clear that any such contribution would ruin the Liberal party in Quebec, probably 75 per cent of English-speaking Canadians also would resist any attempt to narrow the sphere of Canadian self-government, or to place on their backs any portion of the burden of imperial armaments. 'It should be understood, then, that Sir Wilfrid Laurier is not against the New Imperialism because he is a French Canadian, but because he shares with English and French Canadians alike the conviction that its aims are foreign to the genius of the Canadian people, and its ends such as they have no desire to serve.'

The rest of the article was devoted to convincing British readers that Canadians were not simply Englishmen on the other side of the Atlantic but a distinct breed, one that was moving closer to relatives in the United States. It is not surprising that Lord Minto was miffed by some of the language, especially when Farrer returned to a favourite theme of ridiculing imperial honours in the New World. Imperialists, he said, imagined that by distributing titles they could plant an aristocracy that would 'overawe the rough, raw and democratic Canadian farmer and lead him, like a little child, to the altar of Jingo.' Canadians, in fact, did not feel proud when they saw their knights masquerading in Windsor uniforms by the side of untitled American leaders:

... it jars our self-respect to think that the Sovereign, or rather the Colonial Office, which is the real fountain of honour, rates our intelligence so low.

And when we reflect on the career of some of the Canadian politicians knighted in times past – I say nothing of living knights – we are reminded of the old lines: –

L'histoire dit qu'autrefois
On pendait les voleurs la croix [sic];
Aujourd'hui les temps sont meilleurs,
On pend les croix à des voleurs.[4]

Undoubtedly, then, whatever influence Farrer had with Laurier was directed towards reducing the British and accentuating the American connection. Most of his work for Laurier, though, seems to have been not on the major issues of the day but on a host of lesser matters. As far as the Washington work was concerned, he appears to have operated as a recognized lobbyist for Canada, or a quasi diplomat, reporting mainly to Rodolphe Boudreau, Laurier's secretary, although in many cases the wording of his reports was shaped for Laurier's eyes. At home he seems to have performed a number of tasks that, for one reason or another, the prime minister did not want to entrust to regular civil servants. In most cases his job was to research problems, although at times he was also commissioned to influence politicians or newspaper people.[5] According to modern canons, he would be judged guilty of constantly crossing the line between detached journalism and press agentry. In the values of the day he was a legitimate party journalist, although uncommonly knowledgeable and influential within the party.

While scores of Farrer's letters remain on file, a large number were discarded, as gaps in the correspondence make clear. Farrer himself seems often to have assumed that his letters would be treated as current intelligence, to be absorbed and destroyed. In many cases he dated them only by the day of the month, or even of the week, and as result some sequences are not certain. Routinely, too, he advised that he had information that could not be written down. With all these limitations, however, the letters provide occasional clear glimpses of his range of activities.

In the early months of the Laurier government, for instance, Farrer played a complex role in an international effort to curb alcohol smuggling in the Gulf of St Lawrence. He shuttled back and forth from Quebec City to Washington, reporting directly to Laurier or to Sir Richard Cartwright, now minister of trade and commerce. In Quebec

City he set up a network of informers with the aim of getting evidence on leading merchants and officials without exposing the informants to revenge. In Washington he arranged with special agents of the treasury department a system under which the agents would tip Canadian authorities when alcohol shipments were leaving U.S. ports. While the outcome of the case is not clear, the following partial sequence shows something of how the inquiry proceeded:

Toronto, Dec. 24 [1896?]

Dear Sir Richard Cartwright: My friends in Quebec are taking hold of the smuggling traffic with much zeal and skill. They all agree that the first thing to be done is to strike a blow at the rich merchants who are its principal beneficiaries. With this object they are working up cases against leading men, against one leading man in particular. It takes time but the job will be done and done well. Mr Laurier knows the name of the person I am referring to.

But in order that progress may be made they recommend and so do I:

(1) That the Government should, sub rosa, appoint some good criminal lawyer like Mr Lemieux a commissioner ad hoc, with power to take evidence under oath etc.

(2) This commissioner should be entrusted with a small fund for the payment of witnesses, informers, and general expenses. My friends, as you can readily understand, can have nothing to do with the regular Customs and Inland Revenue officials.

(3) The names of the informers etc. to be given by me to this commissioner but on no consideration shall they be revealed to any one else – certainly not to the department at Ottawa. You can imagine that the existing system whereby the informers are disclosed to the Ottawa officials and to Inspector McMichael is a bad one. In almost every instance their names get out and then, of course, their usefulness is gone. Some indeed have had to quit the country. Apart from this, the position of my friends relative to informers would be singularly delicate.

(4) Any small sum which my friends may need from time to time to be supplied by the commissioner through myself or some other outside person i.e. some person in no way connected with the Government, under proper representations ...[6]

A month later Farrer reported that he had made arrangements with the special agents branch of the Treasury aimed at putting down the alcohol smuggling. Under the deal Canadian officials would give the Americans information on attempts to defraud the revenue of the

United States, and in exchange the special agents would wire to Canada whenever a cargo of alcohol was shipped to the Gulf smugglers.[7]

This sequence of letters overlapped with another series that shows a quite different facet of Farrer's work, in which he was both acting as a Laurier propaganda agent in the United States and at the same time pressing him, politely, towards closer relations with the Americans (the first line in the first letter may refer to the smuggling operation):

Toronto, Nov. 30 [1896?]

Dear Mr Laurier: I have just got back from Quebec and everything is now serene with our friend, thanks to your intervention.

I am going to New York and Washington at the end of the week. The New York *Tribune* wishes to get a statement of your intentions in regard to closer trade relations and I shall prepare one before leaving, first submitting it to you. It will not, of course, appear as emanating from you. Mr Smalley, the American correspondent of the London Times, and an old Tribune man, is willing to lend a hand on your behalf, both as regards closer trade with the United States and other things, and I shall make it my business to see him. The friendly aid of the Times would, I venture to think, be of some value to your Administration.

And now may I ask if you think of visiting Washington, say, before Christmas? If you do, I can easily arrange in advance a meeting with the right men ... there is to be a special session of Congress in April to deal with the tariff, and it is important that you should have a talk in a general way with the Republican leaders before they set about arranging their programme & policy ...[8]

Other letters of this kind covered a variety of political events. In December 1896, for instance, Farrer reported on a pro-reciprocity meeting of Liberal, Patron, and 'New Movement' farmers that had wound up with a request to Farrer to write a statement for the finance minister. 'They all agreed that you and Sir Richard should go to Washington, if at all possible. Of course I said nothing of your intentions. But I am sure that if you yourself are unable to go, it would be well that Sir Richard should ...'[9] A month later he was in Washington, still working for closer relations with the Americans:

Personal Willard's Hotel, Washington
Jan. 14 [1897]

Dear Mr Laurier: It would greatly clear the air here if, now that the arbitration treaty between the United States and England is signed (though not yet passed) and both sides are fraternizing, you could manage in some way to let it be known that you favor a relaxation of the policy of overhauling and seizing American fishing schooners. That policy, as Mr Dingley [Nelson Dingley, author of the Dingley tariff act passed in 1897] told me today, keeps up a constant ill-feeling against Canada in New England and renders it difficult for the New Englanders in Congress to discuss the subject of closer trade relations in public ... I had hoped to see Mr Charlton but he has not turned up yet. Mr Dingley will not draft the agricultural schedule of the new tariff for some time yet. He is exceedingly well disposed towards Canada but is bound to get Christian treatment, as he puts it, for American fishermen ...[10]

As this letter suggests, Farrer's Washington business sometimes meshed – or collided – with that of John Charlton, now a member of the Canada-U.S. Joint High Commission that had been set up after Laurier took office.[11] On this occasion a small contretemps developed because Charlton's late arrival combined with Farrer's early departure. On Friday, 15 January, the day after his arrival, Farrer evidently fed to the New York *Tribune* correspondent a story designed to indicate Canadian readiness to deal with a number of problems. He either implied – or the reporter assumed – that Charlton was already in Washington. The result was a thoroughly muddled story, made worse by the fact that Farrer was identified as a Liberal MP, exploring unofficially the prospects for a commercial treaty. 'Yesterday Mr Farrer talked with Mr Dingley of Maine, the Chairman of the Ways and Means Committee, with reference to this matter, and during the day he saw several other members of the committee,' the story said. 'He and Mr Charlton continued their missionary work to-day, but so far as could be learned the results have not been satisfactory.'[12] The story went on to quote Farrer at length on areas where relations between the two countries could be improved. Charlton was naturally puzzled by it all. 'I see the papers credit me with having been here with Mr Farrer last week,' he wrote to Laurier. 'I have not seen that gentleman. He had left the city before I came. I do not know how the report originated.' Charlton added that a newspaperman had told him Farrer had gone to Ottawa to see Laurier about the seizure of an American fishing vessel.[13]

While he might justifiably have been miffed by this mix-up, Charlton, perhaps because of a long relationship with Farrer, seems not to have minded. In a longer report to Laurier the next week he spoke highly of Farrer's potential as a Washington lobbyist. Americans, Charlton said, showed a good deal of ignorance about Canada, and this was made more apparent as Canadian affairs began to excite more attention:

No opportunity should be lost to impress facts bearing favorably upon our side of the case upon the American public, and use should be made so far as possible of the American newspaper press ... In this connection I may say that Mr Edward Farrar is in a position to render us very important services, and is doing so at the present time. While it would not be prudent or judicious in my opinion to associate Farrar publicly with any work in connection with negotiations, or for you to hold direct public communication with him to any considerable extent, yet it is well I imagine to let him know that his services are appreciated, and that the value of the service he is capable of rendering is thoroughly understood. I find he stands well with newspaper men in Washington, and is intimately acquainted with the leading newspaper correspondents in that city. He also has a wide acquaintance with American public men, and I think that he is disposed to use his influence loyally for the benefit of Canada, and that he has given up the idea of persisting in the presentation and urging of his political union sentiments. He is a regular correspondent for the 'New York Tribune' and for the 'New York Sun' and an occasional correspondent for the 'Washington Post' and for other American papers. He is also a writer for the 'London Chronicle' and he is about to furnish Mr Smalley, the United States correspondent of the 'London Times' with an article on the Canadian Reciprocity Question to be inserted in that journal. His knowledge of the question you are aware is thorough and intimate, and in the capacity I refer to his services will be of prime value to Canada ...[14]

Significantly, Charlton did not assume that Farrer had given up on his political union sentiments, but only that he had put them in the background. In his years with Laurier, Farrer became increasingly impatient with American heavy-handedness, in the Alaska boundary dispute and other issues, but his efforts remained conciliatory. In the main he simply reported on American views, as in a 1900 report of a discouraging meeting on the boundary issue, at which Hay argued that he had gone as far as American public opinion would allow him to go, had 'come to the end of his tether,' and 'would not budge.'[15] Sometimes he seemed to be counselling Canadian patience, as in a

1902 report on the reasons why Republicans were reluctant to agree to arbitration in the dispute. The party, Farrer said, had 'a good deal to answer for' and would hesitate to draw the Democratic fire by granting arbitration. '... they say it would be suicidal to do so as matters stand. You may rely, however, that the President will strain a point to bring about arbitration so soon as the elections are over in November ...'[16]

If in these matters Farrer sounds very much like a diplomat, specializing in U.S. affairs, other letters make him seem to be a detective or political fixer. A sequence of letters to Boudreau during 1899–1900, for instance, shows that Farrer was investigating corruption on Quebec and Maritimes rail lines. One letter, dated 16 August, apparently 1899, asked for details – 'with as little delay as possible' – on subsidies to Quebec lines. Another, dated Sunday 1 October, reported that key documents on the Temiscouata Railway might be obtained from a former superintendent of the Intercolonial named McDonald. If Boudreau could not get them quickly through some Quebec contact, Farrer himself would go to Rivière du Loup, because the documents were important for government speakers and newspapers. 'Of course, McDonald has a grievance against the government; still, that, I am told, can be overcome ...'[17]

A similar letter from Trois-Rivières in May 1900 also seemed to promise political ammunition, and it may be significant that the investigation was large enough for at least two researchers:

Dear Mr Boudreau: I think I have got the bottom of the St. Charles branch matter. McCaskill, who has done good work, has attended to the case of those who sold land in Levis to the Government. I have had to do with the construction, and, so to say, the financial part of the job.

The state of things revealed is simply dreadful – worse even than that which came out regarding our old friend Tom McGreevy. But it would not be prudent to hold an inquiry. I think I can use the material I have through the newspapers at the proper time, but it is quite impossible to investigate through a committee.

The letter went on to outline a kickback scheme under which an Intercolonial inspector who was a nephew of Sir Charles Tupper, then railways minister, had worked with a government official to siphon off construction money, some of which was stolen while most was sent to Ottawa.[18]

Typically, Farrer in such letters was a model of discretion. He did not spell out, for instance, how McDonald's grievance could be 'overcome' or why an inquiry on the St Charles line 'would not be prudent.' In a note to Willison late in 1900 he remarked (apparently in response to a request) that he had collected most of the Temiscouata papers before the 3 November election, but that 'friends at Ottawa' had opposed making them public.[19]

At times, no doubt, in the rough world of turn-of-the-century politics Farrer traded in influence or in cash, but the essence of his skill remained his remarkable talent for getting information from people and records, and synthesizing complex issues to create a clear picture. That talent was never better illustrated than in the major *La Presse* scandal of 1904–5, when Farrer's investigative work seems to have helped Laurier score a major tactical victory.

The case in question was complex enough to tantalize a Sherlock Holmes. Even now the circumstances are not fully known, but the best account seems to be that of O.D. Skelton, who evidently had inside information from Laurier.[20] As Skelton told it, the case amounted to a conspiracy to unseat Laurier in the election of November 1904 and brought together Hugh Graham (later Lord Atholstan, publisher of the Montreal *Star*) with railway promoters William Mackenzie and Donald A. Mann. At the time Mackenzie and Mann were fighting Laurier's design to make the Grand Trunk Railway pivotal in plans for a second transcontinental route, and the aim of the anti-Laurier alliance was to put Robert Borden into office and secure reorganization of rail lines in a way that would bring immense profit.

A key element of the plot lay in buying up Liberal or independent papers, especially *La Presse*, to turn them against the government. The plotters also planned to launch a scandal campaign against cabinet members, to buy off Liberal candidates in Quebec, and to turn A.G. Blair, former railways minister, against his former chief. The moving spirits, Skelton wrote, were promoter David Russell, of Saint John and Montreal, and J.N. Greenshields, a Liberal Montreal lawyer who worked for Mackenzie and Mann. Also involved were the Forgets, a prominent Montreal financial family, and *La Presse* editor Arthur Dansereau, a sometime ally and classmate of Laurier. (It was Dansereau who, according to Farrer, manipulated the purchase of the Liberal-leaning *La Presse* from owner Trefflé Berthiaume – for a staggering $1 million. The story was that Dansereau had induced

Berthiaume to sign after an all-night champagne party, at a time when, Berthiaume claimed, his mind was 'a perfect blank.')

Again, no complete file of correspondence on the issue is available, but one long interim report, undated, provides an extraordinary glimpse both of Farrer's detective skills and of the intense, and venal, relationships among political parties, the railways, the banks, and the press:

The Montreal conspiracy to overthrow the Government appears to have been formed early in September [1904]. Messers Greenshields, Dansereau, and Russell were the moving spirits from the first ... From all that I can gather from inside sources Mr Hugh Graham of the 'Star' and Mr Greenshields were the first to get together. Greenshields then brought in Russell and Dansereau. Graham on his part brought in the Canadian Pacific, Mackenzie and Mann, and the Forgets. The project which was developed bit by bit finally took this shape: –

'A.' To defeat the Government and hang up the Grand Trunk Pacific scheme.

'B.' To make Mr Blair Minister of Railways under Borden.

'C.' To lease the Intercolonial to the C.P.R.

'D.' To bring about the purchase by the Government of the Canadian Northern lines west of Lake Superior at a good figure.

'E.' To purchase from Russell and Greenshields derelict railways in the Maritime provinces, such as the Caraquet and Temiscouata, on which Russell had options, and make them part and parcel of the Intercolonial.

'F.' Also to purchase through them the Dominion Atlantic Railway in Nova Scotia and the South Shore Railway of Nova Scotia now being built between Yarmouth and Halifax by Mackenzie and Mann.

'G.' To extend the South Shore from Halifax eastward to connect with the Cape Breton extension, the road built a few years ago by Dr Seward Webb, and now controlled by Mackenzie and Mann.

'H.' In short, all the independent lines in the Maritime provinces were to be bought by the Government, either through Russell and Greenshields, or Mackenzie and Mann, and annexed to the Intercolonial which was to be leased in whole or in part to the Canadian Pacific.

'I.' As said above, the Grand Trunk Pacific project was to be suspended indefinitely on the ground that the surveys did not warrant the construction of the line, the country traversed being too poor, while construction in some places between Quebec and Moncton would be impracticable ...

The report went on to relate how Blair was to be turned against Laurier, and how twenty Liberal candidates were to be bribed (at

$10,000 apiece) to withdraw 'on account of the scandals' at the last moment. Farrer acknowledged that the plan sounded like the program of a parcel of lunatics but insisted that these were indeed the objectives. Hugh Graham, he observed, was cool enough in his own business, 'but in politics he is excitable, almost hysterical, and can be made to believe anything that promises to bring the Conservative party to power.' On the actual dealings to buy *La Presse* Farrer provided an impressively detailed reconstruction:

Dansereau was employed to manipulate Berthiaume. They met at the concert of the Garde Republicaine in the Arena on the night of October 11, and went from there to Greenshields' house, where they remained until six o'clock in the morning of the twelfth. Russell and Mr A.J. Brown, of Hall, Cross & Co., lawyers, were also present, together with Mr Beaudin, lawyer for Berthiaume. A draft agreement for the purchase of the paper had been prepared in advance by Brown. A good deal of liquor was consumed during the night. Berthiaume says he had not drunk liquor before for a long time, that two or three glasses of champagne overpowered him and his mind was a perfect blank when he signed the contract about five in the morning. He signed it, he says, because Dansereau told him everything was all right. In the draft contract made by Brown, no provision was made for Dansereau. It was not until the party had assembled at Greenshields' house that a separate clause was drawn – drawn on a separate sheet of paper – whereby Russell covenanted to pay Dansereau $1,000 per month for ten years, whether he worked for 'La Presse' or whether he did not. It would appear that the drafting of this special clause satisfied Dansereau, as well it might, and thereupon he told Berthiaume to sign. But the story told by Berthiaume, that his mind was a blank, that he imagined Russell and Greenshields were acting for Sir Wilfrid Laurier in purchasing 'La Presse,' and so, on, is ridiculous and false on its face ...

Farrer's report went on to tell how the conspirators immediately pressured the paper to abandon attacks on the Forget interests, and to lean towards the Tories. Berthiaume was required to deny that the paper had passed from his control, while Dansereau, the fixer, was quietly shipped off to Paris, with a well-paid year's leave of absence. The report wound up with detailed analysis on how the money had been raised through banks sympathetic to the Tories, promised more investigation (with the aid of a detective agency), and said that the interim report meanwhile 'shows that the conspiracy was probably a more formidable one than any of us first supposed.'

While the outcome of Farrer's work is not known, Laurier received enough timely information to frustrate the plot. Two Saint John newspapers, the *Telegraph* and the *Evening Times*, had been bought by Russell before the *La Presse* incident, Skelton says, but no other newspapers were purchased, no scandals were launched, and no anti-Laurier attack came from Blair. Skelton, perhaps on the basis of information direct from Laurier, concluded that 'the bomb had failed to go off.' He said Laurier bluntly informed the new managers that if *La Presse* changed its policy, he would expose the sale of the chief French-Canadian journal to a group of English-speaking speculators and denounce it throughout the province.

After the fact, some of the plotters scrambled frantically to get back in Laurier's good graces, as a number of items in Laurier's files make clear. There is, for instance, an astonishing telegram from Dansereau, saying: 'Happy to greet you with welcome news. Sole master of the situation, La Presse at your service.' There is also evidence that the prime minister carried on subtle negotiations with Graham, through 'a friend.' And there is an explicit undertaking from Mackenzie and Mann that as a condition of the takeover, *La Presse* 'is not to be a Tory organ, that it is to be independent, and that it is to give Sir Wilfrid Laurier a generous support.'[21]

While reporting to Laurier on the issue, Farrer undoubtedly fed material to the newspapers as well. A series in the *Globe* from 12 to 20 December parallels a number of the exposures of his report and appears to have been written by him. Needless to say, the series gave no hint of the government's, or Farrer's, role in the drama.

One of Farrer's oddest assignments – and one that extended over several years – was the attempt to work out a deal in the volatile schools issue in Winnipeg. It was an issue already loaded with more than a decade of bitterness and one which, ironically, owed some of its intractable quality to Farrer's work at the *Mail*. When he returned to the issue in 1900, the task was to implement the so-called Laurier-Greenway compromise of 1896–7, a complex plan to permit limited religious and language instruction in the public schools, where a demand existed, and to bring into the public system some of the teachers from the former separate system. The Manitoba Liberal government of Thomas Greenway had since been defeated by Hugh John Macdonald's Conservatives, who resisted implementation of the agreement in the provincial capital, although it had been put into effect in other parts of the province.

The problem was that the agreement was unpopular with the extreme elements in both religions. Farrer's task was to bring subtle pressures to bear on both sides to effect a compromise undermining the resistance of Archbishop Langevin of St Boniface. In doing so, he seems to have gone to the lengths of offering inducements, in the form of trips abroad, to certain key priests whose cooperation he wanted to enlist.

Despite his reputation from the *Mail* days, Farrer apparently still had friends among Manitoba priests. In one early report from Winnipeg, on 29 July 1900, he wrote:

Dear Mr Boudreau: I spent a couple of hours at St. Boniface yesterday talking to some clergy whom I knew years ago when I lived here. So far as the School question is concerned, the facts, as I gather them, are as follows: –

(1) The attempt to revive the issue here in Winnipeg is being made by certain Irish Catholics with a party object in view. But, speaking generally, the French Catholics of Winnipeg and St. Boniface are not desirous of seeing it raised again.

(2) The chairman of the Public School Board in Winnipeg is ready to go as far as he can to bring about a reasonable adjustment, but the agitators referred to are not in a reasonable frame of mind; they want too much.

(3) The present Provincial Government would like to see Sir Wilfrid injured over the question, and is undoing the good effect of the Greenway concessions by ignoring them and seeking to enforce the law as it stood originally.

(4) While the Archbishop feels very strongly on the subject, he is kept down partly by the presence of the Papal Legate, partly by the indifference manifested by the mass of the French Catholics. Then again he sees, what indeed was obvious to all, that Greenway suffered for the concessions he made, the Orangemen returning to the Tory party at the recent Provincial Elections, and being now hostile to the Liberals, because of the Greenway concessions ...

(5) The Archbishop is undoubtedly working quietly by letter etc., to stir up the hierarchy in Quebec. The minor clergy at St. Boniface are of the opinion that Sir Wilfrid will, for this reason, lose ground in Quebec ... It looks, therefore, as if it were a case of 'Anything to beat Laurier' with His Grace ...[22]

The following February Farrer was back in Winnipeg, this time apparently trying to implement a tacit agreement between Laurier and the new premier, Rodmund Roblin, not to exploit the schools issue. Evidently not wanting to make the agreement directly with the Tory premier, Laurier sent Farrer a letter that was to be kept confidential, but could be shown to Roblin. In it Laurier said he would be 'happy to contribute my fullest share' to have the difficulties removed. 'I will see that no political capital is made out of this question, in so far as my Party is concerned, and I hope that the same attitude will be maintained by the Leader of the Conservative Party.'[23]

A week later Laurier also wrote a curious pair of letters that seem in effect to offer rewards to priests who were helpful in seeking a settlement. The offers were hardly significant enough to be considered bribes, but there is a suggestive fit between the names of those offered assignments abroad and those whom Farrer mentioned as being among the helpful. Laurier's letters said:

Private and *Confidential*.   Ottawa, 25th Feb. 1901
My dear Farrer,
I understand that [Sir Clifford] Sifton has a special work in connection with emigration amongst Canadians in the Western States, to be done next summer. I have taken the liberty of suggesting Father Drummond's name for the purpose. Would you ascertain from Father Drummond if he would accept the work which would involve an absence of about three months ...

Private and *Confidential*   Ottawa, 25th. Feb. 1901
My dear Farrer,
I have a special work which I want to have done in Paris, which would consist in the searching of old archives in the several Departments and which would probably involve an absence of two months from Canada. I have thought that Father Cherrier would be a good man for that work. Would you ascertain if he would accept the task ...[24]

Farrer had already been pressing by wire for these letters,[25] and a hint of their purpose shows up in a letter he wrote to Boudreau, dated only 27 January, apparently from 1901:

Father Cherrier will, I am sure, accept the chance of going to France for a few months provided he can get the Archbishop's permission. I told him today, purely as a guess, that you probably desired to have the archives at Paris searched for documents relating to the North West ... Father Cherrier and Father Drummond will be glad to co-operate with Mr Bole for a settlement. I am now trying to get certain influences to work upon the Tory members of the Public School Board, and have hopes of succeeding. But it will take me at least a fortnight more.

Mr Sifton gave me leave to offer Brother Mulvilhill of the Christian Brothers a journey to Ireland on Immigration business. He lives at St. Laurent but the Jesuits have sent for him and he will be here in a day or two. He is quite an important man in Irish Catholic circles.

I really believe that, if only the Archbishop will keep quiet, a settlement can be brought about ...[26]

The following summer Farrer again visited Winnipeg and reported (from Montreal, between trips to Winnipeg and Washington) that progress was being made on the issue. The archbishop had been away, he noted, and it seemed likely a settlement could be reached 'if he will only keep his hands off.'[27] That hope collapsed, however, and Farrer eventually had to report failure in a long 1903 report notable for its praise of moderates and condemnation of extremists on both sides. That stance may not have been surprising for a government agent seeking compromise, but anyone familiar with his performance on the *Mail* would have been astonished by the reference to 'the clamour of the extremists in the Protestant population.' The report praised individual members of the board from both sides of the dispute but again attacked the archbishop and suggested finally that his resistance was politically motivated:

I feel bound to add that both in Winnipeg and St. Boniface the belief prevails, be it well or ill founded, that His Grace does not desire to see the controversy quieted through the instrumentality of Sir Wilfrid Laurier and the law of 1897, that he dislikes Sir Wilfrid personally, that he is too ardent in politics on the Conservative side, and that his past utterances on this subject have embittered the Protestant majority so that a lasting reconciliation will be difficult to accomplish while he remains at the head of the Diocese. On the other hand, there is no question that the Conservatives of Winnipeg, including Mr Roblin himself, would like to see the question left unsettled in order that it may continue to afford Catholics a grievance against the Liberal Party.[28]

By 1906 Farrer clearly had an unusual reputation not only for quiet 'fixing' but also for unearthing political or business skulduggery – a reputation built partly on his extensive network of contacts and partly on his ability to sift patiently through mountains of accounts and to make a detective's connections. In that year he appears to have been engaged in some sort of investigation of corruption on the government-owned Intercolonial rail line. In that year, too, he urged Laurier in one letter on political corruption to 'punish offenders, high and low, relentlessly.' In view of this moralistic tone, it is the more surprising that Farrer's papers contain a mystery letter written to him that year which, on the face of it, appears to implicate him in a massive deal to sell inside information to a contractor. The files give no hint of Farrer's reply to the letter, or the circumstances surrounding the case. It is conceivable, perhaps, that Farrer may have been trying to smoke out the intentions of the man who wrote him, apparently a broker named Abel H. Gilbert of Gilbert and Company in New York. It is conceivable (but not likely) that the broker misread something in Farrer's earlier correspondence. It is also conceivable that Farrer, now in his mid-fifties, with no permanent appointment or pension in the offing, with evidence all around him that others were making fortunes from political deals, succumbed to temptation.

The year had not been a good one for him. In February his only son, Henry, a railway clerk in Montreal, had died at the age of thirty-two. He had left a widow and daughter, presumably the relatives Ham spoke of when he said Farrer was generous with family members dependent on him. He may well have felt the press of financial problems. He may also have had a return of the problem of depression. Henry's body had been buried in Beechwood Cemetery on 8 May, four days before Farrer wrote the mysterious Mr Gilbert, evidently to ask for a pay-off, and twenty-one days before he advised Laurier to punish offenders relentlessly.

Whatever the circumstances, the letter has a damning appearance – so much so, in fact, that it is surprising Farrer kept it in his files through the remaining decade of his life:

PRIVATE May 17th. 1906
Mr E. Farrer
488 Wilbrod Street,
Ottawa, Ont., Canada.

My dear Mr Farrer:

If your letter of May 12th means anything it is that money is required in the immediate future to 'hold' your friends. I am greatly surprised that you should make this demand so soon after your emphatic declaration that money was not and would not be required. It was the rock we split on before, and we may all of us face the situation now as well as at any other time. Neither Mr Barrett nor myself is in a position to procure money for the purpose you intimate and if its use is a pre-requisite to further negotiations we may as well end the business right now.

We offer you on the signing of a contract an amount variously estimated to be equivalent to from $200,000. to $300,000., according to the extent of the work secured. We also tender your friend and his associates sub-contracts which on fair terms will mean their independence for the remainder of their lives.

Political influence may have its value, but it is problematical, and while we want all interests with, rather than against us, we are not in a position to pay for it, we are content with that of yourself alone properly exerted.

The whole matter can be reduced to a very simple proposition. When ready place your friends in communication with our principals, let them show their willingness to furnish the desired information and we can do business. Otherwise, I think it would be only a waste of time to continue negotiations.

If you can induce Mr M to meet our principal, and submit to a square talk, our end will be accomplished. We do not ask him to give us any information until he is satisfied that it is in his interests to do so.

The matter of bidding, whether through Canadians or Americans, is a matter of detail which can be arranged later.

An early reply will greatly oblige,

Yours very truly,
A.H. Gilbert[29]

The letter Farrer wrote to Laurier a week or so later is in startling contrast, amounting to an act of extreme hypocrisy unless the Gilbert letter was something other than what it appeared to be:

488 Wilbrod,
Ottawa,
May 29th, 1906

CONFIDENTIAL
Dear Sir Wilfrid Laurier

I dislike troubling you about such matters, but, as you like to hear the truth, I am sure you will allow me to say that the present scandals are creating a painful impression on the minds of Liberals of the better class. I do not know what facts Mr Borden may have concerning the management of the Interior Department, but the Tories say that an investigation will bring to light graver scandals than any yet produced ... From all I can gather, they contemplate at the Fall Session asking for a special Committee on Intercolonial affairs. You may recollect my telling you about the Eastern Supply Company. Its operations are being investigated for the Tories by W.C. Milner. He is a journalist and an able fellow. He belongs to the Maritime Provinces and has been pursuing the inquiry for a year past. I was over a good portion of the Intercolonial in March last and met him in several places. When I saw him he was investigating the relations between the coal companies and the Intercolonial. What he told me was very similar in substance to the charges made by Mr A.H. Harris, at one time Traffic Manager of the Intercolonial, in a private report to Mr Blair, namely, that the companies club together and put in different tenders, all of which, however, are exorbitant; then they divide the contract amongst themselves in accordance with their capacity of output. Harris declared that in this way they robbed the Intercolonial of $60,000 a year over and above a fair profit ... As you are aware, there is more or less boodling on the Grand Trunk, the Canadian Pacific and other Corporation railways of which the public knows nothing. I found in March traces and indications of such boodling on the Intercolonial. What I found and suspected was not any worse than one could find on the Corporation roads. But the public will view any rascality on the Intercolonial with stern displeasure. I surmise that the Opposition will put a budget of Milner's discoveries before the House at the next Session and argue therefrom that gigantic swindling can be unearthed if you will only grant a special enquiry. I do not believe any gigantic swindling has taken place since Mr Blair left. I am tolerably sure that Mr Emmerson [Henry R. Emmerson, minister of railways] and Mr Butler have done all that men could do to stop leaks and abolish irregularities; and am quite certain that they have no knowledge of the petty boodling now going on, and which, as I have said, characterizes Corporation roads no less than the Intercolonial.

The painful revelations that came to light in the latter days of the [G.W.] Ross administration in Ontario, have made Ontario Liberals – I am speaking of the rank and file – extremely sensitive on the subject of scandals. If I may make a suggestion, the wise policy would be to punish offenders, high and low, relentlessly ...

With great respect
E. Farrer[30]

Farrer's kind words on Henry Emmerson raise the question of whether the railways minister could have been the mysterious 'M' mentioned in the Gilbert letter. At the time, Emmerson was deeply engaged in plans for the National Transcontinental rail line. The scope of that project and the level of Emmerson's position provide one of the few combinations that would have justified kickbacks on the scale Gilbert mentioned. Emmerson, too, was something of a scapegrace, and his career was about to founder. Like Farrer, he had a drinking problem. He pledged abstinence to Laurier but failed to live up to it, and the prime minister in 1907 forced his resignation, during a flurry of scandal charges. (At one point Emmerson solemnly informed the Commons that he had 'never been in a hotel in Montreal with a woman of ill repute.'[31] One account also suggested that he was castrated by an Ottawa surgeon who, equipped with chloroform and his surgical implements, discovered the minister sleeping with his wife.)[32]

Even if Emmerson was 'M', of course, the Gilbert letter proves nothing about his own honesty or about Farrer's. It could be that Farrer was hoping to make a deal with the minister but failed to do so. It could even be possible that Farrer was acting for Laurier in setting a trap for the minister. If indeed the Gilbert letter does represent an act of barefaced corruption on Farrer's part, it appears to be unique; other letters in his own papers or in other collections show an element of political manipulation, but not of a corrupt kind. There appears to be nothing else on the record that sheds light on Farrer's intentions in the Gilbert affair, or indicates whether it was part of a pattern.

While investigating, negotiating, lobbying, and 'fixing' for Sir Wilfrid, Farrer also at times fed propaganda to newspapers in an organized way. This work seems to have come mainly at election times. In 1904, for instance, a few months before Laurier's second election as prime minister, Farrer submitted to him a copy of fact sheets being sent out, together with a list of newspapers, ranging from the Winnipeg *Free Press* down to the Cayuga *Advocate*. The sophistication of the operation is shown by Farrer's comment that there were about 320 such newspapers, plus a second list of 46 newspapers, independent or semi-Conservative, to which 'matter of a somewhat different kind' was sent.[33] During the election campaign, too, Farrer may have run some sort of propaganda bureau within the party organization. A routine letter of recommendation written for a young Quebecker early in 1906 suggests this. Farrer said he had known the young man for about a year, and added: '... during two periods I employed him to translate campaign articles for the French-Canadian press, and to perform other work of a confidential nature, which he did in admirable fashion.'[34] Farrer's letters also make clear that at times he used his own judgment in feeding information to specific newspapers. A case in point was the 1900 railway scandal when he said he would 'use the material I have through the newspapers at the proper time.' Another was a 1910 note to E.J. Lemaire of Laurier's office, attaching a story he was sending to the London *Daily News* 'by way of making Sir Wilfrid's attitude on the navy question clear to the English reader.'[35]

Farrer also wrote speeches for Sir Wilfrid, and it was this activity, according to Hector Charlesworth, that led in one case to embarrassment for the prime minister. The incident, Charlesworth wrote, came during a 1903 debate on construction of the Grand Trunk Pacific and National Transcontinental lines. Promoters of the National Transcontinental wanted to build the line well north of Lake Superior to broaden settlement up to the 'clay belt,' Charlesworth said, and Farrer added a flourish to their propaganda, quoting from an alleged report of a Jesuit missionary who had grown roses in the region. Laurier was challenged on the reference, and thereafter had a 'verbal encounter' with Farrer – an encounter that was 'only saved from becoming a bitter altercation by the sense of humour which was a marked characteristic of both men.'[36]

This story raises another contradiction: while Laurier's long 1903 speech on introduction of the National Transcontinental bill does indeed look like Farrer's work, especially in a section dealing with studies of terrain through which the line would pass, there is no reference to clay-belt roses. It is interesting to note, though, a hint by Conservative leader Robert Borden that Farrer had 'drynursed' the prime minister through the speech – and had quoted and rebutted material he himself had written in the New York *Sun* on the bonding privilege.[37]

Whatever the truth of these implications, Farrer certainly did on occasion write Commons speeches for Laurier. At times these can be identified from Farrer's very distinctive handwriting. One such, entitled 'Notes on the Naval Proposal,' is notable for the way it subtly promotes an anti-imperial line, beginning:

It would be easy, I think, to show that the course of the Government in asserting the right and duty of Canada to control her naval enterprises and whatever expenditures they may entail, is in line with the course of a former Liberal administration, which held it to be a cardinal part of Responsible

Government that she should control her Militia force and Militia expenditure down to the last man and the last dollar, rather than leave them to the supervision of the Imperial authorities ... It is strictly in line, too, with the policy of such eminent Conservatives as Sir John Macdonald and Sir Alexander Galt, who successfully resisted the view that the Imperial authorities should be allowed to manage or to interfere with the Canadian tariff, and who enabled us in the end to enjoy full and absolute self-government in that as in other matters, subject, of course to the maintenance of British connection to which every Canadian, whatever his race, creed or party, is pledged.

Taking them in order of time, let me direct the attention of the House for a moment to ... [38]

Material of this kind, set against Charlesworth's story, again points up the contrast between Farrer's reputation for mischievousness and the actual quality of his performance. The myth – created in part by Farrer's own yarn-spinning – is one of obstreperousness and irresponsibility. The hard evidence paints him otherwise: as a serious, tireless investigator and negotiator and analyst and propagandist. There seems no doubt from the record that Laurier trusted Farrer over a period of at least twenty years, in a manner hard to credit if he was indeed untrustworthy, or if he indeed had betrayed the party and led it into ambush back in the election of 1891.

15 A More Natural Passion

What sort of man *was* Edward Farrer? Behind the guise of amiable mercenary, behind the charm that won easy friendship, behind even the massive competence that so impressed colleagues, what lay at the core of the man? Could he be called an arrogant intellectual, playing mischievous mind games? A true internationalist, ahead of his time? A committed anti-imperial agent? A clever but weak man, ready to prostitute his skills? A philosopher, detached from the petty games around him?

None of these adequately sums up Farrer. As nearly as can be seen, from the thousands of hours he put into his writing, from the testimony of those who knew him, from the papers he left behind, he was a man with a rich inner life, detached from the world's values despite his engagement in it. He was in the best sense a scholar, absorbing and analysing knowledge in a dozen areas. His command of communications matters alone – his encyclopaedic knowledge of freight rates and duties and subsidies and comparative routes – is worthy of awe, even though the matter is largely irrelevant to a later age.

None of this, of course, gives a final answer on what sort of man he *was* – but his work record shows a great deal about what he was *not*. He was not (like Martin Griffin) a sycophant. While he was unfailingly courteous, there is nothing on the record that shows him grasping for approval, for social status. He was not (like Nicholas Flood Davin) a braggart. There is nothing on the record that shows him boasting of his own talents or accomplishments. He was not (like George Brown or John Ross Robertson) a bully. While he hit hard occasionally at scoundrels above him, there is nothing that shows him using his position to damage anyone gratuitously.

The question of Farrer's character, or morality, or integrity, remains, however, a frustratingly difficult one, with much to be said on both sides. The case for the prosecution might be headed with the charge that he was unprincipled and irresponsible in using race and creed issues to try to break up Confederation and bring on annexation. The case for the defence might start with the point that he gave up a great deal for his belief in political union, even though he abhorred the role of martyr or fanatic and seemed to hold the belief lightly. When he left the *Globe*, he was at the peak of his powers and reputation, and could have gone on, if he had chosen to conform, to a prosperous career as the country's leading journalist. It is not surprising, of course, that some of his generation stigmatized him as a traitor and turncoat, but it could also be argued that he showed endurance in supporting an unpopular cause. History has little time for losers, and if political union had been achieved, his later reputation would undoubtedly have been quite different.

Farrer's role in the *Mail*'s 'race and creed' fury is more difficult to defend – or even to understand – although some points might be made in extenuation of the offence. It appears that he did indeed believe the central tenets of the campaign: that the Catholic hierarchy was a threat to liberal democracy, and that the country had no future as a bilingual state. There is fairly clear evidence that he tried to limit the campaign to these areas, avoiding the extremes of bigotry shown by Goldwin Smith and Christopher Bunting. The evidence elsewhere in his career points to a genuine interest in, and sympathy for, French-Canadian culture. There seems little doubt, though, that he exploited the race and religion differences for his own purposes. And the mysterious Gilbert letter leaves an equally dark question against his record for integrity. His friend Walter Gregory found he lacked character, and these two episodes seem to support the criticism.

Farrer did not, however, lack conviction, despite the doubts of his friends. He chose to wear his convictions lightly, and he had tasted and discarded too many ideas ever to be a fanatic. But the record is clear that he believed in liberal humanism – in enlightenment. He believed that education, knowledge, and free thought were intrinsically better than aristocratic or religious authority; that the New World ought to be a new world, shaking off the nationalism and militarism and feudalism and clericalism that had protected the ruling classes of Europe while crushing all others. But even these beliefs he mingled with a certain wryness – a recognition that human nature and idealism seldom mixed.

So while many questions about him must remain open, it can be said with confidence that he was a man of marked individuality, of outstanding intellect – and of conviction. The debate among his friends on his lack of convictions means only that he did not share *their* convictions, and dealt with the problem by putting on a guise of amiability. Even on his religious views, his friends' confusion probably arose not because he was inconsistent but because he was unusual – neither orthodox nor atheist. His personal credo, stated often in various shadings throughout his career, was perhaps never better summed up than in the conclusion of an 1892 *Globe* editorial on fundamentalism:

The important question for each man is not whether he gives his merely intellectual assent or his merely intellectual denial to this or that doctrine as to the inspiration of the Scriptures, but what parts of the Scriptures have sunk into his heart, have saturated his thought, and are the motives of his actions. Those passages, at least, are for him inspired and inspiring. Our forefathers who believed that the sun revolved around the earth nevertheless got along very well; in spite of their error the sun warmed them, gave them light and health, and made their grain grow and their flowers bloom. The mortal error in this case would be to shut out the rays of the sun, as the mortal error in the other would be to shut out the rays of Divine truth ...[1]

These words are not those of a man who was uncertain about his religious views, just as his writing about aristocracy or imperialism or militarism, over four decades and more, are not those of a man who lacked conviction.

Tracing the 'true inwardness' (to use one of his own favourite phrases) of Farrer's beliefs or motives in the important writing of his first two decades in journalism is exceedingly difficult. He was known, of course, as an immensely prolific writer, and he may well have published, during that period, more words than anyone else in the country. To some extent his 'real' viewpoint emerged in the shadings of his argument, even when he wrote on both sides of an issue. Without the guidance of his later, bylined writing, though, attempts to define his views would be difficult and dangerous.

Ironically, this later writing is relatively unimportant, except as an indication of his true thoughts. In the 1880s and early 1890s he had worked at a crucial headwater of opinion formation, creating editorial pages read by everyone of influence – at least in the relevant party.

No politicians, certainly no editor, could afford *not* to read the long leaders of the *Mail* or the *Globe*. And their impact was immediate, in the rapid change of events and alliances. Other writers might in time produce more thoughtful and detailed analyses, but they would be read after opinions had hardened or decisions had been taken. The *Mail* and *Globe* worked on readers' minds while the metal was still hot. In an age before broadcasting, before wire services, they were given remarkable attention. Their readers included all the most influential people in the country.

By contrast, in the early years of the new century Farrer was writing from the periphery of the political world. And the game itself had changed: journalism had become more decentralized. Even the *Globe* and its counterpart, the *Mail and Empire*, no longer spoke, or were heard, as gospel. The leading journalists of the day, the Atkinsons or Dafoes or Willisons, wrote from a stance somewhat detached from party, albeit sympathetic. Although close to government, Farrer at that point was far from the centres of journalistic influence.

Nevertheless, some of his long, scholarly – and signed – articles after the turn of the century are of interest because they show his mature and independent views on the main issues that concerned him, and cast light on his earlier views. In these writings he remained hostile to British imperialism, while showing warm respect for British liberal institutions. He was still convinced that Canada would be better off as part of the United States but mildly criticized American tendencies to browbeat smaller neighbours. He detected rising nationalism in Canada but felt any future as an independent state would be unhappy and short, largely because of the difficulty of operating what he considered to be a bi-racial state. Only in his very late writing is there detectable softening in that view. One such instance came in a 1910 article in which he praised Sir Alexander Galt's efforts to detach Canada from Britain and condemned the 'immense claptrap' of imperialists in both parties. In the final paragraph of that column he seemed to have come some way towards acceptance of Edward Blake's view that Canada had a 'higher though more arduous destiny' than union with the United States. Galt's dream of an independent Canada, he conceded, had much to recommend it. Loyalty to Empire was all very well, but loyalty to Canada was a more natural passion, and therefore bound to be in the end the dominating passion with Canadians.[2]

This statement must be taken with caution, though, since it is doubtful whether Farrer saw loyalty to Canada as separate from loyalty to his North American or New World vision. It would be too easy to assume Farrer had experienced a late-in-life conversion to devout Canadian nationalism; the weight of his signed writing leaned very much the other way.

One of Farrer's most thorough and reasoned arguments for political union was set out in an article entitled 'The Future of Canada,' a long essay that started by reviewing his well-known hostility to imperial centralization and then turned to the continental prospects:

Assuming then that Imperial Federation and Imperial Reciprocity are undesirable and impracticable, what is to be the future of Canada? I had better begin by saying that there is no feeling in favour of annexation to the United States. A good many Canadians regard annexation as our ultimate destiny, but, for the present, side with those who believe that, although bisected in race, language and religion, Canada has a future as an independent nation.

Some of us, a feeble minority indeed, think she should join the United States without waiting to experiment with independence, which could not fail to be a short and turbulent existence ...

Farrer argued that Confederation had been resorted to partly to save Canada from drifting into the United States, partly to 'furnish more ample means of swamping the French.' But if the growth of Western Canada failed to meet the expectations of those who wanted to see French influence obliterated, he said, it would be unwise for Canada, as a house divided, to set up as an independent state:

Lastly, annexation would give us what we most need – population, capital, a rich market for our wares, more opportunities of employment, a future free from perplexity, and uplifting national ideals in place of the sordid ones native to every colony. We should not enter the Republic strangers, a multitude of Canadians are there already, and we can fancy them greeting us with a full heart, 'My brethren and my father's house have come unto me.'³

While Farrer thus had no compunction about advocating annexation, his writing was more often directed against the imperial fervour that was so widespread in Canada in the early years of the century. It was not an easy period in which to be pro-American or anti-British. Canadians – or, at least, English Canadians – had responded with a surge of imperial fervour to Victoria's jubilee and to the Boer War, while finding the Americans bumptiously chauvinistic in such events as the Spanish-American War or the Alaska boundary dispute.

Farrer was of course appalled by Canada's part in the Boer War, but his views were so out of step with the hysteria of English-language Canadian media (to say nothing of politicians) that he had no effective platform. Even the *Weekly Sun* – the former *Farmers' Sun*, now edited by Walter Dymond Gregory and still sponsored by Goldwin Smith – had to tone down Farrer's already cautious material. A Farrer manuscript in Gregory's files, heavily edited, illustrates how sensitive the media of the day were to the imperialistic mania. The editor eliminated entirely a lead saying Canadian MPs were 'playing to the bleachers' and trying to outshine each other in a display of Empire loyalty. It picked up into a section where Farrer explained that Laurier, as a French Canadian, had been squeezed into pre-war support for the British position because the Tories otherwise would have impeached his loyalty. Thereafter several sections were excised in which Farrer made sarcastic reference to bellicose officers, slavish newspapers, and unprincipled politicians.[4] In the mood of the times heavy editing of that sort was probably the best treatment Farrer could expect, and he does not seem to have taken issue with Gregory. The following May Gregory boasted to him that the *Sun* controllers had been 'standing to our guns very well' in the face of heavy attack over their war policy, and he twitted Farrer for his outspokenness on the issue. 'It is rumored that you left with the First Contingent determined to insist on British supremacy in South Africa,' he wrote, 'and your continued absence gives color to the rumor.'[5]

While his anti-imperialist views were thus well known, they were usually stated in reflective and low-key language. The depth of his feeling was perhaps best stated in an article entitled 'A Canadian View of Imperialism,' contained in his files in manuscript form, and possibly not published. Courageous in the context of the times, the article separated the 'sane and moderate' imperialist from the mindless jingo, and appealed calmly to the former while excoriating the latter in terms that came as close to anger as anything in Farrer's writing:

The Imperialist party in England consists, apparently, of two groups, one represented by the common or music-hall Jingo, who clamours for 'little wars' and the annexation of territory from the mere love of excitement; the other composed of high-minded men, with a strongly developed sentimental side, who honestly believe that their schemes of imperial union are called for by the exigencies of the times. The former, who used to delight in reading about prize fights at home and now has an equal relish for newspaper accounts of the slaughter of breech clout enemies abroad, seems to be dangerous only when played upon in the mass by the yellow press ... Jingoism may be roughly defined as a perversion of the moral vision of a considerable body of Englishmen due in the main to the excessive indulgence of the race in the putting to death of inferior races. In the last half century, several hundred thousand Zulus, Afghans, Kafirs, Maoris, Arabs and what not, must have been shot for being in the way of the extension of the Empire, and multitudes were doomed to speedy extinction. As incidents of the universal combat in nature, these campaigns possess a melancholy interest; but, as a test of skill and prowess in war, they amount to little, the spear and matchlock having no sort of chance against a machine-gun, with the resources of England behind it ... If full-blooded Jingoes should ever reach office, therefore, the Empire would be no place for communities like Canada or Australia; we should have to get out to save ourselves, if not from danger, from disrepute. As it is, the Jingo has led England into adventures which have entailed a great increase of taxation, and we Colonists suspect that his slobbering affection for us is prompted by the hope that we may be induced to share the burden.

The modern colonist, Farrer wrote, was radically different from the colonist of former times, who was regarded as a below-stairs Englishman, ready if 'tipped' to perform any sort of drudgery for the Empire:

True, seven or eight thousand Canadians served, at the expense of the British Treasury, in the Boer War; but that does not prove him to be an Imperialist any more than the fact that 30,000 Canadians fought for the North in the American Civil War convicts him of being a Republican. He went to both wars from love of adventure, to see something of the world. Those who fought for the North can now boast that, under God and His servant, Abraham Lincoln, they were instruments in the emancipation of several millions of slaves. On the other hand, those who fought against the Boers ask themselves what, after all, has been accomplished for humanity, what interest they, as Canadians, had in such a quarrel, and whether the United States if so minded might not be able to trump up just as good an excuse for attacking Canada ... Canadians of all origins have the greatest respect for England, as distinguished from the Empire, and if she should ever be in real peril, what little they could do for her would be done with a good heart. With them, however, the chief end of man is not war and destruction but peace, industry and colonization.⁶

Over the next few years themes of this kind turned up regularly in Farrer's writing. In a 1905 article for *Fortnightly Review*, for instance, he condemned the idea of Canadian troops fighting Empire battles, as 'swashbucklers of the British Jingo.' He opposed a centralized imperial command, saying Canada had gained nothing in recent English wars that justified handing over £5 million a year – one-third of all its present revenues – to the British War Office, to be spent thousands of miles beyond Parliament's jurisdiction, on military objects about which Canadians would not be consulted. And he said the imperialists' proposals for unified trade systems made no more sense: they insisted that it would not injure Canadian manufactures, yet told the British artisan it would immensely extend the colonial market for his wares. They said it would not raise the price of food in England, yet would put more money in the pocket of the colonial food-grower. 'To us, the whole project appears to be a bundle of contradictions such as our Protectionists, who do not stick at trifles, would be ashamed to father.'⁷

Five years later, in his columns for *Canadian Century*, Farrer was still writing the same anti-imperialist line, although the tone was somewhat muted. In the magazine's first issue, on 8 January 1910, for instance, he wrote of the coming naval debate, endorsing Laurier's plan to build a Canadian navy rather than contributing to the imperial navy. In his usual way he used the issue to review Canada's progress towards independence and to warn – but in a mild tone – against imperial bullying. He recalled that Aristotle considered some races fit only to be subjects, who benefited from coming into contact with the superior intelligence of the Greeks, and said the average Englishman had once entertained much the same sort of belief about Canadians. But this attitude was changing: 'Instead of being a remote possession constantly looking to him for help, we are on a fair way to become a great and powerful ally, although he must allow us to put Canadian interests first and to be always true to ourselves as the essential condition of our being useful to him.'⁸

Over the next few weeks Farrer returned several times to the naval issue. 'We are now in the full swing of an imperialist reaction in which the colonies are playing a considerable part,' he wrote on 26 February. 'It remains to be seen whether they can be induced to participate in the wars of England as a regular occupation, and how they are likely to fare in the double role of self-governing New World nations and tributary states of the Old.' The following week he produced an article entitled 'The Loyalty of Canadians' – the article wherein he condemned the nonsense of all-out support for Empire and praised Alexander Galt's vision of an independent Canada. That point, though, was made only after a very careful and subtle discussion of changing conceptions of loyalty. On first reading, in fact, the article seemed to be unrelated to current concerns and intended only as a *defence* of the United Empire Loyalists against attack by a reviewer who had found them a 'poor-spirited caste, always on the side of the monarch, always against the people.' It was only in the middle of the piece that readers might realize that Farrer was painting the Loyalists as admirable but misguided – a curious anachronism. And it was many paragraphs later before they would realize the Loyalists were being used as a parallel to the modern imperialists:

When the reviewer says the Loyalist descendants reverse the natural order and profess a greater loyalty to the Empire than to Canada, he is doubtless speaking from what he has read of the immense clap-trap in which Parliament has been indulging over the Naval Policy. Members, Liberal and Conservative, assert in the conventional manner that they would vote our last shilling and last man for the defence of England and the Empire; but in almost every instance they do it with a considerable mental reservation, for it occurs to them, as to the rest of us, that perhaps England, India, Australia, New Zealand and South Africa might not rush to our assistance with equal alacrity, or, indeed, rush at all, were Canadian territory coveted by the United States.

Farrer then went on to review the work of Sir Alexander Galt in promoting Canadian autonomy, as a lesson in self-reliance:

He believed in a strong Canadian militia – there was no talk of a Canadian navy then – and frequently said that if we were not prepared to defend ourselves we need not look for help elsewhere since it would not be forthcoming. He was under no illusions. He did not imagine we could prevent the Americans from overrunning Canada if they chose to attack us; but at any rate we could show that we were not base metal ... Shortly before his death he expressed the belief that when the gust of Imperialism, then beginning to sweep over England and Canada, had spent its force, most intelligent Canadians would come round to his way of thinking.

Whatever may be said against it, Galt's dream of an independent Canada has something uplifting about it. His speeches are genuine and from the heart and far better reading even now than the wholesale make-believe which has been going on at Ottawa. By all means let us be loyal to England and the Empire, but loyalty to Canada is the more natural passion, and therefore bound to be in the end the dominating passion with Canadians. There is a good deal of truth in the old dictum that if, next to the love of God, the land where we were born and live does not occupy the chief place in our affections, we are not fit to live at all.⁹

Despite his antagonism for British imperialism Farrer admired some English qualities, especially the restraint and urbanity of English politicians. In fact, nothing so well demonstrates his distaste for the brawling dimension of Canadian politics – and Canadian journalism – as his comments on the English approach. A 1910 essay on English campaign oratory, for instance, seemed mainly directed at Canadian politicians, but made its points in a kindly and indirect way:

It is said that the habit of stuttering was cultivated in England out of respect for the Hanoverian Kings, who could not speak English well and hesitated while thinking for the proper word. The halting manner in which most Englishmen speak when addressing an audience greatly amused some of the Canadian and American correspondents engaged in watching the recent election campaign ... Yet I am afraid the verdict of an impartial tribunal would be that the spoken matter of the Englishmen is out of sight superior to the best article in that line which our most eminent orators could produce. It is a humiliating confession, but there is no help for it. Take, for instance, the campaign speeches of Mr [A.J.] Balfour. We all know that years ago he wrote books on metaphysical subjects and made a name for himself in Parliament at a critical time. Nevertheless he is a poor speaker in one sense, halts and limps and hesitates and stammers; added to which he is wretchedly inadequate at quoting by the yard from Hansard to show that the other fellows have been among the Sons of Belial from the beginning. But if anyone wishes to read speeches full of matter of an extremely high order of intellectual excellence let him procure those delivered by Mr Balfour during the last five or six weeks. One may consider his premises unsound and his conclusions economically evil, but there is no denying the charm of his moderation and frankness or the winning way in which he states his case in language at once simple and beautiful, and therefore extraordinarily powerful.

Farrer concluded that public speaking of this superb English kind could not be expected in Canada until it had attained cultural maturity:

> An old Greek observed of eloquence that it does not, as some vainly imagine, consist of the outward manner, of the copiousness of the language, or of the arrangement of the argument, but essentially in the pith and virtue of what one has to say, which in turn is the product of intellectual and social cultivation. Just now we in Canada are so busy laying the foundations of a New World nation that we have not had time to develop the highest sources of true eloquence; but all that will be remedied by and by ...[10]

That article, written when Farrer was nearing sixty, and showing no partisan undertones, can perhaps be considered vintage work, containing as it does so many of the qualities that drew respect for his craftsmanship. Most striking, perhaps, is the ability to differentiate, to savour Balfour's language and debating skills while finding his ideas 'economically evil.' It was the same quality that allowed him to feel affection and admiration for Macdonald while condemning his at-times corrupt policies. It was the quality that enabled him to attack the Roman Catholic hierarchy while retaining friends in the priesthood. Most politicians and journalists of the day painted in blacks and whites; Farrer commanded a more sophisticated palette.

Technically the article also shows a number of more specific skills. Most obvious are the range and simplicity of language and the unostentatious use of literary and historical allusion. There is also the knack of identifying with the readers, of drawing them into the discussion and sharing perceptions, rather than talking down to them ('*We* all know that years ago he wrote books on metaphysical subjects ...'). There is the graceful technique of starting out with a little parable or anecdote to catch interest ('It is said that the habit of stuttering was cultivated in England ...'). Finally there is the range of contemporary knowledge – in this case, the close familiarity with British politics. Beyond that there is a curiously gentle, reflective quality – a quality that often appeared in his writing, and showed the ultimate paradox of the thoughtful inner man caught up in the harsh realities of Canadian politics.

In his final years Farrer appeared for a time to be emancipated from the chains of party journalism, able at last to write from the heart.

But the record indicates this was not always the case. Manuscripts left in his personal papers, unsigned but edited in his distinctive handwriting, make clear that at least between 1911 and 1913 he once more went over to the other side and wrote Conservative propaganda. When and why he broke with Laurier is unknown, but in the writings he not only attacked Laurier's revival of the reciprocity dream but, incredibly, his naval policy and his 'straddling' in the Manitoba schools issue. More especially he attacked Laurier's lieutenants, whom he characterized as weak and incompetent, interested only in making 'another dash for the fleshpots' of office.

The first sign of the volte-face came in the late summer of 1911, as Laurier was fighting his last, disastrous campaign as prime minister. The voting was set for 21 September, and Laurier had brought out of storage the twenty-year-old banners of reciprocity, so badly stained by Farrer's pamphlet in 1891. But this time, almost beyond belief, it was Farrer who was arguing that American openness to free trade really meant annexation, and that the Americans could not be trusted.

Granted, the Americans had given him cause when they seriously undermined Laurier's policy after a promising package deal had been negotiated earlier in the year. President Robert Taft himself had delivered the most lethal shaft when he declared that reciprocity would make Canada 'only an adjunct to the United States.' House Speaker Champ Clark had put salt in the wound with his famous statement of hope that he would one day see the American flag flying clear to the North Pole. Taft had also signed a bill that discriminated against Canadian shipments of west coast wheat through the Panama Canal.

Once again, as in 1891, the manufacturers, the banks, and the CPR were hostile to reciprocity, and this (since the CPR was a major client at this point) may provide a clue to Farrer's switch. As recently as the previous fall, Farrer's journalism, particularly in the *Economist*, had shown his usual leaning towards free trade.[11] But on 28 August he filed to the CPR a 'western letter,' date-lined Winnipeg, that started out with seeming sympathy for Laurier and went on to cut away the props from his platform. The story began by explaining that Laurier had delayed a planned western trip, and called it a wise move. 'Although an exceedingly adroit platform orator, he could not very well talk reciprocity at this time when it is being disowned by Mr Taft's supporters in the border States, and when Mr Taft himself, as if to crown the bad taste and bad faith displayed in his "adjunct" letter, has signed the bill ... excluding the Canadian West from equal participation in the advantages of the Panama Canal.'

The actions of Taft and of Congress, Farrer wrote, raised questions on whether Canada would be safe in any kind of negotiations with the United States. When Laurier was dealing with Taft for reciprocity, it would never have entered his head that the president was scheming to bring about political union. 'Yet not the "adjunct" letter only but his speeches after the close of negotiations showed that the President had political union in view quite as much as the extension of commerce, being in this respect no better than Champ Clark or any of the other spread-eaglers of this period.' Furthermore, Laurier had now been shown that Congress was capable of overriding a treaty in order to advance American interests. 'How, then, can he ask us anymore to put our commercial future in the hands of Congress, since that is what reciprocity would really involve?'[12]

Even more breathtaking than the attack on reciprocity was Farrer's turnaround on naval policy, which left him supporting, at least indirectly, the same kind of imperialism he had attacked for years. Yet Farrer's editing is unmistakable on a column in his papers from December 1912, supporting the plan introduced that month by Prime Minister Borden for the sponsoring of three British dreadnoughts. By all the laws of consistency Farrer should have resisted this move to imperial centralization and backed Laurier's rejection of it. Instead, while never endorsing Borden's plan on its own merits, he deftly cut apart Laurier's position. The Liberal stand, he wrote, was merely a ploy designed to get the party back into office. Unanimous approval of the Borden plan would have had considerable moral effect the world over; as it was, German papers were gloating over the division among Canadians. 'If Sir Wilfrid had good or even plausible reasons for objecting to it, no one could complain. But it is a poor business indeed for Canadians to have to explain today that what he wanted, and all he wanted, was to precipitate a general election on the remote chance of his party being returned to office.'

In a second article from the same period Farrer was even more personal, saying the issue showed Laurier's tendency to shape different messages for the two parts of the country: in English Canada he had argued that Borden was not going far enough, while in Quebec he insisted there was no real emergency. 'From long practice he has become adept in the art of straddling, and, as was said of someone else, seldom enunciates a truth without guarding himself against being supposed to exclude the contradictory.'[13]

Even in the opening days of war, though, when a new surge of Empire loyalty swept the country, Farrer's distrust of imperialism resurfaced. In the main he confined himself to neutral topics, such as questions of shipping or financing, but in at least one article the old antagonism showed. Canadians were willing and eager to make their present sacrifice, he said, adding: 'It would be a mistake, however, for Imperialists in England to imagine that hereafter they can draw on us for men and money ad lib, that we shall jump into war after war with the same buoyant spirit ...'[14]

Farrer's papers do not make clear the nature of his relationship with the Conservative party in this period. A letter to him early in 1913 gives a hint that he was writing for a network of papers – possibly the network of CPR sympathizers, or possibly a Conservative grouping. The letter in question pressed the Senate candidacy of one Alex Might, and added: 'Don't hurt him in your 35 papers.'[15] Another letter, from W.H. Aldridge of Trail, BC, sought Farrer's help with the Tory government in securing grazing leases.[16] In mid-1914 there is a letter to Farrer that indicates he was working for the minister of railways. It is from F.P. Gutelius, general manager of government railways, Moncton, and it evidently responds to a Farrer letter asking what questions might be used by the opposition in an attack on the Intercolonial management.[17]

In the pre-war years Farrer's health problems may have slowed his output of writing. A pair of notes in his files from the *Manchester Guardian* (certainly a prestigious client) pressed him, politely, for long-promised material.[18] Until his death in 1910 Goldwin Smith also continued to draw on Farrer's research skills, in notes that reveal something of the tone of the relationship between the two. In 1909, for instance, there was a note that must have amused Farrer, asking ammunition for a possible new outbreak of the ancient war with George Taylor Denison – ammunition in the form of information about the colonel's part in Confederate raids from Canada during the American Civil War.[19] A month earlier Farrer had advised Smith to ignore the 'gross personal insults' heaped on him in Denison's new book, *The Struggle for Imperial Unity*. 'But pray do not let his crazy insolence disturb you,' Farrer wrote. 'Fifty years hence, when the two countries are joined, this book will be a joke and a curiosity, while your name will be revered ...' In the fall of the same year, just after the death of Smith's wife, there was a rather peremptory request for Farrer to come to the Grange, Smith evidently believing, this time with reason, that the inevitable dissolution was at hand. 'I should like very much to have you with me for a few days,' Smith wrote, adding: 'This probably is about our last chance of meeting.' After the visit Farrer wrote apologetically to ask whether he could use some of their conversations as the basis for an article the *Manchester Guardian* had just requested. Smith replied that the material should be held until after his death, since anything written sooner would be sure to 'bring down something unpleasant' in the way of political controversy. 'But be assured I heartily feel this kind manifestation of your friendship. I am always here; always delighted to see you; and to talk over with you the little incidents of my history.'[20]

Reading between the lines, it is not hard to imagine the two ill-matched nonconformists, both near the end of their lives, reassuring each other that their campaigns had not been entirely in vain.

Like Smith, Farrer seems in his final years to have tried to avoid controversy. While his unsigned *Economist* articles still drew respect, especially on rail or financial issues, he was fading from the Canadian public eye. Old associates remembered him fondly, however. 'You are the king of us all yet,' P.D. Ross, now one of the country's leading publishers, wrote in a note to Farrer in 1913, enclosing a cheque for an article he had reprinted in the Ottawa *Journal*.[21] A year earlier a Canadian biographical handbook had quoted the Montreal *Gazette*, once a harsh critic, as calling him the ablest writer on the press of Canada, adding: '... it would scarcely be hyperbole to say that he is the peer of any writer on the American press.'[22] The same sketch had featured a fulsome comment from Willison that must have caused its subject a moment of amusement or chagrin: 'In dignity of style, in grasp of economic questions, in steadiness of purpose, in maturity of mind, and in command of all the resources of his craft, he has few peers in Canadian journalism.'

Why (Farrer must have wondered) had Willison chosen to use that phrase about 'steadiness of purpose'? It was Willison, after all, who had played by the rules and used his opportunities shrewdly, rising now to a position of solid respectability in the land. True, Willison like Farrer had broken with the Liberal party, but not until he was assured a place as editor of the hopefully independent Toronto *News*.

True, Willison had deserted his old idol, Laurier, and thrown all his weight against the reciprocity effort of 1911, but no one called Willison a traitor or a mercenary. In fact, the crossover earned him a knighthood.

From where Farrer stood, it might have seemed that Willison had risen farther with less ability. But if Farrer had any such feeling, it did not stop him from sending congratulations when Willison's knighthood came through in 1913. And Willison, perhaps mindful of shared radicalism of the past, or of Farrer's views about imperial honours, replied in almost apologetic tones. 'You will know that I did not seek knighthood,' he wrote, 'but when it was offered I accepted and so must take the consequences ... I still think you should have got me the position of master of the weigh scales at the market.' At the end of the letter, though, Willison dropped the bantering tone to end on a note of respect and affection: 'I never forget our two years together,' he wrote. 'I knew then and I know better now how much I was and am your pupil and your debtor.'[23]

Farrer's papers show little sign of journalistic or other activity in the last year or two of his life, and it appears that by this time he must have been seriously ill. But he seems even in the final months to have maintained his delight in friendship, as witness the pressing invitations to George Ham. When he died in the spring of 1916, friends not only contributed toward the purchase of the 'Master Craftsman' tombstone but ensured that the same theme was struck in newspaper tributes. For instance, an anonymous and unidentified editorial left in his papers (presumably by his wife, who outlived him by a year) observed:

Every knight of the pen in Canada will bow his head before the bier of, perhaps, the greatest master-craftsman of his art that this country has ever seen. Edward Farrer was in the days of his supreme power the most effective writer of opinion on the Canadian press. A man of wide and accurate knowledge, he possessed the gift of convincing expression to an extraordinary extent ... public opinion in Canada has been more swayed by the genius of Edward Farrer than it has ever suspected.

Mr Farrer was, however, far more than an advocate of causes – he was the creator of policies. Few men had more influence on those who came into immediate contact with them, and his hand shaped many a program which has long since passed into action and into history. His genial personality won him friends in abundance; but his titanic mental powers won him admirers and followers. That he was mistaken in some of his opinions is but the common lot of mortals. Some of his causes became 'lost causes' – in our opinion, properly so. But his pen was ever a power on whatever side it was employed; and only those who have been in a position to pierce his anonymity know how many worthy and successful causes it served.[24]

Other writers were similarly kind. Willison in the *News* offered some of the praise that would show up in his later book, and Annie Farrer was grateful. 'You have read his character better than anyone,' she wrote. 'You have not said one word too much, he deserves the best his friends can say of him.'[25] But Willison was not alone in offering remarkably strong assessments – much more than courtesy demanded. The Toronto *Star*, for one, devoted its lead editorial to Farrer – an indication, given the heavy budget of news that day from both the war and the Irish rebellion, that the tribute may have been written by publisher Joseph Atkinson, who had worked with Farrer on the *Globe*:

Mr Edward Farrer, whose death was announced yesterday, was a great journalist and a man of extraordinary range of intellect. His mind could grasp the most intricate financial question, thrust aside what was of minor importance, and explain what was material in an easy, yet masterful way ... But Mr Farrer was not only an exponent of serious things. He was a humorist of the first rank. He was not conceited about this quality, and he showed it more in his conversation than in his writing.

Always, however, whether in his writing or in his social intercourse, Farrer gave the impression of a master mind. He assimilated information and ideas easily, and yet what he gave out was his own. In whatever he said or wrote, the impression created was of a tremendous, almost infinite, reserve of power. The reader always got the impression that, whatever Farrer said, he could easily have said a great deal more. He did not always agree with the prevailing opinion in Canada, but that does not lessen our regret that he retired from editorial work too soon. We need the influence of vigorous minds, even on the unpopular side.[26]

The *Star*'s front-page headline also saluted Farrer as 'Dean of Journalists,' even though the title was, in a sense, a quarter-century out of date.

The Ottawa *Journal*, in a thoughtful editorial probably written by P.D. Ross (since it echoed the 'king of us all' phrase), had both high praise and also mild censure for the damage Farrer had inflicted on the Conservative party:

If eminence in the ranks of newspaper men is to be judged by power of editorial expression, Edward Farrer was the king of newspaper men in Canada throughout his life, and has had few superiors in any country or clime. An article by Farrer was to the average newspaper editorial as a diamond to a pebble. Compact of logic, thoroughly accurate, pungent with humor, illuminated by wide knowledge of books and men and affairs, the matter of his writing was phrased in clearest English, virile but never coarse, beautiful but never florid. In Mr Farrer's prime every newspaper writer in Canada cheerfully took off his hat to 'Ned' Farrer.

'De mortuis nil nisi bonum,' and so if the Journal offers anything but a tribute of admiration to a great journalist who has crossed the last divide, it is done in only the interests of information regarding an exceptional personality. Ned Farrer had apparently a strong streak of mischief in his powerful make-up. His influence and articles were sometimes suspected to be aimed to breed trouble where trouble was not necessary. At times his phrases bit like vitriol, as for instance the famous sentence, 'then, so much the worse for British connection,' appearing in a leading article in the Toronto Mail threatening what might be done by Canada to the imperial tie if a certain alleged imperial interference with our autonomy were to be attempted.[27] Again, Farrer's influence with C.W. Bunting, managing director of the Toronto Mail in the eighties, when Farrer was editor, was popularly blamed for the disastrous break between the Mail and the Conservative party which was followed by the establishment of the Toronto Empire by Sir John Macdonald. A quarter of a million dollars was lost, together with a lot of the fighting force of the Conservative party, before the Mail and the Empire amalgamated a considerable time afterwards. Farrer was also attacked by political opponents in later years on the ground that he was helping to make trouble at Washington for Canada in connection with reciprocity questions. No doubt he had a right to his own opinions to such matters. The sharpness of the assaults on him in this and other respects illustrated at least the intellectual power of the man who without money or office or party aid or noise made his force much felt in the important affairs of Canada for a considerable era.

A man of powerful physique until his later years, Mr Farrer was kindly and gentle in his manner and we imagine never made a personal enemy.[28]

Other editorial writers struck similar notes. 'Probably no one equalled him in intimate knowledge of what has gone on behind the scenes in Canada's political life for a generation,' the Montreal *Gazette* said.[29] The Edmonton *Journal* spoke of his unique influence,[30] while the Vancouver *Sun*'s writer called him a man of deep learning and marvellous powers of expression, and recalled being present when Goldwin Smith had told a university audience that 'few can hope to write like Edward Farrer.'[31] The *Globe*, for two years Farrer's own paper, also had warm praise; it reviewed the annexation episode and concluded: 'Mr Farrer's marvellous memory, his prodigious industry, and his remarkable gift for the coining of striking phrases were the qualities that made him one of Canada's greatest journalists.'[32]

The anonymous *Globe* writer, perhaps sensitive to the fact that he was writing from Farrer's old chair, also mused, as he wrote, on how influential Farrer had been as a young man. He noted that Farrer was only sixty-six at the time of his death, a fact that would seem 'almost incredible to those who remember that over forty years ago he was a power in the land no political leader could afford to ignore.' Without quite saying it, though, the *Globe* writer implied that Farrer was a man of the past. He seemed to echo a comment by Sir John Willison that Farrer belonged to an earlier period – to the time of Sir John A. Macdonald and Confederation.

And indeed, from the perspective of 1916, Farrer's era must have seemed a much different one: an almost forgotten period of railway building and of Louis Riel, a time of the Pacific Scandal and of the National Policy, of commercial union and imperial federation, of the Orange Lodge and of the Jesuits' Estates – a time of the curious election of 1891, when, for a short period, a continental union had actually been a possibility.

In 1916, in the midst of war, all of that must have seemed very far in the past.

Note on Attribution

Although Edward Farrer was an exceedingly prolific writer, analysis of his work is made difficult by the fact that most of it was unsigned. Some of this anonymous writing can be attributed to him with certainty or near certainty on the basis of his own letters or those of colleagues. Some can be identified with confidence by comparison with signed articles. For instance, the parallels between the following excerpts are striking (the first selection is from a signed *Atlantic Monthly* article in 1881, the second from an unsigned 1882 editorial in the Winnipeg *Times*):

THE HABITANT OF LOWER CANADA

At the conquest in 1760, Lower Canada contained seventy-two thousand French Canadians, the descendants of less than ten thousand emigrants from France. This was a marvellous increase, considering that the little colony had twice recruited the army of Montcalm, waged unceasing war for a century and a half against the Indians, and sent out settlers and traders to the uttermost confines of New France ... the sixty-five thousand peasants left to shift for themselves in the abandoned colony which Voltaire described as 'a few arpents of snow' have increased until their number in North America is not short of two million souls ... Feudalism and religion walked hand in hand in those days, and the colony waxed strong with a pious, thrifty, and prolific people ...[1]

ST. JEAN BAPTISTE DAY

Two hundred and fifty years ago this day was celebrated at Quebec by a little colony of Norman and Breton emigrants. To-day that little colony is represented by over twelve hundred thousand descendants. New France received less than ten thousand emigrants, all told, from Old France, and there were no more than sixty thousand people in Lower Canada at the time of the capitulation. So vast an increase, so prolific a development, was only possible to a virtuous and thrifty race. There is nothing like it in the world's records since Israel 'multiplied before the Lord' in the land of Egypt. That little colony, which Champlain planted and Laval watered, waged unceasing war for nearly two centuries with the Indians, who sought to exterminate it, twice recruited the army of Montcalm, sent pioneers into the wilds of the West and Northwest, established trading posts everywhere, and opened up the larger portion of the North American continent to Christianity and civilization ... The French Canadians have rendered incalculable service to Canada since that time. When Montcalm fell and the King abandoned the colony, which Voltaire sneeringly described as 'a few arpents of snow,' they accepted the situation and, although harshly treated by some of the early British Governors, were ready to offer their lives for British connection during the American revolution ... [2]

Some other Farrer material can be identified fairly closely by topic. It is known, for instance, that he was hired by the *Globe* primarily for his demonstrated skill in promoting free trade with the United States. After his departure the *Globe* director noted that the paper found it difficult to deal with 'questions which Mr Farrer alone had been handling for two years.'[3] Similarly, it seems likely that during his *Mail* editorship Farrer wrote most of the paper's editorials on commercial union and the Jesuits' Estates issue – with the important exception of those written by Goldwin Smith, which have been identified from Smith's files. In general, too, one would expect that most of the editorials in the small and struggling Winnipeg *Times* and Winnipeg *Sun* would have come from the editor, at least in those periods when he was not ill or drinking.

Farrer's style, too, is strikingly distinctive. It may be relevant to report that when I first read the editorial page of the Winnipeg *Sun* for the summer of 1884, I did so on the mistaken assumption that Farrer had not left the paper until November. I became convinced, from a change in editorial tone, that he had actually left in September, and only later found documentary evidence of this.

Something of the distinctiveness of the style is shown by the following passages on the exodus of Canadians to the United States.

Note on Attribution 291

The first is from a *Globe* editorial, almost certainly Farrer's work, and the second is from a pamphlet attributed to Farrer by W.D. Gregory:

What we have lost in a moral or material sense by the exodus, no one can calculate. The boldest and most enterprising depart year after year after we have reared and fitted them for the battle of life, leaving the second best behind. This culling of the fittest is the most cruel and wasting process to which a people could be subjected. A barbarian who had overrun the Dominion with fire and sword could do no worse against its future than exact an annual tribute of its choicest youth ...[4]

The exodus is a process of selection which leaves the unfittest to survive. An invader who had overrun us could not do worse than exact a yearly tribute of the choicest men and women ... The fusion of the two peoples is going on in spite of political boundaries, only with things as they are Canada is being bled to death.[5]

Despite this distinctive style a purist approach would probably demand more or less constant attribution, to the effect that such-and-such a piece had been printed in the *Sun* or the *Mail* at a time when Farrer was editor, and was probably written by him. Such constant qualification would, I think, be as annoying to the reader as to the writer, and I therefore offer this general qualification: I cannot guarantee that everything herein attributed to Farrer was from his pen, but I have limited the device of casual attribution to those viewpoints that were repeated during his editorship.

Notes

The National Archives of Canada and the Archives of Ontario are abbreviated throughout the Notes as NA and AO respectively. The majority of sources are cited in the Notes in short form only; full bibliographic information is given for these sources on pages 321–6.

PREFACE

1 *New England Magazine*, Dec. 1891
2 *Saturday Night*, 18 Jan. 1890

CHAPTER 1 The Traitor

1 Toronto *Empire*, 18 Feb. 1891
2 Toronto *Mail*, 18 Feb. 1891
3 Toronto *News*, 18 Feb. 1891
4 Ibid.
5 Ibid.
6 Quoted in Macpherson, *Life of Sir John A. Macdonald*, 2:409
7 Willison, *Reminiscences*, 209
8 *Empire*, Montreal *Star*, 19 Feb. 1891
9 Queen's University Archives, Gregory Papers, Unpublished Memoir, 100–1
10 *Grip*, 5 July 1890
11 *Empire*, 18 Feb. 1891
12 P.B. Waite (*Arduous Destiny*, 223) reports a rumour that Ritchie put up as much as $50,000 through the *Globe* for campaign funds. Waite cites Fred C. Denison to Macdonald, 30 Dec. 1890 (NA, Macdonald Pa-

pers, 17694–7). However, Denison's evidence was second-hand and ambiguous. The deal reported between Ritchie and Robert Jaffray, *Globe* president, may have been a routine business transaction.
13 NA, Laurier Papers, Willison to Laurier, 5 Jan. 1891, 1197–1204. This letter is dated 5 Jan. 1890, but internal evidence makes clear it was written in 1891.
14 NA, Willison Papers, Ham to Willison, 9 Jan. 1919
15 Willison to Ham, 13 Jan. 1919, quoted in Colquhoun, *Press, Politics and People*, 32

CHAPTER 2 The Partisans

1 Bilkey, *Persons, Papers and Things*, 54
2 Ross, *Retrospects*, 271
3 Ottawa *Journal*, 28 April 1916
4 Willison, *Reminiscences*, 271
5 J. Lambert Payne, 'Big Canadians of Yesteryear,' Ottawa *Citizen*, 6 March 1937
6 Clippingdale, 'J.S. Willison, Political Journalist,' 73
7 Journalistic titles of the time can not be easily compared to present-day titles. Farrer's function was like that of an editorial page editor of today, but in political journals of the time the job carried much greater weight. Farrer was often referred to as the paper's editor, although Willison was officially 'editor-in-chief.'
8 Willison, *Reminiscences*, 205–6
9 Ibid., 214
10 Ross, *Retrospects*, 269
11 One account (Toronto *News*, 18 Feb. 1891) says he was born in England of Irish parents. Cemetery records also list his place of birth as England, and his father's name as James. English birth records list no Edward Farrer born in 1850. However, an Edward James Farrer, son of James Farrer, was born in Chelsea North West, Middlesex County, in 1846, the year given as Farrer's birth date in the 1891 *News* profile. The date of birth is 28 June; the mother's name is given as Fanny Blake (or Blaker), and the father's occupation is listed as porter.
12 *A Cyclopedia of Canadian Biography* (Toronto: Hunter and Rose 1886), 378–9
13 Institutions checked include the Pontifical Gregorian University, the College of the Propaganda, the Irish College, and the English College.
14 Willison, *Reminiscences*, 211–12

15 Ham, *Reminiscences*, 172
16 The references to Donegal may be a coincidence, but it is curious that one of the few seminarians whose Rome documents could fit Farrer's career was a native of Donegal. He was one Edward MacFadden, born 15 August 1846, in 'Culboy' (Coolboy?), in the diocese of 'Rapotensis' (Raphoe). He attended the College of the Propaganda from 1 December 1862 to 3 March 1867, received a doctor of philosophy degree, and took his preliminary vows in 1865, but left the institution two years later 'discessit def. vocat.' – for lack of vocation.
17 The Bundoran/Tullaghan connection was reported in a *Grip* satire, 7 August 1875. The Maynooth connection was mentioned by the same magazine in a satirical poem, 6 July 1889, in which Farrer was portrayed as singing to cronies about his background. The poem began:

'Twas in Ireland I was born,
   An' passed me youthful days, sirs,
'Twas there I got me wit,
   An' all me Irish ways, sirs

...

When I was but a bie
   They meant me for the altar,
(Tho', whisper in your ear,
   More like 'twill be the halter).
An' so they packed me aff
   To get me sacred knowledge,
At old Maynooth beyant –
   The famous Jesuit College

18 Winnipeg *Times*, 16, 19, 20, and 21 March 1883
19 Ham, *Reminiscences*, 172–3
20 Toronto *News*, 18 Feb. 1891
21 *Atlantic Monthly*, Dec. 1881
22 Willison, *Reminiscences*, 212
23 Toronto *Empire*, 7 Oct. 1890
24 Willison, *Reminiscences*, 214–15
25 Toronto *Leader*, 4 Feb. 1870
26 AO, T.C. Patteson Papers
27 NA, order-in-council 1665, 12 Dec. 1873
28 NA, Laurier Papers, Farrer to Laurier, 19 June 1903, 74181–7
29 While Farrer died intestate, court records show that his wife left an estate of just over $30,000, mostly to her granddaughter, when she died a year after him (AO, Surrogate Court records, County of Carleton).

296 Notes to pages 22-31

30 One ledger-style book written in shorthand has been partly deciphered, from idiosyncratic Pitman, and appears to be a draft or copy of a history of England. It is not clear whether Farrer undertook this as a serious project or merely as a mental discipline – or, indeed, whether it is even his work. Roughly deciphered (by Mabel Charlesworth of Oxfordshire), the work begins: 'I propose to write a history of England from the accession of King James II down to the time which is within the memory of men still living ...' (NA, Farrer Papers, vol. 4).
31 *A Cyclopedia of Canadian Biography* says: 'Mr Farrer, who is a very finished scholar, has made much careful study of the language of our Indian tribes, and the kindness of Archbishop Taché [of St Boniface] has opened many desirable doors to him in this direction. We are promised that, should Mr Farrer find time, he will some day put the result of his researches on Indian philology into permanent shape' (378).
32 Willison, *Reminiscences*, 214
33 Queen's University Archives, Gregory Papers, Unpublished Memoir, 99
34 Skelton, *Laurier*, 1:372
35 *News*, 6 March 1881
36 *Empire*, 19 Feb. 1891
37 Willison, *Reminiscences*, 208-11
38 Preston, *My Generation*, 182
39 *Saturday Night*, 21 June 1890
40 Ottawa *Citizen*, 28 July 1892
41 Bilkey, *Persons, Papers*, 54
42 Ham, *Reminiscences*, 172
43 Preston, *My Generation*, 182
44 Pope, *Public Servant*, 36
45 NA, Laurier Papers, Cartwright to Laurier, 8 Aug. 1889, 1005-7
46 Ham, *Reminiscences*, 171
47 Ibid., 173. An interesting sidelight on this story is the suggestion that Ham would have accepted Farrer as speaking for Sifton.
48 Ross, *Retrospects*, 271
49 Ham, *Reminiscences*, 174-5
50 Willison, *Reminiscences*, 211-12, 120, 213, 210; Ham, *Reminiscences*, 171-4
51 NA, Macdonald Papers, Rowe to Macdonald, 7 April 1884, 193921
52 Gregory, Memoir, 111
53 Willison, *Reminiscences*, 19
54 Charlesworth, *Candid Chronicles*, 120-2

55 Henry Farrer, a CPR clerk in Montreal, died on 8 February 1906 at the age of thirty-two, from what cemetery records describe as 'acute menritis.' His only child, Kathleen, born in 1899, apparently shared her grandfather's adventurous nature. She served as an ambulance driver in the First World War (at a time when she could have been no more than eighteen), married a Belgian army officer, and also had one child, a son. She was later estranged from both husband and son and lived in various parts of the world before dying in Montreal in 1978. Nothing more is known of the son (interview with estate executor Gerry Maas, Montreal).
56 Gregory, Memoir, 98–100
57 Gregory, Memoir, 99; Willison, *Reminiscences*, 214; NA, Willison Papers, Ham to Willison, 9 Jan. 1919

CHAPTER 3 'Scalps Must Be Taken'

1 Smith, *Reminiscences*, 433. Brown's biographer, J.M.S. Careless, rejects the 'legend' that Brown introduced 'journalistic terrorism' into Canada. In fact, he says, Brown merely outplayed rivals in a well-established game (*Brown of the Globe*, 1:44).
2 NA, Farrer Papers, vol. 4, newspaper clipping, dated 10 Feb. 1910, reporting on Farrer article in *Canadian Century*, apparently 29 Jan. 1910 (original unavailable)
3 Winnipeg *Times*, 10 July 1882
4 Quoted in Poulton, *The Paper Tyrant*, 25
5 Ibid., 56. *The American Newspaper Directory* for 1872 lists 'E.H. Farrer' as editor of the *Telegraph*, and 'Thos.' [John Ross] Robertson as publisher. There is no other available evidence that Farrer ever was editor of the *Telegraph*.
6 Macdonald to Carling, 24 Nov. 1871, quoted in Poulton, 57–60. After the *Mail* was in operation, Tory 'friends' apparently turned the screws on the *Telegraph* and crushed it by early summer. The *Leader* lasted until 1878.
7 While his biographer makes much of Robertson's boldly independent approach, it is clear that concrete plans to set up the *Mail* prompted him to try to ingratiate himself with the party. On 18 December 1871 John Carling wrote to the prime minister suggesting that if he were to meet with Robertson, he would not find him difficult to deal with (NA, Macdonald Papers, 137713–16). On 21 February 1872 Sir David Macpherson wrote to Macdonald that Robertson 'thought it very hard that

a new paper should be established in opposition to him: that if at any time the writing [on the *Telegraph*] was not sufficiently vigorous or satisfactory that writers might be employed and paid by a Committee; that this would cost much less than manning a new paper, etc., etc.' (NA, Macdonald Papers, 111469–72).
8 AO, Patteson Papers, Macdonald to Patteson, 22 March 1872
9 Ibid., 8 April 1872
10 Toronto *Mail*, 30 March 1872
11 AO, Patteson Papers, Macdonald to Patteson, 2 April 1872. 'Them's my sentiments' refers to the story of the backwoods politician who said: 'Them's my sentiments, but if they don't suit you, they kin be changed!'
12 Smith, *Reminiscences*, 435
13 AO, Patteson Papers, 29 Oct. 1872
14 Willison, *Reminiscences*, 210–11
15 AO, Patteson Papers, Macdonald to Patteson, 13 and 16 July, 1872; 15 Aug. 1872
16 Ibid., Macdonald to Patteson, 16 Sept. 1872; *Mail*, 20 Sept. 1872
17 *Mail*, 20 Sept. 1872
18 Toronto *News*, 18 Feb. 1891
19 The case, interesting mainly because of *Mail* charges that the Ontario Liberals perverted justice and packed the jury, arose from a criminal libel charge brought against Patteson by one Creasy Whellems, an Englishman of shady past who had worked as an immigration agent (*Mail*, 7 April 1873, 8 Oct. 1874).
20 *Grip*, 7 Aug. 1875. For background on the 'Little Mrs Blank' episode, see 'The Chief Mourners' cartoon in *Grip* of 12 September 1874, along with Bengough's explanation in his *Caricature History of Canadian Politics*, Toronto: Grip Printing and Publishing Co. 1886, 1:232.
21 *Canadian Century*, 29 Jan. 1910
22 NA, Farrer Papers, vol. 5
23 Some accounts say Farrer became editor after the paper was sold in 1877 to its principal creditor, paper manufacturer John Riordan (Masters, *The Rise of Toronto, 1850–1890*, 163). A city directory of 1879, however, continues to list him as night editor. In 1880 and 1881 he was listed as editor.
24 *Mail*, 4 Dec. 1880
25 Ibid., 8 Dec. 1880
26 Ibid., 2 Dec. 1880
27 *Grip*, 13 Nov. 1880

Notes to pages 43–50 299

28 Two writers, Joseph Pope and P.D. Ross, place Farrer on the *Mail* in the spring of 1882, and Ross says he was at the time editor-in-chief. There are other indications, though, that Martin Griffin remained in the editorship while Farrer wrote for both the party and the *Mail* before going on to Winnipeg. Dwight's letter to Wiman in the Pew case (see ch. 4) suggests Farrer went from New York to Ottawa, and then to Winnipeg. The questionable *News* profile implies the government brought Farrer back from New York in the spring of 1882 to prepare election campaign material, and then, with the CPR sharing the cost, sent him to Winnipeg (18 Feb. 1891).
29 *Grip*, 8 April 1882
30 Toronto *World*, 17 June 1890
31 NA, Macdonald Papers, Rowe to Macdonald, 2 May 1882, 180036
32 Ibid., Rowe to Macdonald, 22 Aug. 1882, 182797–8

CHAPTER 4 Making Mischief

1 For a good account of the Manitoba boom of 1880–1, see Morton, *Manitoba*, 199–233.
2 NA, Macdonald Papers, William Bathgate to Macdonald, 15 Nov. 1879, 167643
3 Winnipeg *Times*, 7 Sept. 1882. Captain Goodridge's letter did not make the *Times* any more respectful of the British military. A few days later it observed that British officers sent out to command Canadian militia had 'never been especially distinguished for military skill or common sense,' and that the current adjutant-general, Major-General Luard, was the most signal failure of them all (*Times*, 11 Sept. 1882).
4 Ibid., 15 Aug. 1882
5 Ibid., 16 Feb. 1882
6 Ibid., 9 April 1883
7 Ibid. 19 May 1883. See also 23 and 27 April 1883.
8 Toronto *Globe*, 12 Sept. 1890. Farrer's hostility to Dewdney was probably reciprocated. An 1884 letter from Dewdney to Macdonald appears, though the handwriting is not clear, to refer to Farrer as a 'blackmailer of the deepest dye' (NA, Macdonald Papers, 24 June 1884, 90082–7).
9 *Times*, 11 April 1883
10 Ibid., 5 June 1883
11 *Debates*, House of Commons, 7 May 1883, 1028–30
12 *Grip*, 12 May 1883

13 Quoted in J.K. Johnson, ed., *Affectionately Yours: The Letters of Sir John A. Macdonald and His Family* (Toronto: Macmillan 1969), 148
14 Manitoba *Free Press*, 6 Sept. 1883
15 John W. Dafoe, 'Early Winnipeg Newspapers,' in Clifford Wilson, ed., *Papers Read before the Historical and Scientific Society of Manitoba*, 3d ser., no 3 (Winnipeg: Advocate Printers 1947), 14–22
16 NA, Macdonald Papers, Rowe to Macdonald, 7 April 1884, 193921
17 Ibid., Fahey to Macdonald, 23 April 1884, 200778–81
18 Ibid., Farrer to Macdonald, 19 Feb. 1883, 186222–4
19 Winnipeg *Sun*, 6 June 1884; 11 Aug. 1884
20 NA, Macdonald Papers, Davin to Macdonald, 6 and 13 June 1884, 195272, 195468
21 *Sun*, 11 June 1884
22 Ibid., 30 and 31 May 1884; 2 June 1884
23 Ibid., 8 and 30 Aug. 1884; 1 Sept. 1884
24 Macdonald's papers contain a considerable file of correspondence on this episode (145390ff). For a fuller account of it, see Carman Cumming, 'The Plot to Buy the Northwest,' *Beaver* (Autumn 1984).
25 *Sun*, 23 and 30 June 1884
26 NA, Macdonald Papers, McDougall to Macdonald, 21 July 1884, 145391–4
27 *Sun*, 16 Aug. 1884
28 Ibid., 9 and 13 May 1884; 22 Aug. 1884
29 Ibid., 7 July 1884
30 *Canadian Century*, 5 March 1910
31 *Sun*, 12 May 1884
32 *Ibid.*, 23 and 11 Aug. 1884
33 Ibid., 25 Aug. 1884
34 Regina *Leader*, 26 June 1884
35 *Times*, 14 May 1883
36 *Grip*, 19 Jan. 1884; *Leader*, 10 Jan. 1884
37 *Times*, 12 July 1882
38 *Sun*, 8 May 1884. Similar references to Mayo families showed up in the Toronto *Mail* after Farrer returned to that paper. See, for instance, 'An Old Issue Revived,' *Mail*, 7 Aug. 1885.
39 *Times*, 22 July 1882. The same fascination for miracles and the same gentle scepticism showed up in some of Farrer's later, signed writing. See, for instance, 'Miracles in French Canada,' *Popular Science Monthly*, Dec. 1895.
40 *Times*, 20 June 1883

41 *Free Press*, 23 and 30 Sept. 1884; 1 and 8 Oct. 1884

CHAPTER 5 Splendid Isolation

1 *Saturday Night*, 10 Dec. 1927
2 Willison, *Reminiscences*, 118
3 For a discussion of technological change in newspapers in this era, see Kesterton, *A History of Journalism in Canada*, 50–4.
4 The pattern of 'scalping' news from other papers was common, but particularly shameless cases of theft by the *Telegram* were detailed in *Globe* attacks of 5 and 12 October 1886.
5 *Grip*, 25 Jan. 1890
6 Reprinted in Toronto *Mail*, 21 Feb. 1889
7 Tennant, 'Policy of the Mail,' 110
8 AO, Patteson Papers, Unpublished Memoir, 6
9 *Mail*, 2 Aug. 1880
10 Chalmers, *A Gentleman of the Press*, 20–31; Charlesworth, *Candid Chronicles*, 72–8. Kit Coleman was apparently hired after she impressed Farrer with a column offering an unorthodox view of Adam and Eve (*Women's Tribune*, 11 Sept. 1897, quoted in Freeman, *Kit's Kingdom*, 24).
11 NA, Griffin Papers, vols 1–3, 12. At one point after his return to Ottawa, Griffin wrote, from the Parliamentary press gallery:

> To Sir John Macdonald
>
> Here in my old accustomed place
>   I sit with heart as true
> As when your foes I used to face
>   And break a spear for you
> ...
> Good luck, God speed my chief.   MJG
>   The Gallery (NA, Macdonald Papers, 219134)

12 NA, Macdonald Papers, 187644–45
13 Morgan, *Canadian Men and Women*, 388
14 Sir Charles G.D. Roberts and Arthur Tunell, eds., *Canadian Who Was Who, 1875–1937* (Toronto: Trans-Canada Press 1938), 2:145
15 For instance, Paul Rutherford (*A Victorian Authority*, 60) says 'madness struck' the paper after it had built itself up to be the loudest Conservative voice in the Dominion and had overturned the *Globe*'s hegemony in western Ontario. Rutherford says the *Mail* chose inde-

pendence because abusing French Canadians 'proved so popular.' He describes the *Mail*'s editorials on its various policies as brilliant but makes no direct link between the race/creed campaign and the commercial union agitation.

16 Toronto *Globe*, 18 Feb. 1890
17 Montreal *Gazette*, 23 Jan. 1890
18 NA, Macdonald Papers, Hughes to Macdonald, 25 May 1887, 17199
19 R.S. White to Willison, 19 June 1890; quoted in Clippingdale, 'J.S. Willison, Political Journalist,' 29
20 A pro-annexation letter in the New York *Sun*, 2 Jan. 1890, is signed 'W. Blackburn Harte, Toronto *Mail*.'
21 *New England Magazine*, Dec. 1891. Harte said Farrer's 'versatility' was shown by the fact that before working for the *Mail* he had written for the ultramontane paper *L'Etendard*. Harte also described him as a convert to Unitarianism. Neither statement can be confirmed.
22 Ottawa *Journal*, 28 April 1916
23 Willison, *Reminiscences*, 208–9
24 Toronto *News*, 28 April 1916
25 *Globe*, 5 and 23 Nov. 1886
26 Rutherford, *Victorian Authority*, 60
27 NA, Macdonald Papers, McCarthy to Macdonald, 7 March 1887, 98373
28 NA, Tupper Papers, Griffin to Tupper, 25 July 1888, 3905–9
29 NA, Macdonald Papers, Griffin to Macdonald, 17 Aug. 1885, 203044
30 Bunting's letters to Macdonald were generally tractable. 'Agreeably to your request I have instructed our Montreal correspondent to abstain from attacking Senecal and his schemes,' one letter said. 'I would have done so before had I known you desired it' (NA, Macdonald Papers, Bunting to Macdonald, 24 Dec. 1883, 191695).
31 P.B. Waite (*The Man from Halifax*, 316–17) discusses Bunting's bids for party support.
32 *Grip*, 18 April 1885, 13 Nov. 1886
33 NA, Macdonald Papers, Griffin to Macdonald, 1 Nov. 1883, 190744–52
34 Ibid., Griffin to Macdonald, 1 May 1884, 194453
35 Ibid., Bunting to Macdonald, 9 May 1884, 194601
36 Ibid., Griffin to Macdonald, 2 June 1884, 195129
37 NA, Griffin Papers, Griffin to Martin Griffin, Jr., 6 July 1901. John O'Donohoe, the same man who had been condemned by Macdonald when he ran for the Reform party in 1872, was appointed to the Senate 12 May 1882.
38 Willison, *Reminiscences*, 210–11

39 *Grip*, 22 Nov. 1884. A Toronto city directory for 1885 lists Farrer as an associate editor, but he apparently resumed the editorship during the summer of that year. A *Grip* comment of 16 August referred to a recent change of editorship at the paper, and Griffin's appointment as parliamentary librarian was announced about the same time.
40 NA, Macdonald Papers, Griffin to Macdonald, 17 Sept. 1883, 190067–8
41 Koester, *Mr. Davin, M.P.*, 59
42 NA, Macdonald Papers, Griffin to Macdonald, undated (apparently February 1885), 199234–6
43 *Mail*, 11 Feb. 1885
44 *Grip*, 11 April 1885
45 See *Mail* of 30 March 1885 for original reference. O'Soup's role is described in Bob Beal and Rod McLeod, *Prairie Fire: The 1885 North-West Rebellion* (Edmonton 1984), 82–4.
46 NA, Macdonald Papers, Griffin to Macdonald, 20 July 1885, 202463
47 *Mail*, 8 July 1885
48 *Grip*, 23 Jan. 1886
49 NA, Macdonald Papers, Griffin to Macdonald, 17 Aug. 1885, 203044–51
50 See *Mail* editorials of 6 May and 9 Oct. 1885.
51 *Mail*, 23 Nov. 1885; cited in Schull, *Laurier*, 178–9
52 Ibid., 11 Dec. 1885
53 Pope, ed., *Letters*, 380
54 *Grip*, 11 Sept. 1886
55 *Mail*, 23 Sept. 1886
56 *Grip*, 25 Sept. 1886
57 *Globe*, 18 Sept. 1886
58 *Mail*, 20 Sept. 1886
59 Montreal *Star*, 2 Oct. 1886
60 *Globe*, 5 Oct. 1886. The *Globe* was probably right about Bunting's part in the whisky ring. In 1883 Bunting had written Macdonald asking for a regulation change that would allow 'several of our best friends here' to set up a warehousing company and import whisky in carload lots – a step that would 'see much profit for all concerned' NA, Macdonald Papers, Bunting to Macdonald, 19 June 1883, 188686).
61 Ibid., 3 Sept. 1886
62 Baker, *Anglin*, 246, citing AO, Edgar Papers, Cartwright to Edgar, 9 Aug. 1886
63 *Mail*, 4 Nov. 1886
64 Baker, *Anglin*, 235

65 Winnipeg *Times*, 8 June 1883
66 Baker, *Anglin*, 247
67 *Globe*, 5 Nov. 1886
68 Ibid., 23 Nov. 1886
69 *Atlantic Monthly*, Dec. 1881
70 *Mail*, 23 Sept. 1886
71 *Grip*, 30 Oct. 1886
72 *Globe*, 2 and 22 Oct. 1886. At times, however, the *Mail* had been an effective critic of the liquor trade. See 17 Sept. 1885, for instance.
73 *Grip*, 9 Oct. 1886
74 *Star*, 7 Oct. 1886
75 Ibid., 9 Oct. 1886
76 NA, Macdonald Papers, J.H. Beaty to J. White, 30 April 1887, 219102
77 NA, Laurier Papers, Gorman to Laurier, 26 Sept. 1887, 208145
78 NA, Tupper Papers, vol. 6, Macdonald to Tupper, 22 Dec. 1886
79 NA, Macdonald Papers, Meredith to Macdonald, 24 Dec. 1886, 99212
80 *Grip*, 27 Nov. 1886
81 NA, Minto Papers, Macdonald to Melgund, 5 April 1887
82 Pope, ed., *Letters*, 392
83 *Mail*, 8 Jan. 1887

CHAPTER 6 The Hidden Message

1 Toronto *Mail*, 11 March 1889
2 Ibid., 14 March 1889
3 NA, Macdonald Papers, McCarthy to Macdonald, 17 April 1889, 98615–18
4 NA, Laurier Papers, H.H. Cook to Laurier, 29 Dec. 1888, 208340
5 See, for instance, Miller, *Equal Rights: The Jesuits' Estates Act Controversy*; and Dalton, *The Jesuits' Estates Question, 1760–1888*.
6 Toronto *News*, 24 Feb. 1891
7 *Mail*, 23 March 1889
8 Ibid., 10 Jan. 1889
9 Ibid., 30 Nov. 1888
10 Ibid., 1 June 1889
11 Ibid., 29 Jan. 1889
12 Ibid., 3 March 1890
13 Ibid., 28 Nov. 1888
14 *Canadian Century*, 29 Jan. 1910
15 Toronto *World*, 28 Nov. 1887; 14 Feb. 1888, and 21 March 1888

Notes to pages 102–17   305

16 *Mail*, 31 Aug. 1885
17 Ibid., 9 Sept. 1885
18 Ibid., 7 Aug. 1885
19 Ibid., 9 Oct. 1885
20 Ibid., 23 Nov. 1885
21 Ibid., 5 Jan. 1887
22 Skelton, *Laurier*, 1:372
23 Willison, *Reminiscences*, 166–7
24 Tansill, *Canadian-American Relations*, 386 (citing Bayard MS)
25 Ibid., 390
26 NA, Macdonald Papers, Macdonald to Tupper, 15 Jan. 1888, 17363. In a letter to one of his editors in July 1887 Macdonald wrote that the Tory press should not attach undue importance to commercial union. 'Congress will doubtless squelch the whole thing ... The course of the Toronto World in dealing with it as a matter for ridicule is the true course for the present' (NA, Acton Burrows Papers, Macdonald to Burrows, 15 July 1887).
27 NA, Laurier Papers, Cartwright to Laurier, 8 July 1887; AO, Cartwright Papers, Laurier to Cartwright, 8 Aug. 1887 (quoted in Brown, *Canada's National Policy, 1883–1900*, 163–4)
28 *Mail*, 27 Oct. 1887
29 Ibid.
30 Ibid., 20 March 1888
31 *Grip*, 7 July 1888
32 NA, Lansdowne Papers, Lansdowne to Sir Henry Holland, 29 Oct. 1887; quoted in Brown, *Canada's National Policy*, 147
33 Denison, *Struggle for Imperial Unity*, 82–3
34 For a fuller discussion, see Brown, *Canada's National Policy*, 130–1.
35 Thomas Fisher Rare Book Library, University of Toronto, Charlton Diaries, vol. 3, 13 Dec. 1888
36 Toronto *Empire*, 31 Jan. 1891
37 Denison, *Struggle*, 99–101; Warner, *Continental Union*, 171
38 *North American Review* 151 (Aug. 1890), 212–13
39 *Empire*, 24 Feb. 1891
40 NA, Justice Department Files, RG 13, B 7, vol. 963, 'Secret Files on American Annexationists, 1893–94,' T. Burke Grant to David Creighton, 8 March 1894
41 *Report of Senate Select Committee on Relations with Canada*, Senate Report 1530, 51st Congress, 1st session, vol. 2712
42 NA, Laurier Papers, Cartwright to Laurier, 8 Aug. 1889, 1005–7

43 Wallace, *Goldwin Smith: Victorian Liberal*, 96. On commercial union the dates are: 20 May, 18 and 21 June, 1, 9, 17, and 23 Sept., 1 Oct., 5 Nov., 7 and 24 Dec. 1887; 1 and 24 Feb., 16 March, 8 June, 13 July, and 10 Nov. 1888. On the Jesuits' Estates the dates are: 26 Jan., 5 and 9 Feb., 2, 9, 11, and 13 March, 18 and 25 May, 22 and 27 June, and 6 and 13 July 1889.
44 *Mail*, 2 and 9 March 1889
45 Ibid., 16 March 1889. Farrer seems, however, to have been ill about this time. A report of a Toronto 'Irish press dinner' on 17 March quoted the chairman as saying Farrer was 'on a fair way to recovery' and added a laudatory comment from Nicholas Flood Davin: 'Soon, I hope, will we have again in fullest activity that teeming brain and that giant power for work' (*News*, 18 March 1889)
46 *Mail*, 11 March 1889
47 Ottawa *Journal*; quoted in *Mail*, 21 March 1889
48 NA, Laurier Papers, Thomson to Laurier, 5 Jan. 1890, 1210–11
49 *Grip*, 30 March 1889
50 Willison, *Reminiscences*, 170–1
51 *Grip*, 23 Feb. 1889
52 Ibid., 23 March 1889
53 Ibid., 24 Aug. 1889
54 *Mail*, 26 March 1889
55 *Debates*, House of Commons, 28 March 1889, 2:872
56 Ibid., 2:903
57 *Mail*, 29 and 30 March 1889
58 Ibid., 27 March 1889
59 Ibid., 3 April 1889
60 Ibid., 21 and 27 May 1889
61 NA, Laurier Papers, Thomson to Laurier, 9 Aug. 1889, 1013–14
62 NA, Macdonald Papers, Creighton to Macdonald, 14 June 1889, 80460. Some time afterward, Creighton cited the Jesuit issue as the main reason for the *Empire*'s failure to achieve financial success, saying the agitation that swept the province 'simply dashed all our hopes, leaving us at its close to regain our lost ground as best we could' (NA, Thompson Papers, Creighton to Sir John Thompson, 26 July 1894).
63 NA, Macdonald Papers, John Riordan to Macdonald, 22 Aug. 1889, 237114
64 *Grip*, 12 Oct. 1889 and 4 Jan. 1890
65 Willison, writing of the genesis of the Manitoba issue, observed that McCarthy 'was not only consulted but probably directed, and there is

no doubt that Mr. Edward Farrer had knowledge of what was contemplated.' However, Willison probably exaggerated the role of the Toronto clique in creating the Manitoba schools crisis when he wrote: '... it is curious that Mr. McCarthy, Mr. Farrer and Mr. Goldwin Smith, united against the Roman Catholic hierarchy, created conditions in the country which finally destroyed the unity of the Conservative party and gave victory to the Liberals under a Roman Catholic leader' (*Reminiscences*, 247). Later scholars have tended to see the Manitoba schools issue not as a McCarthy creation but as a local issue. See, for instance, Friesen, *The Canadian Prairies*.
66 *Mail*, 22 Jan. 1890
67 Ibid., 24 Jan. 1890
68 This excerpt is from an article entitled 'Religious Toleration' left in Farrer's files partly in proof form and partly in his handwriting. It appears to have been written as part of the Liberal propaganda for a Saskatchewan election early in the twentieth century (NA, Farrer Papers, vol. 4).
69 For a detailed and reflective version of Farrer's views on Quebec and Catholicism, see 'New England Influences in French Canada,' *Forum* (May 1897), 308–19.
70 J.R. Miller, for instance, says the *Mail* had been 'a-whoring after the strange god of continental free trade' and had turned to the Jesuits' Estates issue only after election of a protectionist Congress forced it to 'look about for a new cause to champion' (*Equal Rights*, 49). P.B. Waite echoes that interpretation: 'The torch that lit the [Jesuits' Estates] fire was the Toronto *Daily Mail*. The *Mail* was looking for something to do that summer of 1888; the commercial union agitation had gone stale, and something new was needed ...' (*The Man from Halifax*, 235).

CHAPTER 7 Master Craftsman

1 Toronto *Mail*, 8 Feb 1889; 12 March 1889
2 Ibid., 12 March 1889
3 Colquhoun, *Press, Politics*, 127
4 Tennant, 'Policy of the Mail,' 274
5 Ottawa *Journal*, 28 April 1916
6 *A Cyclopedia of Canadian Biography* (Toronto: Hunter and Rose 1886), 378–9
7 *Mail*, 21 March 1888

308 Notes to pages 131–46

8 Ibid., 19 March 1888
9 Ibid., 20 March 1886
10 Ibid., 12 March 1889
11 Ibid., 8 July 1885
12 Ibid., 6 Jan. 1886
13 Ibid., 30 Jan. 1886
14 Ibid., 4 Jan. 1886
15 Reprinted in *Manitoba Free Press*, 14 Nov. 1884
16 NA, Macdonald Papers, Davin to Macdonald, 7 Jan. 1885, 198204–5
17 *Mail*, 3 Jan. 1885
18 Ibid., 8 Dec. 1884; 19 Jan. 1886
19 *Mail*, 11, 18, and 19 Jan. 1886; *Globe*, 16 Jan. 1886. The 'Ontario' poem was printed in the *Mail*, 6 Feb. 1886. The 'Blake' poem was an atrocious bit of campaign doggerel that went as follows:
   Oh, Blake is the man for the nation,
   A statesman most excellent and true,
   The determined enemy of all kinds of taxation
   And the Tories too.
   Mail, 3 Sept. 1885
20 *Grip*, 30 Jan. 1886
21 Charlesworth, *Candid Chronicles*, 196–7
22 *Mail*, 8 March 1889
23 Ibid., 12 March 1889
24 Ibid., 1 March 1889

CHAPTER 8 The *Globe*, the *Mail*, and the *Empire*

1 NA, Arthur Boswell Papers, Macdonald to Boswell, 3 Feb. 1887
2 NA, Macdonald Papers, T.C. Patteson to Macdonald, 5 Jan. 1887, 213256. At one point late in 1886 Macdonald and McCarthy discussed buying the *World*, either as an official or an unofficial organ. It is notable that Macdonald preferred a secret link and McCarthy resisted this, on the grounds of a need to convince the public that the *Mail*'s course 'was not the result of an understanding with you' (ibid., McCarthy to Macdonald, date unclear [apparently October 1886] 98329). As late as October 1887 *Empire* directors met Maclean in an attempt to buy the *World*, but the price was too high (ibid., Boswell to Macdonald, 12 Oct. 1887, 146542; David Creighton to Macdonald, 13 Oct. 1887, 146514).
3 NA, Macdonald Papers, McCarthy to Macdonald, 28 Feb. 1887, 98364; 7 March 1887, 98373; 3 Sept. 1887, 98424

Notes to pages 147–64 309

4 NA, Alexander Campbell Papers, Macdonald to Campbell, 5 Oct. 1887
5 Charlesworth, *Candid Chronicles*, 149. Kribs was described as 'one of the kindest-hearted men who ever lived,' a bulky, blond German from Waterloo who played the oboe, adopted waifs, and wrote humour columns signed 'Henry Pica' (ibid., 76–9).
6 NA, Thompson Papers, Creighton to Thompson, 11 Oct. 1892, 20482
7 Toronto *Globe*, 7 Jan. 1890
8 NA, Laurier Papers, Wiman to Laurier, 2 Jan. 1890, 1174–5
9 *Globe*, 7 Jan. 1890
10 Toronto *Mail*, 8 Jan. 1890
11 Reprinted in the Toronto *Empire*, 7 and 19 Feb. 1891; Denison, *Struggle*, 162
12 *Grip*, 18 and 25 Jan. 1890
13 *Saturday Night*, 18 Jan. 1890
14 NA, Macdonald Papers, Creighton to Macdonald, 21 Jan. 1890, 88511–12
15 *Empire*, 22 and 23 Jan. 1890
16 *Mail*, 23 and 24 Jan. 1890
17 *Grip*, 8 Feb. 1890
18 *Globe*, 24 Jan. 1890
19 Reprinted in *Empire*, 27 Jan. 1890
20 *Saturday Night*, 1 Feb. 1890
21 *Mail*, 25 Jan. 1890
22 NA, Macdonald Papers, Creighton to Macdonald, 26 Jan. 1890, 88514–15
23 *Empire*, 27 and 28 Jan. 1890
24 *Grip*, 8 Feb. 1890
25 *Empire*, 29 Jan. 1890
26 *Mail*, 11 June 1890
27 Toronto *News*, 15 July 1890
28 NA, Macdonald Papers, Creighton to Macdonald, 21 July 1890, 151078–9
29 *Empire*, 4 Feb. 1890
30 NA, Macdonald Papers, Creighton to Macdonald, 29 March 1890, 88543
31 *Saturday Night*, 8 March 1890

CHAPTER 9 The Mercenary

1 *Saturday Night*, 21 June 1890
2 AO, Goldwin Smith Papers, R.R. Hitt to Smith, 30 June 1890

3 Toronto *Globe*, 4 Oct. 1890. The expression 'double-leaded editorials' referred to a practice of emphasizing major editorials by putting extra space (leads) between the lines.
4 *Grip*, 28 June 1890; 5 July 1890
5 NA, Willison Papers, White to Willison, 19 June 1890
6 Colquhoun, *Press, Politics*, 20
7 Queen's University Archives, Gregory Papers, Unpublished Memoir, 98–9
8 Rutherford, *Victorian Authority*, 59
9 Jaffray to Blake, 20 March 1889, quoted in Clippingdale, 'J.S. Willison, Political Journalist,' 55–6
10 Toronto *Empire*, 29 Jan. 1890
11 Willison, *Reminiscences*, 204–5
12 Toronto *World*, 17, 23, and 30 June 1890; 2 July 1890
13 NA, Farrer Papers, vol. 4, handwritten article draft
14 NA, Laurier Papers, Willison to Laurier, 23 June 1890, 1329–34
15 NA, Willison Papers, Laurier to Willison, 26 June 1890, quoted in Clippingdale, 72–3
16 NA, Laurier Papers, Willison to Laurier, 23 June 1890, 1329–34
17 Ibid., Willison to Laurier, 14 Dec. 1892, 2360
18 Willison to Sifton, 29 Jan. 1901, quoted in Colquhoun, 99–100
19 *Saturday Night*, 21 June 1890
20 Willison, *Reminiscences*, 206–7
21 *Grip*, 23 Aug. 1890
22 NA, Macdonald Papers, Creighton to Macdonald, 21 July 1890, 151078–9
23 NA, Laurier Papers, Willison to Laurier, 22 Oct. 1890, 1519
24 Willison, *Reminiscences*, 210
25 *Globe*, 6 Oct. 1890
26 Toronto *Mail*, 7 Oct. 1890
27 Quoted in *Mail*, 7 Oct. 1890
28 *Empire*, 7 Oct. 1890. In fact, the coverage in the *Times* of the Battle of Tel-el-Kebir seems straightforward. The paper carried a long editorial fleshing out the cable dispatches with background and a measure of surmise, but there is no evident fabrication (Winnipeg *Times*, 13 Sept. 1882). The story on the 'French-Canadians' may be the *Atlantic* article discussed in chapter 5. It, too, shows no demonstrable fabrication.
29 *Globe*, 6 Oct. 1890
30 *Mail*, 8 Oct. 1890
31 *Globe*, 8 Oct. 1890

32 *Empire*, 9 Oct. 1890

CHAPTER 10 The Plot

1 Denison, *The Struggle for Imperial Unity*, 161–7. Denison describes Sherwood as a colonel, but in fact his promotion to lieutenant-colonel, and his knighthood, were still some years off.
2 Toronto *Telegram*, 28 July 1892
3 NA, Denison Papers, vols. 3–4, 1773–4
4 Berger, ed., *Imperialism and Nationalism*, 12
5 NA, Macdonald Papers, Stanley to Macdonald, 31 Jan. 1891, 35276–8
6 Tansill, *Canadian-American Relations*, 427, quoting Blaine message of 22 Dec. 1890
7 See Brown, *Canada's National Policy*, 203–4, for a thorough discussion of this sequence.
8 Creighton, *John A. Macdonald: The Old Chieftain*, 551–2
9 Thomas Fisher Rare Book Library, University of Toronto, Charlton Diaries, vol. 6, 16 Jan. 1893
10 NA, Macdonald Papers, Pauncefote to Stanley, 2 Feb. 1891, 35279–83
11 Ibid., Creighton to Macdonald, 30 Jan. 1891, 88654
12 Toronto *Empire*, 30 Jan. 1891
13 'Canada and the United States,' *Contemporary Review*, Oct. 1906, 550–63
14 *Empire*, 14 and 18 Feb. 1891
15 NA, Laurier Papers, Willison to Laurier, 2 Sept. 1892, 2228–30
16 Willison, *Reminiscences*, 234–5, 227–8
17 NA, Laurier Papers, Willison to Laurier, 5 Jan. 1891, 1197–204
18 NA, Macdonald Papers, 27473–89
19 Liberal MP John Charlton, who was associated with Farrer for many years, made the following comment in his diary entry of 22 December 1896, after an hour-long meeting with Farrer: 'He gave me a good deal of information about American matters. He is in touch with public men in Washington and has their confidence. He was employed for four months by Mr. Blaine a few years ago in making inquiries about the fishery question, and he knows most of the plans of American public men at Washington about Canadian matters. I hope to be able to make advantageous use of his services if I go to Washington as Canadian commissioner for the purposes of attempting to negotiate a reciprocity treaty ...' (Charlton Diaries, vol. 9).
20 Toronto *Globe*, 18 Feb. 1891

21 *Empire*, 19 Feb. 1891
22 *Globe*, 19 Feb. 1891
23 *Empire*, 18 Feb. 1891
24 Montreal *Star*, 24 Feb. 1891
25 Toronto *Mail*, 25 Feb. 1891
26 NA, Macdonald Papers, undated, 27579
27 *Empire*, 19 and 20 Feb. 1891
28 Toronto *World*, 18 Feb. 1891. *Grip* reacted to Maclean's campaign by calling him a 'bunco-steerer' who 'would advocate Annexation tomorrow if he thought there was anything in it financially for himself' (*Grip*, 18 April 1891).
29 Halifax *Herald*, Toronto *News*, 19 Feb. 1891
30 *Empire*, 18 Feb. 1891
31 NA, Macdonald Papers, Kribs to Macdonald, 19 Feb. 1891, 27505–6
32 *Empire*, 24 Feb. 1891
33 *Globe*, 20 Feb. 1891
34 *Empire*, 24 Feb. 1891
35 *Globe*, 25 Feb. 1891
36 *Week*, 27 Feb. 1891
37 *Mail*, 25 Feb. 1891
38 *Saturday Night*, 28 Feb. 1891
39 Howard A. Scarrow, *Canada Votes: A Handbook of Federal and Provincial Election Data* (New Orleans: Hauser Press 1962), 22. R.C. Brown (*Canada's National Policy*, 211) reports different figures, compiled by the Dominion statistician in 1891, which show the government winning only 48.9 per cent of the popular vote in Ontario, and 51.1 per cent overall, compared with the Liberals' total of 51.1 per cent in Ontario and 48.9 per cent overall.
40 Quoted in Waite, *Arduous Destiny*, 225
41 Pope, *Public Servant*, 77
42 Macdonald to Stephen, 31 March 1891, in Pope, ed., *Letters*, 485
43 Charlesworth (*Candid Chronicles*, 109) said Clark was found to have stolen personal letters of his ministerial chief, John Haggart.
44 NA, Laurier Papers, Clark to Laurier, 31 July 1895, 3825–7. Clark offered Laurier an exposé on 'the Haggart-Craig scandal of 1891, which will demonstrate by evidence how a man whose family will provide a prostitute for a minister can secure promotion.'
45 NA, Abbott Papers, vol. 3, Tupper to Abbott, 22 Feb. 1892
46 R.C. Brown (*Canada's National Policy*), while not finding the evidence conclusive, implies a connection with the comment: 'McDougall did not

get his senatorship but Macdonald got Farrer's pamphlet and put it to good use' (206–7). At least one other historian, citing Brown, echoes this interpretation: '... what seems to have determined Macdonald to dissolve [Parliament], was the discovery, through William MacDougall [*sic*] of the famous proof sheets of Farrer's pamphlet ...' (Waite, *Arduous Destiny*, 222).

47 NA, Tupper Papers, Wiman to McDougall, 25 April 1889, 4064; McDougall to Tupper, 11 May 1889, 4067–8
48 NA, Justice Department Files, RG 13, B 7, vol. 963, 'Secret Files on American Annexationists, 1893–94,' file 1, T. Burke Grant to David Creighton, 26 Feb. 1894 and 8 March 1894, 41–4 and 46–54
49 E.M. Saunders, *The Life and Letters of the Right Hon. Sir Charles Tupper, Bart., K.C.M.G.* (London: Carswell 1914), 150

CHAPTER 11 A Wicked and Ungovernable Force

1 NA, Denison Papers, Denison to Salisbury, 19 Dec. 1891, 2078–80
2 Toronto *Globe*, 26 Sept. 1891, 3 Nov. 1891, and 14 Dec. 1891
3 NA, Laurier Papers, Mowat to Laurier, 26 and 31 Dec. 1891, 2041, 2042–3
4 *Globe*, 31 Dec. 1891
5 Toronto *Empire*, 14 Feb. 1891
6 Queen's University Archives, Gregory Papers, Unpublished Memoir, 105
7 Thomas Fisher Rare Book Library, University of Toronto, Charlton Diaries, vol. 5, 31 Dec. 1891
8 NA, Laurier Papers, Willison to Laurier, 5 April 1891, 1791
9 *Grip*, 29 Aug. 1891
10 NA, Laurier Papers, Cartwright to Laurier, 11 Nov. 1891, 1951–7
11 Ibid., Farrer to Laurier, 24 Oct. 1891, 1903–6
12 Ibid., Farrer to Laurier, 2 Nov. 1891, 1934–6
13 Charlton Diaries, vol. 5, 12 and 16 March 1892; cited in Brown, *Canada's National Policy*, 244–5
14 Ibid., vol. 6, 30 March 1892
15 See Tansill, *Canadian-American Relations*, 434, for a discussion of this point.
16 *Debates*, House of Commons, 7 April 1892, 1134, 1143
17 *Grip*, 9 April 1892 and 9 Jan. 1892
18 *New England Magazine*, Dec. 1891
19 *Globe*, 18 March 1892

20 Ibid., 27 July 1892
21 Toronto *News*, 27 July 1892
22 Toronto *World*, 28 July 1892
23 Toronto *Telegram*, 28 July 1892
24 Halifax *Herald*, 29 July 1892
25 Willison, *Reminiscences*, 206. The salary figure given by the *News* also disagreed with an earlier *World* story, 18 June 1890, saying Farrer had moved from the *Mail* to the *Globe* for an increase to $5,000 from $3,400, and that this was highest amount ever paid to an editorial writer on a Canadian daily. If Farrer's salary was indeed at this level, it was far above the going rate. Edward Toker, chief editorial writer on the *Empire*, earned $1,560 a year in 1891 (NA, Macdonald Papers, Creighton to Macdonald, 10 Jan. 1891, 88638-41).
26 *Saturday Night*, 30 July 1892. 'Mack' is identified as Joseph T. Clark by Fraser Sutherland (*The Monthly Epic*, 90).
27 *Grip*, 13 and 6 Aug. 1892
28 Ottawa *Citizen*, 28 July 1892. The *Globe*'s coverage of Macdonald's death was in the main sympathetic, although its summation of his career was critical: 'When his whole work comes to be examined, it will be found that he spent most of his time not in rearing a permanent structure but in erecting scaffoldings held together by means of compromises supplemented with bribery, and that on his disappearance some tumbled down of their own rottenness while others had to be dismantled out of consideration for the national safety' (17 June 1891).
29 *Saturday Night*, 30 July 1892
30 *Empire*, 28 July 1892
31 NA, Laurier Papers, Smith to Laurier, 2 Aug. 1892, 2202-6
32 Ibid., Willison to Laurier, 4 Aug. 1892, 2207-10
33 *News*, 29 April 1916
34 NA, Laurier Papers, Farrer to Laurier, 16 Aug. 1892, 2214-17
35 Ibid., Willison to Laurier, 2 Sept. 1892, 2230
36 *L'Electeur*, 26 Aug. 1892: 'Le Globe n'est plus que l'ombre de lui-même. Il nous semble que ce journal a sensiblement perdu de son originalité et de sa vigueur depuis les changements survenus dans la rédaction.'
37 NA, Laurier Papers, Willison to Laurier, 5 April 1891, 1792
38 Ibid., Willison to Laurier, 4 Aug. 1892, 2207-10; Willison, *Reminiscences*, 228-35.
39 *World*, 28 July 1892

CHAPTER 12 The Forlorn Hope

1 Queen's University Archives, Gregory Papers, Unpublished Memoir, 104
2 The Farrer material, often signed 'E. Farrer' or 'E.F.,' peaked late in 1892 and early 1893. See, for instance, 27 Nov.; 5, 11, 18, and 25 Dec.; and 1 and 3 Jan. Some details of the *Sun* arrangement are also contained in the Gregory papers, box 1, Farrer to Gregory, 27 Nov. 1892; and Wiman to T.M. White, 15 Dec. 1891 (Queen's University Archives).
3 Willison says: 'Goldwin Smith had no genius for research. He never had the laborious, continuous patience of the historian. Mr. Farrer had those qualities, and Goldwin Smith often sought his advice and cooperation' (*Reminiscences*, 207–8).
4 Smith, *Canada and the Canadian Question*, 212
5 Gregory, Memoir, 108
6 *Canadian Century*, 26 Feb. 1910
7 Toronto *Globe*, 29 Nov. 1892
8 See, for instance, *Globe* reports of 3, 12, 15, and 21 Dec. 1892.
9 Toronto *Empire*, 29 Nov. 1892
10 Continental Union Association of Ontario, *Our Best Policy* (Toronto: Hunter, Rose 1895)
11 New York *Sun*, 27 Nov. 1892; 11, 19, and 25 Dec. 1892
12 Gregory, Memoir, 109
13 Brian J. Gilchrist, ed., *Inventory of Ontario Newspapers, 1793–1986* (Toronto: Micromedia 1987), 180
14 NA, Laurier Papers, Smith to Laurier, 4 Dec., 1892
15 The *Empire* on 11 January 1893 printed a long list of U.S. newspapers supporting outright annexation. For a fuller discussion of the U.S. movement, see Warner, *Continental Union*, 234–9.
16 Gregory, Memoir, 111
17 Queen's University Archives, Gregory Papers, E.A. Macdonald to Farrer, 5 April 1893; Glen to Farrer, undated but contained in 1893 file; Gen. James H. Wilson to Farrer, 13 June 1893
18 NA, Thompson Papers, Creighton to Thompson, 11 and 18 Jan. 1894, 24585, 24662. Creighton apparently reported first to the prime minister in person, since references to the issue do not show up in his letters until mid-January.
19 NA, Justice Department Files, RG 13, B 7, vol. 963, 'Secret Files on

American Annexationists, 1893–94' (hereafter cited as 'Annexationist Files'), Glen to Farrer, 20 Jan. 1894; Glen to Mercier, 3 April 1894
20 Ibid., Grant to Creighton, 26 Jan. 1894; 6 and 17 Feb. 1894; 8 March 1894
21 Ironically, Glen was jailed for fifteen days in 1904 over debts to another typist (*Globe*, 21 Nov. 1904). At that time he was described as the promoter of a North American union.
22 Annexationist Files, Grant to Creighton, 26 March 1894; 9 May 1894; 28 Sept. 1894; also 7, 11, and 19 April 1894
23 Ibid., Glen to Farrer, 20 March 1894; Glen to Myers, 30 April 1894
24 Ibid., Grant to Creighton, 22 Oct. 1894
25 AO, Goldwin Smith Papers, Smith to Gen. James. H. Wilson, 10 Nov. 1894
26 Gregory, Memoir, 110

CHAPTER 13 Remarkable Connections

1 NA, Laurier Papers, Edgar to Laurier, 24 Nov. 1893 and 2 Dec. 1893, 2689–91, 2692
2 Ibid., Mulock to Laurier, 25 Jan. 1894, 2819–20
3 Ibid., Cartwright to Laurier, 3 Feb. 1894, 2850–2
4 Ibid., Gorman to Laurier, 4 and 7 Feb. 1894, 2853–7, 2863–8
5 Ibid., Cartwright to Laurier, 8 Feb. 1894, 2871
6 Ibid., Edgar to Laurier, 20 Feb. 1894, 2878–9
7 Ibid., Edgar to Laurier, 8 March 1894, 2936–8
8 Ibid., Farrer to Laurier, 3 April 1895, 4203; cited in Crunican, *Priests and Politicians*, 83
9 For accounts of this episode, see S.E.D. Shortt, 'Social Change and Political Crisis in Rural Ontario: The Patrons of Industry, 1889–1896,' and Carman Miller, 'Mowat, Laurier and the Federal Liberal Party, 1887–1897,' in Swainson, ed., *Oliver Mowat's Ontario*.
10 Ottawa *Citizen*, 8 June 1896
11 *Canada Farmers' Sun*, 10 June 1896
12 *Citizen*, 15 June 1896
13 Toronto *News*, 8 June 1896
14 Queen's University Archives, Gregory Papers, Unpublished Memoir, 112–13
15 *Citizen*, 8 June 1896. The *Farmers' Sun* itself insisted that no politician had an interest in the paper.
16 Cited in Shortt, 'The Patrons of Industry,' 230

17 Senator W.E. Sanford of Hamilton wrote that the paper was in a very demoralized condition and that he had been approached by two parties with a view to controlling its policy. 'I am almost inclined to think this can be done without its being known to be under the control of Conservative interests[,] the articles being liberal, at the same time of a mild type' (NA, Thompson Papers, Sanford to Thompson, 19 March 1894, 25506).
18 Charlesworth, *Candid Chronicles*, 163
19 This effort is explored in Waite, *The Man from Halifax* 316–7
20 Toronto *Empire*, 25 Nov. 1892
21 NA, Laurier Papers, Edgar to Laurier, 25 Nov. 1894, 3373–5
22 Charlesworth, *Candid Chronicles*, 160–3
23 Toronto *World*, 25 June 1896
24 AO, Goldwin Smith Papers, Smith to Gen. Lloyd Bryce, 16 Jan. 1895; Isaac L. Rice to Smith, 23 July 1895

CHAPTER 14 Backstairs Agent

1 Winnipeg *Tribune*, 28 April 1916
2 NA, Laurier Papers, 3 March 1897, 13541
3 NA, Minto Papers, Letterbook 4, Minto to Marquess of Lansdowne, 12 Jan. 1904; cited in Munro, *The Alaska Boundary Dispute*, 112. In his diary Minto recorded that Laurier had told him about Farrer's activities in a meeting of 25 February 1903: 'He [Laurier] spoke to me quite openly about his private means of communication with Washington – his agent is a Mr Farrer, who was originally a leader writer for the "Mail and Empire" [*sic*] and though belonging to a different political party to Sir Wilfrid he has long been a great friend of his and believes him to be thoroughly reliable. He is now chiefly employed in newspaper work for the C.P.R. and appears to pass backwards and forwards frequently between Ottawa and Washington. He is personally acquainted with [Henry Cabot] Lodge, and I think also with [John] Hay ...'
4 E. Farrer, 'Canada and the New Imperialism,' *Contemporary Review*, Dec. 1903
5 For instance, Charlton recorded an occasion when Farrer 'came to me to talk about railroad policy and I found that Sir Wilfrid had sent him to try and influence me to support the Government policy [on a second transcontinental line] ...' (Thomas Fisher Rare Book Library, University of Toronto, Charlton Diaries, vol. 14, 6 July 1903).

6 NA, Laurier Papers, Farrer to Cartwright, 117101a–c. This letter is labelled by the archives as possibly from 1906; it is more likely from 1896 since it meshes with a sequence identified as from early 1897, written from 36 Woodland, Toronto, where Farrer lived only until 1898 or 1899.
7 Ibid., Farrer to Laurier, 25 Jan. and 25 Feb., presumably 1897, 11412–13, 11414–15. The dates are virtually confirmed by a 7 April 1897 letter in Farrer's files, written by a U.S. treasury agent to his superiors and confirming the arrangement (NA, Farrer Papers, vol. 3).
8 NA, Laurier Papers, Farrer to Laurier, 19152 (identified by the archives as possibly from 1898, but more likely from 1896)
9 Ibid., Farrer to Laurier, 28674 (identified by the archives as possibly 1898, but more likely 1896)
10 Ibid., Farrer to Laurier, 41083–4 (identified by the archives as possibly 1900, but almost certainly 1897, in view of complementary references by Charlton and the New York *Tribune*)
11 On 13 Jan. 1892, for instance, Charlton wrote in his diary that he had gone to Toronto, had had a long talk with Farrer, and 'concluded not to go to Washington at present and feel relieved because it would be very inconvenient for me to leave now' (Charlton Diaries, vol. 5).
12 NA, Laurier Papers, 11153 (clipping from New York *Tribune*, dated Saturday, 16 Jan. 1897)
13 Ibid., Charlton to Laurier, 19 Jan. 1897, 11176
14 Ibid., Charlton to Laurier, 26 Jan. 1897, 11180–3
15 Ibid., Farrer to Lelievre, 11 July [1900?], 47416–19
16 Ibid., Farrer to Boudreau, 11 July 1902, 66508
17 Ibid., Farrer to Boudreau, 52023–K, 52023–L. These letters are dated only 'Aug. 16' and 'Sunday, Oct. 1.' They are listed by the archives as possibly from 1901, but the second is more likely from 1899 since 1 Oct. fell on a Sunday in that year, but not in 1900 or 1901. The dating of the first letter is more difficult, but it is associated in the files with the second letter and is dated at 174 Park Road, Toronto, where Farrer was listed as living in 1899.
18 Ibid., Farrer to Boudreau, 4 May 1900, 45280–1
19 NA, Willison Papers, vol. 14, Farrer to Willison, 26 Nov. 1900
20 For a fuller account of this episode, and extensive excerpts of Farrer's report, see Skelton, *Laurier*, 2:203–16.
21 NA, Laurier Papers, Dansereau to Laurier, 3 Jan. 1905, 93358; Graham to Laurier, 14 Jan. 1905, 93720; Laurier to Graham, 12 Jan. 1905, 93722; Mackenzie and Mann statement, 93729

22 Ibid., Farrer to Boudreau, 29 July 1900, 47881-6
23 Ibid., 53536. This letter is unsigned, but is in the form used for copies of Laurier's letters.
24 Ibid., 53653-4. These letters are also unsigned copies.
25 Ibid., Farrer wire to S. Lelievre, Privy Council, 22 Feb. 1901; and undated Lelievre reply to Farrer, 53615
26 Ibid., Farrer to Boudreau, 27 Jan. [1901?], 69585
27 Ibid., Farrer to Boudreau, 9 July 1901, 57467
28 Ibid., Farrer to Laurier, 19 June 1903, 74181
29 NA, Farrer Papers, vol. 1, Gilbert to Farrer, 17 May 1906
30 NA, Laurier Papers, Farrer to Laurier, 29 May 1906, 110614
31 Schull, *Laurier*, 458-64
32 Gwyn, *Private Capital*, 418-20
33 NA, Laurier Papers, Farrer to Laurier, 31 May 1904, 86299-306
34 Ibid., 16 Jan. 1906, 10605a-d
35 Ibid., Farrer to Lemaire, 11 Oct. 1910, 175604
36 Charlesworth, *More Candid Chronicles*, 111-12
37 *Debates*, House of Commons, 30 July 1903, 7672, 7702
38 NA, Laurier Papers, 219849ff and 219856ff. This document is preserved both in Farrer's handwriting and in typescript.

CHAPTER 15 A More Natural Passion

1 Toronto *Globe*, 20 Jan. 1892
2 *Canadian Century*, 5 March 1910
3 NA, Farrer Papers, vol. 6. This article is contained in Farrer's files in the form of a signed manuscript, with indications it was published in the early 1900s.
4 Queen's University Archives, Gregory Papers, box 1
5 Ibid., Gregory to Farrer, box 5, 2 May 1900
6 NA, Farrer Papers, vol. 5, 'A Canadian View of Imperialism'
7 E. Farrer, 'The Next Colonial Conference,' *Fortnightly Review*, Dec. 1905, 1022-36
8 *Canadian Century*, 8 Jan. 1910
9 Ibid., 26 Feb. and 5 March 1910
10 Ibid., 12 Feb. 1910
11 See, for instance, 'Sir Wilfrid's Fiscal Policy,' an unsigned article, very much in Farrer's style, in the *Economist* of 17 September 1910.
12 NA, Farrer Papers, vol. 1
13 Ibid., vol. 5

14 Ibid., vol. 6, unsigned article dated 14 Sept., apparently 1914
15 Ibid., vol. 1, Walker C. Bonwell to Farrer, 7 Feb. 1913
16 Ibid., vol. 1, W.H. Aldridge to Farrer, 13 Sept. 1912
17 Ibid., vol. 1, F.P. Gutelius to Farrer, 22 July 1914
18 Ibid., vol. 1, 29 March 1912; 18 April and 21 May 1913
19 Ibid., vol. 1, Smith to Farrer, 30 May 1909
20 Ibid., vol. 1, Smith to Farrer, 23 Sept. and 19 Oct. 1909; NA, Goldwin Smith Papers, Farrer to Smith, 26 April and 18 Oct. 1909
21 NA, Farrer Papers, vol. 1, Ross to Farrer, 20 Dec. 1913. The article apparently was an editorial column of the same day defending Bob Rogers, the Conservatives' controversial interior minister, and deriding 'Billy' [William Lyon Mackenzie] King.
22 Morgan, ed., *Canadian Men and Women of the Time*
23 NA, Farrer Papers, vol. 1, Willison to Farrer, 21 Jan. (apparently 1913)
24 Ibid., vol. 2, unsourced and undated editorial
25 NA, Willison Papers, vol. 14, Annie Farrer to Willison, 4 May 1916
26 Toronto *Star*, 28 April 1916
27 This phrase apparently emerged in the 1878 election campaign, and it is not clear whether it was indeed from Farrer's pen.
28 Ottawa *Journal*, 28 April 1916
29 Montreal *Gazette*, 28 April 1916
30 Edmonton *Journal*, 28 April 1916
31 Vancouver *Sun*, 28 April 1916
32 Toronto *Globe*, 28 April 1916

NOTE ON ATTRIBUTION

1 *Atlantic Monthly*, Dec. 1881
2 Winnipeg *Times*, 24 June 1882
3 NA, Laurier Papers, Willison to Laurier, 2 Sept. 1892, 2230
4 Toronto *Globe*, 26 Sept. 1891
5 Continental Union Association of Ontario, *Our Best Policy* (Toronto: Hunter, Rose 1895), 10–11

Sources

The material for this book is drawn principally from the newspapers on which Farrer worked (especially the Winnipeg *Times* and *Sun*, the Toronto *Mail* and *Globe*, and the New York *Sun*), from other contemporary newspapers and magazines (especially *Grip*), and from the papers of the two political leaders under whom he worked, Macdonald and Laurier. A number of other collections of personal papers at the National Archives of Canada (NA) have also been used, including those of Martin J. Griffin, George Taylor Denison, Sir John Willison, Sir John Thompson, and of Farrer himself. (The latter were useful but limited, comprising a mixed collection of manuscripts, clippings, and notebooks; few were valuable in defining Farrer's personality or his political connections.) Other papers that proved somewhat rewarding included those of T.C. Patteson in the Archives of Ontario (AO), of Walter Dymond Gregory at Queen's University, of Goldwin Smith (microfilm copies in both the National Archives and the Archives of Ontario), and of John Charlton (diaries only) at the University of Toronto. Justice Department documents provided much of the material on the annexation movement of the 1890s. With the permission of the *Globe and Mail* I was able to consult the unpublished history of the *Globe*, by M.O. Hammond and Hector Charlesworth, held in the newspaper's library. Attempts were made in London, Dublin, and Castlebar, and at Stonyhurst School in Lancashire, to trace Farrer's family and educational connections, but without success. Dr Paola Ludovici MacQuarrie made similar efforts in Rome to discover Farrer's connections there. Research in Washington to trace Farrer's U.S. political connections was also unproductive, except for limited benefit drawn from papers of the U.S. Senate Select Committee on Relations with Canada (the Hoar Committee), for which Farrer worked in 1888 while he was editor of the *Mail*. A good deal of Farrer's bylined work was also accessible in such magazines as *Canadian Century, Fortnightly Review, Contemporary Review, Forum, Atlantic Monthly,* and *Popular Science Monthly.*

John Willison's memoirs (*Reminiscences Political and Personal*) were a crucially important secondary source: they first prompted my interest in Farrer and provided convincing evidence of the essential paradoxes of his nature and work – along with a wealth of anecdote. Memoirs of several other journalists, including Hector Charlesworth, George Ham, Paul Bilkey, W.T.R. Preston, and P.D. Ross were useful, but often unreliable. Scholarly studies that were particularly rewarding included Richard T. Clippingdale's PHD dissertation on John Willison and G.R. Tennant's MA thesis on the Toronto *Mail*'s policy in the 1880s. The writing of Professor Wilfred Kesterton (*A History of Journalism in Canada*) and Professor Paul Rutherford (*The Making of the Canadian Media* and *A Victorian Authority*) were important in helping me to understand general journalism context in the late nineteenth century.

ARCHIVAL SOURCES

Archives of Ontario (AO)
Sir Richard Cartwright Papers
T.C. Patteson Papers
Goldwin Smith Papers (microfilm)

National Archives of Canada (NA)
Sir John Joseph Caldwell Abbott Papers, MG 26C
Arthur Radcliffe Boswell Papers, MG 27 I, I 2A
Charles Acton Burrows Papers, MG 27 II, 24
Sir Alexander Campbell Papers, MG 27 I, C 2
George Taylor Denison III Papers, MG 29, E 29
Edward Farrer Papers, MG 30, A 4
Martin Joseph Griffin Papers, MG 30, D 37
Justice Department Files, RG 13, B 7, vol. 963, 'Secret Files on American Annexationists, 1893–94'
Rt Hon. Sir Wilfrid Laurier Papers, MG 26, G
Sir John Alexander Macdonald Papers, MG 26, A
Sir Gilbert John Elliott (Lord Minto) Papers, MG 27 II, B 1
Philip Dansken Ross Papers, MG 30, D 98
Oscar Douglas Skelton Papers, MG 30, D 33
Goldwin Smith Papers (microfilm), MG 29, D 69
Rt Hon. Sir John Sparrow David Thompson Papers, MG 26, D

Rt Hon. Sir Charles Tupper Papers, MG 26, F
John Steven Willison Papers, MG 30, D 29

Queen's University Archives
Walter Dymond Gregory Papers

Thomas Fisher Rare Book Library, University of Toronto
John Charlton Diaries

BOOKS

Baker, William M. *Timothy Warren Anglin*. Toronto: University of Toronto Press 1977
Berger, Carl, ed. *Imperialism and Nationalism, 1884–1914: A Conflict in Canadian Thought*. Toronto: Copp Clark 1969
Biggar, E.B. *An Anecdotal Life of Sir John Macdonald*. Montreal: Lovell 1891
Bilkey, Paul. *Persons, Papers and Things*. Toronto: Ryerson 1940
Brown, R.C. *Canada's National Policy, 1883–1900*. (Princeton, NJ: Princeton University Press 1964
Careless, J.M.S. *Brown of the Globe*. 2 vols. Toronto: Macmillan 1959
Chalmers, Floyd S. *A Gentleman of the Press*. Toronto: Doubleday 1969
Charlesworth, Hector. *Candid Chronicles*. Toronto: Macmillan 1925
– *More Candid Chronicles*. Toronto: Macmillan 1928
Colquhoun, A.H.U. *Press, Politics and People*. Toronto: Macmillan 1935
Creighton, Donald. *John A. Macdonald: The Old Chieftain*. Toronto: Macmillan 1955
Crunican, Paul. *Priests and Politicians: Manitoba Schools and the Election of 1896*. Toronto: University of Toronto Press 1974
Dalton, Roy C. *The Jesuits' Estates Question, 1760–1888*. Toronto: University of Toronto Press 1968
Denison, Col. George Taylor. *The Struggle for Imperial Unity*. London: Macmillan 1909
Desbarats, Peter, and Terry Mosher. *The Hecklers. A History of Canadian Political Cartooning and a Cartoonists' History of Canada*. Toronto: McClelland and Stewart / National Film Board of Canada 1979
Freeman, Barbara M. *Kit's Kingdom*. Ottawa: Carleton University Press 1989
Friesen, Gerald. *The Canadian Prairies*. Toronto: University of Toronto Press 1984

Gwyn, Sandra. *The Private Capital*. Toronto: McClelland and Stewart 1984

Ham, George. *Reminiscences of a Raconteur*. Toronto: Musson 1921

Haultain, T. Arnold. *Goldwin Smith: His Life and Opinions*. London: T. Werner Laurie Ltd n.d.

Kesterton, W.H. *A History of Journalism in Canada*. Toronto: McClelland and Stewart 1967

Koester, C.B. *Mr. Davin, M.P.* Saskatoon: Western Producer Prairie Books 1980

Macdonald, Capt. John A. *Troublous Times in Canada*. Toronto: W.S. Johnston 1910

Macpherson, Lt. Col. J. Pennington. *The Life of Sir John A. Macdonald*. 2 vols. Saint John: Earle Publishing Houses 1891

Manitoba Library Association. *Pioneers and Early Citizens of Manitoba*. Winnipeg: Peguis 1971

Masters, D.C. *The Rise of Toronto, 1850–1890*. Toronto: University of Toronto Press 1947

Miller, J.R. *Equal Rights: The Jesuits' Estates Act Controversy*. Montreal: McGill-Queen's University Press 1979

Morgan, Henry James, ed. *The Canadian Men and Women of the Time*. Toronto: William Briggs 1912

Morton, W.L. *Manitoba: A History*. Toronto: University of Toronto Press 1957

Munro, John H.A. *The Alaska Boundary Dispute*. Toronto: Copp Clark 1970

Neatby, H. Blair. *Laurier and a Liberal Quebec: A Study in Political Management*. Toronto: McClelland and Stewart 1973

Pope, Sir Joseph, ed. *Correspondence of Sir John Macdonald* Oxford: Oxford University Press, n.d.

– *Public Servant: The Memoirs of Sir Joseph Pope*. Edited and compiled by Maurice Pope. Toronto: Oxford University Press 1960

Poulton, Ron. *The Paper Tyrant: John Ross Robertson of the Toronto Telegram*. Toronto and Vancouver: Clarke, Irwin 1971

Preston, W.T.R. *My Generation of Politics and Politicians*. Toronto: D.A. Rose 1927

Ross, P.D. *Retrospects of a Newspaper Person*. Toronto: Oxford University Press 1931

Rutherford, Paul. *A Victorian Authority: The Daily Press in Late Nineteenth-Century Canada*. Toronto: University of Toronto Press 1982

- *The Making of the Canadian Media.* Toronto: McGraw-Hill Ryerson 1978
Schull, Joseph. *Edward Blake.* 2 vols. Toronto: Macmillan 1975-6
- *Laurier.* Toronto: Macmillan 1965
Senior, Hereward. *The Fenians and Canada.* Toronto: Macmillan 1978
Skelton, Oscar Douglas. *Life and Letters of Sir Wilfrid Laurier.* 2 vols. Toronto: S.B. Gundy / Oxford University Press 1921
Smith, Goldwin. *Canada and the Canadian Question.* 1891; reprint, foreword by Carl Berger. Toronto: University of Toronto Press 1971
- *Reminiscences.* New York: Macmillan 1910
Sutherland, Fraser. *The Monthly Epic: A History of Canadian Magazines 1789-1989.* Markham, Ont.: Fitzhenry and Whiteside 1989
Swainson, Donald, ed. *Oliver Mowat's Ontario.* Toronto: Macmillan 1972
Tansill, Charles Callan. *Canadian-American Relations, 1875-1911.* Gloucester, Mass: Peter Smith 1964
Waite, P.B. *Canada 1874-1896: Arduous Destiny.* Toronto and Montreal: McClelland and Stewart 1971
- *Macdonald, His Life and World.* Toronto: McGraw-Hill Ryerson 1975
- *The Man from Halifax: Sir John Thompson, Prime Minister* Toronto: University of Toronto Press 1985
Wallace, Elisabeth. *Goldwin Smith: Victorian Liberal.* Toronto: University of Toronto Press 1957
Warner, Donald F. *The Idea of Continental Union.* Lexington: University of Kentucky Press 1960
Weir, George M. *The Separate School Question in Canada.* Toronto: Ryerson 1934
Willison, Sir John. *Reminiscences Political and Personal.* Toronto: McClelland and Stewart 1919
- *Sir Wilfrid Laurier and the Liberal Party.* 2 vols. Toronto: Morang 1903

ARTICLES

Beaven, Brian P.N. 'Partisanship, Patronage, and the Press in Ontario, 1880-1914: Myths and Realities.' *Canadian Historical Review* 64, no. 3 (Sept. 1983), 317-51
Blackburn Harte, Walter. 'Canadian Journalists and Journalism.' *New England Magazine* 5 (Dec. 1891), 411-41
Cumming, Carman. 'The Toronto *Daily Mail*, Edward Farrer, and the

Question of Canadian-American Union.' *Journal of Canadian Studies,* 24, no. 1 (Spring 1989), 121–39

Graham, W.R. 'Sir Richard Cartwright, Wilfrid Laurier and the Liberal Party Trade Policy, 1887.' *Canadian Historical Review* 33, no. 1 (March 1952), 1–18

MacKirdy, K.A. 'The Loyalty Issue in the 1891 Federal Election Campaign and an Ironic Footnote.' *Ontario History* 55, no. 3 (1963), 143–54

Miller, J.R. '"As a Politician He Is a Great Enigma": The Social and Political Ideas of D'Alton McCarthy.' *Canadian Historical Review* 58, no. 4 (Dec. 1977), 399–422

– 'The Jesuit-Mail Libel Case: An Example of Nineteenth-Century Anti-Catholicism.' *Studies in Religion* 7, no. 3 (Summer 1978), 295–303

Shortt, S.E.D. 'Social Change and Political Crisis in Rural Ontario: The Patrons of Industry, 1889–1896.' In *Oliver Mowat's Ontario.* Ed. Donald Swainson. Toronto: Macmillan 1972, 211–35

Wallace, W.S. 'The Journalist in Canadian Politics.' *Canadian Historical Review* 22, no. 1 (March 1941), 14–24

THESES

Clippingdale, Richard T. 'J.S. Willison, Political Journalist: From Liberalism to Independence.' PHD diss., Toronto, 1970

Lapierre, Laurier. 'Politics, Race, and Religion in French Canada: Joseph Israel Tarte.' PHD diss., Toronto, 1962

Tennant, Glenn R. 'The Policy of the Mail 1882–1892.' MA Thesis, Toronto, 1946

Index

Abbott, Sir John, 202, 209, 212
Academy of Music, 3, 7
Alaska boundary question, 249, 255–6, 275
Anglin, Timothy Warren, 86–8, 105
annexation movement, 6–10, 177–80, 204–9, 225–37
Atholstan, Lord. *See* Graham, Hugh
Atkinson, Joseph T., 227, 286
Atlantic Monthly, 88, 289

Balfour, A.J., 279
Barnard, Angela, 235–6
Bayard, Thomas F., 106
Bayard-Chamberlain treaty, 188
Beaty, James, 36
Belford, Charles, 18–19, 36–7
Bengough, John W., 41, 65, 70, 90, 91–2, 94, 124–6, 141–2, 151, 157, 165, 214
Bering Sea dispute, 180
Berthiaume, Trefflé, 257–9
Biggs, Samuel Clarke, 52, 56
Bilkey, Paul, 26
Birchall, Reginald, 171–6
Blaine, James G.: and Canada-U.S. relations, 7, 111–16, 181–8, 209, 211–12; and Farrer, 52–3, 148, 155–6, 179, 311n.19
Blair, Andrew George, 257–8, 260, 266
Blake, Edward, 12, 63, 79, 103, 107–8, 116–17, 141, 166–7, 186, 204, 212, 224, 273, 308n.19
Boer War, 274–6
Bonaparte, Prince Pierre, 19
Borden, Robert, 257–8, 265, 268, 282
Bothwell (riding), 38
Boudreau, Rodolphe, 251, 256, 261–2
Bowell, Mackenzie, 245
Brock, W.R., 159
Brown, George, 13, 34–5, 66, 105, 130, 142, 270, 297n.1
Buffalo *Courier*, 150
Bundoran, Donegal, 16
'Bunters,' 69, 85, 88
Bunting, Christopher, 68–94; and annexation / commercial union, 106, 116, 149, 230; and Farrer, 164–6; and Jesuits' Estates, 97, 99, 120–1; and Macdonald, 302n.30, 303n.60; and Toronto

Mail, 50, 65, 146, 158, 216, 239, 245, 271, 287
Butterworth, Benjamin, 111, 149
Bystander, 162

Cameron, John, 114, 120, 157
Campbell, Sir Alexander, 146
Canada and the Canadian Question, 226
Canada Farmers' Sun, 241–4
Canada-U.S. Joint High Commission, 254
Canadian Century, 22, 248, 277
Canadian Pacific Railway, 22, 44–5, 51–3, 55, 61–2, 107, 192, 201, 229, 235, 248, 258, 266, 281, 283, 299n.28, 317n.3
Careless, J.M.S., 297n.1
Carling, Sir John, 297n.7
Carnegie, Andrew, 116, 150, 230–4
Caron, Adolphe, 238–40
Cartwright, Sir Richard: and commercial union, 106–7, 116–17, 162, 178, 184–9, 207–8, 211–12; and election of 1891, 194–6, 199–201, 204–5; and Farrer, 7–9, 24, 27, 40, 86, 192, 209–10, 240–1, 243–4, 251–3; and Toronto *Globe*, 166–7, 170
Castlebar, 14
Chapleau, Joseph Adolphe, 236
Charlesworth, Hector, 30–1, 141–2, 147, 245, 268–9
Charlton, John, 111, 187, 189, 208, 211–12, 254–5, 311n.19, 317n.5
Churchill, Manitoba, 76–7
Clark, Champ, 281–2
Clark, Christopher, 177–8, 202
Clark, Joseph T. [pseud. Mack], 218, 222

Cleveland, Grover, 228
Cleveland *Leader*, 150
Coleman, Katherine ('Kit') Blake, 66, 301n.10
College of the Propaganda, 14, 17
Colquhoun, A.H.U., 63–4, 166
commercial union, 8, 71, 95, 102, 106–18, 225, 243. See also unrestricted reciprocity
Connolly, Nicholas, 238, 240
Conservative party, 71–4, 287
Contemporary Review, 22, 185, 249–51
Continental Union Association of Ontario, 21, 226
Cook, H.H., 97
Creighton, David, 124, 147, 152, 158–9, 161–2, 170–1, 179, 182, 216, 232–4, 244
Creighton, Donald, 181

Dafoe, J.W., 50
Daley, T.M., 38
Dana, Charles, 116, 150, 225, 230–1
Dansereau, Arthur, 257–60
Davin, Nicholas Flood, 52–3, 58–9, 74, 135–6, 138, 270, 306n.45
Denison, Fred C., 293n.12
Denison, Lt-Col. George Taylor, 57, 111, 158, 161, 177–9, 203–5, 208, 283
Detroit *Tribune*, 185
Dewdney, Edgar, 48–50, 52, 58–9, 299n.8
Dingley, Nelson, 254
Dolph, Senator Joseph, 152, 154–5
Dominion Police, 177
Donegal, County of, 16
Dun, R.G. & Co., 235
Dwight, H.P., 55

Economist, 22, 281, 284
Edgar, J.D., 86, 108, 139–41, 165, 211, 238–40, 245
Edmonton *Journal*, 288
Egan, John M., 61
L'Electeur, 224
Ellis, J.V., 201
Emmerson, Henry R., 266–7
equal rights movement, 124, 126, 168
Essex County, 205
L'Etendard, 302n.21

Fahey, Thomas, 50
Falconbridge, Mr Justice William, 161
Farrer, Annie, 16, 29, 31–3, 286
Farrer, Edward: and annexation / commercial union, 5–11, 23, 42, 95, 106, 108–17, 148–56, 177–92, 205–8, 226–36, 274 (*see also* 'two-bites' letter); and Birchall case, 171–6; and election of 1878, 41–2; and Gilbert letter, 264–7; and humour, 28–31, 59, 76–7, 134–43; and imperialism, 45–6, 56, 80, 98–100, 103, 132–3, 250–1, 274–9; and Irish nationalism, 39–40, 60; and Jesuits' Estates, 117–27; and Laurier, 209–11, 247–69, 281; and Macdonald, 7–9, 35, 38–43, 51–2; and McGreevy scandal, 238–40; and Manitoba schools, 124–5, 260–3; and New York *Sun*, 225–30; and party press, 47, 56, 91–3, 169; and Patrons of Industry, 241–4; personal background, 6, 12–22, 32–3, 294n.11, 295nn.16, 17, 29; and religion, 23, 32, 35, 57–8, 60–1, 67, 127–8, 131–2, 272; and social / cultural issues, 22–3, 129–34; and Toronto *Globe*, 163–71, 189–94, 213–24; and Toronto *Mail*, 38–43, 66–71, 74–80, 86–92; and Western separatism, 53–6; and Winnipeg *Sun*, 52–8; and Winnipeg *Times*, 43–50; and writing skills, xii–xiii, 97–105, 129–31, 280
Farrer, Henry, 22, 33, 264, 297n.55
Farrer, Kathleen, 33, 297n.55
Fenians, 18–19, 30, 60
Fenton, Faith. *See* Freeman, Alice
fisheries dispute with United States, 180, 192
Forgets (Montreal financial family), 257–9
Fortnightly Review, 22, 277
Forum, 22
Foster, George, 212
Foster, J.W., 211
Freeman, Alice [pseud. Faith Fenton], 5

Galt, Sir Alexander, 273, 278–9
Gilbert, Abel H., 264–7, 271
Glen, Francis Wayland, 230–6
Gorman, Thomas P., 93, 240
Gould, Jay, 111
Graham, Hugh (Lord Atholstan), 257–60
Grand Trunk Pacific Railway, 258, 268
Grand Trunk Railway, 257–8, 266
Grange, The (Goldwin Smith home), 30–1
Grant, George M., 119, 164
Grant, T. Burke [alias Marcus Robinson; spy in annexation move-

ment], 116, 203, 232–7
Greenshields, J.N., 257–9
Greenway, Thomas, 260–1
Gregg, George, 18–19
Gregg, Thomas A., 157
Gregory, Walter Dymond, 6, 23, 30–2, 166, 208, 225–7, 230–2, 237, 271, 275
Griffin, Martin J., 66, 72–80, 87, 270, 299n.28, 301n.11
Grip magazine, 65, 157, 160; and commercial union, 111–12, 114–15; and Farrer, 15, 41, 43, 59, 70–2, 74–5, 77, 141, 150–2, 164–5, 170, 199–200, 209–10, 213–14, 219–21; and Jesuits' Estates, 99, 120–2, 124–6; and Toronto *Mail*, 42, 50, 78, 79, 81–3, 90–2, 155
Grit party. *See* Liberal party

Halifax *Herald*, 195–6, 216
Ham, George H., 11, 16–17, 26–30, 32, 133, 248, 285
Hamilton *Spectator*, 36, 46–7
Harrison, Benjamin, 111, 184
Harte, Walter Blackburn, xiii, 69, 106
Hay, John, 249, 255, 317n.3
Haycock, Joseph, 31
Hitt, Robert R., 113, 155, 164, 179, 182–3, 185, 197–8, 203
Hoar, George F., 113–16, 148–9, 153–4
Hughes, Sam, 68–9
Hunter Rose & Co., 9, 177, 196

imperial federation, 248
Inglis, William, 86
Intercolonial Railway, 256, 258, 264–6
Irish Canadian, 229
Irish College, 14, 16

Jaffray, Robert, 164–6, 169, 179, 208, 213, 217, 223, 293n.12
Jeffery, Thomas W., 142
Jesuit College, 14
Jesuit Order, 17, 67, 96–8, 104
Jesuits' Estates question, 71, 91, 117–26, 197–9
Journalist (New York), 65

King, William Lyon Mackenzie, 320n.21
Kingsmill, George, 36–7
Kribs, Louis P. (Pica), 147, 152–4, 158, 159–61, 174, 196, 309n.5

Laflamme, Rodolphe, 138–9
Langevin, Sir Hector, 238–40
Langevin, Archbishop J.P.F. Laforce, 261–3
Lansdowne, Marquess of, 111, 249
Laurier, Sir Wilfrid: and annexation, 149, 184–9, 202, 207–14, 234, 236; and Farrer, 21, 27, 167–9, 199–201, 212–14, 222–4, 247–69, 275; and Jesuits' Estates, 97, 123–5; and *La Presse*, 257–60; and McGreevy scandal, 238–40; and Manitoba schools, 260–3; and naval policy, 268–9, 277–8, 282; and Northwest Rebellion, 103; and Toronto *Mail*, 93; and trade with United States, 106–7, 117, 281–2; and Willison, 10, 12, 167–71, 222–4
Laurier-Greenway compromise, 260
Laval University, 104

Lemaire, E.J., 268
Liberal-Conservative party, 35
Liberal-Nationalist party, 107
Liberal party: and annexation, 8, 116, 204–9; and commercial union, 107; and election of 1896, 26, 241–4; and Farrer, 21, 186–8; and McGreevy scandal, 238–40; and Toronto *Globe*, 12–14, 34, 66, 168–9
Lindsay (Ont.) *Expositor*, 18
Lindsay (Ont.) *Post*, 156
'Little Mrs Blank,' 41
Lodge, Henry Cabot, 317n.33
London (Ont.) *Advertiser*, 123
London *Chronicle*, 255
London *Daily News*, 268
London *Times*, 195, 253, 255
Longley, J.W., 187
Luxton, W.F., 56
Lynch, John Joseph, archbishop of Toronto, 60, 72–3

McCarthy, D'Alton, 21, 26, 69, 72, 74, 96, 118, 120, 123–7, 145–6, 168, 238, 241–3
Macdonald, E.A., 230–2
Macdonald, Hugh John, 50, 260
Macdonald, Sir John A.: and election of 1891, 3–10, 177–82, 188–92; and Farrer, 21, 41–2, 51–2, 111–12, 314n.28; and party press, 49–50, 145–8; and Toronto *Mail*, 34–43, 63–95
Macdonald, John Sandfield, 36
Macdonnell, D.J., 122
McDougall, William, 55–6, 178, 197, 202–3
McGreevy, Thomas, 180, 209–10, 238–40, 256

'Mack.' *See* Clark, Joseph T.
McKellar, Archibald, 41
Mackenzie, Alexander, 40, 79
Mackenzie, William, 257–8, 260
McKinley tariff, 180–1, 197
Maclean, John Bayne, 66
Maclean, W.F. (Billy), 64, 102, 146, 157, 164, 195, 245
McMicking, W.J., 160
Macpherson, Sir David, 48, 297n.7
McTavish, J.H., 61
Mallory, C.A., 241–4
Manchester *Guardian*, 22, 283–4
Manitoba Farmers Union, 52
Manitoba Free Press, 45, 50, 60–2
Manitoba schools issue, 21, 124–7, 241, 306n.65
Mann, Donald A., 257–8, 260
Marsh, A.H., 159
Maynooth seminary, 16
Mayo, County of, 14–16, 60, 134, 300n.38
Mercier, Honoré, 107, 117, 120, 210, 225–6, 230–1, 233–4, 237
Meredith, William R., 94–5, 124, 126
Methodist church, 142
Métis, 58, 77–80
Miller, J.R., 307n.70
Mills, David, 123–4
La Minerve, 195
Minto, Gilbert John Elliott, 4th Earl (Viscount Melgund), 94, 249–50, 317n.3
Montreal *Gazette*, 68, 69, 81–3, 164, 288
Montreal *Star*, 85, 91, 93, 257
Montreal *Witness*, 156
Morison, John, 233, 236
Mormon church, 131

Mowat, Sir Oliver, 24, 63, 94, 167–8, 179, 193, 201, 204–9, 212–13, 215–24, 236
Mulock, Sir William, 239
Myers, Elgin, 216–17, 221, 227, 230, 236

National Continental Union League, 230
National Library of Ireland, 14, 16
National Policy, 7, 42–3, 65, 129
National Transcontinental Railway, 266, 268
'Native' (Montreal *Star* columnist), 85, 91, 93
New England Magazine, 69, 213
Newfoundland, 181
newspaper technology, 64–6
New York *Herald*, 183
New York *Sun*, 150, 175, 225, 227–30, 236, 255, 268
New York *Tribune*, 185, 187, 216, 253–5
New York *World*, 21, 150, 155, 174
Noir, Victor, 19–20
Norquay, John, 45, 51, 53–4
North American Review, 113
Northwest Mounted Police, 59
Northwest Rebellion, 18, 48, 77–9
Northwest Territories, 48, 53–4, 76, 127
Nova Scotia, 191–2

O'Donohoe, John, 39, 73, 302n.37
'Ontario, Ontario!' (campaign song), 139–42
Orange Order, 50, 73, 87, 93, 228, 261
O'Soup, Louis, 77
Ottawa *Citizen*, 26, 221–2, 243

Ottawa *Free Press*, 93, 240
Ottawa *Journal*, 71, 120, 284, 286–7
Oxford County, 205

Pacaud, Ernest, 210, 224
Pacific Scandal, 38, 40–1, 45
Panama Canal, 281–2
Patrons of Industry, 21, 26, 31, 238, 241–4, 253
Patteson, Thomas Charles, 37–9, 65
Pauncefote, Sir Julian, 182
Payne, Henry, 113
Pew, E.A.C., 54–6, 113
Pope, Joseph, 24, 27, 80, 201, 299n.28
Portage La Prairie *Review*, 76–7
Presbyterian Review, 86
La Presse, 257–60
Preston, W.T.R., 24–7, 117
prohibition, 88–91

Reform party. *See* Liberal party
Regina (Pile of Bones), 48, 59, 135
Regina *Leader*, 52, 58–9
Riel, Louis, 54, 80, 99, 103–4
Riel Rebellion. *See* Northwest Rebellion
Riordan, Charles, 66, 69, 72, 74, 87, 93, 117, 129, 146
Riordan, John, 65–7, 298n.23
Ritchie, Samuel J., 10, 55, 106
Robertson, John Ross, 35–7, 64, 130, 157, 270, 297n.7
Robinson, Marcus. *See* Grant, T. Burke
Roblin, Rodmund, 261–3
Ross, G.W., 179, 266
Ross, P.D., 14, 28, 66, 71, 284, 286–7, 299n.28

Rossin House, 10
Rowe, Amos, 43, 50, 56
Royal Military College, 56
Russell, David, 257–9
Rutherford, Paul, 301n.15
Ryan, Peter, 240

Saint John *Evening Times*, 260
Saint John *Telegraph*, 260
Salisbury, Robert Arthur Gascoyne-Cecil, 3rd Marquess of, 205
Salvation Army, 57–8
Saturday Night, 64, 66, 124, 152, 156–8, 169, 218–19, 222
Saunders, E.M., 203
scoopograph, 142–3
Sheppard, E.E. (Ned) [pseud. Don], xiii, 25–6, 64, 66, 86, 129, 152, 157, 162–3, 169, 201, 218, 225
Sherman, John, 113
Sherwood, Maj. Percy, 177–8, 202
Sifton, Clifford, 28, 262–3
Sitting Bull, 174
Skelton, O.D., 23–4, 106, 257–60
Smith, Alex, 241–2
Smith, Donald A., 45
Smith, Frank, 73
Smith, Goldwin: and annexation movement, 162, 199, 202, 208, 225–6, 230–1, 233–4, 237; and commercial union, 106–7, 115, 118, 211–12; and Farrer, 21, 23–5, 30–1, 34–5, 164, 196, 222, 245, 275, 288, 315n.3; and Jesuits' Estates, 97, 118–19, 271; and Patrons of Industry, 241, 244; and Toronto *Mail*, 37–8, 69
smuggling, 251–3
Spanish-American War, 275
Stanley, Frederick Arthur, Baron Stanley of Preston, 101, 180, 182
Stephen, George, 201
Stonyhurst school, Lancashire, 14, 16
Stratford *Herald*, 38

Taché, Archbishop Alexandre A., 296n.31
Taft, Robert, 281–2
Tait, Joseph, 165, 217
Tarte, J. Israel, 236
Tel-el-Kebir, Battle of, 174, 310n.28
Temiscouata Railway, 256
Tennant, G.R., 65, 130
Thompson, Sir John S.D., 232–3, 244
Thomson, E.W., 120, 124, 178–9
Tilley, Sir Leonard, 47–9
Tillsonburg *Liberal*, 229
Toronto *Empire*: and Birchall case, 173–6; and Farrer, 152–62, 182–5, 193–9, 216, 222, 227; founding of, 145–8; and Jesuits' Estates, 122, 124, 306n.62; and Macdonald, 3, 69; and merger with Toronto *Mail*, 64, 244–5; and Toronto *Mail* court case, 158–61
Toronto *Globe*, 93, 137, 244, 273; and annexation, 5, 10, 148–50, 189–91, 204–8; and attacks on Toronto *Mail*, 68, 83, 85–7, 91; and Birchall case, 171–6; and George Brown, 13, 34, 66; and Farrer, 71, 155–6, 163–71, 199, 241–3, 260, 288; and fire of 1895, 244; and Jesuits' Estates, 120–2; and Liberal party, 3, 168–9; and McGreevy scandal, 209; and Willison, 12–14
Toronto *Leader*, 18–19, 36

334 Index

Toronto *Mail*, 34, 129–34, 136; birth of, 36–8; and commercial union, 106–17; and court case against Toronto *Empire*, 158–61; and Farrer, 9, 18, 20–1, 38–43, 66–71, 74–80, 86–92; and independence from Conservative party, xiii, 3, 6, 63–95; and Jesuits' Estates, 117–26; and Macdonald, 36–43, 50, 73–6, 81–5, 145–6; and merger with Toronto *Empire*, 244–5, 287; and Roman Catholic church, 84–5, 96–102, 104–5
Toronto *Mail and Empire*, 245, 273
Toronto *News*, 3, 63–4, 66, 74, 129, 161, 244, 284; and election of 1891, 24, 194, 196; and Farrer, 17–20, 40, 215–18, 286, 299n.28; and Jesuits' Estates, 97
Toronto *Star*, 64, 66, 227, 286
Toronto *Sun*, 230
Toronto *Telegram*, 63–4, 129, 178, 216
Toronto *Telegraph*, 18, 35–7, 297n.7
Toronto *World*, 43, 50, 64, 102, 129, 146, 156, 164, 166–7, 195, 215–18, 224, 245, 308n.2
Tupper, Sir Charles, 4–5, 7, 72, 93–4, 177–8, 197, 199, 202–3, 256
Tupper, C. Hibbert, 177
'two-bites' letter, 113–16, 185, 197–9, 203

Unitarian church, 302n.21
United Empire Loyalists, 56–7, 278
United States: and annexation 8; and Senate Committee on Interstate Commerce, 248; and Senate Committee on Relations with Canada (Hoar Committee), 113, 148–50; and trade policy, 106, 150, 254
unrestricted reciprocity, 108, 224. *See also* commercial union

Vancouver *Sun*, 288

Waite, P.B., 307n.70
Wallace, Elisabeth, 118
Washington *Post*, 255
Week, 65, 199
Weekly Sun, 275. *See also* Canada Farmers' Sun
Welch, L.A., 241–2
White, Richard S., 69, 164
White, Thomas, 36
Willison, Sir John: and annexation / commercial union, 5, 11, 106, 120, 191, 208–9; and Farrer, 6, 18–19, 23–5, 29–30, 32, 64, 71, 74, 164, 166–71, 186–7, 217, 222–4, 257, 284–6, 288; and Liberal party, 10, 204, 213–14, 239; personal background, 12–13
Wiman, Erastus, 8, 55–6, 106, 111–16, 148–9, 153–4, 178–9, 184, 187, 197–8, 201–4, 233, 235
Winnipeg *Free Press*. *See Manitoba Free Press*
Winnipeg *Sun*, 21, 42, 44–5, 52–61
Winnipeg *Times*, 21, 30, 43–53, 59–61, 174, 289
Winnipeg *Tribune*, 248
Wood, E.B., 30, 40
Woodstock, 171–5
Woodstock *Sentinel-Review*, 173

Made in the USA
Charleston, SC
12 April 2014